POUND
WILLIAMS

THE CORRESPONDENCE OF EZRA POUND

Pound/Ford: The Story of a Literary Friendship
Edited by Brita Lindberg-Seyersted

Pound/Joyce: Letters & Essays
Edited by Forrest Read

Pound/Lewis: The Letters of Ezra Pound and Wyndham Lewis
Edited by Timothy Materer

*Pound/*The Little Review:
The Letters of Ezra Pound to Margaret Anderson
Edited by Thomas L. Scott and Melvin J. Friedman,
with the assistance of Jackson R. Bryer

Ezra Pound and Dorothy Shakespear: Their Letters 1909–1914
Edited by Omar Pound and A. Walton Litz

Pound/Williams:
Selected Letters of Ezra Pound and William Carlos Williams
Edited by Hugh Witemeyer

Pound/Zukofsky: Selected Letters of Ezra Pound and Louis Zukofsky
Edited by Barry Ahearn

THE CORRESPONDENCE OF EZRA POUND

POUND
WILLIAMS

Selected Letters of Ezra Pound

and William Carlos Williams

Edited by Hugh Witemeyer

A NEW DIRECTIONS BOOK

The illustration in Letter 19 was provided by the Lilly Library, Indiana University; the illustra-
tions and ideograms in Letters 27, 55, 120, and 152 by the Beinecke Rare Book and Manuscript
Library, Yale University; the ideograms in Letter 87 by the Poetry/Rare Books Collection, University of Buffalo.

Manufactured in the United States of America
New Directions Books are printed on acid-free paper.
First published clothbound by New Directions in 1996
Published simultaneously in Canada by Penguin Books Canada Limited

Library of Congress Cataloging-in-Publication Data

Pound, Ezra, 1885–1972
    [Correspondence. Selections]
    Pound/Williams : selected letters of Ezra Pound and William Carlos
Williams / edited by Hugh Witemeyer.
        p.   cm.—(The correspondence of Ezra Pound)
    Includes bibliographical references and index.
    ISBN 0–8112–1301–3
    1. Pound, Ezra, 1885–1972—Correspondence.   2. Williams, William
Carlos, 1883–1963—Correspondence.   3. Poets, American—20th
century—Correspondence.   I. Witemeyer, Hugh.   II. Williams,
William Carlos, 1883–1963. Correspondence. Selections.
III. Title.   IV. Series: Pound, Ezra, 1885–1872. Correspondence.
PS3531.O82Z4976   1996
811′.52—dc20
    [B]   95–38462
                                                                          CIP

New Directions Books are published for James Laughlin
by New Directions Publishing Corporation,
80 Eighth Avenue, New York 10011

Contents

Introduction

The correspondence of Ezra Pound (1885–1972) and William Carlos Williams (1883–1963) began in 1907 and continued until 1963. It provides an unparalleled documentary record of developments in modern literature and culture. It is also a tribute to the enduring friendship of two towering figures in American poetry.

Pound and Williams took part in a far-reaching artistic revolution during the first half of the twentieth century. Their letters contain a wealth of information about their own lives and works. We learn a great deal, as well, about the activities of other important writers and artists of the time. The correspondence vividly evokes the yeasty milieu of small presses and little magazines, of shifting groups and short-lived movements, that sustained experimental modern literature in Europe and the United States.

The letters also register the impact of larger public events upon the lives of artists in this century. During the 1930s, the economic and political crisis that led to the Spanish Civil War and World War II strained the friendship of Pound and Williams to the breaking point. Pound became an advocate of Benito Mussolini and Italian fascism, whereas Williams was a left-leaning Democrat, sympathetic to socialism and communism. After 1945, both poets were much in the public eye. With Pound incarcerated in a Washington mental hospital on charges of treason, the award to him in 1949 of the Bollingen Prize provoked a major national controversy. Williams also received several prestigious awards, and his political allegiances came under scrutiny when he was subjected to a loyalty investigation during the McCarthy era.

Through these vicissitudes, the friendship of the two men was remarkably resilient. Forged during their impressionable undergraduate years at the University of Pennsylvania, it lasted for the rest of their lives, surviving geographical separation, infrequent meetings, and numerous quarrels. Pound left for Europe in 1908; there he led the Bohemian life of a full-time artist in glamorous surroundings, and espoused a cosmopolitan ideal of culture. Williams stayed in New Jersey; there he led the workaholic life of a full-time obstetrician and pediatrician, and espoused a local, distinctively American ideal of culture. Pound once described them as complementary selves, "the two halves of what might have made a fairly decent poet" (September 11, 1920).

For more than three decades, each was the other's window upon a relinquished world across the Atlantic. Pound kept Williams in touch with the avant-garde adventures he might have enjoyed in London, Paris, and Italy. Williams constantly measured his own career against Pound's, using his friend's accomplishments to goad himself to a higher level of achievement. Conversely, Williams provided Pound's most enduring contact with the American literary scene he had left behind. "Ole Bull" was Pound's staunchest ally in the ongoing war against American philistinism. In a letter of March 5, 1928, to Louis Zukofsky, Pound describes Williams as "the best human value on my murkn. visiting list."

The friendship was an unpredictable saga of collaboration and conflict. Mutual cooperation and inspiration could give way with astonishing rapidity to temporary antagonism. Both men enjoyed a good squabble, and liked to display their affection, as boys do, by needling and provoking. The correspondence could be brutally frank, and survived some plain speaking that would wither most friendships.

Yet it could also be curiously reticent and impersonal. The letters contain little of an intimate or confessional nature, for example. Even when the conversation turns toward women and sexual experience, it is couched in veiled and general terms. By the same token, the poets say less about the private creative processes that gave rise to their work than about the channels of transmission by which it was (or might be) publicly disseminated. The bass line of most of the letters is a disinterested, tough-minded dedication to a shared poetic vocation. This selfless commitment helped to sustain both men through trying times and formed the true bedrock of their friendship.

The correspondence also testifies to the loyalty of its publisher, James Laughlin. As a student at Harvard, Laughlin met Pound in 1933 and Williams in 1935. At Pound's instigation, Laughlin founded New Directions in 1936. He soon became the principal American publisher of both Pound and Williams, relying upon their reputations to attract younger and lesser-known talents to his list. New Directions has continued its commitment to the work of Pound and Williams, by keeping old titles in print and issuing collections of new writings, including the series of letters of which the present volume is one.

In the pages that follow, the letters of Pound and Williams are grouped chronologically in five sections. Each section is preceded by an introduction that places the letters of that period into biographical and historical contexts. The principles governing the selection, transcription, and annotation of the letters are explained in the "Notes on the Text." The edition contains no letters from Williams to Pound prior to 1921 because either they were not saved or they were lost when Pound moved from London to Paris in that year. Moreover, no letters were exchanged between December 1941, when the United States entered World

War II, and December 1945, when the war was finally over and Pound had been brought to Washington. Except for these gaps, however, enough of the correspondence has survived to offer a sustained perspective upon an era marked by savage destruction and brilliant creation.

Hugh Witemeyer

Notes on the Text

The surviving correspondence of Ezra Pound and William Carlos Williams consists of approximately 535 items. Most are housed in three principal archives: the Poetry/Rare Books Collection of the University of Buffalo, the Lilly Library of Indiana University, and the Beinecke Rare Book and Manuscript Library of Yale University. A few letters may also be found in the Harry Ransom Humanities Research Center of the University of Texas at Austin, the Alderman Library of the University of Virginia, and the private collection of Dr. William Eric Williams of Rutherford, New Jersey. In the present edition, these collections are identified by the following place names: Buffalo, Indiana, Yale, Texas, Virginia, and Rutherford. Photocopies of the letters in these collections served as the copytexts of this edition, and all photocopies have been checked against the original manuscripts. From references in the surviving correspondence, it is clear that many other letters were written that have since been lost.

For readers interested in the locations of the original letters, the following table may be of use. In the present edition, the letters are numbered in chronological sequence. Buffalo houses the originals of letters 1, 2, 3, 4, 5, 7, 8, 9, 10, 11, 12, 13, 14, 15, 16, 18, 20, 23, 39, 43, 47, 49, 50, 67, 69, 81, 83, 86, 87, 110, 112, and 115. Indiana holds the originals of letters 17, 19, 21, 24, 25, 26, 80, 102, 104, 105, 107, 108, 109, 111, 113, 114, 116, 117, 118, 119, 122, 123, 124, 127, 128, 129, 130, 131, 132, 134, 136, 137, 139, 141, 142, 143, and 146. The original of letter 61 is housed at Virginia. Yale holds the originals of all other letters in this edition. In some cases, only carbon copies have survived; in this edition, carbons have provided the copytexts of letters 64, 66, 71, 74, 77, 79, 88, 91, and 96.

The present edition contains 169 items of the extant correspondence, or slightly more than 30% of the total. In making a selection, I have tried to choose letters that contain important information about (1) the genesis, authorial intention, and publication history of the works of Pound and Williams; (2) their artistic, political, and philosophical principles; (3) their reading and their evaluations of the works of others; and (4) significant developments in their lives and their relationship. Because Pound's wife, Dorothy, handled much of her husband's correspondence after his incarceration, several of her letters to and from Williams are included in this edition. Because this is a selected edition, however, letters of importance have unavoidably been omitted.

In preparing the letters for publication, I have employed the following guidelines. Every letter in the selection is reproduced in its entirety, without editorial abridgement. Each item is preceded by a headnote, which gives its number in the present edition, its form, and the number of its leaves. To designate epistolary forms, I have used the following abbreviations: TLS (typed letter signed), TL (typed letter unsigned), ALS (autograph letter signed), AL (autograph letter unsigned), and ACS (autograph postcard signed). Printed letterheads and return addresses have been omitted, as have directions to readers (*e.g.,* "over").

Some further standardizations have been applied to the texts of the letters. The positions and spacing of dates, salutations, closings, and signatures have been regularized. Dates supplied by the editor from postmarks on envelopes or from internal evidence are given in square brackets. Where the evidence is inconclusive, conjectural dates are followed by a question mark. I am indebted to Dr. Emily Mitchell Wallace and D. D. Paige for their tentative dating of many undated and partially dated items.

The idiosyncratic spacing of Pound's letters poses a major editorial problem. As in his poems, spacing provides an important expressive dimension, yet it cannot be reproduced accurately in anything but a facsimile edition. Because most readers will be more interested in the content of the letters than in their aesthetic effect, I have not attempted to preserve their exact layout.

Paragraph indentations have been standardized. The spacing between paragraphs and lines has been regularized, and unconventional typed or hand-drawn symbols used to indicate spacing and paragraphing have been omitted. The spacing before and after punctuation, and between initials used in names and abbreviations, has been regularized; and all dashes have been standardized to a single en dash, the form preferred by both Pound and Williams.

Authorial insertions, deletions, and corrections have been silently incorporated. Characters missing because a typewriter key failed to strike in the middle of a word have been supplied, and apparently accidental duplications of words have been eliminated. Otherwise, however, the original spelling, capitalization, and punctuation of the letters have not been altered. Both Pound and Williams often employed idiosyncratic and apparently erroneous forms for expressive purposes. Much would be lost if these deviations were to be regularized. The present edition even reproduces apparently unintended errors in spelling, punctuation, and capitalization, marking misspelled or mistyped words with a [*sic*] to indicate that they appear thus in the original.

Other editorial insertions also appear in square brackets. Foreign-language and archaic-English terms are translated, and standard-English equivalents of slang, technical terms, and idiosyncratically spelled words are sometimes given. Some proper names and missing words are provided, and some abbreviations are spelled out. Peculiarities of the copytext, such as illegible words, cut-off pages, and ambiguous placement of addenda, are also explained in bracketed interpolations.

Nearly every letter is followed by a set of explanatory notes. Each note is keyed to the text of its letter by the repetition in italics of a word or phrase from the letter. The names of Ezra Pound and William Carlos Williams are abbreviated in the notes as EP and WCW, respectively. In the interests of economy, some of the explanatory notes refer the reader to an appendix entitled "Biographical Notes." These notes contain information, arranged alphabetically by surname, on key figures mentioned in the correspondence. Many of these entries pertain to more than one letter. They are not rounded biographical sketches but summaries of information selected for its particular relevance to the letters in this edition. Finally, some notes contain abbreviated citations of primary and secondary source materials. The bibliographical key to these abbreviations will be found in the appendix entitled "Abbreviations of Works Cited."

Some of the items in the present edition have been published before. D. D. Paige's edition of *The Letters of Ezra Pound* (1950) contains versions of letters 2, 3, 4, 8, 12, 13, 14, 15, 16, 18, 20, 23, and 50. John C. Thirlwall's edition of *The Selected Letters of William Carlos Williams* (1957) includes versions of letters 30, 34, 37, 40, 41, 45, 51, 54, 60, 84, 117, and 159. Neither Paige nor Thirlwall provides explanatory notes, and in some cases their transcriptions of the letters differ significantly from mine. James Laughlin's "A World of Books Gone Flat," *Grand Street* 3:2 (Winter 1984), pp. 103–09, contains lightly annotated versions of letters 102, 105, 111, 123, and 130. Mary Ellen Solt has also published lightly annotated versions of letters 102, 105, 111, 123, 130, 132, and 141 in *Dear Ez: Letters from William Carlos Williams to Ezra Pound* (1985). In "The Exiles' Letters: The Correspondence between Ezra Pound and William Carlos Williams," *In'hui* 14 (Winter 1980–81), pp. 32–59, Emily Mitchell Wallace quotes selected passages from a number of letters. Brief excerpts have also appeared in other books and articles too numerous to mention here.

I am much indebted to the published researches of other scholars. In addition to the sources listed in the appendix entitled "Abbreviations of Works Cited" and to the works by Solt and Wallace just mentioned, the following studies have been indispensable. Emily Mitchell Wallace, "Pound and Williams at the University of Pennsylvania: 'Men of No Name and with a Fortune to Come,'" *Pennsylvania Review* 1:2 (Spring 1967), pp. 41–53; *A Bibliography of William Carlos Williams* (Middletown, Conn.: Wesleyan University Press, 1968); and "Penn's Poet Friends," *The Pennsylvania Gazette* 71:4 (February 1973), pp. 33–36; Geoffrey H. Movius, "Caviar and Bread: Ezra Pound and William Carlos Williams, 1902–1914," *Journal of Modern Literature* 5 (September 1976), pp. 383–406; Daniel

Hoffman, ed., *Ezra Pound and William Carlos Williams: The University of Pennsylvania Conference Papers* (Philadelphia: University of Pennsylvania Press, 1983); Thomas Parkinson, "Pound and Williams," in *Ezra Pound among the Poets,* ed. George Bornstein (Chicago: University of Chicago Press, 1985), pp. 149–67; and Carol H. Cantrell, " 'Sufficient Ground to Stand On': Pound, Williams, and American History," in *Omnium Gatherum: Essays for Richard Ellmann,* ed. Susan Dick *et al.* (Gerrards Cross: Colin Smythe, 1989), pp. 153–60.

I have received valuable assistance from other quarters as well. My principal obligations are to Mr. and Mrs. James Laughlin, to the late Dr. William Eric Williams, and to Mrs. William Eric Williams, whose encouragement, cooperation, and hospitality have sustained the project from its inception. The letters of Pound and Williams are published by permission of Dr. Williams, Paul H. Williams, the Ezra Pound Literary Property Trust, and New Directions Publishing Corporation acting as agents for the Pound Trust and the Estate of William Carlos Williams. The letters of Dorothy Pound are published by permission of Mr. Omar S. Pound. The managers and editors of New Directions—Peggy L. Fox, Peter Glassgold, and Griselda Ohannessian—have been wonderfully helpful, patient, and cordial.

I owe a great deal to the following libraries and their librarians, who have provided copies of the correspondence, permission to reproduce them and to quote from other unpublished materials in their collections, and full cooperation during my research visits: the Beinecke Rare Book and Manuscript Library, Yale University (Patricia C. Willis), the Poetry/Rare Books Collection, University of Buffalo (Robert J. Bertholf), the Lilly Library, Indiana University (Saundra Taylor), and the Harry Ransom Humanities Research Center, University of Texas at Austin (Cathy Henderson and Richard Oram). I wish also to thank the University of Virginia Library (Sharon Defibaugh and Michael Plunkett) for its assistance in connection with letter 61, the original of which is manuscript 8207 in the Ezra Pound Collection, Clifton Waller Barrett Library, Manuscripts Division, Special Collections Department, University of Virginia Library. I am no less grateful to the Van Pelt Library of the University of Pennsylvania (Nancy M. Shawcross) for patiently answering many queries, to the New York Public Library, to the British Library in London, and to the Inter-Library Loan Department of the University of New Mexico.

In a project of this magnitude, one relies upon the kindness of strangers, friends, students, casual acquaintances—a wide array of generous folk. At the University of New Mexico, three intelligent and hard-working graduate assistants have collaborated with me at various stages of the project: Russell Day, Leslie Hatcher, and Mary Friedman. I have also received information, advice, and material assistance from the following persons: Massimo Bacigalupo, George Bornstein, Fred Bunker, Ron Bush, Carol H. Cantrell, Julie Cunico, Michael Fischer, Donald Gallup, David M. Gordon, Mary Haight, Archie Henderson, Lois G. Hendrickson, Laureen Larson, A. Walton Litz, Marilyn Rae McClellan, Kris McCusker, Christopher MacGowan, Paul Mariani, Timothy Materer, A. David Moody, Antonio Pantano, Jami Peelle, Gail M. Pietrzyk, Omar S. Pound, Mary de Rachewiltz, Lawrence S. Rainey, Tim Redman, Neil Roberts, M. L. Rosenthal, Dieter Schulz, Mary Ellen Solt, Leon Surette, Richard Taylor, E. P. Walkiewicz, Emily Mitchell Wallace, Margaret Wimsatt, Donald Woodward, and Judy Woodward. These gracious people have helped the book come into being, but none of them is responsible for its errors and omissions.

For financial support of this project, I am indebted to the American Philosophical Society, the Ball Brothers Foundation, and the Mr. and Mrs. Robert Wertheim Charter Companies. The University of New Mexico's Department of English and College of Arts and Sciences have contributed in many ways, and I am grateful to the University for a sabbatical leave in the fall of 1994, when much of my editorial work was completed.

I would like to dedicate that work to the wonderful Watkins women: Molly, Mary Ann, Su, and my wife, Barbara.

Hugh Witemeyer

PART ONE

1907–1920

Pound and Williams first met at the University of Pennsylvania in the autumn of 1902. Pound, who turned seventeen in October, was a sophomore student of Romance languages from nearby Wyncote, a suburb of Philadelphia. Williams was a nineteen-year-old freshman student of medicine from Rutherford, New Jersey. Though younger, Pound was more precocious and self-confident, and took the lead in the relationship. The two young men shared interests in poetry, theater and acting, French and Spanish literature, fencing, tennis, and pretty girls. Both were enamored, for example, of Hilda Doolittle, the soulful and strikingly beautiful daughter of a professor of astronomy at the university.

In 1903, Pound transferred to Hamilton College in Clinton, New York, where the curriculum in foreign languages was superior to that of Penn. He remained there until his graduation in 1905, but kept in touch with Williams during vacations in Wyncote. Pound returned to Penn for M.A. work in 1905–06, Williams' final year of study; and he stayed on for Ph.D. studies in 1906–07, while Williams undertook an internship in New York City. In the autumn of 1907, Pound accepted a position as a teacher of foreign languages at Wabash College in Crawfordsville, Indiana. The surviving correspondence begins at this juncture.

Pound did not teach at Wabash for long. In the spring of 1908, he was fired for indecorous behavior. He left the United States, convinced that a serious American artist could flourish only in Europe. He went first to Venice, where he published a book of poems at his own expense, and then to London. There he found publishers for four more books in the next two years and began to cultivate a distinguished literary acquaintance. With financial support from his parents, he became a full-time man of letters.

Williams, meanwhile, finished his medical training in New York and set up a private practice in obstetrics and pediatrics in his home town of Rutherford. In 1909, he, too, published a volume of poems at his own expense. The friends exchanged copies of their books and criticized each other with great gusto. No less determined than Pound to be an important writer, Williams realized that his talent would take longer to develop. He needed a second career to support himself and to maintain his artistic independence.

In the course of the year 1910, the friends met on both sides of the Atlantic. Williams spent several weeks in Leipzig, Germany, attending lectures in medicine at the university. On his way home in March, he stopped for a week in London. There, Pound introduced him to William Butler Yeats and other writers, and to

3

the young woman whom Pound would marry in 1914, Dorothy Shakespear. Williams went on to visit Italy, where his brother was studying architecture in Rome, and Spain before returning to the United States.

That summer, Pound came home to recuperate from a prolonged illness. He stayed seven months, until February 1911. After he was well again, Pound lived mainly in New York, so as to promote his stateside literary career. He frequently visited the Williams family in Rutherford, just across the Hudson River. He renewed his friendship with Williams' parents, and took an officious interest in his friend's neglected literary education. From the books and conversation exchanged during these months, Williams drew inspiration of various kinds for the next ten years.

Back in London, Pound dedicated his new book of poems to Williams. He titled it *Ripostes* (1912), perhaps to commemorate their mutual love of fencing with one another, both literally and figuratively. Meanwhile, Williams put down even deeper roots in Rutherford by marrying a local girl, Florence ("Floss") Herman, and buying a big house, which also served as his medical office. Pound was summoned to the wedding, but regretfully declined the invitation.

He was now immersed in the Imagist movement of 1912–14. This influential, avant-garde campaign emphasized the spare, economical presentation of poetic images in free verse, without authorial commentary or philosophizing. Pound's immediate allies in the movement were English and expatriate American poets who lived in London, such as Hilda Doolittle ("H. D."), Richard Aldington, and F. S. Flint. Pound used his new appointment as Foreign Editor of *Poetry* magazine to promote the Imagist program in the United States as well, and resolved to enlist the talents of Williams in the cause.

In 1913, Williams sent Pound a book-length manuscript of poems entitled *The Tempers*. Having verified their Imagist merit, Pound promptly arranged for an edition of the poems by his own London publisher, Elkin Mathews. Pound generated advance publicity by placing seven poems in Harold Monro's *Poetry Review*, and he reviewed the volume favorably when it appeared. In 1914, Williams officially became an Imagist poet when his work appeared in Pound's anthology, *Des Imagistes*, and in *The Egoist*, the principal London journal of the movement.

This partnership initiated a period of close collaboration that lasted through the end of the Great War of 1914–18. The work of Pound and Williams appeared regularly in *The Egoist, Poetry, The Little Review*, and *Others*, a New York poetry magazine with which Williams was editorially associated. Moreover, the collaboration entailed a creative dialogue. Mutually inspired and challenged, each wrote poems in response to those of the other. They shared an interest in translating Spanish Renaissance poetry and drama. They also edited one another's published works, each compiling a list of poems by the other suitable for inclusion in a one-volume selection.

As the Great War subsided, long-suppressed literary conflicts broke out. One of these culminated in Williams' first public difference of opinion with Pound. In 1918, Pound, exasperated by the editorial policies of *Poetry,* prompted the English critic Edgar Jepson to attack the magazine. Jepson's essay first appeared under the title "Recent United States Poetry" in *The English Review* for May 1918 and was reprinted as "The Western School" in *The Little Review* for September 1918, with an approving introductory note by Pound. In the essay, Jepson criticizes *Poetry* and its editor Harriet Monroe for awarding prizes to Vachel Lindsay, Edgar Lee Masters, and Robert Frost, all of whom Jepson accuses of verbal posturing and poor workmanship. In Jepson's view, the best recent American poetry is that of T. S. Eliot, especially "The Love Song of J. Alfred Prufrock" and "La Figlia Che Piange."

Jepson's polemic provoked a storm of controversy. Williams entered the fray in 1919. Having published a book of poetry without Pound's help (*Al Que Quiere!,* 1917), Williams now declared his literary independence. In the Prologue to *Kora in Hell: Improvisations,* which he published separately in *The Little Review,* Williams took on the expatriate American poets—Pound, Eliot, and H. D. The expatriates, Williams argued, were too Europeanized, too cosmopolitan and deracinated, to be representative of American verse. Instead, Williams championed not the Chicago school but the New York school to which he himself belonged. Thus, the Prologue celebrates the work of Marianne Moore, Wallace Stevens, Mina Loy, Alfred Kreymborg, and Maxwell Bodenheim.

The Prologue also makes a momentous public use of Williams' private correspondence with Pound. Williams directly quotes several passages from a letter Pound wrote him on November 10, 1917. In this letter, Pound defends cosmopolitanism and argues that Williams' mixed ancestry compromises his nationalistic aesthetics. The quotations show how early and how firmly racialist assumptions were established in Pound's thinking, although that was not the point Williams wished to illustrate. The Prologue was the first, but by no means the last, occasion on which Williams made creative use of Pound's letters to him. Pound could hardly object, since he had started the game by quoting one of Williams' lost letters to him in *The Little Review* for October 1917.

That Williams' early letters to Pound are lost is a pity. Their disappearance means that we do not have Williams' views on many of the issues, persons, works, and events that he and Pound discussed between 1907 and 1920. The absence of one side of the correspondence makes the record of the friendship seem more of a Poundian monologue than it probably was. No doubt Williams gave as good as he got in their high-spirited exchanges.

1. TLS-1

Feb. 6 [1907]

Bear Bill.

At last I have some decent news for you. One Miss Viola Baxter . who made hell homelike for me during my exile in upper new york.

One of the few girls I have fallen in love with (and one of the rarer few, the unkissed – this in your private ear, that you may know her afar off

Well – as her looks will speak for themselves unless she has changed greatly in the last few years.

To cut it short she is on the job in the great and wicked city of Gotham [New York] and as soon as I get her adress [*sic*] I will submit it.

Your habit has not been to object to my lady friends . and As the child is alone and lonely I want you to call once or twice out of decency to me – don't object that you are bussy [*sic*]. DAMN It, I know all about being bussy. . If you dont like her you can send your little brother. Please dont go expecting too much . just a simple country girl. I am very uncritical you know. Never see the flaws in women . girl children etc.

I shall also notify Bob. in case you think you will have a sinch [*sic*] on the line – you might not tell your little brother and try to run the monopoly – I am opposed to trusts you know.

I am comeing [*sic*] over myself some time too. It may take you some time to get acquainted. Of course you understand, I know nothing of the lady's present habits. She may have learned to chew and smoke and say darn and. . . . during the last year or so. but as soon as I get her adress I will send it to you. . By the way dont you want to run over for a dance this Saturday. I will gladly give you eat and sleep. and the ladies will be fussed to death to see you mug.

So lond [*sic*] I am in a darneder hurry than the length of this note would lead you to think.

So long you dear old devil.

Ezra

Viola Baxter: See "Biographical Notes" on JORDAN, VIOLA SCOTT BAXTER. In a letter to her of February 6, 1907 (Yale), EP asks for her "receiving address" and describes WCW as "brother in arms, one of the real friends that I have managed to get to endure the strain of my charming society." In a letter to WCW of February 11, 1907 (Buffalo), EP gives Viola's address as 143 E. 83rd Street.

my exile: From September 1903 to June 1905 EP was a student at Hamilton College in Clinton, New York.

your little brother: See "Biographical Notes" on WILLIAMS, EDGAR IRVING. In an amusing letter to Edgar of February 27, 1907, WCW describes his first visit to Viola Baxter; see Mariani, pp. 57–58.

Bob: Bob Lamberton was a classmate of EP and WCW and a varsity football player at the University of Pennsylvania; see Mariani, pp. 51, 59.

2. ALS-22

[October 21, 1908]

Dear Bill

Glad to hear from you at last. Good Lord! of course you dont have to like the stuff I write. I hope the time will never come when I get so fanatical as to let a mans like or dislike for what I happen to 'poetare' interfere with an old friendship or a new one.

Remember of course that some of the stuff is dramatic & in the character of the person named in the title.

The "Decadence" which is one of the poems I suppose in your index expurgatorius is the expression of the decadent spirit as I conceive it.

The Villonauds are likewise what I conceive after a good deal of study to be an expression akin to, if not of, the spirit breathed in Villons own poeting.

Fifine . is the answer to the question quoted from Brownings own 'Fifine at the fair'.

Will continue when I get back from an appointment.

&

once more to the breech.

I am dam glad to get some sincere criticism any how. Now let me to the defence,:   It seems to me you might as well say that Shakespeare is dissolute in his plays because Falstaff is, or that the plays have a criminal tendency because there is murder done in them.

To me the short so called dramatic lyric – at any rate the sort of thing I do, is the poetic part of a drama the rest of which – to me the prose part – is left to the readers immagination [*sic*] or implied or set in a short note – I catch the character I happen to be interested in at the moment he interests me – usualy [*sic*] a moment of song, self-analysis, or sudden understanding, or revelation. & the rest of the play would bore me & presumably the reader . I paint my man as I *conceive* him. et voila tout [and that's all] . . ! Is a painter's art crooked because he paints hunch-backs

I wish you'd spot the bitter personal notes; & send 'em over to me for inspection.

personaly [*sic*] I think you get 'em by reading in the wrong tone of voice – however you may be right. Hilda seems about as pleased with the work as you are. Mosher is going to re-print W. B. Yeats applys [*sic*] the adjective charming but they feel no kindly responsibility for the morals & future of the author.

As for preaching poetic anarchy or any thing else – heaven forbid. I record symptoms as I see 'em. I advise no remedy, I dont even name the disease usualy   Temperature 102 3/8   pulse 78 tongue coated etc.   eyes yellow etc.

as for the "eyes of too ruthless public". . damn their eyes. No art ever yet grew by looking into the eyes of the public ruthless or otherwise.

You can obliterate yourself & mirror God, Nature, or Humanity, but if you try to mirror yourself in the eyes of the public woe be unto your art.

– at least that's the phaze [*sic*] of truth that presents itself to me.

I wonder whether when you talk about poetic anarchy you mean a life lawlessly poetic & poetically lawless, mirrored in the verse, or whether you mean a lawlessness in the materia poetica & metrica.

Sometimes I use rules of Spanish, Anglo-Saxon, & Greek metric that are not common in the english of Milton's or Miss Austin's [*sic*] day.

I doubt however if you are sufficiently au courant [up to date] to know just what the poets & musicians & painters are doing with a good deal of convention that has masqueraded as law.

Au contraire [on the contrary], I am very sure that I have written a lot of stuff that would please you & a lot of my personal friends more than A. L[ume]. S[pento]. but, mon cher [my dear], would a collection of mild, pretty verses convince any publisher or critic that *I* happen to be a genius . and deserve audience. I have written bushels of verse that could offend no one except a person as well read as I am who knows that it has all been said just as prettily before. – Why write what I can translate out of renaissance latin.   . or crib from the sainted dead.

Here are a list of facts on which I and 9,000,000, other poets have spieled endlessly,

1 Spring is a pleasant season.

  the flowers, etc. etc. sprout bloom etc. etc.

2. young mans fancy | lightly

               |

               | heavily

               |

               | gaily etc ect.

3. love, a delightsome tickling.

    indefinable etc.

    by day , etc. etc . etc,

    by night, etc. etc. etc.

4 trees, hills, etc. are by a provident nature arranged

    diversely in diverse places

5 winds, clouds, rains, etc.

    flop thru & over 'em.

6 men love women.

    (more poetic in singular, but the verb retains the same form.)

(in Greece, & pagan countries men loved men, but the fact is no longer mentioned in polite society except in an expurgated sense.) I am not attracted by the pagan custom but my own prejudices are not materia poetica.

Besides I didn't get particularly lascivious in A.L.S.

however in the above 6 groups I think you find the bulk of the poetic matter of the ages.

– wait.

7. men fight battles. etc. etc.

8. men go on voyages.

Beyond this, men think & feel certain things. & see certain things not with the bodily vision. about this time I begin to get interested & the general public too ruthlessly goes to sleep?

To however quit this wrangle. If you mean to say that A. L. S. is a rather gloomy & disagreeable book, I agree with you. I thought that in Venice. Kept out of it one tremendously gloomy series of ten sonnets à la Thompson [sic] of the "City of Dreadful night," which are poetically rather fine in spots   wrote or attempted to write a bit of sunshine, some of which – too much for my critical sense got printed. however the bulk of the work (say 30 of the poems) is the most finished work I have yet done.

I dont know that you will like the "Quinzaine for this Yule" any better.

Again as to the unconstrained vagabondism. = If any body ever shuts *you* in Indianna [sic] for four months & you dont at least *write* some unconstrained something or other, , I give up hope for your salvation –

Again if you ever get degraded branded with infamy etc. for feeding a person who needs food . . you will probably rise up and bless the present and sacred name of Madame Grundy for all her holy hypocracy [sic].

I am not getting bitter. I have been more than blessed for my kindness & the few sheckles [sic] cast on the water have come back ten fold and I have no fight with any body.

I am amused. the smile is kindly but entirely undiluted with reverence.

to continue. I am doubly thankful for a friend who'll say what he thinks . – after long enough consideration to know that he realy [*sic*] thinks – and I hope I'm going to be blessed with your criticism. for as long as may be. – I wish you'd get a bit closer. I mean make more explicit & detailed statements of what you dont like.

Bitter personal note???

Grace Before Song. – certainly not.

La Fraisne – the man is half– or whole mad. . pathos certainly but bitterness. I cant see it.

Cino. – the thing is banal he might be any one. besides he is catalogued in his epitaph.

Audiart – nonsense.

Villonaud for Yule. ''

Gibbet. – personal???

Mesmerism – impossible.

Fifine.   ''

Anima Sola.

Senectus. – utterly impossible.

Famam Librosque. self critisism [*sic*] but I dont see it as bitter.

Eyes. – nonsense.

Script. Ig.   ''

Donzella Beata ''

Vana –

Chasteus.

Decadence. – writ in plural. even if not it is answered & contradicted on the opposite page.

The Fistulae – nonsense.

Where are they. I may be the blind one . .

Now to save me writing.

Ecclesiastes. 2. 24

Proverbs. 30. 19. . this is the arrant vagabondism. the soul. from god. returns to him – but any one who can trace that course or symbolize it by any thing not wandering –

perhaps you like pictures painted in green & white & gold & I paint in black & crimson & purple.

however. speak out & dont become "powerless to write that you dont like". there is one thing sickly-sweet. to wit. the flattery of those that know nothing about the art. & yet adore indiscriminately.

To your "ultimate attainments of poesy". what are they.? I of course am only

at the first quater [*sic*] post in a marathon. – I have of course not attained them.
but I wonder just where you think the tape is stretched for Mr Hays [*sic*], "vittore
ufficiale" and Dorando Pietri hero of Italy . . – that was by the way delightful to
get in Italy & to get here   one of the men who arranged the events. one of the
trainer sort who said Pietri would have never got there if he hadnt been helped.). I
wish no fooling that you would define your ultimate attainments of poesy.

Of course we wont agree   that would be *too* uninteresting.

I don't know that I can make much of a list.

1. To paint the thing as I see it.

2. Beauty.

3. Freedom from didactisism [*sic*].

4. It is only good manners if you repeat a few other men to at least do it better
or more briefly. – utter originality is of course out of the question.

besides the Punch Bowl covers that point.

then again you must remember I dont try to write for the public.

I cant. I haven't that kind of intellegence [*sic*]. .

   "to such as love this same beauty that I
   love somewhat after mine own fashion."

Also I dont want to bore people. that is one most flagrant crime at this stage of
the worlds condition.

19 pages of letter ought to prove that. – I am hopeless. "ma cosí son io" [but
that's how I am]

Your letter is worth a dozen notes of polite appreciation.

Eccovi [here is] an honest man. / Diogenes put to shame./.

Write now that the bars are down. & tare [*sic*] it up. you may thereby help me
to do something better. – flattery never will.

My days of utter privation are over for a space.

adress [*sic*].

48 Langham St

London WC1

                              Ezra

P. S. the last line page 3. of A. L. S. ought to answer some of your letter.

The "Decadence": The poems discussed in this letter were published in EP's first book, *A
   Lume Spento* (Venice: A. Antonini, 1908).

index expurgatorius: In 1546, the Roman Catholic Church promulgated the first *Index
   Librorum Prohibitorum* (List of Prohibited Books), which named books and authors

forbidden to Catholics because of their pernicious effects. The *Index Librorum Expurgatorius* (List of Expurgated Books) named books that could be read only after the deletion or emendation of specific passages.

The Villonauds: "Villonaud for This Yule" and "A Villonaud: Ballad of the Gibbet" imitate the work of the medieval French poet François Villon (1431–*c.* 1463).

Fifine: "Fifine Answers" is a response to *Fifine at the Fair* (1872) by EP's favorite Victorian poet, Robert Browning (1812–1869). The question quoted in EP's epigraph is, "Why is it that, disgraced, they seem to relish life the more?"

Shakespeare: Sir John Falstaff is the pleasure-loving braggart soldier in William Shakespeare's *Henry IV, Parts One and Two* (1598–1600). He appears also in *The Merry Wives of Windsor* (1602).

Hilda: See "Biographical Notes" on DOOLITTLE, HILDA.

Mosher: Thomas Bird Mosher of Portland, Maine, was the leading American publisher of *fin-de-siècle* poetry. He declined, however, to reprint *A Lume Spento*.

W. B. Yeats: See "Biographical Notes" on YEATS, WILLIAM BUTLER. EP had sent him a complimentary copy of *A Lume Spento;* see Carpenter, pp. 94–95.

Milton's or Miss Austin's day: John Milton, author of *Paradise Lost,* lived from 1608 to 1674; Jane Austen, author of *Pride and Prejudice,* from 1775 to 1817.

young mans fancy: In "Locksley Hall" (1842) Alfred, Lord Tennyson memorably declared that "In the spring a young man's fancy lightly turns to thoughts of love."

in Venice: EP lived in Venice from March to August of 1908; he then he moved to London.

Thompson: The Victorian poet James Thomson (1834–1882) published a melancholic sequence entitled "The City of Dreadful Night" in 1874. EP's imitations of Thomson were not published.

"Quinzaine for this Yule": The title of EP's second book of poems, published in London by Pollock & Co. in December 1908.

Indianna: From September 1907 to February 1908, EP was employed as an instructor in Romance Languages at Wabash College in Crawfordsville, Indiana. He was dismissed by college authorities after giving shelter to a stranded female entertainer; see Carpenter, pp. 71–81.

Madame Grundy: In Thomas Morton's play *Speed the Plough* (1798), Mrs. Grundy personifies propriety in British public opinion.

Grace Before Song: The first poem in *A Lume Spento.* EP proceeds to list the titles of other poems in the order of their appearance in the volume.

Ecclesiastes 2. 24: "There is nothing better for a man, than that he should eat and drink, and that he should make his soul enjoy good in his labour. This also I saw, that it was from the hand of God."

Proverbs 30. 19: "The way of an eagle in the air; the way of a serpent upon a rock; the way of a ship in the midst of the sea; and the way of a man with a maid."

Mr Hays . . . and Dorando Pietri: In the marathon at the London Olympic Games of 1908, Dorando Pietri of Italy entered Shepherds Bush stadium well ahead of his nearest rival but collapsed five times during the final lap and was helped across the finish line. Pietri was disqualified and the next finisher, John Joseph Hayes of the United States, was declared the official winner ("vittore ufficiale"). Pietri became an international celebrity and the subject of a hit song by Irving Berlin.

the Punch Bowl: A student publication at the University of Pennsylvania.

to such as love: EP quotes from the dedication of *A Lume Spento.*

Diogenes: Greek philosopher (c. 412–323 B.C.) of the Cynic school, famed for his asceticism and bluntness.

the last line page 3: The line is from "La Fraisne": "For I know that the wailing and bitterness are a folly."

3. ALS-2

[February or March 1909]

Deer Bill:

May I quote "Steve' on the occasion of my own firing: "Gee!! wish I wuz fired!' Nothing like it to stir the blood & give a man a start in life. Hope you shine the improving hour with poesy.

Am by way of falling into the croud [*sic*] that does things here.

London, deah old lundon is the place for poesy.

Mathews is publishing my 'Personae' & giving me the same terms he gives Maurice Hewlett. As for your p'tit frere. I knew he'd hit the pike for Dagotalia [Italy] when does he come over, I shall make a special trip to Ave Roma immortalis [Hail immortal Rome] to rehear the tale of "Meestair Robingsonnh'

If you have saved any pennies during your stay in Nueva York you'd better come across & broaden your mind. american doctors are in great demand in Italy especialy during the touring season.

Besides youd much prefer to scrap with an intellegent [*sic*] person like myself than with a board of directing idiots.

Once more Deer Bill.

Being in a facetious mood I tell you.

re V[iola]. S[cott]. B[axter]. to kiss & make up and also – I quit before I say anything ridikulous.

Eturnaly
EP

Steve: Carey Stevens was an instructor in English at Wabash College in 1907–08. In an undated letter to his mother (Yale), EP describes Stevens as "a very sane and joyous companion."

firing: In March 1909 WCW resigned his internship in obstetrics and pediatrics at Nursery and Child's Hospital in New York City. According to the account in WCW's *Auto-biography,* pp. 102–05, the hospital's Board of Governors expected him to sign patient records that were falsified in order to increase the hospital's state funding. On EP's firing, see the notes to Letter 2 above.

Mathews: See "Biographical Notes" on MATHEWS, ELKIN. In April 1909 Mathews published both EP's *Personae* and *Artemisian: Idylls and Songs* by the English novelist and poet Maurice Hewlett (1861–1923).

p'tit frere: See "Biographical Notes" on WILLIAMS, EDGAR IRVING (WCW's "p'tit frere" or little brother).

"Meestair Robingsonnh': Edgar's bawdy tale of Mr. Robinson, who cuckolded a Frenchman and pissed in his eye, was well known among WCW's family and friends. In a letter to EP of December 19, 1932, Louis Zukofsky refers to it as "Bill's brother's joke" (see Pound/Zukofsky, p. 140); and EP alludes to it in a letter to James Laughlin of February 27, 1935 (Yale).

4. ALS-8

[May 21, 1909]

I hope to God you have no feelings   if you have burn this *before* reading.

Dear Billy,

Thanks for your Poems   What, if anything, do you want me to do by way of criticism.?

? is it a personal, private, edtn [edition], for your friends, or ??

As proof that W. C. W. has poetic instincts the book is valuable. au contraire [on the other hand]. if you were in London & saw the stream of current poetry, I wonder how much of it you would have printed. – Do you want me to criticise it as if were my own work.?

I have sinned in nearly every possible way – even the ways I most condemn   I have printed too much. I have been praised by the greatest living poet. I am after eight years hammering against impenetrable adamant become suddenly somewhat of a success.

From where do you want me to shove the sharpened "blade". – Is there anything I know about your book that you dont know. Individual, original it is not. great art it is not. Poetic it is – but there are innumerable poetic volumes poured out here in Gomorah [*sic*]

There is no town like London to make one feel the vanity of all art except the highest. To make one disbelieve in all but the most careful & conservative presentation of one's stuff.

I have sinned deeply against the doctrine I preach. Your book would not attract even passing attention here. There are fine lines in it but nowhere I think do you add anything to the poets you have used as models.

If I should publish a medical treatise explaining that arnica was good for bruises (or cuts or what ever it is) it would show that I had found out certain medical facts but it would not be of great value to the science of medicine. you see I am getting under weigh –

If you'll read Yeats, & Browning, & Francis Thompson, & Swinburne & Rosetti [*sic*] you'll learn something about the progress of Eng. poetry in the last century .

And if you'll read Margaret Sackville, Rosamund Watson, Ernest Rhys, Jim G. Fairfax, you'll learn what the people of second rank can do & what dam good work it is.

you are out of touch. – thats all –

Most great poetry is written in the first person (i.e. it has been for about 2000 years)   the 3d is sometimes usable & the 2nd nearly always wooden. (millions of exceptions.!) What's the use of this.

Read. Aristotles. Poetics. Longinus "on the Sublime". De Quincey, Yeats, essays.

(Lect I. learn your art thoroughly. if you'll study the people in that lst. lecture. & then reread your stuff. – you'll get a lot more ideas about it than you will from any external critique I can make of the verse you have sent me

Vale et me ama [farewell and love me]
E

And remember a mans real work is what *he is going to do* not what is behind him.

Avanti e coraggio [forward and courage]!

your Poems: WCW's *Poems* was privately printed at the author's expense by Reid Howell of Rutherford, New Jersey, in May 1909. In his *Autobiography,* p. 107, WCW apparently forgets this letter when he writes of *Poems:* "Ezra was silent, if indeed he ever saw the thing, which I hope he never did."

the greatest living poet: See "Biographical Notes" on YEATS, WILLIAM BUTLER.

Gomorah: Biblical city of wickedness, destroyed by fire and brimstone in Genesis 19.

arnica: Medicinal tincture made of the mountain tobacco plant and used in the treatment of bruises.

Francis Thompson: English poet and critic (1859–1907), whose best-known work is "The Hound of Heaven" (1893).

Swinburne: The poetry of Algernon Charles Swinburne (1837–1909) was an important influence upon EP's own early work.

Rosetti: EP was likewise inspired by the poetry, painting, translations, and Bohemian lifestyle of Dante Gabriel Rossetti (1828–1882).

Margaret Sackville: When this letter was written, the English poet and dramatist Lady Margaret Sackville (1881–1963) had published *Poems* (1901) and *A Hymn to Dionysus* (1905). In *Profile* (Milan: John Scheiwiller, 1932), p. 14, EP writes, "I doubt if any one else can quote Margaret Sackville's 'The night forgets the day.'"

Rosamund Watson: The English poet, essayist, and editor Rosamund Watson (1863–1911) was the author of *A Summer Night* (1891), *Vespertilia* (1895), *After Sunset* (1903), *Tares* (1906), and *The Heart of a Garden* (1906).

Ernest Rhys: The English poet and editor Ernest Rhys (1859–1946) was a member of the Rhymers' Club and the editor of J. M. Dent's Everyman's Library series. He was instrumental in Dent's publication of EP's *The Spirit of Romance* (1910).

Jim G. Fairfax: The Australian-born poet and translator James Griffyth Fairfax (1886–1976) was the author of *The Gates of Sleep* (1906) and *Poems* (1908). He was an Oxford student when EP met him in 1909.

Aristotles. Poetics: The *Poetics* of the Greek philosopher Aristotle (384–322 B.C.), a study of the principles of Greek tragedy, is antiquity's best-known work of literary criticism. In a letter to his father of August 4, 1909 (Yale), EP says, "please send the little paper copy of 'Aristotle's Poetics' Longinus 'On the Sublime' bound with it." This was probably Henry Morley's edition, published in London in the Cassell's National Library series (1898, 1901).

Longinus: The Greek critical treatise "On the Sublime" is traditionally attributed to the 3rd-century philosopher Longinus. In an undated early letter to Bert Hessler (Texas), EP writes: "Remember tha [*sic*] since Longinus you have in the field of literary criticism . Dante, Dequinsey [*sic*] and Coleridge, and 'your humble servant' the rest are mere revisers and re-sayers of truism." In his *Autobiography,* p. 65, WCW says that he read "On the Sublime" at EP's behest.

De Quincey: Thomas DeQuincey (1785–1859), English essayist and critic, author of *Confessions of an English Opium-Eater* (1822). In his *Autobiography,* p. 65, WCW says that he still has a volume of DeQuincey's *Literary Criticisms* [*sic*], signed by EP. "I see no sign in them that he ever read them. . . . Maybe he once gave them to me and told *me* to read them. It would be like him."

Yeats, essays: At this time Yeats had published two important collections of essays, *Ideas of Good and Evil* (1903) and *Discoveries* (1907).

5. ALS-2

[October 26, 1912]

Deer Bull.

Yrs. to hand. too tired to enter aesthetic discussion.

I'm foreign correspondent of the Enclosed.

I advise you to subscribe as it contains Yeats, Tagore, me, H. D. & every one of interest.

I've just written to Remy de Gourmont.

Want the best foreign stuff as well as the best London.

tell Welsh & boom the show for all its worth.

We won't be really in full swing till the Dec. no. but never mind.

We're *the only* serious Potery [*sic*] show printed in English & thank Gord there seems to be a little sense at the Chicago end as well as here.

Send yr. stuff. if you ever do anything more that's fit to print, to the Chicago office, or to me, as you like. (tell Welsh to do same. His Deirdre chorus & tell 'em I used to like it. or the whole g[od]. D[amned]. Deirdre. They're going to have a play put on also.)

We are the light in Darkness   see that you boost our subscription list.

> yrs. T H F O [Till Hell Freezes Over]
> Ezry

Has that shit Monro sent you yr copies of the Poetry *Review?*

foreign correspondent: The first monthly number of *Poetry: A Magazine of Verse,* published in Chicago under the editorship of Harriet Monroe, appeared in October 1912. EP was named as the Foreign Editor of the magazine.

Yeats: See "Biographical Notes" on YEATS, WILLIAM BUTLER. *Poetry* for December 1912 carried five poems by Yeats: "The Mountain Tomb," "To a Child Dancing upon the Shore," "Fallen Majesty," "Love and the Bird," and "The Realists."

Tagore: Poetry for December 1912 carried prose translations of six poems by the Bengali writer Rabindranath Tagore (1861–1941), followed by EP's essay on "Tagore's Poems." Tagore's *Gitanjali,* with an introduction by Yeats, was published in 1912, and Tagore was awarded the Nobel Prize in 1913.

me: Poetry for October 1912 contained two poems by EP, "To Whistler, American" and "Middle-Aged: A Study in Emotion." A group of twelve poems entitled "Contemporania" appeared in the number for April 1913.

H. D.: See "Biographical Notes" on DOOLITTLE, HILDA. *Poetry* for January 1913 contained three of her poems, signed "H. D., Imagiste."

Remy de Gourmont: See "Biographical Notes" on GOURMONT, REMY DE. Gourmont's earliest contribution to *Poetry* was two French "Epigrammes" in the issue for January 1915.

Welsh: The American poet, playwright, and journalist Robert Gilbert Welsh (1869–1924) was the drama editor of the *New York Herald* and the author of *Azrael and Other Poems* (1925). EP met him in New York in 1910. Welsh's published works do not appear to include a poetic drama on the subject of "Deirdre."

Monro: Harold Monro (1879–1932) was the owner of the Poetry Bookshop in London, the editor of the *Georgian Poetry* anthologies (1912–22), and the founding editor of *The Poetry Review*, which ran from January to December 1912. Seven poems by WCW, with an introductory note by EP, appeared in *The Poetry Review* for October 1912 under the title, "A Selection from *The Tempers.*"

6. ALS-6

[November 29, 1912]

Deer Bull:

I am slowly digesting *it.* Your prose style is not remarkable for its lucidity.

Still I am, here & there, convinced that you are driving at something or other. And that you usualy [*sic*] mean something or other even where you don't say it.

I recognize that this or that poem, whereon you comment, is distinct from the rest by this or that quality which might be – more or less – defined as you define it.

The "Salve" is early work, it has rhythm & is included solely for the rhythmic structure & because I shall never have anything more to say on that particular matter. – It is "historicaly' [*sic*] out of place in this book

Your theory – I dont say you *express it,* but theory you seem to have back of your truly awful welter of words – is interesting. You've got hold of something or other.

Its odd you don't mention what are usually counted the 2 best poems in the book.

Its odd, what you say of "N. Y." True it is the only poem in the book where I solicit anything. – Would you have had me say "12 years old and flat chested"

Your theory of the invisible force squirting onto the ϱανταστιϰον [phantastikon] is interesting. & very profound – very objective

You are quite right about the Phasellus. I was trying the latin trick of *one* beautiful line in an unpoetic composition.

Also it was rather a lark, as it has become the most scholarly of traditions to parody that poem of Catullus' – A joke so thoroughly abstruse as to require pages of foot-notes – an utter snobbery.

Your perception of the "unit" is the most gratifying. That of course is the artistic triumph. – To produce the whole which ceases to exist if *one* of its component parts be removed or permuted = or make the "whole" that has no "parts". Yes. yes. very flattering. Perhaps true, only my modesty should forbid me to accept such flagrant compliment.

Oh well, you've seen a lot that I suppose nobody else will. – if that's any comfort to you. So I suppose you've earned the bloody dedication. Which by the way I chucked at you free of charge in return for the hope which you some months since inspired. i.e. that you would your self parturate.

I tell you by cock a poem that you will like and that is Wilfred Scawen Blunt's double sonnet beginning.

> "He who has once been happy is for aye
> Out of destructions reach. His fortune then
> Holds nothing secret; and Eternity
> Which is a mystery to other men
> Has like a woman given him its joy.
> Time is his conquest. Life, if it should fret
> Has paid him tribute.

Its in the Oxford book of verse – but beware lest you get drunk on it & take to writing wholly in the Elizabethan manner.

Which he in this sonnet overcomes, but which too often elsewhere swamps him.

I wonder what you'll say to my next book. which is *modern* – ehem!, yes, *modern*.

I'm afraid your *mss* has been lost some where or other. I had it up till a month or so ago. but it seems now to have disappeared.

As my publisher has just gone bust I shall send you nothing but felicitations anent [upon] your approaching nuptuals [*sic*].

By the way, returning to "Ripostes" the "Seefarer" [*sic*] is translated & dam well translated, it is not adapted.

I'd like a 10 page commentary on your epistle.

sic the phrase.

"sublimated to mere being together"

which might have various meanings.??

Yes, I think you are succeding [*sic*] in finding a basis for criticism.

Metaphysical.

Et maintenant assez [and that's enough for now].

E.

it: Apparently a lost letter from WCW containing a critique of EP's *Ripostes,* which was
published in October 1912.

The "Salve": "Salve Pontifex (A. C. S.)," a poetic tribute to Swinburne, had already
appeared in EP's *A Lume Spento* (1908).

"N. Y.": The closing lines of this poem read as follows: "My City, my beloved/ Thou art
a maid with no breasts,/ Thou art slender as a silver reed./ Listen to me, attend me!/ And
I will breathe into thee a soul,/ And thou shalt live for ever."

ϱαντασtικον: The *phantastikon* is the image-making faculty of the mind. In *The Spirit of
Romance* and the 1917 version of Canto 1, EP likens the *phantastikon* to a soap bubble
or "filmy shell," which surrounds the mind and mirrors the outside world. It seems to
be an agency both of perception and of creation.

the Phasellus: EP's " 'Phasellus ille' " (That pinnace) borrows its title from an epitaph for
an old boat by the Roman poet Catullus (*c.* 84–*c.* 54 B.C.). EP's poem, however, is a
satirical epigram about a London editor. The *"one* beautiful line" is, "Come Beauty
barefoot from the Cyclades."

the bloody dedication: Ripostes is dedicated "To William Carlos Williams."

Blunt's double sonnet: EP quotes the opening lines of "With Esther" by the English poet
Wilfred Scawen Blunt (1840–1922). The poem appears in *The Oxford Book of English
Verse 1250–1900,* ed. Arthur Quiller-Couch (Oxford: Clarendon Press, 1912), p. 998.
EP praises it again in "Status Rerum," *Poetry* 1:4 (January 1913), pp. 123–27. Blunt
was a favorite of EP and his London friends, who paid homage to him during a visit to
Blunt's home on January 18, 1914; see Carpenter, pp. 228–29. Blunt is also celebrated
in EP's Canto 81.

my next book: EP's next book of original verse was *Lustra* (1916), which collected the
work of his Imagist and Vorticist periods.

my publisher: Ripostes was published in London by Stephen Swift & Co. In a letter to his
parents of November 5, 1912, EP reports that " 'Swift' is busted. they caught the
manager in Tangier with *some* of the goods"; see Gallup, A8a.

your approaching nuptuals: WCW was married to Florence Herman (1890–1976) in
Rutherford on December 12, 1912. EP received an invitation but did not attend.

the Seefarer: EP's version of "The Seafarer (from the early Anglo-Saxon Text)" first
appeared in "I Gather the Limbs of Osiris—I," *The New Age* 10:5 (November 30,
1911), p. 107. Whether it is a translation or an adaptation of the Old English original is
still debated.

7. TLS-2

Monday may 26. [1913]

Deer Bull.

Just back from Italy on Thursday. Found your wad of stuff. Have taken same to Mathews who will publish it provided you take 250 copies for America. That is he'll publish about half of it. In either the Saville [*sic*] or the Vigo Cabinet series. The Saville is very small, but neat. and well bound.

The trouble with the Vigo is (a) that its only paper back, (b) more serious, he has already printed a lot of muck in that series and nobody expects to find anything good in it. The Saville is a new series with one or two unobjectionable things in it.

The 250 copies will cost you fifty dollars (20 cents per copy) and you may be able to sell some @ about fourty [*sic*] cents, I should say. or perhaps Kennerley would take 'em off your hands, as many as you didn't want to give away. de looks [deluxe] would be twice as much & I don't know that he'd do it.

£10 about covers printing and binding, Mathews does the distribution, reviews adv[ertising]. etc. on his oown [*sic*] would print about 500. There's no dam chance of his making a fortune on the deal.

E. M. wants your Coroners Children, which I used to revive his spirits when he moaned over one of your worst and more pseudo philosophic pieces.

Have you anything more to send over for stimulus. Am just back u. a. d. e. and haven't had time to breathe. Quartely [*sic*] article hadn't been forwarded and that has taken me all my breath, and Seymour is waiting for me to do my Patria Mia, into shape for a book, to the press as soon as I can turn it out, and. . . . .

Oh well. I'll discant [*sic*] later. "They take to slandering me" is more casual and natur'l than the line you've got in that all a [*sic*] etc. I haven't had time to score up the stuff in detail. you'll hear from Mathews, and I'll have a go at the bloody proofs, if you wish it.

Yrs. hell for leather.
Ezry

AND salutations to the lady.

your wad of stuff: The manuscript of *The Tempers,* published in London by Elkin Mathews on September 13, 1913. EP reviewed it in *The New Freewoman* for December 1913.
the Saville or the Vigo Cabinet series: See "Biographical Notes" on MATHEWS, ELKIN.
Kennerley: Mitchell Kennerley (1878–1932) managed the New York branch of the John

Lane publishing company. Between 1910 and 1916, he also published *The Forum*. EP met Kennerley in New York in 1910.

your Coroners Children: The correct title of the poem is "Hic Jacet" (Here Lies).

Quartely article: EP's "Troubadours: Their Sorts and Conditions" appeared in the *Quarterly Review* for October 1913.

Patria Mia: EP's "Patria Mia," a report of his visit to the United States in 1910–11, was serialized in *The New Age* in 1912. These articles, together with "America: Chances and Remedies," were to be issued in 1913 by Seymour, Daughaday, and Co. of Chicago, publishers of *Poetry*. However, the firm dissolved in 1915, without having published EP's book. The manuscript disappeared but came to light again in 1950, when it was published by Ralph Fletcher Seymour; see Gallup, A63a.

"They take to slandering me": The third of WCW's "Translations from the Spanish, 'El Romancero'" in *The Tempers* has the following refrain: "All are slandering me." WCW did not adopt the revision suggested here by EP.

8. ALS-11

[December 19, 1913]

Deer Bull

Thanks for your good letter. Almost you make me think for a moment that I might come to America. Dolce nido [home, sweet home], etc. – There are still a half dozen people there.

I suppose you've seen Demuth about the Glebe. – if not take my introduction to Alfred Kreymborg (the Glebe) 94 Fifth Ave. .

They ought to do yr. book   They're doing the anthology.

I am very placid & happy & busy. Dorothy is learning chinese. I've all old Fenollosa's treasures in *mss*.

Have just bought to [*sic*] statuets [*sic*] from *the* coming sculptor Gaudier Brzeska. I like him very much. He is the only person with whom I can really be "Altaforte." Cournos I like also. we are getting our little gang after five years of waiting. You must come over & get the air – if only for a week or so in the spring.

Richard is now running the N. F. which is now to appear as . "The Egoist" you must subscribe as the paper is poor. i.e. weak financially.

The "Mercure de France" has taken to quoting us, however.

It is the best way to keep in touch.

I wish Gwen could study with Brzeska

Yeats is much finer *intime* [on an intimate basis] than seen spasmodically in the midst of the whirl. We are both, I think, very contented in Sussex.

He returned $200 of that award with orders that it be sent to me. – & it has been. Hence the sculptural outburst & a new typewriter of great delicacy.

About your 'La Flor'': It is good. It is gracious also but that is aside the point for the moment.

Your vocabulary in it right. Your syntax still strays occasionally from the simple order of natural speech.

I think I shall print 'La Flor'' in the Egoist.

I think 'gracious'' is the word I should apply to it also as a critic.

it is dignified. It has the air of Urbino.

I don't know about your coming over. I still think as always that in the end your work will hold. After all you have the rest of a life time. Thirty real pages are enough for any of us to leave. There is scarce more of Catullus or Villon.

You may get something slogging away by yourself that you would miss in the Vortex – and that we miss.

It would be shorter perhaps if one of us would risk an Atlantic passage.

Of course Gwen ought to come over. I haven't heard from her for long & from V only a news paper cutting.

Damn! why haven't I a respectable villa of great extent & many retainers?

Dondo has turned up again after years of exile. He is in Paris, has met De Gourmont. We printed a page of his stuff verse in the N. F. last week. I think he will do something.

If you haven't had that paper, send for back numbers since Aug. 15th.

Cournos has just come in.

Shall mail this at once.

E.

Salams [*sic*] to Madame

Demuth: The American painter Charles Demuth (1883–1935) came to know both EP and WCW in Philadelphia in 1903–05. EP had recently seen Demuth again in London.

the Glebe: A little magazine edited in 1913–14 by the American writer Alfred Kreymborg (see "Biographical Notes" on KREYMBORG, ALFRED) and by the American photographer Man Ray (1890–1976).

the anthology: Des Imagistes, edited by EP, was an anthology of Imagist poems, among them WCW's "Postlude." The collection first appeared as an issue of *The Glebe* for February 1914. In March, it was brought out as a book by Albert and Charles Boni.

Dorothy: See "Biographical Notes" on POUND, DOROTHY.

Fenollosa's treasures: The Harvard-trained linguist and art historian Ernest Fenollosa (1853–1908) became Imperial Commissioner of Art in Tokyo. Among the manuscript "treasures" left at the time of his death were uncompleted translations of classic

Chinese poems and Japanese Noh plays, and an essay on the Chinese written character as a medium for poetry. Fenollosa's widow Mary entrusted these manuscripts to EP, whom she met in London in September 1913. EP's completions of Fenollosa's translations were published in *Cathay* (1915) and *"Noh," or Accomplishment* (1916).

Gaudier Brzeska: See "Biographical Notes" on GAUDIER-BRZESKA, HENRI.

"Altaforte": "Sestina: Altaforte" is a dramatic monologue first published in EP's *Exultations* (1909). Ostensibly a war song declaimed by the Provençal poet and soldier Bertrans de Born, its tone is flamboyant and obstreperous. EP impressed Gaudier-Brzeska by reciting the poem at the top of his lungs shortly after their first meeting.

Cournos: John Cournos (1881–1966) was a poet, novelist, playwright, critic, and translator. Born in Russia, he was taken to New York at the age of ten, where he learned to speak and write in English. From 1912 to 1930 he lived in London.

Richard: See "Biographical Notes" on ALDINGTON, RICHARD.

the N. F.: The New Freewoman, edited by Dora Marsden and Harriet Shaw Weaver, began in London in 1913 as a journal devoted to philosophic individualism and feminism. EP became its literary adviser and Richard Aldington its assistant editor late in 1913. On January 1, 1914, the journal changed its name to *The Egoist.* Between March 1914 and December 1919, *The Egoist* published a number of poems by WCW.

the "Mercure de France": EP's review, "Rabindranath Tagore: His Second Book into English," *The New Freewoman* 1:10 (November 1, 1913), pp. 187–88, is cited by Henry-D. Davray in "Lettres Anglaises," *Mercure de France* 106:396 (December 16, 1913), p. 840.

Gwen: Gwen Baxter (d. 1935), American sculptor and sister of Viola Baxter Jordan ("V"). See Thirlwall, p. 27, and an undated letter of 1913 from EP to Viola: "I have found a sculptor, one Gaudier Brzeska, he is so good that I came very near to insisting that Gwen should emigrate and study under him" (Yale).

Yeats: See "Biographical Notes" on YEATS, WILLIAM BUTLER.

that award: Poetry magazine awarded Yeats $250 (£50) for the best poem to appear in its pages during its first year of publication ("The Grey Rock"). Yeats returned £40 of the award, insisting that it go to EP instead.

'La Flor": WCW's "La Flor" appeared in *The Egoist* for August 15, 1914.

Urbino: Under Duke Guidobaldo da Montefeltro, the court of Urbino was a center of culture and manners during the Italian Renaissance. Castiglione's *The Courtier* (1528) was a product of the Urbino milieu.

the Vortex: EP's name for prewar London and other centers of dynamic creative activity. Early in 1914, he devised the term "Vorticism" to designate a movement toward energetic abstraction in the arts of painting, sculpture, poetry, and music.

Dondo: Mathurin Marius Dondo was a friend of EP and WCW at the University of Pennsylvania. He later taught French at several universities in the United States. In 1906, he took EP to the Bal Tabarin in Paris; the occasion is recalled in Canto 104. Dondo's French poems "Le Vent qui passe" and "Les Grelots" appeared in *The New Freewoman* 1:13 (December 15, 1913), p. 252.

9. ACS

[January 27, 1916]

You will find a longer article on De Gourmont by me in the "Fortnightly Review" for Dec. 1915.

Reread "Sordello" & then get the ten vols. of Walter Savage Landor. Converse with no one until you have read all save a few of the dialogues on politics & orthography. He is the best mind in English literature. Dont hand this on to the mob yet.

Yrs.

E

Dent's edition is not expensive. There are few books worth owning.

Read his Tsingotti [*sic*], "Pericles & Aspasia. Southey & Porson" Richelieu Normanby. Pentameron "Chaucer Boccacio [*sic*] Petrarch"

Y/.

E.

article: See "Biographical Notes" on GOURMONT, REMY DE.

Sordello: Long, difficult poem by Robert Browning, published in 1840 and based upon the life of the Provençal poet Sordello of Mantua (*c.* 1200). Browning's *Sordello* was one of the models for EP's early Cantos.

ten vols.: The English poet, translator, and prose writer Walter Savage Landor (1775–1864) published most of his *Imaginary Conversations* between 1824 and 1829. During the winter of 1915–16 at Stone Cottage, EP and Yeats read Charles G. Crump's ten-volume edition of Landor's *Imaginary Conversations, Poems, and Longer Prose Works* (London: J. M. Dent, 1891–93).

Tsingotti: EP refers to the following *Imaginary Conversations:* "Emperor of China and Tsing-Ti" (VI, 291–374); "Pericles and Aspasia" (IX, 117–410); "Southey and Porson" (III, 185–259); "Duke de Richelieu, Sir Firebrace Cotes, Lady Glengrin, and Mr. Normanby" (V, 326–418); "The Pentameron" (X, 3–147); "Chaucer, Boccaccio, and Petrarca" (IV, 66–108). Titles, volume numbers, and page numbers are from Crump's edition.

10. TLS-2

[May–June 1916]

Deer Bull

I will seeee what can be done. I have, as you know, naught but me pen wherewith to pay the rent, requests for unpaid contributions are not a treat. ARRRRIET [Harriet Monroe] has got the last lot of stuff that is any good, the silly old bitch is fussing about the best poem in the lot, I dont know whether she is going to throw it out, even if she does I should have to try to sell it.

I dont know whether I may not have another BLAST coming out too, which would use anything else I had ready. However something may turn up before August, or July first, or whenever the stuff has to be ready.

Certainly don't exclude anything good that you can find. Some creatures, like the amiable Holley, can't produce anything good, but then. . . .

Why the hell dont you answer my question about Bodenheim?? What sort of animal is he?

Re/ your Aug. number. keep a space open for some poems by Iris Barry. I am pretty sure I can get you a good group of them. I have already sent one set to Harriet.

I enclose the only work not at present engaged. I think Kreymborg refused it once before. My french translator was delighted with it. I dare say the french version will appear before the English. ma che [but what can I do]!

Perhaps you too will reject it as unworthy of my higher self. It is however more than good enough for a dung continent that keeps Wilson as president. passons [let's change the subject].

Not Harriet but ''The Drama'' would be the place for your ''Nuevo Mundo''. If you can get it through Hinckley, the editor, T. B. Hinckley, you can tell him that I'll do an introduction or a note on Lope, or anything you like, if that's any inducement.

Possibly a scene or two from a translation I have made of 'El Desprecio Agredecido' [sic]. I am not satisfied with the play as a whole but the opening scenes are entertaining.

Thanks for having a go at selecting my early wanderings.

If you can't stand my ''search for the national type'', something else may turn up before the Aug. number has to go to press. Something else or something additional. I do think the ''Search'' ought to be printed.

Of course you are welcome to print the two little squibbs [sic] I sent to A[lfred]. K[reymborg]. privately in my last letter, for his own amusement. They are of not the slightest importance however, and there is no need to print 'em.

Iris Barry stuff will be the first of it in Others. you can have that little score for your number. any way.

god be with thee.

yrs

EP

requests: In his role as associate editor of *Others: A Magazine of the New Verse* (1915–19), WCW has asked EP to contribute to the August number. This eventually became the July number, with EP's *Cathay* translation of "To-Em-Mei's 'The Unmoving Cloud'" on pp. 31–32. Although this letter to EP is undated, WCW sent a comparable request to Marianne Moore on May 4, 1916 (Thirlwall, pp. 34–35).

the last lot: A group of eight poems by EP appeared in *Poetry* for September 1916. He withdrew the poem to which Harriet Monroe objected, "To a Friend Writing on Cabaret Dancers" (see Paige, pp. 81–82).

BLAST: The first two numbers of *BLAST,* the organ of the Vorticist movement, appeared in June 1914 and July 1915. There was no third number.

Holley: Horace Holley (b. 1887) was a contributor to *The Egoist* and to *Les Soirées de Paris,* where he is described in the number for July–August 1914 as an American living in Paris. Holley was the author of *The Stricken King and Other Poems, Bahaism: The Modern Social Religion, The Social Principle, The Inner Garden* (all 1913), and *Creation: Post-Impressionist Poems* (1914).

Bodenheim: Maxwell Bodenheim (1892–1954) was an American poet, novelist, dramatist, critic, and editor. Neither EP's "question about Bodenheim" nor WCW's answer to it has survived, but they may have concerned Bodenheim's race; see Letters 11 and 12 below.

Iris Barry: See "Biographical Notes" on BARRY, IRIS. EP sent WCW six poems by Barry (see Paige, p. 82), but only "The Daughter" appeared in the July number of *Others.*

the only work: EP refers to "Stark Realism: This Little Pig Went to Market (A Search for the National Type)," which was eventually published in *The Little Review* for August 1917.

Kreymborg: See "Biographical Notes" on KREYMBORG, ALFRED.

my french translator: Unidentified. No French translation of a work by EP appears to have been published in France before 1920.

Wilson: In 1916, Woodrow Wilson (1856–1924) was elected to a second four-year term as President of the United States. EP detested Wilson for a number of reasons; see Pound/Quinn, pp. 71, 72, 84, 89, 181, and Pound/Cutting, pp. 6, 29–30, 50, 54, 57, 61, 106–07.

"The Drama": The Drama, edited in Chicago by Theodore Ballou Hinckley, published EP's translations of several Japanese Noh plays in May 1915 and August 1916.

your "Nuevo Mundo": See "Biographical Notes" on VEGA CARPIO, LOPE FELIX DE.

'El Desprecio Agredecido': See "Biographical Notes" on VEGA CARPIO, LOPE FELIX DE.

my early wanderings: See Letter 11 below.

11. TLS-1

10/6/16 [June 10, 1916]

Deer Bull

Thanks for your list of pomes. I think you have probably got the guts of the matter. At least in the first books. One or two inclusions and omissions surprise me a little. But in the main I think you have hit the mark pretty well. I dont know that it will be practicable to print the selections as you have made them but I certainly will keep the list and make it in some was [*sic*] the basis of the single vol. when the time comes for it. Just now LUSTRA is all set up in print, it contains Cathay and all the new stuff since Ripostes.

Quinn is trying to place a big vol. with MacMillan containing LUSTRA and most of Ripostes with a few things from Canzoni. Excluding what is in "Provenca", including the other five you have chosen, and some translations.

I see you have kept no translations save "Rome" *see Farer* [Seafarer] & *Cathay*. I am a little surprised that you pick "Sestina for Isolt" instead of the "Laudantes" which I had always tacitly supposed were much better.

In you [*sic*] new book I should certainly keep at least part of the Tempers. Certainly Postlude, the longer version, and Hic Jacet.

I think you had better include the poems on pages 7. 8. 10. 11. 12. 15. 16. 17. 30. 31 though this selection is made rather in a hurry. Very possibly 18. Franco Cologne it will give variety to the book.

I think the book will certainly be stronger if you select it from all your stuff, rather than from the new by itself.

I am afraid Eliot has sent all his unused stuff to Arriet [Harriet Monroe] to get printed if possible before his book comes out. Rodker has made a bloody ass of himself and been tucked into quod [jail]. He has been running with a beastly crowd of objectors. I hope it will teach him sense. I sent Iris Barry's stuff a few days ago. She is better than Rodker, at least she has more in her.

About the nun-like young woman. I don't know that we shall get to Spain. Certainly not unless the war is over. Is she coming to London also? You know I prefer them Bacchic. Still one can not always have these matters chosen to order. I dont mind the enormous if it isn't carried to the point of enormity.

Bill Davis (W. H. Davis [*sic*]) was in yesterday for the first time. Stayed four hours. I like him. You would like him very much.

Thanks for the note on Bodenheim. *I was afraid so.*

I have just heard that W. G. Lawrence, a fine chap from Oxford who had walked over my parts of Provence and whom I liked very much though I had not seen much of him, has been shot down in an aeroplane. Thank God the Russians a [*sic*] smashing up Austria.

yours ever

E

your list of pomes: In a letter to his mother of April 27, 1916 (Princeton), WCW writes: "I have been looking over Pound's work – all he has ever written – for he has asked me to make a selection of all he has ever done to be published in a single volume."

LUSTRA: EP's *Lustra* was published in London by Elkin Mathews in September–October 1916 and in New York by Alfred A. Knopf in October 1917. WCW's "list of pomes" may have helped EP determine the contents of the American edition, which differs considerably from the English; see Pound/Henderson, pp. 198–99.

Quinn: See "Biographical Notes" on QUINN, JOHN.

Canzoni: EP's *Canzoni* was published by Elkin Mathews in 1911.

"Provenca": *Provença: Poems Selected from Personae, Exultations, and Canzoniere of Ezra Pound* was published by Small, Maynard & Co. of Boston in 1910.

"Rome": EP's "Rome, from the French of Joachim du Bellay" appeared in *Canzoni*.

"Sestina for Ysolt": EP's "Sestina for Ysolt" appeared in *Exultations* (1909), as did the sequence entitled "Laudantes decem pulchritudinis Johannae Templi."

you new book: WCW's next book was *Al Que Quiere!* (1917); contrary to EP's advice, it contains no poems from *The Tempers.*

the poems: EP refers to "Peace on Earth," "Postlude," "Homage," "The Fool's Song," "From 'The Birth of Venus,' Song," "An After Song," "Crude Lament," "The Ordeal," "Hic Jacet," "Contemporania," and "The Death of Franco Cologne: His Prophecy of Beethoven."

Eliot: See "Biographical Notes" on ELIOT, THOMAS STEARNS.

Rodker: See "Biographical Notes" on RODKER, JOHN.

objectors: Protestors against Britain's participation in the Great War of 1914–18.

the nun-like young woman: Unidentified.

W. H. Davis: William Henry Davies (1871–1940), English poet and author of *Autobiography of a Super-Tramp* (1908). EP attended a reading by Davies in the first week of June 1916 (see Paige, p. 81), and his review of Davies' *Collected Poems* appeared in *Poetry* for November 1917.

Bodenheim: See Letter 10 above.

W. G. Lawrence: William George Lawrence (1889–1915) was a younger brother of T. E. Lawrence ("Lawrence of Arabia"). He read history at Oxford, and arranged for EP to lecture there. While serving as an observer in the Royal Flying Corps, Lawrence was killed in action in September 1915.

my parts of Provence: In the summer of 1912, EP made an extensive tour of southern France; see *A Walking Tour in Southern France: Ezra Pound among the Troubadours,* ed. Richard Sieburth (New York: New Directions, 1992).

the Russians: In 1916, the Austro-Hungarian Hapsburg Empire, which had allied itself with Germany in the Great War, was on the brink of collapse. On June 4–5, Russian forces under the command of General Brusilov attacked from the east along a 200-mile front with spectacular success. In the next few weeks, some 350,000 Austrian troops surrendered.

12. TLS-5

[November 10, 1917]

B A L L S !!!!!!
- - - - - - - -

BALLS! My dear William. At what date did you join the ranks of the old ladies??

Among the male portion of the community one constantly uses fragments of letters, fragments of conversation (anonymously, quite anonymously, NOT referring to the emitter by name) for the purpose of sharpening a printed argument.

I note your invitation to return to my father land (pencil at the top of your letter sic g. t. h. [go to hell]), I shall probably accept it at the end of the war.

My knoweldge [*sic*] of the (''stet'') American heart is amply indicated in L Homme Moyen Sensuel.

I had no ulterior or hidden meaning in calling you, or the imaginary correspondent an ''American'' author. Still, what the hell else are you? (I mean apart from being a citizen, a good fellow (in your better moments), a grouch, a slightly hypersensitized animal etc??

Wot bloody kind of an author are you save Amurikun (same as me).

And whether, O Demosthenes, is one to be called a ''damn fool'' or a ''person''?

Your sap is interrupted. Try De Gourmont's ''Epilogue'' ('95–'98). And dont expect the world to revolve about Rutherford.

If you had any confidence in America you wouldn't be so touchy about it.

I thought the fuckin' millenium that we all idiotically look for and work for was to be the day when an American artist could stay at home without being dragged into civic campaigns, dilutations of controversy etc. when he could stay in america without growing propagandist. God knows I have to work hard enough to escape, not propagande, but getting centered in propagande.

And America. What the hell do you a bloomin foreigner know about the place. Your pere [father] only penetrated the edge, and you've never been west of Upper Darby, or the Maunchunk [*sic*] switchback.

Would Harriet [Monroe], with the swirl of the prairie wind in her underwear,

or the Virile Sandburg recognize, you a effete easterner as a REAL american.!!?
INCONCEIVABLE!!!!

My dear boy you have never felt the woop of the PEEraries. You have never
seen the projecting and protuberent [sic] Mts. of the Sierra Nevada. WOT can
you know of the country?

You have the naive credulity of a Co. Claire [sic] emigrant. But I (der grosse
Ich) [the great I] have the virus, the baccillus [sic] of the land in my blood, for
neary [sic] three bleating centuries.

(Bloody snob. 'eave a brick at 'im!!!!)

You (read your Freud) have a Vaterersatz [father figure], you have a paternal
image at your fireside, and you call it John Bull.

I of course like your Old Man, and I have drunk his Goldwasser.

Your statement about my wanting Paris to be like London, is a figment of your
own diseased imagination.

"I warn you that anything you say at this time, may later be used against you".
The Arts vs. Williams.

Or will you my head on a platter. Or would you like it brought over to be
punched?? A votre service, M'sieu [at your service, sir]. I am coming to inspect
you.

I was very glad to see your wholly incoherent unamerican poems in the L. R.

Of course Sandburg will tell you that you miss the "big drifts", and
Bodenheim will object to your not being suffiently [sic] decadent.

(You thank your bloomin gawd you've got enough spanish blood to muddy up
your mind, and prevent the current American ideation from going through it like a
blighted collander [sic].

The thing that saves your work is *opacity,* and dont you forget it. Opacity is
NOT an American quality. Fizz, swish, gabble of verbiage, these are echt
Amerikanish [sic, truly American]

And Alas, alas, poor old Masters. Look at Oct. Poetry.

But really this "old firend" [sic] hurt feeling business is to [sic] Skipwithcannellish; it is *peu vous* [not like you]. I demand of you more robustezza. Bigod sir,
you show more robustezza, or I will come over to Rutherford and have at you,
coram, in person.

And moreover you answer my questions, p. 38. before you go on to the p. s.
p. 39 which does not concern you.

Let me indulge the American habit of quatation [sic]:

"Si le cosmopolitisme littéraire gagnait encore et qu'il réussit à éteindre ce que
les différence de race ont allumé de haine de sang parmi les hommes, j'y verrais
un gain pour la civilisation et pour l'humanité tout entière."

L'amour excessif et exclusif d'une patrie a pour immédiat corollaire lhorreur [*sic*] des patries étrangeres. Non seulement on craint de quitter la jupe de sa maman, d'aller voir comment vivent les autres hommes, de se mêler a leurs luttes, de partager leurs travaix, nonseulement on reste chez soi, mais on finit par fermer sa porte.''

''Cette folie gagne certains littérateurs et le même professeur, en sortant d'expliquer le Cid ou Don Juan, rédige de gracieuses injures contre Ibsen et l'influence, helas, trop illusoire, de son oeuvre, pourtant toute de lumière et de beauté.''

et cetera.

lie down and compose yourself.

It's also nonsense this wail that M[argaret]. C. A[nderson]. ''dislikes'' you.

Yrs

EP

---

fragments of letters: A postscript at the end of ''The Reader Critic: Letters from Ezra Pound,'' *The Little Review* 4:6 (October 1917), p. 39, reads as follows: ''An american author writes to me 'You mix your damn foolery with sense, so you continue readable'. Chere Editreuse [dear editor], what does this person want? Does he wish it unmixed and therefore unreadable?'' The ''american author'' was WCW, but the letter from which EP quotes has not survived.

your invitation: The letter to which EP refers has not survived. He did not return to America immediately after the war.

''stet'': ''Let it stand'' is a standard proofreader's command meaning that no correction is called for.

L Homme Moyen Sensuel: EP's poem of this title (The Ordinary Sensual Man) appeared in *The Little Review* for September 1917.

Demosthenes: Greek orator and statesman (*c.* 384–322 B.C.).

De Gourmont's ''Epilogue'': See ''Biographical Notes'' on GOURMONT, REMY DE. Gourmont's *Epilogues* (1903) is the source of the passage in French at the end of this letter.

God knows . . . brick at'im!!!!: Taking EP at his word, WCW quotes extensively from this letter in his ''Prologue'' to *Kora in Hell: Improvisations* (Boston: Four Seas, 1920). This passage occurs on pp. 13–14.

Your pere: See ''Biographical Notes'' on WILLIAMS, WILLIAM GEORGE.

Upper Darby, or the Maunchunk switchback: Locations to the west of Philadelphia, Pennsylvania, where, in the college days of EP and WCW, the city gave way to the country. H. D. lived in Upper Darby.

Sandburg: Like Harriet Monroe, the American poet and biographer Carl Sandburg (1878–1967) was closely associated with Chicago and the American Midwest. He was the author of *Chicago Poems* (1916) and *Cornhuskers* (1918).

Co. Claire: County Clare, in west-central Ireland, provided many immigrants to the United States.

three bleating centuries: EP's grandmother told him that one of his ancestors had arrived in America as early as 1632; see Carpenter, p. 2.

Freud: EP attributes WCW's Anglophobia to an Oedipal conflict with his English father. According to the theory of the Austrian psychoanalyst Sigmund Freud (1856–1939), a son's unconscious childhood rivalry with his father may be transferred in later life to a surrogate father-figure (*Vaterersatz*).

John Bull: In John Arbuthnot's satire *Law Is a Bottomless Pit* (1712), John Bull typifies the English national character.

Goldwasser: A liqueur containing particles of gold leaf. WCW quotes this sentence in the "Prologue" to *Kora in Hell*.

"I warn you . . . ": In these words, American officers of the law are supposed to advise arrested persons of their Constitutional right to remain silent as a protection against self-incrimination.

my head on a platter: In the Gospel of St. Matthew, Chapter 14, the daughter of Herodias asks for the head of John the Baptist in a charger. Eliot had recently alluded to the same episode in "The Love Song of J. Alfred Prufrock."

the L. R.: The *Little Review* began in Chicago under the editorship of Margaret C. Anderson and moved to New York at the end of 1916. EP became Foreign Editor of the magazine in April 1917. Several of WCW's "Improvisations" appeared in the numbers for October 1917 and January 1918. Speaking of them in a letter to Margaret Anderson of February 22, 1918, EP writes: "Bill Wms. is *the* most bloody inarticulate animal that ever gargled"; see Pound/*The Little Review*, p. 190.

I was very glad . . . Oct. Poetry: WCW quotes this passage in the "Prologue" to *Kora in Hell*.

Bodenheim: After "Bodenheim," EP wrote and then crossed out "another American name."

spanish blood: See "Biographical Notes" on WILLIAMS, RAQUEL HÉLÈNE ROSE.

Masters: The American poet and novelist Edgar Lee Masters (1869–1950) published his best-known work, the *Spoon River Anthology,* in 1916. EP had reviewed Masters' work favorably in *The Egoist* for January 1915 and in *Reedy's Mirror* for May 21, 1915; but he expressed reservations about it in *The Little Review* for August 1917. The lead poem in *Poetry* for October 1917 was Masters' "Canticle of the Race."

Skipwithcannellish: Skipwith Cannell (1887–1957), an American poet from Philadelphia, met EP in 1913 and played a role in the London Imagist movement. His work appeared in *Poetry, Smart Set, The New Freewoman, The Little Review, Des Imagistes,* and *Others.* His delicacy is suggested by EP's remark, in a letter to Iris Barry of July 27, 1916, that Cannell was "afraid to read anything for fear it would destroy his 'individuality'" (Paige, p. 88).

robustezza: In his essay on "Mediaevalism and Mediaevalism" (Guido Cavalcanti), EP defines *robustezza* as "masculinity."

my questions: On p. 38 of "The Reader Critic: Letters from Ezra Pound," EP writes: "I would ask you to try to understand WHY American literature from 1870 to 1910 is summed in the sentence: 'Henry James stayed in Paris reading Flaubert and Turgenev.

Mr. William Dean Howells returned to America and read the writings of Henry James.'
And WHY Whistler stayed in Europe, although Chase went back to the Philadelphia
Fine Arts Academy. These are simple questions which the serious reader will not try to
shrink answering.''

Let me indulge . . . compose yourself: WCW quotes this passage in his ''Prologue'' to
Kora in Hell.

''Si le cosmopolitisme . . . beauté'': The passage quoted by EP comes from a section of
Gourmont's *Epilogues* entitled ''1895. Novembre 3. Cosmopolitisme'' (p. 15). The
words are not those of Gourmont, who says he is quoting from a work of 1890 by the
French critic Ferdinand Brunetière (1849–1906).

''If literary cosmopolitanism prevails and succeeds in extinguishing the blood hatred
kindled among men by racial difference, I would see in that a victory for civilization and
humanity as a whole.

An excessive and exclusive love of one country has for its immediate corollary a fear
of foreign countries. Not only is one afraid to let go of his mother's apron strings, to go
and see how other men live, to join in their struggles, to share their labors, not only does
one stay at home, but he ends up by shutting his door.

''This absurdity overcomes certain writers and the same professor who starts out to
explain The Cid or Don Juan compiles genteel grievances against Ibsen and the
influence—alas, all too deceptive—of his work, however full of illumination and
beauty.''

13. TLS-2

[January 28, 1919]

My Dear Old Sawbukk von Grump:

How are your adenoids? Am rejoicing in vacancy; prose collection ''finished''
committed to the gaping maw of the post office; and I freed of its weight. Haven't
heard from you since the pig died.

Is Bodenheistein's book any good? The whirlwind prose hope of Chicago Rabi
[*sic*] Ben Hechtenberg passed by us; his wife said you looked calm and healthy
against the foetid backsideground of Greenitch Village.

Ben very vivid converser, reel jennuine cinema trajectory.

Lewis' show opening Thursday. etc. Manning again in circulation.

All sorts of ''projects'' artoliteresque in the peaceconferentialbolshevikair.
Switzerland bursting into Dadaique manifestos re/ the nothingness of the all.

Fat Madox Hueffer in last evening, Aldington at ''front'' educating Tommies,
Wadsworth and Lewis in town, more or less free;

I think it might be worth while for you to send me any mss. you have by you; there are several schemes in the air re Quarterly, and re a weekly; and something or other will probably start. There is the banked water of several years during which paper restrictions forbade starting of new periodicals; I think something will start cant yet say which or what; was offered a salary two days ago; but that is too wild a fantasy. At any rate shd. like to have some of your stuff by me in case of emergency.

Mgr *said* the first number of a weekly wd. appear in March . . . . . but words of financiers . . . . ??

Am reprinting note on you from "Future" in next prose vol. which Knopf *says* he is bringing out this autumn.

Did a longer note for an America paper which cut down its size on recipt [*sic*] of article, which latter is still floating about in my progenitor's possession. Dont know that you will like it; but I did go so far as to say you weren't a matoid.

Are you capable of doing quarterly notes (1000 words say per three months, on American publications????)

Or is there anybody in the great pure prohibition monarchy capable of writing brief summary criticism of its contemporary abortions?

regards to yr. spouse & offshoots

yrs

EP

Sawbukk: Perhaps a conflation of the American slang terms *sawbuck,* or ten-dollar bill, and *sawbones,* or doctor.

prose collection: Instigations of Ezra Pound, Together with an Essay on the Chinese Written Character by Ernest Fenollosa (New York: Boni and Liveright, 1920).

Bodenheistein's book: Maxwell Bodenheim, *Minna and Myself* (1918), a collection of poems.

Ben Hechtenberg: See "Biographical Notes" on HECHT, BEN.

Lewis' show: See "Biographical Notes" on LEWIS, PERCY WYNDHAM.

Manning: Frederic Manning (1882–1935) was an Australian poet and novelist who served in Flanders and France during World War I. His books include *The Vigil of Brunhild* (1907), *Scenes and Portraits* (1909), *Poems* (1910), and *Her Privates We* (1930).

peaceconferentialbolshevikair: The Versailles Peace Conference of 1919 resulted in the treaty which officially ended World War I. The Bolshevik (majority) faction of the Russian communist party took power after the Russian Revolution of 1917.

Dadaique manifestoes: The Dada movement in art and politics began in Switzerland in 1915–16 and spread across Europe after the war came to an end. Its spirit was anarchistic, iconoclastic, and nihilistic.

Hueffer: See "Biographical Notes" on FORD, FORD MADOX.

Aldington: See "Biographical Notes" on ALDINGTON, RICHARD. In a letter to EP from

Belgium, dated December 8, 1918 (Yale), Aldington writes: "It is bloody back here – I am teaching Tommies [enlisted men] to read the newspaper. I do multiplication sums. O God, O Montreal. This education scheme is bull-shit at its primest."

Wadsworth: The English painter Edward Alexander Wadsworth (1889–1949) was a member of the Vorticist movement and an officer in the Royal Naval Volunteer Reserve.

several schemes: In letters to his parents of December 4, 1918, and January 17, 1919, EP speaks of starting a quarterly review "as soon as paper and periodical restrictions go off" and of becoming the paid editor of "the literary section of a weekly" (Yale). Both of these plans fell through.

note on you: "The New Poetry," *Future* 2:7 (June 1918), pp. 188–90; rpt. *Instigations,* which was published not in the fall of 1919 by Knopf but in April of 1920 by Boni and Liveright.

a longer note: Apparently never published.

my progenitor: Instigations is dedicated "To My Father Homer L[oomis]. Pound." Living in Wyncote, Pennsylvania, and working as an assistant assayer for the United States Mint in Philadelphia, Homer (1858–1942) took a great interest in his son's career and handled some of EP's literary and financial business in the United States.

prohibition: The 18th Amendment to the Constitution of the United States prohibited the manufacture and sale of any drink containing more than 0.5% alcohol. Passed in 1919, Prohibition took effect on January 16, 1920, and remained the law of the land until December 5, 1933.

offshoots: William Eric Williams, born in 1914, and Paul Herman Williams, born in 1916.

14. TLS-7

[September 11, 1920]

My dear old Hugger-scrunch:

Un po di justicia [a little justice]!! Or rather: you're a liar. Precisely I am an "enemy of American verse".

That I swated [*sic*] like a nigger to break up the clutch of the old shit-wall, Harpers etc.

That I tried to enlighten that bitch in Chicago, so as to make a place for the real thing.

That I sent over french models, which have given six hundred people a means of telling something nearer the truth than they wd. have done senza [without].

That I imported U. S. stuff here, to the prejudice of my own comfort (remember I have only what I get by my pen)

And on the contrary, some evidence that I have ever cursed anything but the *faults* of American verse. Produce it, you old village cut-up.

That Jep. is not a fountain of wisdom I admit, but he was a good bolus, or a bad bolus, but at any rate there was no one else whose time wasn't too valuable to waste on trying to penetrate Harriet's crust

That silly old she-ass with her paeons for bilge . . . .

NOT you he-cunt that she matters, but every page of that magazine that goes to BAD stuff is just that much lost to honest work.

You lay back, you let me have the whole stinking sweat of providing the mechanical means for letting through the new movement, i.e. scrap for the mot juste, for honest clear statement in verse.

Then you punk out cursing me for not being in two places at once, and for "seeing no alternative to my own groove".

Which is bilge, just sloppy inaccurate bilge. And you can "take it back" when you get round to doing so.

You get various people who might be honest, who might do a bit of good work, Flattered to hell like Masters, or pouring their stuff into leaky jars for want of someone to tell 'em to plug the leaks, and then when I do, you say I am a plugger, and that I plug, and that left to myself I wd. plug the mouth of the jar before the booze is put in, and vend the vacuous eathenware [*sic*].

Not that I care a curse for ANY nation as such or that so far as I know I have ever suggested that I was trying to write U. S. poetry (any more than you are writing Alexandrine greek bunk, to conform to the ideas of that refined, charming, and utterly narrow minded she-bard "H. D.")

Neither do I have the spinsterly aversion ala [*sic*] Marianne from tutto che non mi piace [everything I dislike].

Can be, on other hand, quite as stubborn as you are; If choose to write about a decaying empire, will do so, and be damned to you. But can't see that it constitutes enmity to your work or to that of anyone else who writes honestly, whether in U. S. or Nigeria.

Amy Lowell's perfumed cat-piss wd. be putrid even if it had been done by a pueblo indian, or written on the highest pinnacle of Harriet's buggerin rocky mts.

It is curious that with the relics of what I suppose was not a scientific education you cant understand the spirit of research; even research into something so dead as a complicated aesthetic of sound . . . . . which ain't dead in the least, though I dare say the canzone is too mumified [*sic*] to walk on its pins ever again.

Also whether I am better alive here, or dead, as I shd. have been from starvation if I hadn't had the remains of primitive animal instinct sufficient to "run" . . . . is a problem which you can answer acc. cons [according to conscience].

Have I ever, on the other hand, tried to pass off Eng. punk on my compatriots?

Have I sent you the dry dung of the Georgians, or the wet dung of the London Murkury?

Have you the adumbrations of intelligence enough to know that the critical faculty which can pick you and Bodenheim, and Loy, and Sandburg (and in earlier phases Frost) out of the muck of liars and shams IS of some use even to poetry in a country so utterly cursed by every fahrt-sided god of the pantheon as to have Woody Wilson for its "choice", and individaual [sic] liberty slowly growing illegal.

If you weren't stupider than a mud-duck you would know that every kick to bad writing is by that much a help for the good.

When did I ever, in enmity, advise you to use vague words, to shun the welding of word and thing, to avoid hard statement, word close to the thing it means.

BUT I don't care a fried fahrt about nationality. Race is probably real. It is real.

And you might in fairness have elaborated my quotation on *virus*. There is a blood poison in America   you can idealize the place (easier now that Europe is so damnd shaky) all you like but you haven't a drop of the cursed blood in you, and you don't need to fight the disease day and night;

you never have had to. Eliot has it perhaps worse than I have – poor devil.

You have the advantage of arriving in the milieu with a fresh flood of Europe in your veins, Spanish, French, English, Danish

You had not the thin milk of new york and new England from the pap, and you can therefore keep the environment outside you, and decently objective

With your slower mental processes, your later development, you are very likely, really of a younger generation, at least of a younger *couche* [stratum];

"The flood of limbs upon eighth avenue," mixed race, semitic goo, opancity [sic] (as I have before remarked).

Different from my thin logical faculty. And thank god from Harriets blow (really the gaseous American period of the generation or two before me . . . . . bluff . . . . . throwing the bull, town prospecting etc.

AND now that there is no longer any intellectual *life* in England save what centers in this eight by ten pentagonal room; now that Remy and Henry are gone and Yeats faded, and NO literary publication whatever extant in England, save what "we" print (Egoist and Ovid Press)

The question remains whether I have to give up every shred of comfort, every scrap of my personal life, and "gravitate" to a New York which wants me as little now as it did ten and fifteen years ago.

Whether, from the medical point of view it is massochism [sic] for me even to stay here, instead of shifting to Paris. Whether self-inflicted torture ever has the slightest element of dignity in it?

Or whether I am Omar.

Have I a country at all . . . now that Mouquin is no more, and that your father has no more goldwasser and the goldwasser no obescent bonhomme [plump, generous man] to pour it out for me?

Or you who sees no alternative?

All of which is, as you have divined, in realtion [sic] to your prologue. I will get on to the Imporvisations [sic] later. for which my thanks.

Have written to Dial that you are the best thing in the country. Can you keep up some push of American stuff, You, Bodenheim, Sandburg, Hecht, Sher. Anderson. etc.

I really can't do the whole show. Beside [sic] I am not supposed to run the American end.

If you want to honour the country, a la your pathriotism [sic], you people who have some guts ought to crowd such whiffle as "Songs of the Pueblo Indians" by A. L. out of the international envoy (Sept. p. 247)

Ez

"enemy of American verse": This letter is a response to WCW's "Prologue" to *Kora in Hell: Improvisations* (1920). The "Prologue" was also published separately in *The Little Review* for April and May 1919. In it, EP is described as "the best enemy United States verse has."

Harpers: EP cites *Harper's Monthly Magazine* (1850–) as a periodical characteristic of the American literary establishment.

that bitch in Chicago: Harriet Monroe, editor of *Poetry*. For the controversy over *Poetry*, see p. 5 above.

french models: EP may be referring to "A Study in French Poets" and several of his other essays on French writers. They were published in *The Little Review* in 1918 and gathered in *Instigations* (1920).

Jep.: Edgar Alfred Jepson (1863–1938) was an English novelist, critic, and editor. He studied classics at Balliol College, Oxford, under Benjamin Jowett.

bolus: A large pill or dose of medicine.

mot juste: The exact word, a phrase used by the French novelist Gustave Flaubert (1821–1880), came to stand for the stylistic ideals of precision and economy that motivated Ford Madox Ford, EP and the Imagists, James Joyce, T. S. Eliot, and other writers of the early twentieth century.

no alternative: In his "Prologue," WCW says: "I praise those who have the wit and courage, and the conventionality to go direct toward their vision of perfection in an objective world where the signposts are clearly marked, viz., to London. But confine them in hell for their paretic assumption that there is no alternative but their own groove."

Masters: For Edgar Lee Masters and EP's view of him, see Letter 12 above.

"H. D.": See "Biographical Notes" on DOOLITTLE, HILDA. In his "Prologue," WCW

makes a point of distancing himself from H. D.'s Hellenism, which he describes as "too staid, too chilly, too little fecundative to impregnate my world."

Marianne: See "Biographical Notes" on MOORE, MARIANNE. In his "Prologue," WCW quotes Moore as saying to him: "My work has come to have just one quality of value in it: I will not touch or have to do with those things which I detest."

a decaying empire: The decay of the British Empire is indirectly suggested in EP's "Homage to Sextus Propertius," part of which appeared in *Poetry* for March 1919.

Amy Lowell's: The American poet and critic Amy Lowell (1874–1925) had been a target of EP's animosity ever since 1914, when, as he saw it, she took over the Imagist movement he had begun. Here, and again at the end of this letter, EP refers specifically to Lowell's "Songs of the Pueblo Indians," *The Dial* 69:3 (September 1920), pp. 247–51.

a complicated aesthetic: In his "Prologue," WCW mocks EP for foisting off "parodies of the middle ages, Dante and *langue d'oc* [Provençal]" as "the best in United States poetry." EP's "Homage à la langue d'Oc" appeared in *The Little Review* for May 1918. It consists of six translations of intricately rhymed poems by Provençal troubadours, including a *canzon* (song) by Arnaut Daniel.

the Georgians: A group of English poets whose work appeared between 1912 and 1922 in a series of five anthologies entitled *Georgian Poetry*. The contributors included Rupert Brooke, John Masefield, John Drinkwater, W. H. Davies, Walter de la Mare, Harold Monro, and Edward Marsh.

the london Murkury: The London Mercury was founded by J. C. Squire in 1919 and ran until 1939. Early in 1920, T. S. Eliot described the magazine as "run by a small clique of bad writers," "despised," "without standing among intelligent people," and "socially looked down upon"; see Eliot, pp. 358, 359, 362.

Loy: The British-born poet, essayist, and artist Mina Loy (1882–1966) belonged to the *Others* circle in New York. In his "Prologue," WCW compares her favorably with Marianne Moore and praises the originality of her work.

Frost: See "Biographical Notes" on FROST, ROBERT.

quotation on virus: In his "Prologue," WCW quotes directly from EP's letter to him of November 10, 1917 (see Letter 12 above).

"the flood of limbs": In "Imaginary Letters. IV. (Walter Villerant to Mrs. Bland Burn)," *The Little Review* 4:5 (September 1917), p. 21, EP writes: "Unfortunately the turmoil of yidds, letts, finns, esthonians, cravats, niberians, nubians, algerians sweeping along Eighth Avenue will not help us. They are the America of tomorrow."

pentagonal room: EP's flat at 5, Holland Place Chambers, Kensington.

Remy and Henry: Remy de Gourmont died in 1915. The American expatriate novelist and critic Henry James died in 1916.

Egoist and Ovid Press: An offshoot of *The Egoist* magazine, the Egoist Press was created in 1916 especially to publish James Joyce's *A Portrait of the Artist as a Young Man.* Other publications included Wyndham Lewis' *Tarr* (1916), T. S. Eliot's *Prufrock and Other Observations* (1917), EP's *Dialogues of Fontenelle* (1917) and *Quia Pauper Amavi* (1919), and Marianne Moore's *Poems* (1921). For the Ovid Press and its publications, see "Biographical Notes" on KODKER, JOHN.

shifting to Paris: EP had just visited Paris in June and July of 1920, and he moved there in the spring of 1921.

Omar: The Rubaiyat of the Persian poet Omar Khayyám (1050–1123) was translated into English by Edward FitzGerald in 1859. Given the melancholy vicissitudes of life, Omar recommends that one enjoy its transitory pleasures to the full.

Mouquin: A French restaurant in New York, located near the corner of Sixth Avenue and 34th Street. EP and WCW frequented Mouquin's before 1914, but the restaurant did not survive the First World War. In "Dr. Williams' Position" (1928), EP speaks of "an American yesterday as gone as les caves des Mouquin," and WCW recalls the place fondly in Chapter 15 of his *Autobiography*.

Dial: New York literary magazine, edited by Scofield Thayer. EP served as salaried Foreign Editor from March 1920 to July 1921.

Sher. Anderson: The American novelist and short story writer Sherwood Anderson (1876–1941) had recently achieved celebrity with his popular stories of Midwestern small-town life, collected in *Winesburg, Ohio* (1919).

15. TLS-4

11 Sept [1920]
later in the day

Deer Bull

Got as far as p. 68. All that can be expected of middle aged european in one day.

Inclined to think it best you have done. Don't know that it is more incoherent than Rimbaud's Saison en Enfer;

nor yet that it cd. be improved by being more intelligible.

STILL, am inclined to think it is probably most effective where most comprehensible.

The italics at any rate dont detract. Not that they, in many cases, much explain the matter either.

Not sure that you wd. lose much or anything by still further exposition.

Not on other hnd. suggesting that clear Maupassant modus wd. serve yr. every turn.

Re the dialog. with yr. old man, which I don't bloody remember . . . . . remember we did talk about "Und Drang" but there the sapphires certainly are NOT anything but sapphires, perfectly definite visual imagination.

However upshot (which you don't, certainly, imply) is that yr. old man was certainly dead right. and that whatever t'ell I said ten yrs. ago, I certainly have since then endeavoured "to why in the hell or heaven" *say it* and NOT zummat else . . . . . . to the whatever t'ell improvement of my whatever t'ell style or modus.

Possibly lamentable that the two halves of what might have made a fairly decent poet shd. be sequestered and divided by the fuckin buttocks of the arse . . wide atlantic ocean.

If I was as ornrey in my clear verse as you are in yourn I'd be up before the beak [magistrate] . . . . .

Dare say Mozart and Brahms had a different personal rhythm in coitu [sexual intercourse] . . . . . but differs acc[ording to]. female component in any case.

I wonder why Lamar lets you thru and pinches the innocent Joyce non-conformist parson from Aberdeen while you . . . . . ("ohe ma-ma" as ma chere [my dear] Xelestine wd. remark under similar . . . .) variant "Mummy"

will say that the cover design IS at any rate purr-fectly clear.

Wholly definite indication of the spirit of the woik as a hole.

(even there, the layman's ignorance . . . . Is there any occult significance in the black eggs?

Not sure Gaudier oughtn't have dedicated the FIRST post-Xtn bust of the century to your rather than to my LIBERATOR.

Le gracieux et souple rhythme de Properce fait croire à une fleuve ou à une verge plutôt qu'a un chêne. (mummy)

If any one has patience enough to read I think the book does manage to convey general sense of what you are meaning . . . . more one can not ask, perhaps.

Problem (not five minute problem): wd. more 3d. person, objective statement . . . . etc . . . Oh HELL . . . . dare say it wd.nt.

ANYHOW blaze away, and more power to yr. elbow. Dont listen to any one else, and above all dont listen to me.

Shd. welcom [sic] yr. candid re both "Homage to S. Prop." and "Mauberley" if you have the texts.

Nobody tells me anything about 'em that I don't know already (and that they usually tell me à rebours [against the grain]) all except [name crossed out] who says . . . . in confirmation of the remark on lunar eclipses . . . etc. that Callimachus is too much, and that the Rubaiyat is properly annotated.

and when I think where I found her.

I must cross the proper names out of this, as youre such a devil for printin ones private affairs.

a toi [yours]

E

p. 68: Page 68 of WCW's *Kora in Hell: Improvisations* (1920) marks the beginning of section XVIII.

Rimbaud's Saison en Enfer: Une saison en enfer (A Season in Hell, 1873) by the French poet Arthur Rimbaud (1854–1891) is, like WCW's *Kora,* an alogical, even delirious, sequence of dissociated fragments, many of them written in a highly poetic prose.

The italics: Every major subsection of *Kora* contains at least one passage that is printed in italic typeface.

Maupassant: The French novelist and short-story writer Guy de Maupassant (1850–1893) employed a lucid, naturalistic prose style.

the dialog: In his "Prologue" to *Kora,* WCW recounts a conversation between EP and William George Williams, the subject of which was the meaning of certain images of precious stones in EP's poem "Und Drang" (*Canzoni,* 1911). According to WCW, EP explained that the "jewels" represented "the backs of books as they stood on a man's shelf," to which Mr. Williams replied, "But why in heaven's name don't you say so then?" The lines in question occur in section VII, "The House of Splendour": "And I have seen her there within her house,/ With six great sapphires hung along the wall,/ Low, panel-shaped, a-level with her knees." WCW also describes this exchange in his *Autobiography,* pp. 91–92, and in Heal, p. 8.

Mozart and Brahms: Austrian composer, Wolfgang Amadeus Mozart (1756–1791), and German composer, Johannes Brahms (1833–1897). Mozart appears in section III of *Kora,* dancing with his wife and "whistling his own tunes to keep the cold away."

Lamar: Judge William Harmon Lamar (1859–1928) was an assistant attorney general and solicitor of the United States Post Office from 1913 to 1921. In that capacity, he was involved in the Post Office's suppression of issues of *The Little Review* containing Wyndham Lewis' "Cantleman's Spring Mate" (1917) and certain episodes of James Joyce's *Ulysses.*

Xelestine: A Parisian mistress? EP has crossed out the name "Victorine" and substituted "Xelestine," for the reason stated at the end of the letter.

the cover design: WCW later said that the cover design of *Kora* "represents the ovum in the act of being impregnated, surrounded by spermatozoa, all trying to get in but only one successful. I myself improvised the idea, seeing, symbolically, a design using sperms of various breeds, various races let's say, and directed the artist to vary the shadings of the drawing from white to gray to black"; see Heal, pp. 28–29, and *Autobiography,* p. 158.

the FIRST post-Xtn bust: Viewed from the rear, Gaudier-Brzeska's *Hieratic Head of Ezra Pound* resembles an erect phallus.

Le gracieux: The source of this quotation has not been identified. The following English version is my own: "The gracious and supple rhythm of Propertius makes one think of a river or of a bank [*berge*] rather than of an oak."

Homage to S. Prop.: EP's "Homage to Sextus Propertius" had appeared in *Poetry* for March 1919 (four sections only), in *The New Age* (June 19–August 28, 1919, six sections only), and in *Quia Pauper Amavi* (1919, entire).

Mauberley: "Hugh Selwyn Mauberley" had appeared in book form from the Ovid Press in June 1920 and in *The Dial* for September 1920 (six sections only).

Callimachus: An Alexandrian Greek poet (*c.* 305–*c.* 240 B.C.), who wrote satires, lyrics, and elegies. He was admired by Propertius and Catullus.

the Rubaiyat: On *The Rubaiyat* of Omar Khayyám, see Letter 14 above.

16. TLS-2

12 Sept. [1920]

(continuing yesterdays)

Voui mon vieux coco [yes, old bean]:

Another point re/ parodies, langue d'oc etc.

To be "historic", the "Homage langue d'oc" was the first thing hit upon by L'Intransigeant as supposedly of popular interest to the populous french public. That's nothing, proves only that populous french are insular, like to think their country is noticed etc. NO importance.

But what the French *real reader* wd. say to your "Improvisations" is

Voui, c(h)a j(h)ai deja (f)vu c(h)a c(h)a c'est de R(h)imb(h)aud [yes, that, I've already seen that; that's by Rimbaud]!!

So much for your kawnscious or unkawnscious. I certainly never put up translations of Provencal as "American"; and Eliot is perfectly conscious of having immitated [*sic*] Laforgue, has worked to get away from it, and there is very little Laforgue in his Sweeny [*sic*] or his Bleistein-Burbank, or his Gerontion, or his Bay State hymn book

And in fact you are talking through your hat when you suggest that I at any time was ever ass enough to have picked La Figlia for the fantastic occasion you hypothecate.

[Edgar Lee] Masters is not as good as Jammes "Existences". Your "representative american" verse will be that which can be translated in foreign languages without appearing ridiculous to us after it has been "accepted" and which will appear new to the french or hun or whatever

Pas de bile [no hard feelings]

E

of course for me to say "you're another" is no argument – its only drawing attention to the vitreous nature of yr. facade on observing the bricks you heave at my conservatory.

mon vieux coco: WCW echoes this greeting in section XI of *The Great American Novel* (1923).

"Homage langue d'oc": For WCW's criticism of EP's "Homage à la langue d'Oc," see Letter 14 above. WCW had suggested that EP wished to pass off "parodies of the middle ages, Dante and *langue d'oc*" as "the best in United States poetry."

L'Intransigeant: A Paris daily newspaper (1880–1940), known for its coverage of politics and art. EP implies that it reviewed his *Quia Pauper Amavi* (1919), but the review has not been identified.

the French real reader: In section III of *The Great American Novel,* WCW quotes from this letter without attribution: "Take the improvisations: What the French reader would say is: *Oui, ça; j'ai déjà vu ça; ça c'est de Rimbaud.* Finis. Representative American verse will be that which will appear new to the French . . . prose the same."

Eliot: In early poems, such as "The Love Song of J. Alfred Prufrock," "The Portrait of a Lady," and "Rhapsody on a Windy Night," T. S. Eliot imitated the tone and imagery of the French Symbolist poet Jules Laforgue (1860–1887). The poems to which EP refers—"Sweeney Erect," "Sweeney Among the Nightingales," "Burbank with a Baedeker: Bleistein with a Cigar," and "Gerontion"—appeared in Eliot's *Poems* (1920) and are less crepuscular.

Bay State hymn book: A book of poems written, like many hymns, in quatrains. In this case, EP probably refers to Eliot's *Poems,* which contains seven satires in that form.

La Figlia: In "The Western School," Jepson describes Eliot's "La Figlia Che Piange" as "the very fine flower of the finest spirit of the United States." In the "Prologue" to *Kora in Hell,* WCW envisions "an international congress of poets" at which "Ezra stands up to represent U. S. verse" and "begins by reading 'La Figlia che Piange.'"

Jammes "Existences": Francis Jammes (1868–1938) is one of the writers discussed in EP's "A Study in French Poets," first published in *The Little Review* for February 1918. EP describes Jammes' "Existences," a poem published in *Le Triomphe de la Vie* (1901), as "the more than 'Spoon River' of France . . . the canvass of an whole small town or half city," and possibly "the most important single volume by any living French poet" (pp. 41, 46).

vitreous: People in glass houses shouldn't throw stones.

PART TWO
1921–1932

Pound and Williams continued to debate the role of the American poet throughout the 1920s. At first glance, their positions seem opposed. On the one hand, Pound maintained his European exile and his cosmopolitan standard. He lived in Paris from 1921 to 1924, and in Rapallo, Italy, from 1924 to 1945. For nearly thirty years (1911–39) he did not set foot on American soil. He was involved in many expatriate publishing projects, and launched his international, multilingual epic, *The Cantos*. On the other hand, Williams staked out an indigenist or nativist position in such works as *Spring and All* (1923), *The Great American Novel* (1923), and *In the American Grain* (1925). The job of the American writer, as he saw it, was not to connect American literature with European or world traditions, but to discover and express what is new and distinctive in the American experience and the American language.

In some ways, however, this opposition was more apparent than real. During the 1920s, Williams reached out toward Europe as never before. He made two trips to the Continent and published a number of works there. As Pound, Eliot, and James Joyce began to produce their postwar masterpieces, Williams resolved that he and his work would not be excluded from the international stage. At the same time, Pound maintained his contacts with periodicals and publishers in the United States, still determined to influence cultural developments in his homeland. Despite the *Kora* conflict, Pound and Williams continued to collaborate on many levels.

Early in the decade, Pound enlisted Williams in the "Bel Esprit" project. The aim of Bel Esprit was to raise enough money from private donations to enable a writer to live and work for a year, free of economic pressures. The first beneficiary was to be Eliot, who was employed full-time by Lloyd's Bank in London. If the plan succeeded, Williams himself might be exported to Europe for a year. After a decade of private practice, the hard-working doctor found the idea of a sabbatical very alluring. He swallowed his reservations about Eliot and chipped in twenty-five dollars. Unfortunately, the scheme never got off the ground.

Meanwhile, Pound had located a talented and wealthy American printer in Paris, William Bird. Together with Robert McAlmon, another U. S. expatriate with money to spare, they established the Three Mountains Press. It specialized in fine, limited editions of innovative British and American writing. McAlmon had known Williams in New York, where they co-edited a little magazine named *Contact*. He and Pound invited Williams to become a Three Mountains author. In

1923, Bird printed two experimental manuscripts by Williams, *Spring and All* and *The Great American Novel*. In 1925, Three Mountains also printed the first volume of Pound's epic, *A Draft of XVI. Cantos*.

Finally, Williams was able to make the extended journey to Europe which he had postponed so often. He and Floss came to Paris early in 1924. There, Williams made or renewed contacts that would shape the rest of his literary career. He met James Joyce, Ernest Hemingway, Ford Madox Ford, Sylvia Beach, Natalie Barney, William Bird, Peggy Guggenheim, George Antheil, Man Ray, Clive Bell, Constantin Brancusi, Jean Cocteau, Louis Aragon, Philippe Soupault, and Fernand Léger; and he enjoyed reunions with H. D., Mina Loy, McAlmon, and Pound. During the rest of their five-month stay, Bill and Floss also visited Italy, Austria, and Switzerland. Upon returning to the United States, Williams began his first novel, an autobiographical account of his travels. Dedicated to Pound, it was entitled *A Voyage to Pagany* (1928). In 1927, Williams and his wife came to Switzerland to put their sons into boarding school for a year. On this occasion, however, Williams spent only a few weeks in Europe and did not meet Pound.

The nativist, it seems, was not working exclusively in the American grain. Indeed, chapters of the book which bears that title were first published in *Broom* (Berlin), *Transatlantic Review* (Paris), and *This Quarter* (Milan). Williams also contributed to *transition* and became the American consulting editor of *Bifur*, both published in Paris. He wanted his name to be as familiar in the cultural centers of Europe as it was in New York and Chicago.

In 1927, Pound himself started up a new literary magazine called *Exile*. Edited in Rapallo, it was published and distributed mainly in the United States. Pound solicited manuscripts from many of his friends, including Williams. With the editorial assistance of Louis Zukofsky, Williams assembled a large group of poems and prose passages; "The Descent of Winter" made up most of the fourth and final number of *Exile*, published in the autumn of 1928. "It is a delight to me to feel a possible bond of workmanship being exercised between us today," Williams wrote to Pound (April 16, 1928).

The bond grew even stronger with Pound's publication, in *The Dial* for November 1928, of an insightful critical essay entitled "Dr. Williams' Position." Williams responded humbly: "Nothing will ever be said of better understanding regarding my work than your article in The Dial. I must thank you for your great interest and discriminating defense of my position" (November 6, 1928). At this time, the editor of *The Dial* was Marianne Moore, a friend of both Pound and Williams. She accepted contributions from both men and saw to it that they received *The Dial*'s annual $2,000 prize in consecutive years: Williams in 1927, and Pound in 1928.

The two were appearing side by side in other American magazines as well. For example, *Pagany,* which had taken its name from Williams' first novel, was serializing his second, *White Mule*. At the same time, it was publishing Cantos and cultural broadsides by Pound. *Poetry, Hound and Horn, The Little Review, Symposium, The New Masses, Blues, 1924,* and *Contempo* all carried work by Pound and Williams during the 1920s and early 1930s.

The two of them patronized individual artists as well as little magazines. For example, Williams shared Pound's enthusiasm for the young American composer George Antheil. As Pound had promoted Antheil's experimental music when it was first performed in Paris in 1926, so Williams boosted it when Antheil's New York premiere took place in 1927. Among the younger writers whose merits Pound and Williams jointly proclaimed were McAlmon, Zukofsky, Ben Hecht, Joe Gould, Emanuel Carnevali, Charles Reznikoff, and Parker Tyler. The senior authors did not always see eye to eye, though. For instance, Williams did not care for the rhymed and metered verse of Pound's protégé Ralph Cheever Dunning. And Pound adamantly refused to join Williams in contributing to Richard Aldington's *Imagist Anthology 1930*.

Another common interest was the literary representation of American history. In a period of moral disorientation, both writers looked to the past for ethical exempla. Pound admired Williams' *In the American Grain,* and Williams was fascinated by the Cantos into which Pound incorporated the correspondence of Thomas Jefferson and John Adams (XXXI–XXXIV). The poets did not choose the same heroes from the annals of American history, but they were both drawn to the Jacksonian Populist-Progressive tradition, with its deep distrust of big business and big banking.

The collaborations of this decade culminated in Pound's editing of two anthologies, *Profile* (1932) and *Active Anthology* (1933). These compilations showcase vital authors and developments in modern poetry, and each includes a substantial representation of Williams' work. For Pound firmly believed that Williams was "the best prose writer and poet in America" (unpublished letter to John Henri Buchi of September 27, 1934, Yale).

17. TLS-1

Jan. 4 – 1921

Liebes Ezrachen [Dear Little Ezra]:

I am nearly crazy with paying attention to halves and quarters (not dollars!) – broken pieces of men that have me sick trying to patch something up out of the mess.

I've fallen in a bit among the piano strings. I'll come out of it – but it takes time – time – time. Best accept the apparition as "something" and blot it down as a dog does with dirty feet – anyhow it occured [*sic*] to me that I might normalize myself by addressing you –

It is growing bitter to think of you there far off where I cannot see you or talk to you. It would be as if – It would be sun coming up to see you again.

Pas de bile – you are right. I had counted on that. I read most of the stuff you are sending over or write yourself.

Nothing to say.

Our new magazine is out. Glad to have you send us a typed page or two from time to time if you want to. I'll send copies as soon as the second issue is printed.

I wish I were in Paris with you tonight. I am a damned fool who sees only the light through a knothole. I resist, it's about the most I can say for myself. Yet I remember moments of intense happiness – no it wasn't happiness.

Take the trouble to send me the names of the Spaniards you spoke of in a former letter, also addresses and the names of a couple of worthwhile spanish books – modern poetry. Please do not forget this as I am now in a position to do a little work along this horizontal.

I feel better – even at this distance.

God be wi' ye.

Yrs.
Bill

Family well. Ed. trying to do architecture – but times are vile.

W

Demuth is painting some good stuff cold – ordered – a little pale but good.

Bill

Our new magazine: Contact, a little magazine produced by WCW and Robert McAlmon, appeared irregularly from December 1920 to June 1923.

18. TLS-6

18 Mars [March 1922]

DEER BULLLL:

The point is that Eliot is at the last gasp. Has had one break down. We have got to do something at once.

I have been on the job, am dead tired with hammering this machine. Steps have been taken. Richard and I, pledged to £10/per year.

This merely to apologize for brevity. I enclose a carbon outline. Get to it. Can you run to 50 dollars yourself???

I wd. try and make it good to you later. I mean the struggle is to get the first man released. "Release of energy for invention and design" acc[ording to]. best economic theories.

AFTER Eliot is freed it will be much easier to get out the secind [*sic*] theird [*sic*]. and tenth prisoners.

I wd. back you for the second, if you wished. BUT I dont really believe you want to leave the U. S. permanently.

I think you are suffering from nerve [*sic*]; that you are really afraid to leave Rutherford.

I think you ought to have a year off or a sxi [*sic*] months vacation in europe. I think you are afraid to take it, for fear of destroying some illusions which you think necessary to your illusions.

I dont think you ought to leave permanently, you [*sic*] job gives you too real a contact   too valuable to give up.

BUT you ought to see a human being now and again.

One might after frreing [*sic*] Eliot, run a yearly trip from america. Or at least you one summer, Mariaannne [Moore] another, etc. when there was someone worth it.

At present, although the necessary 30 for Eliot haven't been found, I can I think offer you a summer home.

The BEL Esprit [Fine Minds] is definitely started. And the "pavillon" was offfered [*sic*] me yesterday for suitable candidate.

It is not the "sanctuaire" on card enclosed.

No hate with the mornibg [*sic*], no satiety with the nightfall,

It is a show down. Those who dont care 50 dollars a year for the arrts, dont care for MUCH. It gags the sassiety muckers.

I want you [*sic*] help. If you cant make the 50 dollars a year pledge, can you organize a group which will do so.

I am writing to Bob McA.; I want you to work in America.

It is the start that is the hardest. Once the nucleus formed. Once the Tom cat and the she-cat, the kittens will arrive. without our worrying.

NO use trying to unite people on critical basis, basis of common taste, or opinion, must unite on basis of common good will.

Anyone dont like choice of Paris branch of Bel Esprit can start local branch, backin local fancy.

If you dont approve sending american poet to Europe, you can invite European poet to U. S. A. . I dont care.

First step is however necessary. MUST free the qualified energies, if we are to get the stuff.

> yours
> Ezra

[carbon-copy enclosure] THERE IS NO organized or coordinated civilization left, only individual scattered survivors.

Aristocracy is gone, its function was to select.

Only those of us who know what civilization is, only those of us who want better literature, not more literature, better art, not more art can be expected to pay for it. No use waiting for masses to develop a finer taste, they aren't moving that way.

All the rewards to men who do compromise worke [*sic*]. No hope for others.

Millionaires all tapped too frequently. Must be those of us who care. We are none of us able to act alone. must cooperate.

Increase production, of the best, by releasing the only energies that are capable of producing it.

Bel Esprit started in Paris. To release as many captives as possible.

Darkness and confusion as in middle ages; no chance of general order or justice; we can only release an individual here or there.

T. S. Eliot first name chosen. Must have thirty guarantors at £10 per year ''for life or for as long as Eliot needs it. (anyone who dont like our choise [*sic*] is at liberty to choose some other imprisoned artist or writer, and start another Bel Esprit group.

Only thing we can give the artist is leisure to work in. Only way we can get work from him is to assure him this leisure,.

As fast as his sales go up, amount of his subsidy will be decreased; this to insure quality; to prevent his being penalized for suppressing inferior work; Every writer is penalized as at present for not doing bad work, penalized for not printing EVERYTHING he can sell.

Wastage of literary prizes. Anatole France deserved the Nobel prize, but no one will claim that giving it to him at age of 74 in any way increases or betters his production.

Eliot, in bank, makes £500// too tired to write, broke down; during convalescence in Switzerland, did "Waste Land, a masterpiece; one of most important 19 page poes [*sic*] im [*sic*] English.

Returned to bank, and is again gone to pieces pyhsically [*sic*].

Pound, Aldington start with £10/ guarantees, if they can afford it others can.

Must restart civilization; people who say they care, DONT care unless they care to the extent of £5 in the spring and £5 in autumn, ridiculous to say they do, if they wont run to that, cant expect a civilization or grumble if they dont [word or words missing]

NOT charity, NOT "pity the poor artist". Eliot wd. rather work in bank than do poor work. Has tried to live by pen and cant. (Poor health, invalid wife).

NOT charity in his case nor in case of any other good artist whom we may later choose.

It is for US who want good work, to provide means of its being done. WE are the consumers and we demand somethg [*sic*] fit to consume.

In the arts quantity is nothing, quality everything.

Only certain men who can produce the grade of stuff we want. They must be in position to do so.

Only certain lands will produce copper, etc. Must go where the stuff is. no gathering figs of thistle bushes.

If not enough good will to release ONE proved writer, how do they expect to regenerate Europe.

Eliot first item on a list. Anyone free to start group for their own choise.

Eliot: For Eliot's breakdown and EP's attempts to help him, see "Biographical Notes" on ELIOT, THOMAS STEARNS.

Richard: Two of EP's letters to Richard Aldington on the subject of Bel Esprit, dated March 12 and 16, 1922, are at Texas.

a carbon outline: EP also circulated another appeal for Bel Esprit; see Paige, pp. 174–75.

you job: WCW's full-time medical practice in obstetrics and pediatrics.

the "pavillon": See Letter 20 below.

Bob McA.: See "Biographical Notes" on MCALMON, ROBERT.

the Tom cat and the she-cat: Eliot and his wife Vivien Haigh-Wood; see "Biographical Notes" on ELIOT, THOMAS STEARNS. Mrs. Eliot suffered from a number of physical and psychological illnesses.

Anatole France: The French novelist and short-story writer Anatole France (1844–1924) was awarded the Nobel Prize in 1921.

Waste Land: WCW had not yet seen *The Waste Land,* the first American publication of which came in *The Dial* for November 1922. For his reaction to the poem ("the great catastrophe to our letters"), see the *Autobiography,* pp. 146, 174–75.

19. TLS-3

March 29, 1922

Dear Esq:–

Oh why don't you go get yourself crucified on the Montmartre and will the proceeds to art? I'll come to Paris and pass the hat among the crowd. What the hell do I care about Elliot [*sic*]?

About my nerves: they've survived you; today more able than yesterday.

I'd enjoy a trip to Paris. But I don't care much to trade my own illusions for yours. By unfortunate circumstance I have stumbled on the few particles of truth about writing that I know, things which you might have pointed out to me in three words if you had the skill or the understanding.

What I see before me in my work needs no special companionship or food other than that which is before it. I long for intelligence and good will, as I detest as the essence of stupidity all your assumptions referable to what I am and what I need.

It is interesting that you have gotten far enough in your understanding to realize that "good will" is all you can give an artist. I am for you there. "Bel esprit" shows the influence of the french spirit on your obtuse soul. Or is that one of my illusions? I think it is.

I need leisure, true, but not money. How I am to get leisure is difficult to say. But having fought the thing out along a single line from the first, without the least assistance from friends, I'll probably get my leisure as I have gotten the rest.

Take the money and stick it up your A. S.

yours
W

P. S. Write again –

You don't explain yourself: Thirty guarantors will keep Elliot [*sic*] alive for life. Will the next candidate be kept alive for life by the same thirty?

Yes, now at last, I should like to go to Paris. I should like to live in your "pavillion" [*sic*] and never see you at all. I should like to have you give me five pounds every spring and autumn and to have you remain anonymus [*sic*] always. That would amuse my soul.

Perhaps I shall come – very soon.

After much pain I have pulled one foot out of the primal ooze, or more properly, the suburban mud, and planted it on something which feels firm. Your "bel esprit" comes at that moment with a song between the valves of iys [*sic*] beak and sings me its song. It would be a lie to say that it does not pull my eyes up in astonishment. With two feet planted on something resistant I will want to go abroad at last. I will want to go to Paris where, unless I am still eye-bogged, I shall see men walking simply about in the sun. If I may walk with them I shall be too happy to wish for other expression.

What you say of invention and design is the best you say.

I begin.

Never until now have I seen what I want. But the realization has been so essentially what I had imagined; it has been made by myself of what I knew it could be and must be made - that (no use to develope [*sic*]) It has not been necessary to go out until today. It was only necessary to strike in deep enough. I have done so.

Tres interessant [very interesting] – american candidate for Bel Esprit – combien [how much]? Cinq cents francs – Les voila [five hundred francs – there they are].

A very beautiful post card. I have a machine for reflecting the image on a sheet on the wall: two incandescent bulbs inside, concave mirrors – shall use picture.

Balieff's Theatre de la Chauve-Souris here: superbly done.

Remember – I shall take your pavillion.

> Yours-in-bud
> Bill

P. S. – 2

The difficulty of my situation is that I cannot leave my practice and keep it. If I leave it, it will crumble away unless I make a certain effort to hold it by having someone her [*sic*] in my plave [*sic*] while I am gone. This I have not been able to arrange to do until now.

I am glad to have had you feel that the work I do is of some value to me. It can now be said to you: I do not want to lose that which is my sole means of sustenance in the world. Romantic starvation for the one thing that deeply concerns me in life – composition, does not appeal to me. I have always rejected it for the definite reason that it defeats its own end, an argument so overwhelming that I have not been able to defeat it.

My pace is a slow one but as I am gifted by nature with an inflexible stubborness [*sic*] and an excessively adherent youthfulness I have not worried about that. If I am to succeed in any kind of valuable work I shall succeed in spite of advancing years.

If I am defeated by sickness or accident I shall always know that I have kept company with my imagination through thick and thin.

Now the time has come when I want to go abroad; I do not say that I feel starved for a trip or cramped in any way. I simply feel a strong desire to move in among a few others more or less like myself. I suppose it is really ridiculous to imagine they are any more in the sun than I am. They cannot be so, not today. But they are more used to it. I like good manners and good company. In fact – if life had been more amenable to reason and more luxurient [*sic*] where I have happened to be in the world reality might have found me – I would have enjoyed the happiest existance [*sic*] conceivable;

The twenty five dollars I enclose were paid me by a Jew named Katz. His wife had a baby last week. They own a steam laundry here. This is her third son. She leaned on the bed post and screamed enough to waken the saints – it was a Sunday afternoon. Before the baby came I made her go to bed. She shit on the bed. Then she bled all over the sheet. It leaked through on the mattrass [*sic*]. When a child is born the scrotum is – a male child – swollen and loose: like yours on a hot day at Lago de [*sic*] Garda. This child had an unusually full bag. Woe unto christianity. The woman's breasts weigh (estimated) five pounds each. She stinks like hell –

the same to you.

Bill

Perhaps I shall come: WCW did not go to Paris until January 1924.

post card: The "card enclosed" by EP in Letter 18 above, showing a view of a "sanctuaire." It does not appear to have survived.

Balieff's Theatre: La Chauve-Souris (The Bat) was a Paris review produced by the Armenian theater director Nikita Balieff (1897–1936). After a successful London run in the fall of 1921, it opened in New York on February 4, 1922. Reviews in the *New York Times* for February 6 and 12 describe it as "a casual, informal Muscovy vaudeville," which originated at the little Bat Restaurant in Moscow, and featured folk singers, dancers, mummers, and clowns. EP saw a performance in Paris in May 1923, and mentioned it in a letter to his mother of May 26 (Yale).

Lago de Garda: Lake Garda, near Verona in northeastern Italy, was one of EP's favorite retreats and "sacred places." The town of Sirmione, at the southern end of the lake, had

been a home of Catullus; it was there that EP met Edgar Williams in 1911 and James
Joyce in 1920.

20. ALS-5

21 May [1922]

See here ole son:

If you hear a report of my death don't fer Xt's sake deny it. Say you expected
as much. Suggest Xifiction or assifiction or any other –
& express perlite regret.

Now as to the Pavhillion = I wrote you from Paris that I hoped to be able to
offer it to you.

The matter i.e. pavilion was broached at a tea fight 3 days before I left Paris & I
was expected to come out & inspect it – hygenicly etc. & pronounce it fit or unfit
for literary habitation.

On receipt of yrs (containing Katz proceeds I wrote to Paris, to see if formality
of my inspection etc. were necessary.

La Baronne de Clauzel responds that it is fit for a european artist but that she
shudders to think of effect it might have on an american

An american to her is evidently someone who wd. shrink from sharing his
privvy [sic] with a chauffeur.

My studio wont hold three, but my spouse goes to Eng. about July 15th. I can
threfore [sic] offer you a room for 6 weeks or 2 months.

During which you cd. have time to inspect the Pavhillion & see if it is habitable
= or worth bothering about for the rest of yr. vacation.

You wd. during the 6–8 weeks have the inconvenience of my presence below
you, balanced by the convenience of getting yr. breakfasts ready made & not
having to struggle with charwomen.

I need scarcely say that the incommodity of yr. presence wd be but a greater
delight to me

am not expecting to give birth to an infant, at least I have shown no symptoms
of pregnancy & there is only 2 to four months in which you wd. be exposed to the
dangers of a hurry call.

You can have a seperate [sic] key to the back entrance, & put a couch in the
wash room if you want to receive female patients without my knowledge.

Thanks for 5 bones [dollars] recd.

I hope you'll come over

Seriously. please don't contradict report of my demise if it has the luck to spread. I want a little quiet.

And let me know probable date of yr arrival & length of yr. time off.   ? you dont want to take a boat to Genoa & come to Lago di Garda for a week first?

Probably not worth bore of extra visas & train trip up to Paris.

I shan't be back in Paris before about 7th July.

[not trying to nurse you or personally conduct you thru Europe – only you can't get into the studio in my absence as the key is here in my pocket & the lease forbids loan or sublet – Hence the meticulous necessity of my being there to open the door if you deign to enter

There is also the very faint possibility that I might have to form a junction with X here in Italy which might (tho' unlikely) delay my return a week or so.

will let you know as soon as pos[sible]. but in any case, in anny kase, so far foresight permits nothing visible at the moment, menaces your having 6 weeks or two months free shelter at 70 *bis* and more in Baronne's back garden IF her shack is good enough.

As you have been so explicit in yr. optation of undisturbed solituted [*sic*] I hesitate to offer to prolong my sojourn in Italy – if you shd. care to shed the lustre of yr. medical knowledge on this land already flavoured with sunlight

Possibly cd. offer you at least four nerve cases – if thats any inducement.

As to Paris. If you take the room off my studio don't fer christ's sake think you need see me except at breakfast or that your quiet need be infected.

I've got (or suppose I have) leave to use a room & garden elsewhere so that we shdn't be cramped.

yrs

Ezra

---

a report of my death: This was a hoax of EP's that fizzled. He had a life mask of himself made by Nancy Cox McCormack. Calling it a death mask, he had photographs of it sent on Good Friday to *The Little Review*. But the editors of the magazine, Margaret Anderson and Jane Heap, were not taken in. See Pound/*The Little Review*, pp. 283, 287.

left Paris: The return address on this letter is "Hothell Savhoy, Venedig" (Hotel Savoy, Venice). In the spring and summer of 1922, EP spent several months in Italy, researching the life of Sigismundo Malatesta in preparation for the writing of Cantos 8–11.

La Baronne de Clauzel: Unidentified, but probably one of Natalie Clifford Barney's circle in Paris (see "Biographical Notes" on BARNEY, NATALIE CLIFFORD). In a letter of March 20, 1922, to Richard Aldington (Texas), EP speaks of "'a somewhat indefinite offer of a pavillion' from the Contesse de Cloisel or summat. I am to go and see her and the pav. when I return from Italy."

5 bones: In a letter to EP of May 5, 1922 (Indiana), WCW enclosed five dollars along with an account of the forceps delivery by which he earned the money.

X: Possibly "Xelestine," mentioned in Letter 15 above.

21. TLS-1

July 13 [1922]

Dear Ezra: –

It's no use. Can't be done. One hundred and seven dollars to Paris THIRD class plus the same for return trip. At least fifty dollars in the city – AT LEAST. And I'd only be there ten days. No.

Next year for three months in the fall. It will have to remain a promise – to myself of course.

I'll continue the contribution as long as I am able but not forever. Another year for the present at least. I want to see more of Eliot's work. After next year I'm to be away from the income end of my activities a twelve month and shall need my savings.

I may want to bring out another book the coming winter. Verse. Also I have a prose thing of book proportions. Nothing to say of that yet. It all takes coin in one way or another.

You I'd like to see. I saw [Charles] Demuth recently. It should be like that. But I can't go to Paris.

I never yet saw anything lost for keeping it – wine, yes. But not wine well kept. I may die this winter but if so – I'll be dead, dancing dead. IT's [*sic*] the only way I'll die except finally. I wish to god I could. Drunk with niggers. Anyhow it sounds well today in this heat after I've been down in the brick yards watching the blacks make and pile bricks.

Marjory [*sic*] Allen Seiffert, Moline, – I've forgotten the state – might come across. She and Mrs. Aldis. I can't see it otherwise. Marion Strobel, the assistant manager of the Poetry stables has a Pa who has millions, they say. Meet David O'Neil in – in Europe and ask him. Arensberg has lost all his money in oil, I hear from Demuth. Ask Loeb of BROOM if his wife won't hock a shirt or something and throw in the proceeds.

To actually see Paris   See what? It is intollerable [*sic*] not to be leaving on the 2nd. August. Maybe I can sell something to the Dial. No. No; no use.

Bill

another book: No book of verse by WCW appeared in the winter of 1922–23.

a prose thing: Probably *In the American Grain* (1925), a series of essays on American history and culture. They began to appear in magazines in January 1923.

Marjory Allen Seiffert: The American poet Marjorie Allen Seiffert (1885–1970) of Moline, Illinois, was the author of *A Woman of Thirty* (1919). She was a contributor to *Poetry* and a financial supporter of *Others.*

Mrs. Aldis: Mary Reynolds Aldis (b. 1872) was a Chicago poet and playwright. Her husband Arthur Aldis was a wealthy real-estate developer and a financial guarantor of *Poetry* and *The Little Review.*

Marion Strobel: Marion Strobel (1895-1966) was the author of *Lost City: Poems* (1928). She worked on the editorial staff of *Poetry.* WCW met her during a visit to Chicago in March 1919 and probably had a brief love affair with her at that time.

David O'Neil: David O'Neil retired from the lumber business in St. Louis, Missouri, and went to live the poet's life in Europe. In 1917, he published a volume of verse entitled *A Cabinet of Jade.*

Arensberg: The New York poet, prose writer, and art collector Walter Conrad Arensberg (1878–1954) was a financial backer of *Others* when it started up in 1915–16. He was the author of *Poems* (1914) and *Idols* (1916).

Loeb: Harold Loeb (1891–1974) was the editor of *Broom* (1921– 1924), which published poems by WCW and several chapters of *In the American Grain.*

22. TLS-2

[July 23, 1922]

Poor ole BUGGSquash

Any use my comin' over to fetch you, or to inspect your teeth.

Endocrinology is humming under this roof at the moment. The G[rea]t. gland sleuth has jest went.

I dont suppose your B[el]. Esp[rit]. 30 bones wd. help.

B. E. espr. cant import you at the moment. What about my coming to N. Y.; I suppose that needs about 5000 (five thousand bones). for expenses and time. And your influence with lecture agencies = = nil???

Of course I wont come to N. Y. unless I can come "first". i. e. class.

Ten days is too short a time to cross for. you must get your locum tenens [reservation] for three months.

Merely I don't refuse to come to the U. S. (on principle), I merely must have honourable terms.

YOU OUGHT NOT TO pay for publication of your stuff. DO confer with me before committing that folly. I dont abs[olutely]. know that I can be of any use, but wd. certainly have a shot at it. (Have I misinterpreted your letter on this point, you say "it all takes money one way or another".

Brining [*sic*] out a book for you NOW ought NOT to take money. The "Tempers" was another matter.

There is Rodker in London with a press, and the Egoist, and also a printer here who wants my "unprintable" stuff.

Loeb? shit. "That man is a god-awful mess, somebody ought to clean him up" said Djuna, apropos of of Loeb's bringing over a poor little bitch as stenographer or secretary to Broom, and then chucking her without funds here in Paris.

For once I can agree with Djuna unqualifiedly.

yrs.

Ez

gland sleuth: Dr. Louis Berman (1893–1946) of New York, author of *The Glands Regulating Personality: A Study of the Glands of Internal Secretion in Relation to the Types of Human Nature* (1922). EP reported favorably on Berman's work in *The New Age* for March 16, 1922. During Berman's visit to Paris in July 1922, he examined James Joyce and concluded that Joyce's eye troubles were due to dental abscesses; see Pound/Quinn, p. 216.

The "Tempers": WCW's *The Tempers* was published by Elkin Mathews in 1913 with the help of a $50 subsidy from the author; see Letter 7 above.

Rodker: See "Biographical Notes" on RODKER, JOHN.

the Egoist: For the Egoist Press, see Letter 14 above.

a printer here: William Bird; see Letter 23 below.

Djuna: Djuna Barnes (1892–1982) was an American expatriate writer who lived in Paris. She contributed fiction to *Others, The Little Review,* and *transition,* but her best-known work is *Nightwood* (1936). WCW met her on the French Riviera in 1924.

23. TLS-2

[August 1, 1922?]

Cher [Dear] Bull:

There s [*sic*] a printer here wants me to supervise a series of booklets, prose (in your case perhaps verse, or whatever form your new stuff is in.)

Gen[eral]. size about 50 pages. (??? too short for you.). Limited private edtn. of 350 copies. 50 dollars down to author, and another 50 later.

Is this any use to you for anything. Appearacne [*sic*] in this series wdnt. interfer [*sic*] with later reprint in pub[lic]. edtn. or inclusion of the 50 pages in some later longer book. It is a means of getting in 100 dollars extra. before one goes to publisher.

Yeats' sisters' press in Ireland has brought him in a good deal in this way. I got nearly as much from my little book with them as from the big Macmillan edtn. of Noh.

I shall keep the series strictly modern. One can be more intimate. The private limited edtn. dont imply that one is talking to the public. but simply to ones friends.

Anyhow. Explode: lets hear what you have and what you thin [*sic*]

I think it is probably better, at point where we have now arrived, than stray contribution to stray magazines.

on peut bien etre soi, et chez soi [one can be himself, and at home]. Also the printing will be good, as the chap is doing it himself. (His name is Willyum Bird)

Also what tips can you give the press re/ American book shops (IF any. And how many contact subscribers wd. be likeley [*sic*] to want your stuff.

Its hell the way I always seem to get sucked into editing something or other.

I suppose the people included in the series wd. more or less pool their lists of likely addresses.

I shall probably use the series for an annual outburst; and only send enough stuff to magazines to pay my rent.

I haven't exactly flooded the world with muck during the last two years, any how.

The series is OPEN: Though I dont at the moment see much more than half a dozen names: Hueffer, you, Eliot, [Wyndham] Lewis, Windeler, Hemingway et moi meme [myself]. that s [*sic*] seven.

I take it Marianne [Moore] never has anything but verse???

This is a prose series. general success or point of the thing wd. lie in its being really interesting.

As Bird says, he can make money issuing bibliographies, that is NOT what he wants.

yrs

E

A printer here: See ''Biographical Notes'' on BIRD, WILLIAM.

my little book: Certain Noble Plays of Japan: From the Manuscripts of Ernest Fenollosa,
   Chosen and Finished by Ezra Pound, with an Introduction by William Butler Yeats was
   published in September 1916 by the Cuala Press of Churchtown, Dundrum, a small
   hand press operated Elizabeth Corbet (''Lolly'') Yeats and Susan Mary (''Lily'') Yeats.

Macmillan of London brought out an expanded version of this book in January 1917 under the title *'Noh' or Accomplishment*.

contact subscribers: Subscribers to *Contact,* the little magazine edited in New York by WCW and Robert McAlmon in 1920–23; see Letter 17 above.

an annual outburst: The Three Mountains Press published EP's *Indiscretions* (1923), *Antheil and the Treatise on Harmony* (1924), and *A Draft of XVI. Cantos* (1925).

half a dozen names: In addition to *Indiscretions,* the series of short prose works organized by EP included WCW's *The Great American Novel,* Ford Madox Ford's *Women and Men,* B. C. Windeler's *Elimus,* B. M. G.-Adams' *England* (all published in 1923), and Ernest Hemingway's *in our time* (1924).

24. TLS-1

Tuesday, Aug. 15, 1922

Liebes Ezrachen: –

. . . . . yes, I said, Yes

Just finished Ulysses. I am satisfied to put it away for the moment. Yes, I'll risk one comment: It encourages me to champion my own particular form of stupidity – or knowledge or intelligence or lackknowledge. It is the first of the return from the desert.

Your proposal, fifty pages prose, attracts me. I should like to publish about fifty pages of prose bits which I have spilled in the past ten years. It would have to be a miscellanious [*sic*] lot. I'll go about it at once. I think it might prove interesting to whatever following I have here. Yes, it would go pretty well.

I'd call it simply: PROSE   That does not involve the presumption of calling a book POEMS. God knows though there's as much presumption I suppose in calling it PROSE (synopsis of the life of W.)

But really I am very much interested and the 100 bones would fit me out a new skeleton with which to walk into a new book of poems. I have always wanted a book of prose things, some place to appear without the necessity of assenting to the editorial nod of some lunar sheet's boss. There is this though to say: some of the stuff would have appeared in magazines. I don't suppose he wants the virginal only. I hope not at any rate. I have some prose in preparation that I want to have come out later but it will be at least a couple of hundred pages.

I am at present writing in the Green Mountains enjoying a change of climate, fishing, looking at the moon, the stars, smelling the dung, the newmown hay, playing with the children, boating, swimming, loafing, reading eating etc. so that I haven't anything handy, but when I return home in September see [*sic*] that you get the CONTACT list. It isn't large but there are some royal souls among the lot, scattered everywhere about the place.

I see Viola occasionally, had a long ride and talk with her in July. She has had a bloody rotten time of it. The blood – her own, three kids. The rot, inherited and married. Her man is not a bad sort either, in fact I like him very much. At present they are living togeter [*sic*] again, in a way. He goes and comes (mostly or entirely inside his stenographer) and V. smokes cigarettes until she is stained yellow almost up to her elbows and eyes. But she is beautiful (sloppy as hell, what the hell, diapers, kitchen) – furious at the world but more furiously virginal than ever. A burning hell. She is however surviving most marvellously. Writes a song, music, now and then.

Bill

Ulysses: See "Biographical Notes" on JOYCE, JAMES.

prose bits: WCW's *The Great American Novel* is divided into nineteen heterogeneous chapters. None was published separately in a magazine.

some prose in preparation: Probably *In the American Grain.*

the Green Mountains: WCW and his family were vacationing in the Green Mountains of Vermont.

Viola: See "Biographical Notes" on JORDAN, VIOLA SCOTT BAXTER.

her man: See "Biographical Notes" on JORDAN, VIRGIL D.

25. TLS-1

Sept. 11 [1922]

Liebes Ezrachen: –

as a lighthouse above the marsh: you before Winesburg. If I yank negroid morons and continue to do so it is only in defeat – knowing that I cannot run on air. If you survive living on nector [*sic*] or the odor of nectar you may step on my neck when you please. I remember the apple the Janizary cuts with his saber while in full gallop: half flies up and half down.

I am overwhelmed by your approval of my NOVEL. I need your critical remarks: God sometimes I feel myself to be the rottenest sham of the artist. "Intuition" does me so well that sometimes I think it is nothing but lack of brains. I work and then float off into emptiness – self critique comes only in flashes, two years apart –

I'd like to cut out the Baroness part if it can honestly be done. You see the hold it has on me. Really, what do you think? Or rather let us wait for the proof – I am afraid my wish to remove the canker may be the worse canker – You see I am still prone to fall inside the piano.

The mountain part – the sugar head – I copied verbatim from the Ladies Home Journal. How shall I make that appear? I court your advice – not saying of course that I'll take it.

Wait for the proof – then, if you want to use the knife, indicate the cuts. It will be of infinite assistance.

I read all you write. I have read the Cantos. I wait impatiently for the modern: it is my loss perhaps – Here and there flashes of the peacock-tail lovliness [*sic*] overtake me –

Come and live in my apartement on the Bosphorus – when I am sixty, dear.

By all means cut out anything that may suggest buggery. It is indeed thoughtless writing if it comes to that. I refer to what you call p. 27. I have no other copy of the MSS. so can't imaginw [*sic*] what you mean. – Coer [*sic*] de Lion; thanks. I thought he wrote a poem.

Gratefully

Weelyum

Winesburg: Small-town America; WCW borrows the name from Sherwood Anderson's *Winesburg, Ohio* (1919).

the Baroness part: The Baroness Else von Freytag-Loringhoven was an eccentric German writer and sculptor whose poetry and prose appeared frequently in *The Little Review*. WCW met her in New York in 1919. The "Baroness part" of WCW's *The Great American Novel* is probably the dialogue between the American narrator and a European woman in section XI. It is a response to Freytag-Loringhoven's "Thee I Call 'Hamlet of Wedding-Ring': Criticism of William Carlos William's [*sic*] 'Kora in Hell' and why . . . ," a long, two-part essay which appeared in *The Little Review* for 1921.

Ladies Home Journal: Section XVII of *The Great American Novel* is plagiarized from an article by Winifred Kirkland entitled "Mountain Mothers" in the *Ladies' Home Journal* for December 1920.

the Cantos: The first installments of EP's epic-length poem had appeared in *Poetry* in 1917; the most recent, in *The Dial* for August 1921 and May 1922.

the MSS: The manuscript of *The Great American Novel* is now at Indiana. Page 27 contains the last part of section VI, from "And this is romance" to the end. No passage has been cut, and none obviously suggests "buggery." Nor were any cuts made in section XI.

Coer de Lion: Richard I (1157–1199), King of England from 1189 to 1199, composed his best-known poem in French during his imprisonment in Germany on his way home from the Crusades. He died of an arrow wound in the neck and shoulder at the siege of Chaluz on April 6, 1199. In section XIV of *The Great American Novel*, WCW conflates these incidents: "Richard Coeur de Lion [Lionheart] shot through the chest with an iron bolt wrote the first English – no, French, poem of importance."

26. TLS-1

Nov. 22 – 1922

Dear Ezrachen:–

Give the whole business to Rudin – I mean the hundred. My last letter went off before the receipt of yours.

Not much chance of my seeing you in Europe before 1924 – the spring of that year. If I live and do not succumb to the fascination of present work too far, so far succumb, that is, that I shall want to stay here and see through what I have started before going to Europe, I'll be in France, May 1924. Of course many things may happen before then. Really I don't care very much any more anyway. I have enough in my head to keep me busy in this province for six years. And for the effect it may have on Europe I care not one least damn. Besides, I am almost forty, will be forty next year – and what the hell? Words have got me at last I suppose. I want only to sit down – anywhere – and do battle.

But of course, as I say, many things may happen. When spring gets me by the balls, as it always does, I may break a spring, or something. Perhaps I wish that were possible. God knows I should like to sit down quietly in contemplation before a few undiseased and naked cunts for a few months – sit down that is until I should recuperate from my last ten years vigil. I should like to come to yourope and fuck my head off (not the head of my cock though) – But that is after all hardly a reason for leaving the good old U. S. A.

Of course (again) there are moments when it is almost insupportable to be here. I feel that I could throw my arms about your neck, yes yours, and weep my heart out for eight weeks. Am I nearly dead? No, I think not. I am not even aclimatized [sic] here. But here I am just the same.

At lest [sic], your [sic] are still interested in facts, in literature that is. How curious? So am I, so is Willie.

Yours
Bill

Rudin: WCW offers the $100 promised by EP for *The Great American Novel* (see Letter 23 above) to the young American sculptor Paul Rudin. EP declined the offer, explaining that "Rudin, thanks to your eloquence, seems to have got an allowance from his family" (Buffalo, n.d.).

27. ALS-4

Dec. 23 – 1924

Dear Ezra: –

The extracts from your notes upon music have just reached my eye via the recent "1-9-2-4". I have culled a great pleasure from them. It is the sense of form which you have so skillfully presented by what you say. I await the book with a great interst [*sic*]. You too have changed.

Bill Bird tells me in a recent letter of his struggles to complete the printing of your Cantos. It is all so slow that at times it drives me to despair. I do not wish to become Hinduistic and wait for all completions to take place in another life – or is that American Indian lore? – The Am. Indians were strayed Asiatics.

Europe seems closer since we have been there but – again – it seems infinitely further off: so great has my wish to be there become intensified by the recent trip.

Paris seems just ⟨sketch⟩ there! Either I must be a tragic

ass, or nothing – or an American – I scarcely know which is the worst.

Hoping to see you again soon

Bill

Answer by a card or as you will. (to give me your true *new* address)

I may want to send you some recent prose of mine to read: your "notes" have greatly encouraged me to trust my studies.

Bill

your notes upon music: "Varia," *1924: A Magazine of the Arts* 4 (December 1924), pp. 132–35. This was an excerpt from EP's *Antheil and the Treatise on Harmony* (Paris: Three Mountains, 1924). The same issue of *1924* contained two prose improvisations by WCW, "Goodbyevienna" and "Reallythesound" (pp. 124–26).
your Cantos: A Draft of XVI. Cantos (Paris: Three Mountains Press, 1925).
the recent trip: WCW and his wife arrived in France on January 18, 1924, and departed on June 12. They visited Italy, Austria, and Switzerland as well.

new address: EP had recently moved from Paris to Rapallo, Italy, where he was to live
   until 1945.
some recent prose: Unidentified, but possibly "An Essay on Virginia," published in *This*
   Quarter for Spring 1925.

28. TLS-4

Feb. 12 [1926]

Liebes Ezrachen: –

Dunning was unknown to me before the receipt of your letter. Since then I have
read his verses in POETRY, also your comments. Walsh's words in THIS
QUARTER also noted.

By myself I should scarcely have looked twice at D's things. Superficially they
are boring. Following your lead I find them interesting. I find them interesting
because as you have pointed out they are superlatively well done from a technical
viewpoint. Your comments are just and illuminating. Your charm, your personal
charm, is still there.

Now cometh the quandry [*sic*]. Or perhaps there should be none. You have not
said that Dunning is the best – But yes you did say it, tentatively. You said he was
one of the four or five best of our poets living and writing today. The quandry
returns.

To me it seems that Dunning has proven, by a route none of the others of us has
taken, that it is still impossible to write work of first excellence in a demoded
form. We abandoned the form, he used it well. He used it superlatively well and
now, by his excellence, proves the failure. He could have proved nothing by
sloppy work. After reading him I still find the form he uses so well, intolerable. It
accords, however, with his stale content;: AN EXCELLENCE.

Thus the quandry increases, for the thing nobody can decide is, what excellence is most excellent. Should he be most admired who adds most to the means
of expression in his art or should he be admired who shows that there is no need
for additions.

Dunning gives me nothing but the old thrill of excellent craftsmanship. If that
is all there is to it, then he is a winner. If there is something more than that then he
is just opium. To me it seems that here is an excellent fellow with nothing much
to say who by dint of fine perception, hard work and great patience has after long
hours hit upon the one dead mode which fits him. Doing this over and over he has

come at last to the distinction of making something precious which fits all the rules of fine practice in his art without stretching them or caring to know where they may be departed from or amended.

This sort of thing is good medecine [*sic*]. But there is an excellence beyond Dunning's dreams which it has seemed to me was the great force behind all the finest work of today.

Or must we revert to neo-classicism –

To me then, Dunning seems no more than a ripple on the big wave of modern achievement in English poetry. I do not mean by this that the wave is big. I mean that Dunning's work seems to me no more than a little drop in the general upslant of the larger rise. He has finished exploring the cul-de-sac that we left in our hurry and proved it a dead end – as we thought.

This is a fascinating discussion. I tremendously admire your continued leads in these things. To call yourself –. to doubt, in public, that you are "not yet gaga" – strikes me as fine. No, you are not yet gaga. You still hold the discussion down to the facts, to the words, to the necessity for exactness, to the need for selection of means and the choice of the best. You are right that many today are losing track of the continual necessity for recapitulation in the rush ahead. Thus your falling upon Dunning. I think however in that case that you went somewhat astray yourself in your prceptions [*sic*], laying too much stress on the down stroke. It is a matter of emphasis.

I myself, feeling more than a little uncertain about all this (though not very uncertain after all) would like very much to see Dunning's mss. Send it on. It should be got out. I'd cheer a bit for it. Let 'em scramble to get over it (as I have for the past few days) 'twill do no harm. Yes, certainly I agree with you "inability to find something in a poem like Cheever's 'Shadows' shows distinct limitation."

Walsh being in a hurry can't be held responsible for lapses (if it is he you are aiming at)   He is out for the big game. He is mad alive. Let him go. Dunning can come in on the other side of the sphere. Walsh has excited me with his mighty shouting. I am committed to the insertion of an ad in The Dial when his This Quarter #3 will be ready to appear.

Haven't written to you before because I didn't know where you were. Some said Vienna, other Perrugia [*sic*] or thereabouts.

Recently I heard that The Dial had made overtures to you, nearly asking you to come again into the fold. There, I thought, is an opportunity for Ezra to do something for the art. He could write for The Dial and send the check he might receive to Walsh. It would be instructive and beautiful! But they say you turned The Dial down. Too bad.

The Dial has two short stories of mine, stuff from my practice but I suppose they will be too broad for that chaste sheaf. They have also a POEM of mine, the first I have done in many a long day, a longish poem. Of course they are printing another poem of mine which, when you see it, I do not want you to mistake for the longish one I am speaking of.

Hemmingway [*sic*] is here. Paul Rosenfeld is giving a dinner. Write again. I'll not wait but do the same

Yours

Bill

Dunning: The expatriate American poet Ralph Cheever Dunning (1878–1930) became a protégé of EP's in Paris. Thirteen poems by Dunning appeared in *Poetry* for April 1925 under the general title "The Four Winds." EP's essay on "Mr. Dunning's Poetry" was published in *Poetry* for September 1925, and Dunning was awarded *Poetry*'s Helen Haire Nevinson Prize. In an undated letter to WCW (Yale), EP asks, "Wotcher think of the Dunning that you have seen? And are you ready to look thru whole mss. Pussnly I think that inability to find something in a poem like Cheever's 'Shadows' shows distinct limitation. Inability to get past the language and to the meaning." "Shadows" is the name of the final poem in the "Four Winds" group.

Walsh's words: Ernest Walsh (1895–1926) was co-editor, with Ethel Moorhead, of *This Quarter*. In an editorial published in the second number (Autumn–Winter 1925–26), Walsh attacked EP's essay on Dunning and *Poetry*'s award to him of the Nevinson Prize. "Dunning never lived, doesn't exist, and never will" (p. 292).

one of the four or five best: In "Mr. Dunning's Poetry," EP says, "I thought, in my enthusiasm when I first read the manuscript of this book: Dunning is one of the four or five poets of our time."

dead mode: The poems in "The Four Winds" are written in iambic meters and rhyming stanzas.

"not yet gaga": In "Mr. Dunning's Poetry," EP says that when he read Dunning's manuscript again, two months after others tried to talk him out of his enthusiasm for it, "I thought, 'Damn 'em, I am not yet gaga.'" From this passage WCW may have derived the title of his 1941 attack on EP, entitled "Ezra Pound: Lord Ga-ga!" (see Letter 96 below).

Dunning's mss: In "Mr. Dunning's Poetry," EP refers to "Mr. Dunning's volume, still in typescript." This is probably the volume published as *Rococo* (Paris: Black Manikin, 1926).

mighty shouting: In the second number of *This Quarter,* Walsh praises WCW and reprints two of his works: "Jacataqua," a chapter of *In the American Grain,* and "Postlude," an Imagist poem which Walsh describes as "a rarity" and "more than this age deserves."

an ad: WCW arranged for a full-page advertisement, costing $75, to appear in *The Dial* for May 1926; see his letters of February 24 and March 31, 1926, in the *Dial*/Thayer collection (Yale). The ad did not appear because Walsh's death delayed the third number of *This Quarter* until 1928.

overtures: Asked by Marianne Moore, assistant editor of *The Dial,* to contribute two book reviews, EP declined the invitation in a letter to her of September 14, 1925 (*Dial*/Thayer collection, Yale).

two short stories: "Sadness" and "The Five-Dollar Guy"; *The Dial* rejected both.

a POEM: WCW's "Struggle of Wings" was published in *The Dial* for July 1926.

another poem: "Tree" appeared in *The Dial* for January 1927.

Hemmingway: See "Biographical Notes" on HEMINGWAY, ERNEST.

Paul Rosenfeld: The American novelist, essayist, and critic Paul Rosenfeld (1890–1946) reviewed musical performances for *The Dial* in 1926–27 and was later a co-editor of *The American Caravan.* WCW eulogizes him in the *Autobiography,* pp. 240, 271–72.

29. TLS-2

February 20 [1926]

Liebstest Ezrachen: –

The amazing thing is not that I am occasionally hysterical but that I am as sane as I am – my faults duly acknowledged, the Chi[cago]. Tribune and all. I enjoy your letters – won't hurt you to shove a stick in my eye, might help you to find where the eye is: helps me to see. – and why should I after all give you the cream of my moods –

– as for your calm "European" who calls me hysterical it is nothing within the confines of his experience that causes my particular brand of hysteria, and I begin to think, nothing in yours. Need what you need and call it what you please, I do not need those things. I need something else, an adequate electrical connection that I can't manage to fix up. This is my hysteria. I know what I want and I know where to get it. IT's [*sic*] coming, maybe – if I don't die first – in the ways one may die.

Certainly I do not want Europe except as a substitute that I know is a fake replica of what I can't get. The Riviera, etc. – all very lovely, nice place to be for a month or two. Paris, very enlightening, in a backhanded way, regarding what evades me here – a thing Paris never could replace really* [*sic*] I'd rather starve here. You and your statement that humanity is *Un peu partout* [somewhat ubiquitous], no use to me.

My hysteria – to please you – or actually, perhaps – is just a matter of cash. I can't live without continuing at my trade and I can't continue at my trade and find time for writing, not just yet. I would not be happy being confined to Europe for life because I didn't have enough cash to live here. I don't want to do it that way. I want to live, but to *live,* here. AFTER I have done that, done it to my own satisfaction, so that there is nothing left for me to do that I want to do here, THEN I may be satisfied to live in Europe. Not before. If I never find it possible to do what I want to do here – then *tant pis* [so much the worse] for me. Nothing that life could give me would be sweet without that first.

Saw SKYSCRAPERS ballet by Carpenter at the Metropolitan last night Amazing how these things set me up. Wish to God it had been Antheil. Glad you are getting on with your opera. Someday I hope to see your work on the Metropolitan stage. I believe it will be soon (10 years – 5?) First will come Antheil, via Carnegie Hall, etc.

Do you know of a N. Y. chap Coblend – a jew I guess. He played and sang something good the other evening. Hemingway was there. Marianne Moore calls Hem. the weakest of American writers. He pressed her hard to find out why The Dial hadn't reviewed his book. She lied valiantly, said it hadn't come into the office. But she is braver without him leaning over her threateningly. Life is rough –

P. S. Instead of railing at me as you do, you oyster too long in the barrel, you should really be rooting for me to stick here even at the cost of my scalp. Can't you see that every damned thing – Well, that's where we differ, isn't it?

Anyhow, if your damned Villon thing ever goes, to amount to anything, it will be HERE. I'm really a stick in the sides of the populace here if you only knew it, a kind of outpost that is trying to make it safe for ART in the lousy country. Do you really think I go around sympathizing with the Presbyterian minister because the girls carry hip flasks?

Come on out of it yourself. I know I make foolish statements when I speak of Paris. I get my "ideal" picture mixed up with the facts. But I am, yes I am getting to know Uncle Sam's back yard which you ain't getting to know at all in spite of your spiritual nature and lovely hair and knowing ways.

Well, come again – I love to be edicated when it is such a dainty hand as yours that dioes [*sic*] it – and I have learned since the war not to "bite the hand that's feeding you"* [*sic*] Sorry you don't always like my pancakes with maple syrup.

Yours

Bill

your letters: The letter from EP to which this one is a response has apparently not survived.

SKYSCRAPERS: WCW was in the first-night audience for the world premiere of the jazz ballet *Skyscrapers* at the Metropolitan Opera on February 19, 1926. John Alden Carpenter's orchestral score included jazz rhythms and Negro folk melodies, saxophones and banjos. Samuel Lee's choreography was influenced by musical comedy, cabaret, and dance hall. The sets by Robert Edmond Jones ranged from a Manhattan street with crowds and skyscrapers, to a factory, to Coney Island. "The fundamental underlying motive is the work and the play of the masses in any great city," according to Olin Downes in the *New York Times* for February 20; "Mr. Carpenter's ballet has a distinctively local and even radical quality" (p. 15).

Antheil: George Antheil (1900–1959) was a young American composer of experimental music. WCW had met him in Paris in 1924. Antheil's *Ballet Mécanique* had its world premiere in Paris on June 19, 1926, and its American premiere in New York on April 10, 1927 (see Letter 33 below).

your opera: In 1921, EP wrote an operatic score entitled *Le Testament de Villon*. It is based upon the life of the medieval French poet François Villon (1431–1463?) and draws its libretto from his works. The composition was first performed in a concert version in Paris on June 29, 1926.

Coblend: Unidentified.

his book: in our time; see "Biographical Notes" on HEMINGWAY, ERNEST.

30. TLS-4

5 March [1926]

Deer Bull:

Have just been rereading your Jacquinta, or however you spell it; VERY good; spurred thereto by a letter from Dad, saying that mother had taken two hours to come to, after being gassed for tooth, and had tried T. Quarter during convalescence. She appears to have been "upset" by the text.

All of which leads me to raise the point of "American" vs. racial, and mondial.

The english wuz so stupid
    they'd fergotten how to . . . .
Till Mrs Dr. Marie Stopes
    come to show them with her book:

"Now, John, you mind the moment when her oviduct is full!
    "And then go in
    and play to win
And show ye are JOHN BULL."

However the English stock is fortunately anti-intellectual, and mistrusts ideas, so it has never been thoroughly corrupted, like the underfed (i, e, on badly cooked fontier [*sic*] food) thinner murkn blood.

SERIEUSEMENT [seriously]: you dont recognize the life impulse in the American who LEAVES THE GOD DAMN PLACE.

You are yourself the only thing IN it; I know that constitutes a distinction and makes you a unique and interesting "CASE" for foreign observation; and that your yell is symptomatic.

Possibly your unique literary value. And that *my* pt. of view, injected into you (supposing that possible) might result in mere silence.

Still: you never answer my argument, that you are a foreigner, and that America interests you as something EXOTIC (damned, but exotic)

2.

The present redoubling and pox of infamy, sfar as I kin see, is all traceable to one thing:

LOSS OF ALL DISCRIMINITATION [*sic*] BETWEEN PUBLIC AND PRI-VATE MATTERS.

The res publica OUGHT to mean the public convenience.

The res publica and the res privata, ought not to be confused one with the other.

It is here that England wins: man's house his castle.

Roman legal sense, sense of govt. still exists in England (despite rotten state of that country)

The rest is the old monotheistic shit. Judah. J[esus]. C[hrist]. tried to kill it, but all the worst features revived (or never let up) with new lable [*sic*].

Half of England worse than U. S.: saddistic [*sic*] maniacs on the judiciary, etc; but always an opposition; the blood of the people;

also great proportion of females above that of males, makes it THE land for the male with phallus erectus. London THE cunt of the world.

Though no Italian ever emigrated there, or had to, save as a waiter or a political exile.

Oh well, you bloomin Exogamist.

I spose I ought to be passin the morning in serious composition. I dont in the least mean that "OUGHT"; but chuck it in as a sop to your "national" feeling.

You called me a cowyard cause I shinned [*sic*] up the tree and ate the bananas?

Young Bobbik is bak from the orieumt. He says our privik lives is sacred and ought not to be revealed to the publicum. (I dont mean that he used those words).

C'mon bak ole soc; plenty of room for you in Rapallo. (very little disease . . . . new English doctor has to spend his time playing tennis.)

Also, I shd think, as diagnostician, you are wrong about kiki. Looks to me like case of exhibitionism, with very little to back it up; all steam at the whistle. The real europe lying deeper and not needing all this visual manifestation.

In fact Man once said so: I dont mean that he rose to the above intellectual generality. He remarked the particular case from experience; as I had already made the diagnostic at sight.

Y a mieux que ça; mong vieux [there are better ones than that, old man]

Ho, wull; I spose you're the keeper of the lonely lighthouse:

stick to your jewty. Is there anything in the way of hard tack and ships beans, that we can send you from the mainland.????

Of course *I* dunno wot you cd. have written abaht if you HAD moved over the 'lantic. Mebbe thass th answer.

Ennyhow, we crown you with bay leaves.

E

Jacquinta: "Jacataqua," a chapter of WCW's *In the American Grain,* appeared in *This Quarter* for Autumn–Winter 1925–26. It criticizes the Puritan-American fear of life and direct physical contact.

mother: Isabel Weston Pound (1860–1948) had a well-developed sense of decorum and propriety.

Dr. Marie Stopes: The English botanist Marie Charlotte Carmichael Stopes (1880–1958) was an advocate of contraception and sex education, and the author of popular manuals entitled *Wise Parenthood* (1918) and *Married Love: A New Contribution to the Solution of Sex Difficulties* (1918; 18th ed., London: Putnam, 1926). EP repeats this jingle in a letter to Wyndham Lewis of March 30, 1926; see Pound/Lewis, p. 167.

Exogamist: One who marries outside his tribe, clan, or family.

Young Bobbik: Robert McAlmon had just returned to Paris from a trip to Egypt, Athens, Constantinople, and Vienna.

kiki: Kiki of Montparnasse (Alice Prin, 1901–1953?) was a painter, writer, cabaret singer, model, and lady of easy virtue. In his introduction to *Kiki's Memoirs,* trans. Samuel Putnam (Paris: Black Manikin Press, 1930), Ernest Hemingway says that she "dominated that era of Montparnasse more than Queen Victoria ever dominated the Victorian era." WCW mentions Kiki in *Spring and All* (1923), and in "Jacataqua" he writes: "I don't suppose there has ever been an American woman like Kiki . . . ."

Man: Kiki was a model and a mistress of the American avant-garde artist and photographer Man Ray (1890–1976).

31. TLS-2

[March 1926?]

I have sold something to The Dial and shall use the cash to put an ad for Walsh in the same. I have told him so. No need to undertake anything for me.

Rebels to your point of view – Jesus Christ, what is the number of your patent? And if I ever tried to make anybody think anything at all – All I ever asked, even of you, is that you SEE me and not through glasses guaranteed and specially fabricated to miscolor and distort everything they come against. I do object to that. Look if you have any eyes at all – and forget for a moment what happens to be itching you at the time. It may for a moment permit you to get a little pleasure without aching to make me something that I ainT.

You talk life [*sic*] a crow with a cleft palate when you repeat your old gag of heredity, where you come from or where I come from. Do you really agree that place matters? Or time either.

Hell, – somedays I can write what I want to and some days I write In. T. Am. Grain – and when I'm very low I can write a letter

The Masses – starting again, minus Floyd Dell, Eastman etc. they have got hold of some cash. I don't know any of them. They have Boni's old place: 39 W. 8th.

There's a place in N. Y. – a printer who wants new stuff McCauley (?) The only drawback is that Kreymoborg [Alfred Kreymborg] is his literary adviser.

I have plans for doing something like small bookshop in N. Y.   special agent, just the books you can't get elsewhere. Trying to fix it up with a machine for getting out a monthly bundle of stuff, anything we want to get out – I don't quite see way clear yet. Maybe nothing will happen. Letn [*sic*] you know how it progresses. Maybe continue *Contact*

Things in general are picking up here, interest, painters, etc.   lots of loose talk but it looks a little as if there may be something of interest going soon – always looks that way here, perhaps. Anyhow thought you might be interested.

Yours
Bill

sold something: WCW was paid $80 for "Struggle of Wings"; see Letter 28 above.
In. T. Am. Grain: WCW's *In the American Grain* was published in New York by Albert and Charles Boni in November 1925.
The Masses: A socialist literary magazine published in New York from 1911 to 1917 under the editorship of the American novelist, playwright, and critic Floyd Dell (1887–1969) and the American poet, translator, essayist, and publisher Max Eastman (1883–1969).

Its successor was *The New Masses,* which ran from 1926 to 1948. The first number of
The New Masses (May 1926) carried WCW's story "The Five-Dollar Guy."
McCauley (?): The Macaulay Company published WCW's *A Voyage to Pagany* (1928)
and his translation of Philippe Soupault's *Last Nights of Paris* (1929).
small bookshop: This scheme did not work out, and *Contact* was not revived until
1932.

32. ALS-4

January 6. [1927]

Dear Ezra: –

Its always good to hear from you. Don't bother about the stuff T[his]. Q[uar-
ter]. may be wanting to bring out. I have nothing to send you now but – if I live,
you'll have the best I can bring up – *etc* my day has been a wild one with
influenza, bad feeding and what not – even though I may have nothing for the first
number.

Florence is reading Bodenheims "Ninth Avenue" a novel. She says it beats
Hemingways The Sun Also Rises, by two laps and one lick.

I won, or was given, the Dial's Award for 1926. That makes 3000 only that
literature owes me.

In self defense I have written a novel in the last six months, thus if I sell it for
3000 I'll be square again and ready to do poetry – (it gives me a thrill to believe I
can do it again) – once more.

Work now obsesses me – I mean my practice of medicine. The day is spent in
sallys [*sic*] and retreats. The work pays. Had I the "five grand" again, plus the
Dial's two, plus what I could get for my house I could live on the income
(modestly) for the balance of my days. But would I do it? I believe not – not yet;
perhaps it would be cutting my throat to cut off this fury of running around from
house to house that somehow fires me with energy even while it exhausts me.

There must be a balance of energy somewhere in my scheme, a place at which I
have the maximum of time for what I most want to do, won at great cost from the
rough.

Well, there you have me – a great fool perhaps.

Yrs
Bill

the first number: EP was planning the first number of *Exile,* four issues of which were
published between Spring 1927 and Autumn 1928. Asked for an "unprintable" contribution to the first number, WCW told EP, in a letter of November 26, 1926 (Yale), that
he had sent his "most offensive" recent work to *This Quarter.*

Bodenheim's "Ninth Avenue": Both Maxwell Bodenheim's *Ninth Avenue* and Ernest
Hemingway's *The Sun Also Rises* were published in New York in 1926.

the Dial's Award: The award to WCW of *The Dial*'s annual prize, worth $2,000, was
announced in the issue of January 1927. A year later, the award went to EP.

3000: WCW had recently lost $5,000 in an out-of-court settlement of a lawsuit against him
stemming from the publication of his short story "The Five-Dollar Guy" (see Letter 31
above). Based upon a real-life incident of attempted seduction, the story appeared with
the actual names of the participants unchanged; see Mariani, pp. 254–55.

a novel: A Voyage to Pagany (1928).

33. ALS-2

Sept. 16, 1927

Dear Ezra:

There is no chance of my seeing you this visit. Next spring, if all goes well, I'll
land in Genoa or at Genoa instead of at Antwerp then you may have your
opportunity to give me my orders for the next ten years. Meanwhile I do hope
your tail is healed for though I am not especially interested in that end of you
(though I have two sons) yet etc, etc. Orrick Johns says Italian nurses are terrible.
Here's wishing you luck at the hospital.

The boys are now at school at Coppet, near this city. Flossie and I will remain
here for another three days before going up to Paris where we do not expect to go
over to the present American side of the river. McAlmon and Bill Bird will there
be regaled by the sight of my graying pol [*sic*; poll, or head].

I aint seen the second issue of *Exile.* Nor have I any new work to show you –
though it is true that you have not recently asked to see any of mine. I will leave a
copy of my novel [*A Voyage to Pagany*], the carbon MSS that is, with Bob. If you
care to see it I will send it on to you at a word from yourself. To write me at 12 rue
de l'Odeon at once would be better perhaps. Though I doubt very much that
you'll be interested in my story.

Transition continues to draw my glances in spite of your innuendos [*sic*]. I
have sent them a couple of critical notes, one on Joyce's new work and one on
Antheil's New York concert.

And now may the spirit of the Lord bless you and keep you and make his (its) light to shine upon you forever and ever and round back again from top to bottom, Amen

> Yours of the Sacred Brotherhood
> xxo, Bill.

this visit: WCW and his wife had enrolled their sons for a year in a private school near Geneva, Switzerland, where this letter was written. After their visit to Paris, WCW returned to Rutherford and Mrs. Williams to Geneva, where she remained with her children until their homecoming in July 1928.

Orrick Johns: The American poet Orrick Johns (1887–1946) contributed to *Poetry, Others,* and EP's *Catholic Anthology* (1915). He is the author of *Asphalt and Other Poems* (1917), *Black Branches* (1920), and *Wild Plum* (1926).

12 rue de l'Odeon: Robert McAlmon's Paris address.

Transition: Between 1927 and 1930, WCW contributed a dozen items to *transition,* a little magazine edited in Paris and the Hague from 1927 to 1939 by Eugene Jolas, Elliott Paul, and Robert Sage. The two articles mentioned here are "A Note on the Recent Work of James Joyce" (November 1927) and "George Antheil and the Cantilene Critics: A Note on the First Performance of Antheil's Music in N.Y.C.; April 10, 1927" (Summer 1928). WCW was in the audience for the American premiere of *Ballet Mécanique* (see Letter 29 above).

34. TLS-1

> April 16, 1928

Dear Ezra:

Your present letter rescued me from an oozy hell. Your offer is generous. I hereby give up any thought of a new magazine. Within two weeks I'll let you know what kind of material – what kind of impetus it is that has been stirring me. If you feel impelled to give me a whole number of Exile when you have the material in hand, well and good. But I'll be content with as much space as comes my way.

But it is a delight to me to feel a possible bond of workmanship being exercised between us today. Damn it why don't – why didn't I seek you sooner. Exile is a good venture, let me from now on really throw my energy into it – not for my name or for myself in any way, but just to do it. I'll do it. For a year at least I'll shower you with anything I can rustle up or squeeze out. I want to. I need to. I have felt sometimes of late that I am sinking forever.

This is just to accept your offer. More later. I heartily support your judgement of Zukofsky's excellence (in the one poem at least) and he seems worth while personally.

Bill

Zukofsky's excellence: See "Biographical Notes" on ZUKOFSKY, LOUIS.

35. TLS-2

May 17, 1928

Liebes Ezrachen:

Yes, yes, you have still ze punch. Issue numero three is even bigger and better than even anyone even I could optimistically have been lead [*sic*] as it were to expect so to speak really.

Verry good Ezrie.

As to my own uncertain certainties. Your spy Zukofsky has been going over my secret notes for you. At first I resented his wanting to penetrate – now listen! – but finally I sez to him, All right, go ahead. So he took my pile of stuff into the city and he works at it with remarkably clean and steady fingers (to your long distance credit be it said) and he ups and choses [*sic*] a batch of writin that yous is erbout ter git perty damn quick if it hits a quick ship – when it gets ready – which it aren't quite yit.

What I have to send you will be in the form of a journal, each bit as perfect in itself as may be. I am however leaving everything just as selected by Zukofsky. It may be later that I shall use the stuff differently.

Permit me to say, sir, that your note, Mediaevalism and Mediaevalism in The Dial presented one of the most telling comments on Christianity that I have ever clapped my eyes upon. If all the god damned pulpit bastards in the world were simultaneously of a certain Sunday to speak, after preliminary personal cleansing, on what you have pointed out – Of course there would be no change in anything – But what a relief there would be from the usual thin shit on that day. Really I was stirred as I have seldom been by spiritual conceptions in vacuuo [*sic, in a vacuum*] . Pop would have liked that –

I am awaiting your translation of Guido's canzon which Marianne [Moore] says is soon to appear in The Dial.

My novel [*A Voyage to Pagany*] – which you will not like – went to press ten days ago.

My family leaves France for Noo Yoik July 6.

Greetings to Dorothy.

Yrs.

Bill

Issue numero three: The third issue of *Exile* contained works by W. B. Yeats ("Sailing to Byzantium" and "Blood and the Moon"), EP (part of Canto 23), Louis Zukofsky ("Poem Beginning 'The'"), and John Rodker (the conclusion of *Adolphe 1920*).

a journal: WCW's "The Descent of Winter" appeared in *Exile* 4 (Autumn 1928), pp. 30–69. A mixture of poetry and prose, it is subdivided into dated entries that run from "9/27" to "12/18." Zukofsky selected and edited the sequence.

Mediaevalism: EP's "Mediaevalism and Mediaevalism (Guido Cavalcanti)" appeared in *The Dial* 84:3 (March 1928), pp. 231–37.

your translation: "Donna Mi Prega by Guido Cavalcanti; with Traduction and Commentary by Ezra Pound," *The Dial* 85:1 (July 1928), pp. 1–20.

36. ALS-8

13 June [1928]

Deer Bull:

Recd. Zuk[ofsky]'s selections. –

very much the sort of block I needed to make No. 4 –

very good things in it. (not yr. magnumest opus [greatest work]). but got fibre.

Wot I suggest is that I shd. either omit the opening underwear or stick it later in the show.

you have waved the undershirt before. (in well known opus). & think it gives the hostile too good a chance to say: or to get the impression –

"Just ole Bill wavin' his shirt again" –

Apart from that, I think the lump shd. go it [*sic*] about as it stands. –

I will leave the underwear at start if you insist or rather. = oh well, consider it, and lemme know. =

I think it is needless hinderance [*sic*] – *in that place.*

no objections to yr. wearing underwear, or mentioning it on occasion.

Praps only the waste of words in four lines.

"What are there . . . I have"
"I touch it and it is"

at least 10 waste words. in the 21.
21 which will go into *8*.
the next four lines contain no such wastage.
Now that you have a publisher or editor (i. e. *me*) and that the stuff is due to appear, I wonder if you care to comb also the rest of it for stray bits of *slag*.
I don't insist – but you might run thru it & see if you have or haven't a chance here & there to improve it.
I don't think there is much to be done, = praps as editorial practice for the Hwgb. Dr. Wms.
on the whole my suggestions may apply only to those 4 lines. –

> Ez
> address Rapallo

my impression is that the prose is O.K. & the slack, what little there is, is in the verse.
too damn many simple *ands* & *is*'s.
look at pages 4, 6, 15, guess the rest is O. K.
VURRY glad to 'ave it (i. e. yr. mss.)

opening underwear: The opening section of "The Descent of Winter" reads as follows: "'*What are these elations I have/ at my own underwear?/ I touch it and it is strange/ upon a strange thigh.*'"
well known opus: Probably "Dance Russe," first published in *Others* for December 1916, in which the speaker dances "naked, grotesquely/ before my mirror/ waving my shirt round my head."
Hwgb.: Hochwohlgeboren (nobly born).
address Rapallo: This letter was written in Vienna, Austria.

37. TLS-1

Jun2 [*sic*] 25 [1928]

deer Editur:

Your suggestions regarding – etc. etc. very welcome. At this time of the day, the week, the month, the year I find myself, however, about as word sensitive as a three toed sloth. I couldn't retouch those poems for any money in the ooniverse.

But I am more than willing to make cuts to this effect that the poems you speak of will be *spurloss versengt* [*sic*]. *Raus mit ihnen!* [sunk without a trace. Out with them!] Thus the following pomes will disappear from the script – and chuck 'em in the waste bucket!

Underwear poem (p. 1)   First poem (p. 4)   pome (p. 6)   pome (p. 15). Yes, that helps a lot.

I'll send *In the Am[erican]. Grain* to your Austrian lady in a few days.

And now, me old frien', lemme tell ya what I done last week. Havin' writ a novel what I always sez I would never in the world do (nothin does, does, does as it use [*sic*] to do, do, do!) Why I sez to myself this is sOmethin. Well, then who shall I hang it onto. Why who else but my old friend and college chum Ezrie, sez I. So this is to let you know that I writ it all out fine and high soundin and it'll be print [*sic*] in the front of that there novel, as nice as you please. What do you think? Why it's dedicated to you. God help me. I hopes you likes it. But if you don't why you can tear out the dedication page in the copy I'm a going to have them send you – as soon as it's printed and as soon as I get around to signing my ugly scrawl into it.

Anybody you think should get complimentary copies? Send me their names. Official publishing date is "after Labor Day". But you should have a copy by end of August. Give me a little blurb will you? That is of course if you don't feel disgraced.

Remember me to Dorothy. I'd like very much to know what her reaction to the novel will be. I'm most anxious to have direct words from all whom I know – since there is to be another one, another novel (already ordered by the publisher! My Jesus.) Please do not think, however that I am going to do it to order. It will be much different from the current one. Meanwhile I have – many other projects. God what a fool. I am sick with work as it is but I suppose the Jew in me likes punishment. Anyhow that's the way I get myself into the terrible mill which writing is sometimes – and must be so. Wish I could find a publisher for a new book of poems.

I'm really delighted that you like Zukofsky's batch of choosings. You'd be amused to see the stuff he didn't take. Yet he did a fine job, believe me; –

Yours
Bill

---

cuts: These cuts were not made when "The Descent of Winter" was published in *Exile* 4.
your Austrian lady: Unidentified.

do, do, do: The title of a popular song by George and Ira Gershwin (1926).

dedicated to you: A Voyage to Pagany was published on September 7, 1928. The dedication reads as follows: "To the first of us all my old friend EZRA POUND this book is affectionately dedicated."

another novel: Macaulay and Company went out of business before WCW could fulfill this commission.

38. TLS-2

July 12 [1928]

Dear Resra: (short for "res erection" – with best wishes)

I sent your last letter to Zukofsky asking him to see them guys as you requested. I myself cannot do the business stunt, never could. I am a hard working suburban doctor with no talent for yankee deals. More than likely I'd ruin any chances for continued success which you may have if I so much as opened my mouth in the presence of business.

Zukofsky, being a Jew, is even worse at it – if I guess rightly.

But if Louis (Z.) has any success after the first visit I stand ready to back him up (and you) by subsequent talks with the business partners. Meanwhile I'll correct the proofs if you'll have them sent to me. I'll look out for the word you mention.

It's been hot as hell here for a week. My family arrives in three days – after a year's absence, nearly. You may imagine that'll [*sic*] I'll be worth little to the world in general for a month or six weeks now.

Louis seems to have an idea once you tire of this magazine that he and I could continue it. Jesus! Well, it may be so nevertheless. All it means just now is that should you contemplate dropping the magazine at any time – leave us know, so we may study the situation preparatory to making you an offer.

Literary news I never have to dispense. Somebody told me one Matthew Josephson had written a life of Zola. They say Hart Crane is – this or that – a crude homo. It puzzles me a little. Marianne [Moore] detests his work, calls it fake-knowledge. Others think he is God Almighty – which naturally offends anyone, like myself, who pretends to the same distinction. Best poet in U. S. say the Kenneth Burkses, Gorham Munsons, etc. I dunno. Ivor [*sic*] Winters is plum gaga over him (Crane) e. e. cummings seems to be drunk most of the time. I had him out here after witnessing his play (at the Provincetown theater) "him" and found him to be a very fine machine busting himself up over nothing as usual.

He is one of the few here of "gentlemanly" charm. I spoke to him of you and some reaction toward him you had expressed, that you thought he probably though [*sic*] of you as sunk in age and cliché. But he said it was unworthy of you, that he only had the most distinguished regard for you but that (being a sensitive person) you had always picked a fight with him when he had seen you.

God knows what will become of him. He is said to have his door open on Patchin Pl. #4 for any woman who wants to be fucked – and he does it all the time. Gossip perhaps. He is to me a feeling of – no use to me. One of the best. He doesn't need me. Going to hell. Wish to god I could see more of him. For what? Just the manners of a graceful (drunken) mind – lost in fucking perhaps, I dunno. Marianne says he is more interested in meeting the Vanderbilts than in writing.

Not much else to say. I see almost no one. They say The Dial is for sale. One Gurdjief [*sic*] is thinking of buying it. If he does he can go to hell as far as I am concerned. That fake system gives me a feeling of chronic loss of manhood – a drip like a leaky cock or breast or something equally bungless.

my nuvel [*A Voyage to Pagany*] aint out yet, I haint even seen the page pruffs. the man [Macaulay] says he's a gonna bring it out sometime efter Labor's day. Who in hell wuz Labor, anyway? Guess he must a bin one of the first presidents, I never seem to a cum acroos his name in the papers anywhere.

I write.

Had a good talk with Louis on Fourth of July. He spent the afternoon and evening here – with me and two of my brother's children (girls) who were staying with me for the day. It was an amusing afternoon. To the boom of toy explosions and the flare of the latest varieties of jigging rockets we talked of writing (to frequent interruptions [*sic*] from the kids begging more matches) until late at night.

I like Louis. He has distinction. He knows and is not puffed up, offensive, perverted by what he has absorbed. He puzzles me. His mind is really silky. God knows if he'll ever do anything with it. He has no job, doesn't seem to be able to get any. They live in a tenement – under trying if not distressing circumstances – yet he is fine. And strong too. I have rarely met a person who can see as clearly, hold as firmly to his point, enjoy excellence and for a clear reason, so gracefully and find fault so convincingly – curious.

Must have some breakfast.

Haven't sent the book to Vienna yet.

Yours
Christofer

them guys: See "Biographical Notes" on COVICI, PASCAL. The letter to Zukofsky with which WCW forwarded EP's request is also dated July 12, 1928 (Texas).

My family arrives: See Letter 33 above.

Matthew Josephson: See "Biographical Notes" on JOSEPHSON, MATTHEW.

Hart Crane: See "Biographical Notes" on CRANE, HART.

Kenneth Burkses: See "Biographical Notes" on BURKE, KENNETH.

Gorham Munsons: See "Biographical Notes" on MUNSON, GORHAM BERT.

Ivor Winters: See "Biographical Notes" on WINTERS, YVOR.

e. e. cummings: See "Biographical Notes" on CUMMINGS, EDWARD ESTLIN. In a letter to Louis Zukofsky of March 5, 1928, EP writes: "Cummings I have met. . . . Believe he regards me as gentle bore and relique, sort of Kris Kringle, very bearded" (Pound/Zukofsky, p. 8).

Gurdjief: The Russian mystic George Ivanovitch Gurdjieff (1872–1949) founded the Institute for the Harmonious Development of Man in 1914. Gurdjieff's "system" emphasized the attainment of a balance among the human faculties through such disciplines as meditation and dance. He did not buy *The Dial.*

39. TLS-4

27 July [1928]

Dear Bill

Am allus ready to make way for youth and strength, but don't believe Cov[ici]. wd. go on pub[lish]ing Xile without the glory of my name. In all these matters the printing BILL . . . . !!!!

Sfar azi know, I am ready to DO about anything you or Zuk. want . . . willing to be mere figurehead etc . . .

Mr Winters, Mr Jo-l-arse etc. explaining to me WHY art has gone on and left me etc.

Johouse is an idiot, Winter's [*sic*] trouble in [*sic*] p[ar]tly analysed – not with ref to Him – in one of Mr Antheils interjections in my work (standard work) on the subjek.

Mr Mat. Josephsohn [*sic*] Putiphar obviously can NOT understand even the simplest declarative sentence; vide [see] his bumble in current no. of transition . . .

at least IF you think that he thinks that he knows why what I said means the opposite of what appears on the page . . . etc.

enlighten us.

Crane has Winters' disease. (vide Antheil on music.)

Your essay on N. Y. crit[ic]s. by the way is damn good and much needed. Why didn't it DIAL at the time of the event, instead of transiting??

If you see Cummings again, assure him that I never picked a quarrel with him.

Am curious of god's handiwork, and ask questions of my minors in order to find out what they think, mean, desire, etc.

As to the possibility of his LIFE damaging his output (apart from septic complications), the simple act!!!

let me plunge into literary history. When ole Uncl. Wm. Yeats, possessed of strict literary conscience and wishing to preserve maximum force for poetic composition consulted his medico about "excess" he was told to procede [*sic*], and that "a few cigarettes will do you more harm than any amount of it."

Whether suburban medical opinion differs from that of Harley St. I leave you to judge, and I expect you to report (to me) the fruits of yr. judgement.

Personally seems to me nature protects one, deep slumber etc. . . . .

though of course, not having seen Cumming's [*sic*] waiting list, cue [queue] or whatsoever, and regarding America, not (vide Mr Josephson) not so as [*sic*] a CRUEL mistress, as an incitement to onanism, I can not judge of the "life in Patchin after these 20 years."

Still, if it is as you say, it must represent a progress in American life and amenities, in relation to what such life was in our youth.

Is it due to Havelock or to Marie Stopes?

There is, on the cuntrary a peculiar sterility about the Cranes, Ivors, Munsons [illegible name] Burkes etc . . . (a little the dryness I used to find in yr. friend Demuth, who has however, I believe, much more talent than any of this lot.

as you say Cummings seems to me good machine . . . but . . . . as you remark . . . . "over nothing"

spose reaction, nacherl, against the moral ferver [*sic*] and Roosveltian [*sic*] era.

heres fer the good old virtues, a heavy load, no morals and no inhibitions.

Erros [*sic*] of ang-sax race have been to degrade word virtu, and synonomyze [*sic*] it with "morals" (mainly negative).

she hath lost her virtue, i,e, she can no more raise the tomwhangus of the buck-male. She hath lost her virtu. she hath lost her latent potential.

I don't know whose money Gurjef will use to buy Dial. In some ways it wd. be highly fitting, though inconvenient, just as that orgum has show [*sic*] disposition to be useful.

If they sell, it shd. be Watson's duty to elevate the Exile into the realm of contributor-paying publications. Wd. be very inexpentszive in comp[arison]. with sumptuous Dial.

(Does it mean that Thayer is worse? I mean "ill".)

What becomes of Mary-ann?

Yrs

Ez

Mr Winters, Mr Jo-l-arse: See "Biographical Notes" on WINTERS, YVOR. The American poet, journalist, essayist, translator, and editor Eugene Jolas (1894–1952) was the principal editor of *transition* from 1927 to 1939. The remarks by Winters and Jolas to which EP refers have not been identified. A "jo-house" is an outdoor privy.

one of Mr Antheils interjections: EP's *Antheil & the Treatise on Harmony,* pp. 42–46, contains notes from Antheil's criticism of other composers. It is difficult to say which of these assessments EP would apply to Winters.

Mr Mat. Josephsohn Putiphar: See "Biographical Notes" on JOSEPHSON, MATTHEW. EP connects Josephson's name with the Old Testament story of Joseph and Potiphar, an officer of the Pharoah of Egypt (Genesis 39).

Your essay: EP wonders why WCW's article "George Antheil and the Cantilene Critics" (see Letter 33 above) appeared in *transition* for Summer 1928 instead of in *The Dial* a year or so earlier, at the time of Antheil's New York concert. In "Dr. Williams' Position" (see Letter 41 below), EP declares it to be "symptomatic of New York that [WCW's] analysis of the so-called criticisms of Antheil's New York concert should appear in Paris, a year after the event, in an amateur periodical."

Wm. Yeats: See "Biographical Notes" on YEATS, WILLIAM BUTLER.

Harley St.: The most reputable private medical practices in London were grouped in the neighborhood of Harley Street.

CRUEL mistress: In his "Open Letter to Mr. Ezra Pound," Josephson urges EP to return to America even though "she is, indeed, a cruel mistress."

20 years: During his visit to the United States in 1910–11, EP called upon H. D., who was then living at 4 Patchin Place in Greenwich Village.

Havelock: Henry Havelock Ellis (1859–1939), English medical student, writer, and editor. His best-known work is *Studies in the Psychology of Sex,* 6 vols. (1897–1910).

Marie Stopes: For Dr. Marie Stopes, see Letter 30 above.

virtu: In the introduction to his 1912 edition of *Sonnets and Ballate of Guido Cavalcanti,* EP writes: "*La virtù* is the potency, the efficient property of a substance or person . . . . Each thing or person was held to send forth magnetisms of certain effect." The comparison of *virtù* with magnetism is repeated in EP's 1928 essay on "Medievalism and Medievalism (Guido Cavalcanti)."

Watson's: Dr. James Sibley Watson, Jr. (1894–1982) was co-owner of *The Dial,* along with Scofield Thayer.

Thayer: Scofield Thayer (1889–1982) was the principal editor of *The Dial* from 1919 to February 1926, when he suffered a collapse that required him to be hospitalized.

Mary-ann: See "Biographical Notes" on MOORE, MARIANNE.

40. TLS-3

Aug. 11, 1928

Dear Ezra:

Thayer seems to have all but nothing to do with the management of The Dial at the present time – from what I am able to infer from a talk I had with Mary Ann. The rumor I heard, that The Dial was for sale and might be bought by G[urd-jieff]., is perhaps no more than a rumor. I have heard nothing more of it since. If The Dial is sold and bought I am sure that it would mean the retirement of our Mary. She will not sell out I know but would probably go back to the library – on starvation wages. Marianne gets little credit for her fight in New York but stands aces high with me for what she is doing, not – though – for what she is able to accomplish, unfortunately. The Dial is a dead letter among the publisher crowd. It almost means that if you are "one of The Dial crowd" you are automatically excluded from perlite society as far as influence in N. Y. goes. Shit! And yet I myself feel so disgusted with The Dial for its half hearted ways that I am almost ready to agree with anyone concerning its worthlessness.

Marianne, however, is never included by me in my condemnations; she is doing quietly all she can to warp things toward a better policy – but she will not succeed. I myself think it is the dead hand of Thayer in the background that ruins everything. It is this, to my mind, that really compells [sic] Watson to sell. I cannot see Thayer for one shutter flash, never could. He is antipathetic to me from start to finish.

If Watson sells I will positively, for once in my life, stir everything about me in an effort to have him support Exile. It is the first sensible proposal of the sort that I have ever encountered.

As to the Hart Crane, Josephson group – to hell with them all. There is good there but it's not for me. As it stands, Crane is supposed to be the man that puts me on the shelf. But not only do I find him just as thick headed as I am myself and quite as helplessly verbose at times but that he comes up into clarity far less often. If what he puts on the page is related to design, or thought, or emotion – or anything but disguised sentimentality and sloppy feeling – then I am licked and no one more happy to acknowledge it than myself. But really I do not feel so violently about the group. I am quite willing that they shall be what they are for there is nothing there that I expect to be caught copying for the next twenty years. To hell with them. But if I can help them, I will. Ha, ha!

I'm on my vacation. Just finished The Education of Henry Adams. Also John Dos Pasos [sic], Orient Express. The first interested me enormously for its information and for the mental balance of Adams. It's [sic] style is probably all the style there was in the U. S. in his day. It was refreshing to me to find how much of what he said is – after all – pure style: never to be understood. Now I want to go at his Mont St. Michel and Chartres. A fine old fellow, credit to his country and any country – or all countries, I should say as any sensible person must be – being international.

I have Soupault's, Dernieres Nuits de Paris with me and the first volume of Gide's, Si le Grain ne Meurt. Also Conditioned Reflexex [sic] by Paclov [sic]. Jesus, Jesus! if only I had time! if only I could devote even ten percent of my days to what writing means to me. Oh well, oh well! if I had all the time in the world to devote to it I'd probably do no more than I do and it wouldn't have, probably, half the taste to it it has now.

I have heaps of undigested notes to thumb through both physically and mentally. Then there is a book of – theories! to design, and a new so called novel to thrash out. Of course it isn't a novel at all. I can't write fiction. All I do is try to understand something in its natural colors and shapes. Since it must have some kind of shape to be seen by me at all it grows to be – if it please – a novel.

The first few pages of Soupault, by the way, are delightful reading. Easy, deceptive, accurate to the rules of conversation (which I am afraid Hem[ingway] doesn't at all understand since it is rarely as expressive as he makes it and almost always twice as succinct) just batting the air effectively and swimming in it – like an airplane. I like the Soupault better than anything of his that I have encountered. Perhaps it will grow foolishly fantastick later in the book –, as much of the little modern french stuff that I have seen does.

What TRANSITION – per Joesphson [sic] – wants to say is that you are a conservative. You are, what of it? It's just a class of radicals whaich [sic] wants to sell what it has high, whereas the rest don't know the value of anything, half the time. Anyhow with you it's constitutional, and being so it hasn't kept you from recognizing the best for twenty years or more before anyone else did so. Naturally you aint God and you are thick headed when there's no need of it – on occasion – but I'll bet my everlasting shirt that if someone with extraordinary brains gave you and anybody else that I can think of half a million to do literature with the Josephsons and Burkses and Cranes and all of them would look so old fashioned they'd half [sic] to wipe their asses with corn cobs to keep in style. That's not flattery but my frank opinion. An [sic] this would be so because you know what you are talking about and they don't. – Or so it seems to me.

Under separate cover you will receive a copy of last Sunday's Tribune Book Section. I was invited up to see this here Isabel Patterson [sic]. She lit into you and wanted to larf you and Antheil.off the stage. I was saying was there anything that could be done to get decent literature through the customs for private libraries without having it stole by the government. Then she started to laugh at your name, says she: All he wants to do is to find fault with something. That's all he ever does. Then says I &$— &%$''! For once I got mad. She and Burton Rasco [*sic*] and a couple of others listened very politely, I thought. Later I quoted them the gist of my article about Antheil. Again they listened. Isable [*sic*] retorted, however, that she had heard the same sort of thing concerning some other N. Y. composer Leo Ornstein ten years ago and where was he now. Says I, You din't hear anything about him from me, did ya? To which she had to admit that she didn't. Which is about as daring as I have ever been in public (sic) in my days. Who knows what the future may be?

The corn is amost [*sic*] ready for our lunch. After storms yesterday, lightning – which is very hopeful, in a way – and oppressive heat which usually makes me think of *South Wind* – etc.

I've nothing finished to send you just now. The nuvel [*A Voyage to Pagany*] should be out in a few weeks.

Remember me to Dorothy.

Glad to have the benefit of Yeats's medical advice. Yes, excess is very necesaary [*sic*] to the literaturist – and America *is* much, oh much, advanced since our youth. Is that the reason, perhaps, that the Crane school is made up of cock suckers – why mince words. And why exaggerate, since Burke has three daughters and Josephson has one. I have at this stage of my days, so many ladies willing to throw their cloaks in the mud at my feet that I am in danger of – No, figuative [*sic*] speech won't do. I have more than I can serve, to be plain.

Best luck.

Yrs.

What you say re. Cummings noted. I'll talk to him.

W.

back to the library: See ''Biographical Notes'' on MOORE, MARIANNE.

vacation: WCW wrote this letter from Monroe, New York, where his wife's parents owned a farm.

Henry Adams: The American journalist, historian, essayist, and diplomat Henry B. Adams (1838–1918) was the author of *Mont-Saint-Michel and Chartres* (1904) and *The Education of Henry Adams* (1907). WCW became interested in his work through Louis Zukofsky (see ''Biographical Notes'' on ZUKOFSKY, LOUIS).

Dos Pasos: In 1927, the American novelist, poet, and playwright John Dos Passos (1896–1970) published a travel book entitled *Orient Express*.

Soupault's: WCW met the French novelist and surrealist Philippe Soupault (1897–1990) in Paris in 1924. He liked Soupault's *Last Nights of Paris* (1928) so well that he translated it into English (New York: Macaulay, 1929). "It was about a very wonderful little French whore, very intellectual, exotic, strange" (Heal, pp. 47–48).

Gide's: The French novelist, dramatist, and critic André Gide (1869–1951) published *Si le grain ne meurt* (If the Seed Doesn't Die) in 1926. It is an autobiographical account of his early years, describing his revolt against a strict Protestant upbringing.

Paclov: The Russian physiologist Ivan Petrovitch Pavlov (1849–1936) was the author of *Conditioned Reflexes: An Investigation of the Physiological Activity of the Cerebral Cortex,* ed. and trans. Gleb Vasilevich Anrep (London: Oxford University Press, 1927).

a book of – theories: Provisionally entitled *On the Humanization of Knowledge* and later retitled *The Embodiment of Knowledge,* this work of WCW's was published post-humously in 1974.

so called novel: An experimental prose work provisionally entitled *January: A Novelette* and later published as *A Novelette* (1932). Three chapters appeared in *transition* for June 1930 (see Letter 44 below).

Tribune Book Section: On July 24, 1928, WCW went to the offices of the *New York Herald Tribune* to be interviewed by the novelist and critic Isabel Bowler Paterson (1885–1961). In her column, "Turns with a Bookworm," published in the *Tribune's* Book Section on Sunday, August 5, p. 16, Mrs. Paterson writes: "We met William Carlos Williams this week, too. He is the author of 'Voyage to Pagany,' which will be published soon. He has an immense enthusiasm for the critical acumen of Ezra Pound, and the musical genius of George Antheil. You may remember that Antheil is the composer of the 'Ballet Mechanique,' scored for sixteen electric pianos and other deadly instruments to suit. A steam riveter, probably."

the customs: See Letter 42 below.

Burton Rasco: The American literary critic and journalist Burton Rascoe (1892–1957) was reviewer, columnist, and/or books editor for a number of periodicals, including the *Chicago Tribune,* the *New York Herald Tribune,* the *New York Sun,* and *The Bookman's.*

my article about Antheil: "George Antheil and the Cantilene Critics"; see Letter 33 above.

Leo Ornstein: The Russian-born composer and pianist Leo Ornstein (b. 1892) emigrated to New York in 1907. He began to attract attention in 1913–14 with futuristic, experimental compositions such as *Dwarf Suite, Wild Man's Dance,* and *Impressions de Notre-Dame.* From 1920 to the early 1930s, he was out of the public eye, but he then made a professional comeback.

South Wind: A novel published in 1917 by the English novelist and essayist Norman Douglas (1868–1952), whom WCW met in Rome in 1924. It is set on a fictitious Mediterranean island named Nepenthe during the season of the "moisture-laden sirocco" (p. 89). WCW mentions *South Wind* in *Paterson,* Book IV, Part 2.

41. TLS-1

Nov. 6, 1928

Dear Ezrie:

Nothing will ever be said of better understanding regarding my work than your article in The Dial. I must thank you for your great interest and discriminating defense of my position. Without question you have hit most of the trends that I am following with the effect that you have clarified my designs on the future which in turn will act as encouragement and strength for me.

Naturally I consider myself a fool for not getting out of Medicine. I do not consider myself a fool for having been a physician for the past twenty years. That was accurately figured out in its relations to my disposition and mental capabilities. It has all turned out precisely as I foresaw, save only that at my present age I planned to withdraw from active competition with the world and close up the gaps in my expositions, continuing at this till I was shovelled under or went daffy or satisfactorily convinced myself that I had failed.

I am now engaged in cutting out much of my medical work under the guise of becoming a ''specialist''. Within a few months I will have done with evening office hours, that hellish drag. But it is not going fast enough. I can't quit cold for I would only torment myself into the grave if I did so. I ain't built that way, I mean to withstand financial worries or to discover ways of living aside from the work of my hands. I simply can't.

But things are moving nevertheless according to the plans. Perhaps I expect too much.

But I am touched by the sobriety of your review, that is what I set out to say meaning to add that I am going on as best I can and that you have helped me there also. You also have grown older – without loss. In fact I like your writing in what you have said of me as well as anything I have seen of yours in prose.

I have the new Cantos but there has been no time in which to read – as yet.

Yours
Bill

your article: ''Dr. Williams' Position,'' *The Dial* 85:5 (November 1928), pp. 395–404.
the new Cantos: A Draft of the Cantos 17–27 of Ezra Pound (London: John Rodker, 1928).
WCW received a copy around October 18; see his letter of that date to Louis Zukofsky (Texas).

42. TLS-2

Oct. 19, 1929

Dear Ezrie:

Intellectual probity be damned, I don't think it involved in this case – of the anthology. It *is* involved in the composition of poems. The collection would be interesting to me, the soul ache, if any, be Aldington's. Though I should have objected to the title "The Last Imagist Anthology" had I thought in time to do so. Why the hell didn't you offer some such criticism and then come in? I think it was less than a matter of intellectual probity which prevented you from so doing, Mr. Lenin.

Be that as it may, I am sorry to see the same damned human stupidities predominant in supposedly intelligent men which have always kept one and one apart when they might have been two and so on to some sort of Elysium. The Chinese ancients seem to have known more of life than we.

Bob McAlmon has been in New York for the last two weeks, I have seen him several times. He has developed in the past two years. Last night he read us two of his newest tales of life among the playboys. He has a gift for characterization which is excellent. The people appear and move about with integrity in a clarity of perception which amounts to an art in itself. It's curious to feel Bob succeeding in spite of an appearance of no art at all. In fact there is no art in the writing, he himself would be the first to say it. But there is an understanding which holds the words in suspension. One gets the impression that no one else is quite as clean about the truth as Bob is, and so he seems, himself, crystaline [*sic*] and from that the quality pervades and distinguishes what he does. And so gets into the words after all. And is an art.

It is an art for the reason that a slip in the feeling would alter the shapes of the words and their position in the sentences. The present stories are better than the earlier one [*sic*], in "Distinguished Air", because the low down quality has been avoided in the drawing and as a result the characters are allowed to come up closer to the eye, to the broader sense of understanding, they seem quite normal in spite of their original twists and quite properly candidates for our approaches.

Saw Bernice [*sic*] Abbott yesterday, she has a photo studio on 67th. St. There's another one worth taking into account.

Chas. Demuth has been in town also. He and Bob and Bernice have been batting around a little. The three of them are going to Phila[delphia]. next week to see what dens of vice they can discover there for their amusement.

Did you read that the Senate has passed a new law permitting foreign books to come into the country uncensored? That is something at least and may influence someone to begin publishing again.

Bob is having little luck with his scripts, no one quite dares take them on. He has seen several representatives of the larger houses such as Scribner's etc. but they just nibbe [*sic*] and squirm away.

I'm writing nothing. I had had hopes that someone would be interested in a "collected poems" but that also seems to have gone by the board. A collection of prose things then seemed to offer some hope but that also faded. Then a person named Hillman was to publish a Novelette which I completed last winter but, again, nix.

Louis Z. has done good work with his second long poem "A" It has a quality of scholarliness and extreme scepticism, combined with a cold certainty of perception in matters of the abstract which flares up icily at times with very unsent8mental [*sic*] distinction. It is clean, hard writing. It is as far from bob's [*sic*] quality as Scot is from Jew. I have not permitted my two friends to see each other as yet, I am keeping them apart. I think Bob would get into one of his impatient, intollerant [*sic*] moods and that Zuke would freeze up and act frail and shy. Shit, what hope is there among you noblemen? In any case they are going to meet whether they like it or not.

Gorgeous weather now, wine, yellow wine, sunlight – but rather warmish, which makes it quite un-wine-like – and so we come back to delightfully soothing air. Wish I could go for a swim. I had the best time swimming this summer that I have ever had. A pool was opened near here to which I went frequently taking lessons and learning to do the crawl fairly well. I can hardly wait for another warm season to come around.

Family's all well. Boys, 15 and 13 are almost as large as I. Mother is thinking of going to Paris in the early spring.

Love to Dorothy.

Yours
Bill

the anthology: *Imagist Anthology 1930: New Poetry by the Imagists* (New York: Covici, Friede 1930). Edited by Richard Aldington, the collection includes works by him, John Cournos, H. D., John Gould Fletcher, F. S. Flint, Ford Madox Ford, James Joyce, D. H. Lawrence, and WCW. EP refused to contribute.

Mr. Lenin: The Russian Marxist leader Lenin (Vladimir Ilitch Ulyanov, 1870–1924) was the head of the Bolshevik Party, which instituted the "dictatorship of the proletariat" after the revolution of 1917. WCW implies that EP, like Lenin, is reluctant to share power in the revolution he incited.

Bob McAlmon: See "Biographical Notes" on MCALMON, ROBERT.

Bernice Abbott: The American photographer Berenice Abbott (1898–1991) worked in
   Paris from 1923 to 1929. She then returned to New York, where she became a successful documentary and portrait photographer.

a new law: On October 11, 1929, the United States Senate, acting as a Committee of the
   Whole, voted in favor of a resolution to alter Section 305 of the United States tariff law
   so as to exempt books from seizure by U. S. customs agents on the grounds of obscenity
   or seditiousness. This resolution did not have the force of a "new law," and was
   modified when the Senate debated the matter again in March 1930; see Pound/Cutting,
   pp. 15–20.

a Novelette: WCW's *A Novelette and Other Prose* (*1921–1931*) was not published until
   1932. "Hillman" has not been identified.

Louis Z.: See "Biographical Notes" on ZUKOFSKY, LOUIS. Zukofsky and McAlmon first
   met on November 2, 1929; see Zukofsky's letter to WCW of November 3 (Yale).

43. TLS-4

5 Nov. [1929]

Yr. elegy rec[eive]d.

All right you greasy MenscheviKK

When Mr A. [Richard Aldington] does anything with as single a purpose as
your stuff in Exile IV, we'll consider the matter of burying his ten years on the
Times and 15 of opposition to EVERY new clean move in sculpture painting or
writing. & of denying everything I have attempted in the past 15 years.

Its one thing to kill the calf and another to be the calf.

Just what meaning (other than that of personal sentimental slobber and absoloot insincerity) do you attatch [*sic*] to a union in print with the appearance of a
manifesto AGAINST Zukofsky; Lewis; Rodker, the newer prose, Eliot as poet
(note that R. A. has always boosted Eliots [*sic*] as god damn academic retrograde
critic and crabbed his poetry) He is now in reaction against T. S. E. for reasons
originating in the 18th. century.

God's ballz the healthy tendency is shown by ole Wyndham getting out and
kussing everyone (me included) not by trying to crwal [*sic*] back into mama's
vagina and investigate the monthly flux.

Anything I can do to assist R. A. to make a living or get OUT of england and
the muck he has lived in for the past ten years/ YES/

BUTT

A dissociation of ideas was made in 1912 and then falsified. Made by me and
falsified by various other people.

I take it there was never any question of an attempt to clean up this mess in a preface to the Aldington Fletcher Lawrence 1930 manifesto. In fact that the artistic impulse to same lay largely in A's relations to his second wife.

And at any rate WHY the balls shd. I be mixed up with Mr Friede????

Of course you can take the position that in art nothing matters; that Mr Erskine, author of the Privvy life of Helen is as good a Hellenist as Mr Cocteau author of Antigone; etc; Polyana.

Perhaps you wd. favour us with a chemical xposition of the dif[ference]. between cockcheez and jism??

Oh yes; thanks very much for the History. It came while I was away. I purchased the English edition of Singer some months ago, and peerused same with interest.

That don't detract from my gratichood to you fer kind thought. Any suggestions as to what I shd. do wiff spare copy?

To return to the other matter. It is not as if R[ichard]. had in any way really cast his skin or caught up with Bob [McAlmon]. and any of the rest. or as if any such associstaion [sic] of semi senile writers didnt (A.) tend to clique and cenacle

(B.) act as grouping against the newer invention as yet ungrouped. Zuk[ofsky]. Vogel; etc.

Note that when one NOW hears the Sacre du Printemps what one hears or notices is NOT its strength but its kinship to the suspended scsch-schcsh ot [sic] Debusy [sic].

Come alive you old zkunk cabbage.

Reading Exile 4. yesterday. the parts Zuk dug out of you I seriously considered printing another number; even tho I have as yet NO means of distributing 100 copies save by free gift.

I at least sent off some of Gould's stuff to a London typist.

Get Bob and Vogel together.

J. Vogel, last known address 12 W. 88

Bob wont scare Vogel or Vogel him.

Mr Zukofsky's writing continues to give me increasing pleasure as Marianne [Moore] wd. write if the idea occurred to her.

> yr. deevoted ole friend
> Alma Tadema

MenscheviKK: EP is responding to WCW's characterization of him, in the preceding letter, as "Mr. Lenin." The Menshevik (minority) wing of the Russian Social Democratic Party lost out in its power struggle with Lenin's Bolsheviks.

ten years on the Times: See "Biographical Notes" on ALDINGTON, RICHARD.

a manifesto: I have not identified a "manifesto" by Aldington against the authors named by EP.

Eliot as poet: In a letter to Eliot of July 18, 1919 (Harvard), Aldington praises his prose criticism but deprecates his poetry as "over intellectual"; see Charles Doyle, *Richard Aldington: A Biography* (London: Macmillan, 1989), p. 90.

the 18th. century: Aldington published many translations of eighteenth-century French literature and did not share Eliot's generally dim view of the period. Aldington's 1931 satire of Eliot, "Stepping Heavenward," in which Eliot is lampooned as Jeremy Pratt Cibber, owes much to the model of Alexander Pope's *The Dunciad* (1743).

ole Wyndham: See "Biographical Notes" on LEWIS, PERCY WYNDHAM.

A dissociation of ideas: In EP's view, the original principles of Imagism, formulated and declared in 1912–13 by himself, Aldington, H. D., and F. S. Flint, began to be distorted in 1914, when Amy Lowell took over the movement.

1930 manifesto: For the *Imagist Anthology 1930,* see Letter 42 above. The American poet and critic John Gould Fletcher (1886–1950) and the English man of letters D. H. Lawrence (1885–1930) appeared in Amy Lowell's anthologies (*Some Imagist Poets,* 1915, 1916, 1917) but not in EP's *Des Imagistes* (1914). In a letter to Glenn Hughes of September 26, 1927, EP says, "Lawrence was never an Imagist. He was an Amygist . . . . Neither he nor Fletcher accepted the Imagist program" (Paige, p. 212).

second wife: See "Biographical Notes" on ALDINGTON, RICHARD. Brigit Patmore was never Aldington's wife, because both were still legally married to others.

Mr. Friede: Donald S. Friede; see "Biographical Notes" on COVICI, PASCAL.

Mr. Erskine: The American novelist, critic, and musician John Erskine (1879–1951) was professor of English at Columbia University and, from 1927 to 1938, president of the Juilliard School of Music. He was also the author of a historical novel entitled *The Private Life of Helen of Troy* (1925).

Mr. Cocteau: See "Biographical Notes" on COCTEAU, JEAN.

Polyana: A person who is naively optimistic, finding cause for happiness in the most disastrous situations. The name derives from the heroine of a series of children's books by the American writer Eleanor Hodgman Porter (1861–1920).

Singer: Charles Joseph Singer (1876–1960) was the author of *A Short History of Medicine: Introducing Medical Principles to Students and Non-Medical Readers* (New York: Oxford University Press, 1928). In a letter of September 11, 1929 (Yale), WCW tells EP that he is sending a copy of this work. In a letter of November 18 (Yale), he suggests that EP forward the superfluous copy to Sylvia Beach in Paris.

Vogel: The American poet, short story writer, critic, and editor Joseph Vogel (1904–) attended EP's alma mater, Hamilton College. He contributed work to *The New Masses, Blues, Pagany, Blast, The Magazine,* and *American Caravan,* and later published two novels, *At Madame Bonnard's* (1935) and *Man's Courage* (1938).

Sacre du Printemps: Revolutionary orchestral work by the Russian composer Igor Stravinsky (1882–1971), which inspired a riot when first performed in Paris on May 29, 1913. EP's translation of *Igor Stravinsky,* a French study by Boris de Schloezer, was serialized in *The Dial* from October 1928 to July 1929. Stravinsky's affinities with the French composer Claude Debussy (1861–1918) are mentioned in the second and sixth installments.

Gould's stuff: Joseph Ferdinand Gould (1889–1957) was an indigent Greenwich Village character, who claimed to be compiling a massive, anecdotal record of personal and popular culture entitled "Oral History of the World" (or "of Our Time"). EP published "A Chapter from Joe Gould's Oral History of the World" in *Exile* (Autumn 1927), and other installments appeared in *The Dial, Broom,* and *Pagany.*

Alma Tadema: Sir Laurence Alma-Tadema (1836–1912) was a well-known Victorian neoclassical painter. His elder daughter, Miss Laurence Alma-Tadema (d. 1940), was a prolific author and translator, some of whose poems were published by Elkin Mathews.

44. TLS-2

March 2, 1930

My dear Mr. Dante Personae Pound, et al. [and others]:

How are ya? Which is no answer to your two recent proposals, via the Zuke [Louis Zukofsky].

The first was that I should send you a script of not more than thirty pages, or so, for The Hours Press. This immediately momopolized [*sic*] my dcanty [*sic*] time and I began to woik like hell to get something ready for you.

This I have succeeded in doing. It is a poem of the specified number of pages which it has taken me two years to complete. But there is a string thereto: its twist is that Mr. Aldington has an incomplete, early version of the same which is to appear in The LAST Imagist Anthology! Also parts of the poem have appeared separately in Hound and Horny, as it were.

Now, Signor, the version of the poem which you will receive in a day or two is the only complete version of the great woik yet offered to the only true agent of the eyes of the woild as yet in the flesh. This is the final copy. I hopes ya likes it. I hopes ya prints it. I hopes there won't be no objections to its having appeared in other form elsewhere. And I 'opes there won't be no objections to my using the same in a collected edition of my woiks (from the waist up) which may or may not appear 'ere there or elsewhere sometime or other. Is that right? Or ain't it?

Well.

There is another woik which you will receive in the same mail as the unique speciment [*sic*] mentioned above. This time you gets prose. It is called, A Novelette. I writ it last year. It was turned down (by the grace of God) by the American (Have you heard how it is that all these american girls are getting pregnant right out of high school without husband – or even a lover – in the proper sense? Well, its the colored toilet paper they are using over here that's doing it. Now what do you think of that!) Caravan.

But there's a string to that also. For Jolas has accepted the first, and perhaps the best, part of this novelette for TRANSITION.

Now thene [*sic*], if your head is still clear, comes your second proposal. It is that I send something, along with a picture of my mug, for this here american number of Variété [*sic*].

Well now, all I can say is that I haven't a nother [*sic*] thing to send you. So, if it suits your divine purpose to bear with this poor miserable sinner and weakling – and to be kind to him in his hour of trouble (if there is ever one that aint) you will patiently select the best chapter from the Novelette – or nove; ette [*sic*] – and have it translated into French for V.

's the best I can do.

I'll write to Bob [McAlmon]. I'll try to get a copy of the Graphic.

– and make the light of his countejance to shine upon your foever [*sic*] more.

I got a woman up in the hospital this afternoon who seems to be having trouble with twins. She wants 'em in and they wants to come out. Tere [*sic*] seems to be no way to compromise. I can hear the heart of one of them (if there are two) beating. It's just seven months since the house party. Too bad, two bad, to bed. Amen.

Yours as ever
Bolicky Bill

Personae: The name of a 1909 volume of EP's poems and of the 1926 collected edition of his early work. "Personae" suggests the multiple identities or masks assumed by EP in his dramatic monologues and lyrics. In "Histrion" (1908), for example, the speaker says, "Thus am I Dante for a space."

The Hours Press: See "Biographical Notes" on CUNARD, NANCY. For the proposal that WCW prepare a book of poems for the Hours Press, see an undated letter from Louis Zukofsky to WCW (Texas). However, no such book was published.

a poem: "Della Primavera Trasportata al Morale" (Spring Moralized). An abridged version of this sequence appeared in the *Imagist Anthology 1930* (see Letter 42 above), and the section entitled "Rain" was published in *Hound and Horn* for October–December 1929.

A Novelette: See Letter 40 above. It was published in 1932, not by the Hours Press but by TO, Publishers.

the American . . . Caravan: The *American Caravan* (later the *New Caravan*) was an annual of new writing founded by Alfred Kreymborg, Van Wyck Brooks, Lewis Mumford, and Paul Rosenfeld in 1927.

Jolas: In *transition* 18–19 (June 1930), pp. 279–86, Eugene Jolas published three sections of WCW's *A Novelette:* "The Simplicity of Disorder," "A Beautiful Idea," and "Conversation as Design."

Variété: Variétés: Revue Mensuelle Illustrée de l'Ésprit Contemporain was edited by P.-G. van Hecke and published in Brussels. Van Hecke wrote to EP on January 30, 1930 (Yale), proposing an American number to complement the Russian number that appeared in March and the German number for May. On February 6, EP sent a round-robin letter to Zukofsky, WCW, and Robert McAlmon, asking for contributions and editorial help (Buffalo). However, *Variétés* was sold in June 1930, and the American number never appeared.

the Graphic: In his round-robin letter of February 6, 1930, EP asked for "a real tabloid" and a sample of current American newspaper headlines. Zukofsky sent a copy of the New York *Evening Graphic* for February 21, 1930, along with a letter dated March 6 (Yale).

45. TLS-1

Mar. 13/30

Dear Ezra:

Your last letter, re. Bifur, etc., received. I'll tend to the various subjects therein mentioned during the next day or two.

As you may possibly have imagined, this is my mad season. Work is that which makes me maddest – not the weather. I'm rushing around trying to keep the medical lid on, only in the free moments between calls rushing to the typewriter to keep within sight of my literary – or what you will.

I've been up since 5.30 certifying the death of a man's wife (he cried) and now finishing the correction of the Novelette.

The latter will go forward to you by the next mail. It is the prime provocation for this letter:

Naturally Nancy [Cunard] will not want to print two books by me this year. And the poem should come first if she prints either. But the novelette is very close to my heart – and no one will handle it here. You see what I mean.

The novelette contains something I have been trying for for half my life, yet – Well, that's about enough of that. I hope you like the thing and that you will be able to find something in it suitable for Variété [*sic*].

What can I do? The answer is: Write.

Oh, Jolas will be using the first four chapters of the novelette in TRANSITION. I'd suggest that you take the chapter called "Conversation as design" – if

I remember it correctly – it's in a drawer behind my back and I can't bother to turn around.

Hope Dorothy has some fun out of the thing. Floss and the ubiquitous Zuke are the only ones in this section of understanding who have fallen for it. And no two people could approach the thing from a more divergent angle.

Yours
Bill

Bifur: Edited by G. Ribemont Dessaignes, this French little magazine published six
numbers between May 1929 and June 1930. WCW was one of its Foreign Correspondents, along with James Joyce and Gottfried Benn.
"Conversation as design": See Letter 44 above.

46. TLS-2

Oct. 6, 1930

Liebes Ezrachen:

's no use talkin to them Black Sun people about me, translations is more in their line than I am. But I thank you, as Lindberg [*sic*] would say, I thank you. Ferget it however. Ef I can't get published here I ain't much interested in gettin published a tall. Not that I wouldn't like to be *printed* but mebbe I'll be able to do that fer myself perty soon. Mebbe. Anyhow, as I sez before – as Lindberg would say, I thank you.

There's a whole lot of things in your letter which I know nothing about. But you alluz wuz like that. I picks what seems good and chucks the rest out. I dunno nothin about all them publishin ventures you mentioned. Something you sez went bust. Is that so. Well now I'm sorry. Better luck next time. I knew a fella had a still up in the country and the same thing happened to him.

Pagany does kind a worry me sometimes becuase [*sic*] of its lack of a fixed critical objective. But it aint from not knowing what we think. Right now we think there aint much use in a fixed critical objective. Right now it seems to us that that's one of the things we aint much interested in. Thar's been too much a that sort a thing around here just lately. But we know what we like which aint eriginal and it aint perticular high toned but anyway it aint Eliot ner it aint houndish nor horny. Tho that aint nuthin against bein horny because we're about as horny as most people we know of around here ever gits.

And did you here [sic] the one about the country fella who took the girl he'd just got married to to a hotel in Portland. He asked the man at the desk fer a room, a kind a nice room where a fella could take a girl he'd just got married to. So the man at the desk told the boy to take him up and show him a nice room. Well sir, when they come back the man at the desk asked how he liked the room. And the fella says, no he didn't like it at all. So the man asked him why and he says to the man, No sir that aint no fit room to take a woman to. Why he says, there's a privy in there and there'd be folks coming and goin all night long.

That fella in Paris, that Frank fella, is no relation to Waldo that I know of. He's just a poor son of a gun who workd [sic] for a guy named Levy who has the money. His magazine is a pretty good lookin magazine I thinks but its all in french and that's a drawback and it don't seel [sic] either. I hear they were pretty close to being on the rocks two months ago and that they're just hanging on by their eyelashes now.

Zuke as you know is teaching in Wis[consin] just now. Bob McA[lmon]. is heading this way again with France in view if he doesn't sell something substantial in N. Y. Which he won't, until he lets someone do the raking of his prose – which he won't do. But he says he's makin em firmer recently – hasn't been drinking for two months. Sounds good. It's a god damned fuckin shittin shame he doesn't get put on – and what's the use of doin anything while that state of affairs exists. The H[ound] & H[orn] especially give me a pain in the hemorrhoids – just as if I didn't have enough pain there already. They turn down all kind of things because they don't come tied up in the right kind of string.

So I sits me down this summer and writes a long-short story for the Scribner's 5000. dollar prize. It had to be 15,000 words in length as a minimum. After mulework of the heaviest kind I managed to get together 15,007 words. So that's the end of that I suppose. It's not a bad story tho. I sent it to Zuke. Ef he likes it and you're interested I'll send you the copy. Nothin especially litrary erbout it. Just a story.

The first six months of this year were more or less knocked out by me mother breakin her hip. She can hobble around now.

I've slightly enlarged my shell by building a big room in my attic. I'm there now. It's a great room. At last I have space to slop around in. Come on tell me what to think so that I won't be lonesome there.

Sorry I can't read Sordello in the original or any other way I suppose. Wish I could. But ef I could I probably wouldn't. One man in each generation is erbout enough I suppose.

Boys are getting bigger. One goes to college in about another year. Grapes are ripe and plentiful up on my mother-in-laws place about 40 miles back in the hills.

And while I'm speaking of her I've been working on a short story, a real short story which she told me this summer. Wanna see that too? Guess not.

Poetry   £   &   % $! Gord how I still loves that gal.

Yours

Bill

Black Sun: The Black Sun Press was founded in Paris in 1927 by the wealthy American expatriates Caresse and Harry Crosby. It published EP's *Imaginary Letters* in 1930. WCW had met the Crosbys in New York on December 7, 1929; see Mariani, pp. 294–95.

Lindberg: The American aviator Charles Lindbergh (1902–1974) made the first nonstop, solo, transatlantic flight on May 21–22, 1927.

your letter: WCW forwarded EP's letter to Richard Johns of *Pagany,* who wrote to EP on October 17, 1930 (Yale). Their correspondence led to EP's contributing an essay to *Pagany* for January–March 1931 under the title, "The First Year of 'Pagany' and the Possibility of Criteria."

Pagany: Pagany: A Native Quarterly was published from 1930 to 1933 in Boston and New York under the editorship of Richard Johns (1904–1970) and John Sherry Mangan (1904–1961). The title was taken from WCW's *A Voyage to Pagany,* and WCW contributed more than a dozen items to it, including the "Manifesto" that opened the first number.

houndish nor horny: Hound and Horn: A Harvard Miscellany ran from 1927 to 1934 under the editorship of Lincoln Kirstein and Varian Fry. The magazine took its name from EP's early poem "The White Stag," but EP often referred to it as *Bitch and Bugle.*

that Frank fella: The Italian playwright and film critic Nino Frank (b. 1904) was the editorial secretary of *Bifur;* see Letter 45 above. Pierre G. Levy was the magazine's proprietor. Waldo Frank (1887–1967) was an American novelist and critic.

Zuke: See "Biographical Notes" on ZUKOFSKY, LOUIS.

a long-short story: WCW's "Old Doc Rivers" did not win the Scribner's prize. It was published in *The Knife of the Times and Other Stories* (1932).

me mother breakin her hip: This accident occurred on January 20, 1930; see Mariani, p. 304.

Sordello: See Letter 9 above.

a real short story: Probably "Pink and Blue," also published in *The Knife of the Times.* For a more detailed account by WCW of the origins of this story, see Hugh Witemeyer, ed., "Williams' Unpublished Introduction to His Short Stories," *William Carlos Williams Review* 16:2 (Fall 1990), pp. 14–16.

47. TLS-3

18 Feb. [1931]

Deer Bull

White Mule a pullin' strong. Mr Caldwell not so good as wuz.

We muss' get AXSHUN. I have just writ. to [Richard] Johns suggesting that IF Pagany, Bitch and Bugle [*Hound and Horn*] and Symposium wd. *each* agree to be responsible for 150 copies of cheap books to be printed in Europe, we cd. break the barrier and get stuff into print without all the goddam bothers and delays.

My prop[osal]s. were 1. six vols. of Bob [McAlmon].

2. anything of yours that was held up.

3. my collected prose (stalled by Aquila failure) IF it were wanted.

You might sound Symposium. If either P. Wheelwright or Johns agrees, I can sound H. & H.

each agreer shd. furnish list of authors considered Drukfahig [*sic*, worthy to be printed].

I rule out the other mags. as either hostile or incompetent to distribute. Also three depots ought to be enough. More wd. create confusion (???)

I shd. count the three 150s on printing and shipping.

Any sales here; or extras wd. go to paying authors. (that's us; the bloody unfed).

the point being to keep sale price of books LOW enuff so'z they'd sell and not clog storage room.

ANY *OTHER* suggestions?

Shdnt. talk MUCH about it. Certainly not yawp to people who can't act.

I think Lowenfels Carrefour Edtns. wd. be glad to have you anonymous if you stand for that.

He prints pretty, has had publicity on the ''idea'' but the two books sent me not up to much. AT least I can't persuade myself to read 'em and see if. . . . . .

Have you the faintest bloody of how much circulation enny ov these highbrow mags. has ?????????????

If the three revoos WONT, can they find anyone who will. I prefer reviews to book shops. . . . in fact I doubt if bksps. are possible.

Certainly NOW no need of any MORE magazines. The next bright beamish boy shd. be put to collaborating in this (or similar) publishing scheme and not Nativitising yet another mugazoon.

Aint it nearly time some MONEY was released somewhere for some useful purpose?

Take money. Yess. TAKE money. Lemme take a nickel. Say aint YOU never met a millyumaire?

E

White Mule: Several chapters of WCW's novel *White Mule* were serialized in *Pagany*. EP refers to the second installment, "A Flower from the Park," which appeared in the number for Winter 1931. The same issue contained a short story entitled "Hours Before Eternity" by the American fiction writer Erskine Caldwell (1903–1987), who contributed to each of the first five numbers of *Pagany*. Caldwell's best-known novel *Tobacco Road* appeared in 1932.

Symposium: The Symposium: A Critical Review ran from 1930 to 1933 under the editorship of James Burnham and Philip E. Wheelwright. WCW reviewed EP's *A Draft of XXX Cantos* in the number for April 1931.

Aquila failure: The Aquila Press of London was to have published EP's edition of *Guido Cavalcanti Rime* in December 1929, but went bankrupt before the project could be completed.

Lowenfels: The American poet, critic, editor, and publisher Walter Lowenfels (1897–1976) was the author of *Episodes and Epistles* (1925), *Finale of Seem* (1929), and *Apollinaire* (1930). His company, Éditions du Carrefour of Paris, published *Bifur* and a series of new works by unidentified authors. In a letter to EP of February 12, 1931 (Yale), Lowenfels writes: "At present Carrefour is committed to Anonymous books only and cannot handle anything else."

Nativitising: Nativity: An American Quarterly, edited by Boris J. Israel in Columbus, Ohio, began publication in the winter of 1930–31. In a letter of January 22, 1931, to Lincoln Kirstein of *Hound and Horn* (Yale), EP writes: "All these bastuds that is starting mags. OUGHT to be herded into one pen and made to coop[erate] in the circulation of pamphlets and cheap books."

48. TLS-1

Sept. 1 [1931]

Dear Ezrie:

Thank's old top, who're the wops? I mean who are they? Must be somebody I ought to know or you wouldn't have stuck in their names. You yourself seem youthful beyond belief in that pichur – you look well. That's always good news.

I been up to Labrador – on a boat with other tourists. Not many though. We rounded the Gulf of St. Laurence [*sic*], took a peek through the Straits of Belle Isle and returned home much rested. Just bare rocks spattered with green. But when you try to climb one of them the green turns into an impassable thicket of dwarf spruces about breast high. And the black flies bite like dragons – a chunk out each time – the blood runs down.

On the so called North Shore where nothing is spoken but an old style french there are fishing villages about twenty five miles apart back of which there is plenty of room and no people until one descends from the pole on the other side and falls on the exiles in Siberia. It's a good feeling to be there and to look off north beyond the villages.

Anyhow I found Pagany on my return, glanced at your Jefferson – no light as yet.

Dusty, dry weather. Had my garage enlarged for a car my son [William Eric Williams] may buy. He took a job as Bell Hop on a boat that went to Frisco this summer. Gonorrhoea, crabs, puke, pineapple tops, sweat – sixteen men in a "glory hole" three decks down – disinduced him to go again. But he saw plenty. Almost had his nuts wrenched loose by eager whores in Panama (through his pants only, howbeit) when walking through the famous Cocoa Nut Grove of Balboa.

Life less interesting day by day – sad but true. Wish many things – mostly to be done with my own trivial nature. Not that I want to be serious in a sense to be dreaded – like Eliot I mean – but really shaved of the "realities"

Yrs
Bill

that pichur: Unidentified.

Labrador: From August 11 to August 25, WCW and his wife took a cruise from Montreal to St. Anthony's, Newfoundland, and back; see *Autobiography,* pp. 274–76, and Mariani, pp. 315–18.

your Jefferson: EP's Cantos 31–33 appeared in *Pagany* for July–September 1931. They focus upon the life and works of Thomas Jefferson (1743–1826), third President of the United States.

49. TLS-2

14 Nov. 1931

Deer Willyum

In response to yrs/ of Sept. 11, 1929 which has just come to surface cause its gotta note about Frachetta's note on G[uido]. C[avalcanti]. on its verso. I have nothing to say because I anser'd [*sic*] the said, at the time.

Just before my las' anniversary I debutted [*sic*] wie bezahlter Komponist [as paid composer], and despite the helexshuns in bloody ole hengland the B. B. C. spotted up, in devaluated paper currency, but still more'n a bloody author gits for ritin books. Nacherly I have started ritin' my nex opry, and tryin' further means of makin written moozik fool proof.

I dunno why I am ritin' all this, except that as the rest of the damn world seems fairly well stuck, I have mostly me own nooz and not it''s.

Have corrected proofs, and been told it wuz to appear last week, of "How to Read". Dead ole Bloody Britain again in advnace [*sic*] of Dreiser's ole tragdey [*sic*].

I fergit wehther [*sic*] you read wop and receive the Indice. Emanuel has did my Canto VIII into the lingua Toscana [Tuscan dialect] or Bolognese or whatever he talks up in Bazzano.

In fact he has done the precedin' 7 but the VIII wuz the first one he seemed to come/through with. Feel he had better go on to finish before one bothers about revisions.

Mr McAlleyman [McAlmon] seems to like Munich. Mr Hemnwy [Hemingway] seems to have been right about Spain. wot ells.

Mr Z' his friends seem to go on contemplating publishing.

Mr [Richard] Johns??

Whatchman wot of the night! Bloody darrk me lllord!

Damn fine autumn but now turned WETT w e (bloody double TT) wet.

Consort just back from Lunnon, brought vol/ called K/in H/ I had fergot yr/ biological cover design.

What about usin it for a anti-national emblem?

Yr/ admired Mr Wyndamn Lewis has been to Morocco and D[orothy]. reports he iz paintin' again and about weaned from the Bri'sh nipple. No other London nooz save that Rodker's new novel is good. Rest of population deceased.

Come to lunch, nex time yr/ over.

EP

Frachetta's note on G. C.: EP was readying his edition of the works of the medieval Italian poet Guido Cavalcanti (*c.* 1255–1300) for publication in January 1932 by Edizioni Marsano of Genoa. WCW's letter of September 11, 1929, with "Frachetta's note" on the verso, is preserved at Yale. Girolamo Frachetta (1580–1620) was the author of a commentary on Cavalcanti, entitled *La Spositione di Girolamo Frachetta sopra la canzone di Guido Cavalcanti. Donna mi prega &c.* (Venice: Gioliti, 1585).

wie bezahlter Komponist: A radio performance of EP's *Le Testament* (see Letter 29 above) was produced by the British Broadcasting Company on October 27 and 28, 1931, a few days before the composer's forty-sixth birthday (October 30). He received a payment of £50 for the performance. A general election also took place in Britain on October 27; it resulted in a landslide victory for the Conservative Party and the formation of the "National Government" of Ramsay MacDonald and Stanley Baldwin.

my nex opry: During the summer of 1932, EP completed a draft of *Cavalcanti,* an operatic setting of poems by Guido Cavalcanti and Sordello; but the B.B.C. decided not to produce it.

"How to Read": EP's *How to Read* was published as a book by Desmond Harmsworth of London on December 2, 1931. The essay had originally appeared in three installments of the *New York Herald Tribune* in January 1929.

Dreiser's ole tragdey: An American Tragedy (1925), a novel by Theodore Dreiser (1871–1945).

Indice: L'Indice (The Index) was an Italian literary periodical edited by Gino Saviotti and published in Genoa. EP contributed a number of items to it in 1930–31. The issue of November 10, 1931, carried Emanuel Carnevali's translation of EP's eighth canto; see "Biographical Notes" on Carnevali, Emanuel.

Mr Z' his friends: See "Biographical Notes" on Zukofsky, Louis. TO, Publishers planned a multivolume edition of EP's collected prose. Only *Prolegomena I* (1932) appeared, however; this volume reprints *How to Read* (1929) and part of *The Spirit of Romance* (1910).

Whatchman wot of the night!: EP echoes the Old Testament, Isaiah 21:11.

K/in H/: WCW's *Kora in Hell: Improvisations* (1920). For the cover design, see Letter 15 above.

Rodker's new novel: See "Biographical Notes" on Rodker, John.

50. TLS-2

22 Nov [1931]

Deer Willyum the Wumpus

How badly does Zuk. want to git to yourup? and how badly OUGHT he. Until his last letter (in which the question is not mentioned) I had held the view that he ought to git some sort of root in N. Y. before wandering. AND I have allus held that sometime somehow GOD DAMN etc. something ought to git started ON THE BLOODY spot (especially as old Europe aint what she wuz.).

However if it merely means killing off yet another generation. . . . . . .

Secondly IF in yr/ judgement he ought to have a breathing spell, can we in any way manage it?

Has he ANY resources (fiscal?)

Question of whether it wd. weaken his fibre etc/ to be helped/ whether to add yet another to an unpaid perfession in which even the old stagers are havin hells own helluva to pay for their beer and sandwiches . . . etc . . .

What sort of degradation is he willing to undergo??

Etc/ first question is whether you think it wd. be a good thing for him to be exported TEMPORARARILY [*sic*]/ or if he once gets his nose out whether he cd. ever stand repatriation????? etc/etc/

God damn it; who are the just men in yr/ transpontine sodom ennyhow ?????

EP

[*1931*]: Paige, p. 229, misdates this letter to 1930.

His last letter: See Pound/Zukofsky, pp. 105–06, 109–10.

sodom: In the Old Testament, Genesis 18, the Lord promises to spare the wicked city of
    Sodom if ten just men can be found there; but only one such man is found.

51. TLS-3

Dec. 8, 1931

Dear Ezra:

Aw can't see that Zuke needs Urup just now, not at any pussonal sacrifice on his friends' part leastwise. And he has a couple uv friens, here and there who might help him. No, his place just now is here facing the harbor and the whited Statue of Miss Liberty – which his cubicle in Brookly [*sic*] faces very pleasantly – if it does face north and a french window his only bulwark against the wind. But he has a private bath and toilet to boot. Leave him lay for the moment at least. In the Spring it may be different. In fact he might need a change by that time if he survives.

He has just completed (during the past month) an anthology which Putnam has. Now I don't know Putnam well, but I've written to him and had no answer after having been led to believe that he might answer very substantially, etc. etc. Now ef you wants Zuke to see Yurup, have Put. bring out that anthology first, and if you can't do the second why think of the first.

Fer meself, I've a book of poums doing a Nurmi around these here book publishers I think they used to call em in Nieu York. It's a nice book too, big and fat and willing to go to bed with almost anyone fer a price. But I don't want no cheap guys. I wants a reglar publisher what knows how to do it, you get me, with a limousine, flowers, a swell feed and, you know, three or four times one after the other, just like that, way up and hard. Thas the kind I wants, right up in the throat. I aint no Lesbian, I doN8t [*sic*] care for violets.

If I get any bids I'll let you know. No real ones yet, but one good nibble at least.

Then Im editor of a new quarterly, Contact! up again and soon to be at 'em. And we got a couple of guys Bob picked up when he was last in New York who are backing it. I say they are backing it, but it's their mag. I'm just the, you know, editor – until we meet again or something. All I does is to pick out what goes into the magazine – if it aint too dirty or lood whatever that means. The first issue is to appear in January. I'll see that you get one.

There are other projects in the offing but none sufficiently certain to talk about. I go on writing White Mule, a few pages every three months and [Richard] Johns goes on publishing it in Pagany. For my interest in Pagany continues tho' I have little or nix to do with it.

My boy Bill goes to college next year if he makes it and I don't get caught by the depression. So far, although I am badly in the hole on stocks I bought, I can still hold my head up tho' not very high. The kid was captain of his Socker [*sic*] team. The other brat played end of [*sic*] the second football team. The wife is well and getting buxom. My mother who lives with me busted her hip two years ago and walks little. We just found out that my grandmother who died in 1920 left sixty dollars in the bank at the time! her total estate. I hope I can get it out.

Any howe, here we er, and there we er and what t'ell. I write all the time and get less done or more or different and I hope my pomes gets published because that would be a help – as they say.

I read what you said about me in the May June July The New Review – and it embarassed [*sic*] me – but I know you're right and it's to the point. It's just a temperamental jibe to feel anything but the force of what is being said, and still I felt embarassed and still you're right. Maybe in this new Contact –

Bill

Urup: Zukofsky's first trip to Europe came in the summer of 1933.

an anthology: An "Objectivists" Anthology, edited by Zukofsky, was rejected by Samuel
   Putnam in February 1932 and published instead by TO, Publishers in the summer of that
   year. The anthology contains seventeen poems by WCW.

Putnam: See "Biographical Notes" on PUTNAM, SAMUEL.

a book of poums: WCW's *Collected Poems 1921–1931* was published by the Objectivist
   Press in January 1934. WCW had assembled the book in the spring of 1931. See also
   Letter 59 below.

Nurmi: The Finnish track star Paavo Nurmi (1897–1973) was the greatest long-distance
   runner of the 1920s. He set twenty-nine official and unofficial world records and won
   nine gold medals in the Olympic competitions of 1920, 1924, and 1928.

Contact!: For the original *Contact* (1920–23), see Letter 18 above. WCW, Robert
   McAlmon, and Nathanael West revived the magazine for three issues in 1932. Its
   publishers were David Moss and Martin Kamin, who owned a bookstore in New York
   City.

my grandmother: Emily Dickinson Wellcome (d. 1920) was WCW's paternal grandmother.

The New Review: In "Our Contemporaries and Others," *The New Review* 2 (May–June–
   July 1931), p. 150, EP writes: "The use of logic in place of perception is hostile to
   principles. The logician never gets to the root. (For orientation observe the growing
   strength of Bill Williams and the progressive desiccation of logicists and the construc-
   tors of superficial sequence.)"

52. TLS-3

18 Dec. [1931]

Dear Wulruss:

Murry Xmas.

I read that Possum is to BBBB Poesy Prof. at Hawvud.

ha haw haw vud.

An a great joke on ole Eliza Schelling and Frozen mug Penniman/
haw hawhawVUD.

I trust you will be nice to our sad sad friend Mr Eliot an' help him to bear his
cross in na Jheezus = like manner.

At any rate a great step up fer murkn kulchuh, from the Storks and Ausslanders [*sic*].

I think you might bury yr/ differences and send him a nice little note of
welcome (especially as he aint yet got there).

A decent; discriminating retroactive academicism is something solider to rebel AGAINST than the mush of Canby's and incertitudes of Ausslanders.

of course   He mustn't be allowed to pizen a whole generation. But I think the opposition might be cordial and amiable/

some sort of decent example of how a difference of belief CAN among decent human beings be conducted. Intransiegeant [*sic*] refusal to have anything whatever to do with this nonsense [*sic*] about kings, episcopacies, and with Mr Eliot's other private predilections. But hearty welcome to your shores, and an appreciation of his *literary* as distinct from his philosophical or religious or social discernment.

at any rate he is not a mere bluff/ windbag: ignoramus/

Keeps up to the Harvard tradition. They invited Henry Adams at a time when no other univ/ wd. have done so.

I fergit whether you have even met the victim. You might be more inclined to lay offn him ef yeou had.

I dont imagine he will have energy enough left to DO anything even if he does get to Cambridge. That remains to be seen.

In the mean time, take five minutes off an write him a nice li'l note of welcome. It wont hurt you very much as the dentist said to the rhino.

address Faber and Faber, 24 Russel [*sic*] Sq. London W.C.1

gord knows the pore chap will feel lonely thinkin' of that god damnd new hengland coast. (which shd. be better for him n London ennyhow.)

Ef you remember the hall = rush, its the first half inch that counts. Ole possum aint got much foot hold, but push onto some solid part of him, not onto the pit of his stummiKKKK.

Yrs

E

Possum: Eliot applied this nickname to himself in a letter to EP of July 19, 1922; see Eliot, pp. 548, 589. The Possum, in turn, called EP "Rabbit"; the nicknames recall the animals in Joel Chandler Harris' Uncle Remus tales.

Poesy Prof.: See "Biographical Notes" on ELIOT, THOMAS STEARNS. His appointment as the Norton Professor of Poetry at Harvard was announced on December 15, 1931.

a great joke: The "joke" was that, whereas Harvard had honored its alumnus Eliot, the University of Pennsylvania refused to honor EP. In 1920, EP's father was rebuffed in an attempt to persuade the university to award him a doctorate or an honorary degree. In 1931, EP's attempt to complete the requirements for his Ph.D. by submitting his edition of Cavalcanti as his doctoral dissertation was likewise unsuccessful. See Paige, p. 237, and Carpenter, p. 464.

Schelling: Felix Emanuel Schelling (1858–1945) was professor of English at the University of Pennsylvania during EP's student days. EP corresponded with him for many years after leaving Penn.

Penniman: At Penn, EP studied the history of literary criticism with Professor Josiah Penniman (1868–1941); it was the only course he failed. Penniman served as Provost of the University from 1923 to 1939.

Storks: The American poet, translator, teacher, and editor Charles Wharton Stork (1881–1971) edited a Philadelphia poetry journal named *Contemporary Verse* from 1917 to 1925. He was also the author of *Day Dreams of Greece* (1908), *Sea and Bay* (1916), and *Sunset Harbor* (1933).

Ausslanders: Joseph Auslander (1897–1965) was a Philadelphia-born poet, translator, and editor. He contributed to *The Dial* and served on the editorial board of the *North American Review*. In a letter to William Bird of December 25, 1937 (Yale), EP writes: "Ten thousand Auslanders matter NOWT to literature, they can't STOP the real work being done/ BUT one or two of the bastids can do a LOT of harm to the general level of intelligence."

Canby's: See "Biographical Notes" on CANBY, HENRY SEIDEL.

this nonsence about kings: See "Biographical Notes" on ELIOT, THOMAS STEARNS.

Henry Adams: For Henry Adams, see Letter 40 above. In 1870, Harvard hired Adams to teach medieval history and to edit the *North American Review* at a time when Adams had made himself unpopular in Washington as a crusading journalist and reformer. He remained at Harvard until 1877.

53. TLS-1

Dec. 30, 1931

Dear Ezra:

Pussonally Eliot can go to hell before I welcome him to these shores. But since your letter is so damned decent, not to say generous, I'll ignore the proff rather than tell him what I think of him. If I must get culchuh I'll take it from some one else. For I'm sure he will pizen a generation by his mere sickly presence – even in New England. Apparently he is sick from what you say. That would at least enlist my interest as a physician – if he weren't a writer as well. No. To hell with him. Harvard without him is bad enough.

But I won't kick him in the stomach. I suppose there'd be no use trying to kick lower.

Jesus Christ, you've got a nerve asking me to do a thing like that, now that I think of it. I think you've been abroad long enough. I'd suggest that you come over her [*sic*] as Eliot's valet.

I've been working on a new magazine, yes, another one – to be called Contact after the recent lamented – It's to be a quarterly, sponsored by a couple of Jewish boys as usual – who own a book shop, not bad examples of the race. The thing is in the press now. Wish I could use your letter verbatim in it but my wife gave me hell when I mentioned it. Will send you a copy. Hope you like it.

1932 next.

Best luck

yours
Bill

Contact: See Letters 18 and 51 above.

54. ALS-6

June 14, 1932

Dear Ezra:

The Profile Anthology, yesterday, no letter or note of explanation, does actually come as new. Really refreshing, more than a little enlightening – I am thinking of the Eliot "Hoo hoo" bit – as well as of others. Certainly you have escaped preciosity. Seem to have been following some sort of consecutive understanding of the matter which is not common. This insures a complete failure – re publicum [as regards the public?] (I make no pretence at Latin).

It's rather a pointed answer – the body of the book, I mean, – to Symon's [*sic*] question with which you open the attack.

I haven't read the thing carefully as yet – I'll probably have a chance to speak of it somewhere soon.

A card from Zukofsky this a.m. saying he is in N. Y. again – after the California jaunt. I've seen little of him in the past year.

Contact I should be on its way to you by this time. No. II should be out next week. Wait for No II before judging No. I. No. III is all made up (roughly) There will be a No. IV – after which what? It's been a task. Unfortunately I cannot take these things lightly. Nothing may come of them – but I carry them strapped to my back while they live.

There are too god damned many things in my life anyhow. Id be better off with a fourth part of them to care for. But this continual writing of letters – about nothing – seems particularly stupid.

Its to some extent the economic stress that is wearying me as it does all about me. I am not precisely pinched but my liberty of movement and feeling – are greatly restricted. Its a sort of invisible constriction that encloses the body as a whole.

I've done some writing but nothing that offers release to me, nothing I can say is new and good. A poem in Contact II somewhat refutes this but that's a year old now.

There seems no where to go, no thought to follow. I have to confess as great confusion within as without. Not that I believe even in that, for I do not. Even confusion seems thoroughly unnecessary – were it not for the order makers who are so intent on imposing order that they never detect it's beshitted existence.

Precisely I mean verse insterests [sic] me as solidly as ever; in the long track which your anthology traces there is a direction both ahead and underfoot. But who can believe it and what's more who can live it –

((to go on) – several hours later) [Beginning with this line, the rest of the letter is typed.]

The New English Review hass [sic] offered space to those who speak well of you, meaning, I presume, precisely nothing.

It seemed to me there were other things to say but apparently I was mistaken.

I've been playing with a theory that the inexplicitness of modern verse as compared with, let us say, the Iliad; and our increasingly difficult music in the verse as compared with the more or less downrightness of their line forms – have been the result of a clearly understandable revolution in poetic attitude. Whereas formerly the music which accompanied the words amplified certified and released them today the words we write, failing a patent music, have become the mucis [sic] itself and the understanding of the individual (presumed) is now that which used to be the words.

This, blasts out of existence forever all the puerilities of the dum te dum vedsifiers [sic] and puts it up to the reader to be a man – if possible. There are not many things to believe but the trouble is no one believes them. Modern verse forces belief. It is music to that, in every sense when if ever and in whoever if [sic] does or may exist. Without the word (the man himself) the music (verse as we know it today) is only a melody of sounds. But it is magnificent when it plays about some kind of certitude.

Floss has just brought me up an apple jack mint julep which I enjoy – We do produce good apple jack in Jersey – and Floss can mix 'em.

Confusion of thought is the worst devilment I have to suffer – as it must be the hell itself of all intelligence. Unbelief is impossible – merely because it is impossible, negation, futility, nothingness – But the shit that is offered by sale by the big believing corporations – (What the hell) I don't even think of them, it isn't that) It's the lack of focus that drives me to the edge of insanity.

I've tried all sorts of personal adjustments – other than a complete letgo –

Returning to the writing of verse which is the only thing that concerns us after all: certainly there is nothing for it but to go on with a complex quantitative music and to further accuracy of image (notes in a scale) and – the rest (undefined save in individual poems) – a music which can only have authority as we –

I'm a little drunk –

Contact can't pay for verse or anything else. I mentioned to West that you had more or less objectionably asked me if I was doing this (publishing editing Contact) in order to offer you a mouthpiece – I told him I had told you to go to hell. He said he'd be mighty glad to have a canto, that he thought them great

But we can't pay a nickel –

(after another two hours)

The Junior Prom at the High School: Bill is taking his first girl (after an interval of five years) The fishing period and girl hating has passed again. This one has taught him to dance – he is getting ready to take a bath – now when it is almost time to leave the house.

Yes, I have wanted to kick myself (as you suggest) for not realizing more about Ford Maddox's [sic] verse. If he were only not so unapproachable, so gone nowadays. I want to but it is not to be done. Also he is too much like my father was – too English for me ever to be able to talk with him animal to animal.

It's the middle of a June evening

No news – much I'd like to do.

Yours
Bill

The Profile Anthology: Profile: An Anthology Collected in MCMXXXI, ed. Ezra Pound (Milan: John Scheiwiller, 1932). It contains four poems by WCW: "Hic Jacet," "Postlude," "Portrait of a Woman in Bed," and "The Botticellian Trees."

the Eliot "Hoo hoo" bit: T. S. Eliot's "Fragment of an Agon" appears on pp. 91–99 of *Profile*. A choral passage on p. 99 reads as follows: "Hoo ha ha/ Hoo ha ha/ Hoo/ Hoo/ Hoo."

Symon's question: Profile opens with "Modern Beauty" by the English poet and critic Arthur Symons (1865–1945). In his introduction, EP justifies the chronological arrangement of authors in the anthology by saying, "In other words, if Cummings is no 'better' than Symons, the 'Georgians' are mere apes void of interest and the official taste of the British and American commercially sustained weeklies is mere excrement such as parasites of all ages have spread where they have parasitified" (pp. 9–10).

Contact: See Letter 51 above, where WCW promises EP a copy of the first issue of *Contact.* But in a postcard to WCW of May 20, 1932 (Rutherford), EP asks, "HAZ your bloomin peeyeerodicule EVER been printed an nif so, why dont you send it to me?" Despite WCW's statement here, there was no fourth number of *Contact.*

a poem in Contact II: The second number of *Contact* contained two poems by WCW: "The Canada Lily" (later retitled "The Red Lily") and "The Cod Head."

New English Review: For the *New English Weekly* (not *Review*), see "Biographical Notes" on ORAGE, ALFRED RICHARD.

West: The American novelist and short-story writer Nathanael West (1903–1940) was the associate editor of *Contact.* An excerpt from his famous story "Miss Lonelyhearts" appeared in the second number.

Ford Maddox: See "Biographical Notes" on FORD, FORD MADOX. *Profile* contains three poems by Ford: "Views," "The Starling," and "In the Little Old Market-Place." Introducing them, EP writes, "Madox Ford brought out a series of volumes of poetry the qualities of which became more apparent with time."

PART THREE

1933–1941

In March 1933, Franklin D. Roosevelt became President of the United States, with an electoral mandate to combat the economic depression into which the nation had sunk since the stock-market crash of 1929. It was a lean time for writers and doctors as well as for ordinary workers. Like many other members of the intelligentsia, Pound and Williams felt a strong historical imperative to involve themselves directly in economic and political action. For a time, they found a common cause in the international Social Credit movement. But as the Thirties unfolded, their politics diverged dramatically and threatened to destroy their friendship.

Social Credit was a halfway house between capitalism and socialism. First propounded in 1919–20 by an English engineer named C. H. Douglas, Social Credit located the economic flaws of modern industrial society not in production but in distribution. Something was preventing consumers from acquiring the food, clothing, housing, and other goods and services that they needed and that modern technology could provide. Douglas attributed maldistribution to the discrepancy between prices and purchasing power brought about by excessive bank interest charges, or usury. This imbalance, he argued, leads to domestic poverty and eventually, through competition for overseas markets, to international war. Douglas proposed to nationalize credit banking and to operate it in the public interest, while preserving private ownership and private enterprise in the rest of the economy. He also advocated price controls and direct consumer subsidies from the national treasury, which he called National Dividends.

Initially conceived to account for the prolongation of World War I and the recession that followed it, Social Credit enjoyed a revival during the 1930s as a plausible analysis of the crisis of Western capitalism. Pound met Douglas in the London offices of A. R. Orage's *The New Age* and was converted to his theories in 1919. At the onset of the Depression, Pound took up the cause again and lobbied for it tirelessly in public manifestoes and private correspondence. To Douglas' program, Pound added other enthusiasms, such as stamped paper money or "stamp scrip" and a four-hour working day. Williams, meanwhile, began to attend Social Credit meetings in New York in 1933. He and Pound both contributed regularly to the leading Social Credit journals of the day, *New Democracy* in New York and the *New English Weekly* in London.

From this common ground, however, the politics of Pound and Williams soon diverged. Williams leaned to the left. He contributed proletarian fiction and poetry to left-wing periodicals, despised the fascist dictators of Germany and Italy, and sympathized with the struggles of workers, peasants, and soldiers in the Soviet Union. Pound, in contrast, leaned to the right. He admired Mussolini, and believed that Italian fascist syndicalism was more likely than any other economic system to achieve economic justice by implementing the principles of Social Credit and guild corporatism.

Pound met Mussolini in 1933. He persuaded himself that Il Duce embodied the principles of the American Founding Fathers, and wrote a book called *Jefferson and/or Mussolini* (1935). Pound did not become an Italian citizen or join the fascist party, but he defended Mussolini's invasion of Abyssinia in 1935. His letters to Williams became more and more programmatic in content and proselyzing in tone as the decade wore on.

The Spanish Civil War of 1936–39 tested the friendship as nothing had done before. Williams became an ardent partisan of the Loyalist or Republican side. He was active in the Bergen County, New Jersey, chapter of the Medical Bureau and North American Committee to Aid Spanish Democracy, an organization that obtained and shipped medical supplies to the Loyalists. The intervention of Mussolini and Hitler on the side of General Franco and the Nationalist forces in 1937 confirmed Williams' dark assessment of the intentions of the fascist dictators. Pound, on the other hand, remained curiously neutral on the subject of the war. When he answered Nancy Cunard's questionnaire for *Authors Take Sides on the Spanish War* (1937), Pound told her, as he also told Williams in correspondence, that the conflict was unimportant, a mere distraction from the larger struggle against the forces of usury.

After 1937, Pound began to speak favorably of Hitler as well as Mussolini and to be more overtly anti-Semitic in his statements. Writing to Rutherford, Pound recommends that Williams read *The Protocols of the Elders of Zion,* he rejoices at the Nazis' arrest of Austrian Jewish banker Louis von Rothschild, and he queries the role of Jews in the Abolitionist movement and the Reconstruction period. In a 1939 review of Pound's *Guide to Kulchur,* Williams publicly accused Pound of anti-Semitism.

By this time, Williams was convinced that his old friend had gone off the tracks, mentally as well as politically. He urged Pound to leave Italy and come home. Pound did, but only for a short visit in the spring of 1939. He came to persuade American leaders in Washington that a few simple economic reforms would restore prosperity, and that Italy was not an enemy of the United States. Williams saw Pound twice during this visit, once in Washington and once in Rutherford. He did not like what he saw—a man with a closed mind, who had come to preach and not to listen.

Yet the two writers disagreed far less over literature than over politics. Even during this period of tension, they collaborated on various literary projects. Each continued to admire the other's published work. Thus, Williams read and favorably reviewed the new installments of Pound's *Cantos* (1934, 1937, 1940), his *Guide to Kulchur,* and even *Jefferson and/or Mussolini.* Pound, in turn, praised and promoted Williams' volume of realistic short stories, *Life Along the Passaic River* (1938). They tried to reach agreement on declarations of poetic principle, and they discussed a number of publishing schemes.

Literary publishing in America was in the doldrums. After twenty-five years of steady production, Williams still had no regular publisher. From 1930 to 1937, new books by Williams appeared only in small editions issued by short-lived publishers. He had no British audience to speak of, and no book of his had appeared in London since *The Tempers* in 1913. Pound, during the same period, depended heavily upon his British connections with T. S. Eliot at Faber and Faber and with the Social Credit publisher Stanley Nott. Between 1933 and 1937, ten different books and pamphlets by Pound were published in London, but only five of them appeared in the United States as well.

The advent of James Laughlin's New Directions upon the American publishing scene in 1936 was therefore timely and welcome to both writers. Within two years, Laughlin had brought out three books by Williams and become his principal American publisher. By 1940 Pound, too, was a New Directions author. Laughlin, still in his twenties, revered his strong-minded elders but was independent enough to hold his editorial ground when they tried to dictate to him.

Medical matters occasionally crop up in the correspondence, too. Pound had dipped into several branches of medicine and biology, and liked to pretend that he was more scientific than "Doc" Williams. Pound had elaborate theories about the physiology and psychology of sex; indeed, both men saw an intimate link between sexual and artistic expression in males. Pound also took an interest in endocrinology and in certain public-health issues such as malnutrition and the prevention of pulmonary diseases.

Thus, in 1937–38 Pound took up the cause of Dr. Tweddell. Francis I. Tweddell, a general practitioner on Long Island, thought he had discovered a cure for tuberculosis. He had observed that workers in plaster-of-Paris factories and in marble quarries seldom contracted the disease. He believed that pulmonary sufferers could be treated by regular inhalations of powdered calcium or gypsum. But he needed a sample of thirty or forty infected patients on whom to test his theory. Pound encouraged Tweddell to contact Williams and tried to browbeat Williams into helping Tweddell find experimental subjects. Williams responded politely but skeptically, and criticized Pound's habit of pretending to professional expertise in fields of which he had only an amateur's knowledge.

Throughout 1940 and 1941, Williams tried in vain to warn Pound of the consequences of the course he was following. From the beginning of the Battle of Britain to the attack on Pearl Harbor, Williams sent a series of blunt and percep- tive letters, to which Pound replied with an insouciant mixture of denial, rational- ization, and evasion. When Pound began to broadcast his views on the overseas service of Rome Radio, Williams publicly attacked him in an article entitled "Ezra Pound: Lord Ga-Ga!" For Williams, the Rome Radio speeches put Pound in the same camp as "Lord Haw-Haw," the British propagandist who broadcast from Berlin on behalf of Nazi Germany.

The final straw was Pound's callous attitude toward the heavy losses suffered by the Soviet Army in the early stages of the German invasion of Russia. "There is a lot of meat lying round on the steppes at the moment," Pound said casually in a letter of October 18, 1941. Williams fired off a furious reply, but the letter never reached its destination. The Post Office returned it because mail service to Italy had been suspended. Japan attacked Pearl Harbor on December 7, and the United States entered the war. The correspondence of Pound and Williams broke off for the next four years. Their friendship, too, had reached a breaking point.

55. TLS-3

Jan. 23
anno XI [1933]

Oliver Twist to Willyam the WalRUSS

Az you've give Zuk/ a hand (Sympozeeum, current)
What about doin a note on Profile? fer th same orgum/
IF you feel about it wot you wrote me at the time.

I think it contains a few facts and few statements that cd/ pro the publik bone be diffused.

also I think the system of criticism by juxtaposition and BY chronology cd. be used more XXXtensively to the killing off the sonzovbitches /

I mean the crit/ by juxtaposition / as opposed to crit/ by shittin flies allover [sic] th place (Rascoe; Phelps, VanBrooks [sic], etc.)

Certain miscalculations OUGHT NOT to be possible to anyone who has read the book.

If that is so, the bk/ is a definite critical act.

In so far as it is polemical it is pro/ Marianne and pro/ Zuk whereas it didn't boost you, but was merely just.

or less than just

/or put it./

You didn't benefit/ except in so far as all the contributors benefited by introduction to a few foreign reders [sic].

whereas Zuk/ and more partic[ularly]/ Marianne; might be said to have an injustice righted.

WHEREFORE you are in a better position to do the rev[iew]/ without suspician [sic] of partiality.

my "error" if any: is the old error of expecting people to SEE what is held up infront [sic] of 'em. instead of xxxxxxplaining at length in words of one syllable that a CAT is a cat

Incidentally you might kick Wheelright [*sic*] for saying/ p 118/119
"theirs is long and two shorts/ ours accented and two unaccented."
second time this week/ an american fails to distinguish between the habitual
and the necessary. (orther case a failure to dist[inguish]/ betw[een]/ economic
habit and econ[omic]/ neces[sity].

must be some shit in the acdaemic [*sic*] sugar bowl.

Tom Lawrence 33% ass evidently. but he had an agreeable brother.   the rest
of T. R. [*sic*] O. K. I suppose; but a bloody tiresome character.

Yrs

E

Again re/ Profile/ Scheiwiller might be MORE useful if encouraged/ he is
perfedtly [*sic*] honest and WANTS to do as much as his means permit.

anno XI: EP met Mussolini in January 1933 and began to date some of his correspondence
  by the fascist calendar, according to which 1922, the year Mussolini seized power, is
  the year 1.
Sympozeeum: WCW reviewed Louis Zukofsky's An *"Objectivists"* Anthology in *The
  Symposium* for January 1933.
pro the publik bone: Pro bono publico (for the public good).
Rascoe; Phelps, VanBrooks: For Burton Rascoe, see Letter 40 above. William Lyon
  Phelps (1865–1943) was professor of English at Yale University and a nationally known
  critic, lecturer, preacher, and columnist. The critic, editor, and literary historian Van
  Wyck Brooks (1886–1963) was the author of *The Wine of the Puritans* (1909),
  America's Coming of Age (1915), *The Ordeal of Mark Twain* (1920), and *The Pil-
  grimage of Henry James* (1925).
pro/ Marianne and pro/ Zuk: Profile contains five poems by Marianne Moore: "Pedantic
  Literalist," "Radical," "Those Various Scalpels," "A Graveyard," and "Old Ti-
  ger." It also includes Zukofsky's "Movements from 'Poem Beginning The.'"
Wheelright: The Symposium for January 1933 also contains Philip Wheelwright's review
  of T. E. Shaw's 1932 translation of Homer's *Odyssey*. In it, Wheelright says, "there
  is still no possibility of achieving in English a dactyl that will sound remotely like a
  Greek or Latin dactyl, for theirs is made of a long and two short syllables, ours of an
  accented and two unaccented" (pp. 118–19).
Tom Lawrence: T. E. Shaw was the adopted name of Thomas Edward Lawrence ("Lawrence of Arabia," 1888–1935). For his brother William George Lawrence, see Letter 11
  above.
Scheiwiller: In a letter to Joseph Vogel of November 2, 1928, EP describes Giovanni
  Scheiwiller of Milan as "employee, publisher and messenger boy . . . . he is a clerk
  in Hoepli's, but he is also publisher of 'Chirico, Prampolini, and I don't know who
  else'" (Paige, p. 220). In a letter to WCW of January 24 [1932?] (Buffalo), EP reports

that Scheiwiller's books "are printed at his own expense, not de luxe, but neat, and he loses a small sum on each."

56. TLS-2

21 Feb [1933]

Deer Bull

As thou hast desisted from bein a neditor you are eligible fer signing/ Manifesto/

My first idea was that editors could each comment in the [*sic*] own orgums. In fact it still is.

Manifesto designed to knock off Criterionism, Dialism, BitchandCornism etc. as you will see. I can't remember whom I asked, signatures to date/ Zuk[ofsky]/ Marianne [Moore]/ Basil [Bunting]

I think the others asked were Parkes, Mangan, Mayor; Rakosi. & Tyler

It was to lead off a special number of some review/ enforcing what I advanced in the Almanacco Letterario to effect that crit[icism]/ in murka/ wuz lookin up.

We dont WANT more than ten sig[nature]s.

I see no use in further waiting. Mangan's invite went to uncertain address and he hadn't rec[eive]d. it when he last wrote.

Ennyhow IF you are in HAR/Mony; stick on yr/ fist and in any case send it to Zabel wiffout delay.

I dont want heterogeneous names. If Zuk/ has had word from anyone about it, ANY of the original invitees are includable, but NOT people who have manifestly lived in open violation.

yrs
Ez P.

Manifesto: See Letter 57 below.

Parkes: Henry Bamford Parkes (1901–1972) was a contributor to *Hound and Horn* and *Fifth Floor Window.*

Mangan: John Sherry Mangan (1904–1961) was an editor of *Pagany.*

Mayor: Alpheus Hyatt Mayor (1901–1980) was an editor of *Hound and Horn.*

Rakosi: Carl Rakosi (1903–) contributed to *Poetry, The Little Review,* and *Hound and Horn.*

Tyler: See "Biographical Notes" on TYLER, PARKER.

Almanacco Letterario: In ". . . Il libro americano: status rerum" (The American book:

where things stand), *Almanacco Letterario [Bompiani]* (1933), pp. 264–67, EP speaks of "il risorgimento della critica americana" (the revival of American criticism) since 1930 by a generation of younger critics writing for little magazines. He names "Mangan, Mayor, Zukofsky, Parkes, Bunting," and he also mentions WCW as an important critic of the preceding generation.

Zabel: Morton Dauwen Zabel (1901–1964) was an editor of *Poetry.*

57. TLS-2

Mar. 4, 1933

Dear Ezra:

Strange that I should have sent off my "sonnet" yesterday and today I receive your letter-manifesto.

I return the m. signed, a salutary and illuminating statement, the first intelligible general declaration concerning the art of criticism that I have ever encountered.

Yours
Bill

THE FUNCTIONS OF CRITICISM

The following manifesto has been under discussion for several weeks but as three signatures are quite enough for any manifesto there seems to be no reason for further delay in publishing it. The original copies were sent by E. P. to a small number of critics whose practice had in the main corresponded with the substance of the manifesto.

MANIFESTO

1. The best type of critic actually causes an improvement in the art he criticizes.

2. The next best critic is the one who most focuses attention on the best work.

3. The pestulence [*sic*] pretending to criticism distracts attention from the best work, either to work of secondary value or to tosh or even to wobbly essays on criticism.

William Carlos Williams

The first version of this statement contained several [rest of document missing]

my "sonnet": Probably "Our (American) Ragcademicians," *New English Weekly* 3:13 (July 13, 1933), p. 309.

58. TLS-4

10 March [1933]

SEE/ree/ YEUSE/ment [seriously]

you ole rich = in = blubber WHALE

Do you think certain defects, soft spots etc/ in yr/ poems of ten years ago are essential to their Americanity?

Problum ov editn' yew, becomes more weighty as I procede [*sic*]. IF you don't go over on this heave/ yew being night [*sic*] on ter 50/ and ought = ing to have 25 or more years WORK purr/formed from which to see/lekt the XXXhibits!!!

As for what the furriner calls your "special sentimentality about america" as destinct [*sic*] from the gneral [*sic*] sentimentality which you share with your father's co = nationals!!!

I have not crabbed you for 15 or 20 years. As fer murka// I doubt it is an END/. As a means it prob[ably]/ helped you to get to where Catullus, Homer, Rimbaud and possibly the sottoscritto [undersigned] have got/ I mean OUT of the particular god damn slop of the XIX century, Victorian era; age of General Grant/etc/ or in nother woids OUT of a particular slice of cultural complication or deformity.

As to AGENDA/ it amounts to no more than rereading a few poems without prejudice. You can't have it both ways/ IF I take all the weight of bein' transplanted FOR certain purposes/ you can't have all the gravy of settin geographically in an out of the worle [*sic*] HOLE for the sake of ROOTS/ *and* all the advantages of getting your soft spots trod on by spoken crizism.

If you had been in a milieu/ or near anybody wot knew anything, some phrases, soft spots of language wd. have been protested AT THE TIME.

Fer ninstince/ Spring an All/ p. 71. XIX / all that is on p. 71 is damn good/ then on p. 72 you end in slop and sugar

sweet heads/ dark kisses//// orrible me deer Willyam the YAM

all Harriet's young ladies cd. or might.

Despite this diabetes/ you have Transmitted, putt over the general feeling or conviction of your being there/ BUT you have got it over ONLY to the few patient admirers who put up with the the stale merangue [*sic*]/ BECAUSE of the roast beef under neath [*sic*] it.

Zuk/ went thru yr/ inedits for Exile. BUT I doubt whether anyone has taken the trouble to go thru you [*sic*] complete woiks/ with BENEVOLENT intentions since ole Ez. had a try back in the be-fo-th-wo [before the war].

I am not doin this corpus poetarum [assemblage of poets] fer mere dillytantism/ the book has got to do work. MY first Imagist anth/ did WORK, as distinct from the Amygist volumettes which merely sabotaged and exploited.

From Sprung and All/ I have listed

as most likely//

I, IX, X, XI, XII, XIV, XVIII.

and I have in my mind the "Corpse" and the "Cod"

The Kore [*Kora in Hell: Improvisations*] is writ as prose: and better be left out for (various reasons, muddle in readers mind about free verse . . . sfar as Eng[land]/ is concerned// also it is probably better editing to use only VERSE, plus the Nuevo Mundo (any short bits printed as prose, wd. muddle re/ the verse and take away the emphasis that I shd. like to throw on the Nuevo Mundo, FORM.

One OUGHT to be able to get 20 pages or 24 pages perfectly SOLID: without repeating from Profile.. must look as if there was *plenty of* you.

The question is more than OF one anthology. America seems to have voluntarily surrendered whatever adv[antage]/ she got by having Little Review pub[lishe]d/ in N. Y. instead of London. May be trifle but a bad sign if I am getting printed in London BEFORE I can get a U. S. pubr/

England may be waking up a bit/ and London publishing may again (gloomy thought) count as it did before the amurikun wake up.

(yaaas, I talk like a public meeting . . . . but putt it into yr/ own words. WE have never had enough influence with the sons of bitches who run the N. Y. pubing/ houses. And you cant wait for the VanDoren fambly to sanction yr/ activity.

MY last two new books have been pubd/ in London and the XXX had to be put thru by MacLeish in N. Y.

A Brit. appearance with success wd. facilitate yr/ dealings with the local mob.??????

ALSO there is yr/ noo stuff thet I haven't seen/ etc.

The advantages of a persistent thymus

                are in some degree

                    neutralized by the persistence

of a softness in linguistic Xpresshun

                  into which the foot of the reading eye

plops.

BEE/sides Bee/hind Bee-behind end.

"The Active Element"/ wants to show that you are still going ON. Thet's th point of the collection/ to gather the ten or or so who have stuck at it/ not resigned.

You cant REMAIN the author of "Portrait of a Woman in Bed." which as you know I have allus considered etc.

immune from defects above mintioned and none the less YOURS for that freedom.

Naow/ try to go to bed sober fer once/ an reflect on what yr/ ageing frien has writ. you.

What I want is 32 pages of yr/ best/ Spring an All I've got on me desk/ any emendations, can be typed as such. no need of retyping hole poem.

love to Flossie

E

editn' yew: In February 1933, Frank V. Morley of Faber and Faber in London commissioned EP to prepare an anthology of contemporary poetry. Initially entitled *The Active Element,* the book was published as *Active Anthology* in October 1933. WCW is represented by fifteen poems (pp. 29–55).

the furriner: See "Biographical Notes" on BUNTING, BASIL.

your father's co-nationals: The English; see "Biographical Notes" on WILLIAMS, WILLIAM GEORGE.

age of General Grant: General Ulysses S. Grant (1822–1885) commanded the Union Army during the American Civil War and served as President of the United States from 1869 to 1877. His Administration was notoriously corrupt.

Spring an All: Section XIX of WCW's *Spring and All* (1923) ends with the lines, "Out of their sweet heads/ dark kisses—rough faces" (p. 72).

Harriet's young ladies: Genteel, sentimentally romantic contributors to Harriet Monroe's *Poetry* magazine.

Zuk/ went thru yr/ inedits: See Letters 34–37 above and "Biographical Notes" on ZUKOFSKY, LOUIS.

ole Ez. had a try: See Letters 7 and 11 above.

be-fo-th-wo: EP alludes to a popular book of poems by A. C. Gordon and Thomas Nelson entitled *Befo' de War: Echoes in Negro Dialect* (1888).

MY first Imagist anth/: Des Imagistes (1914), as distinct from Amy Lowell's *Some Imagist Poems* (1915, 1916, 1917).

I have listed: The list given here differs considerably from the selection of WCW's work that ultimately appeared in *Active Anthology.*

the Nuevo Mundo: The untitled seventh section of WCW's *The Great American Novel* (1923) begins with the words "*Nuevo Mundo* [New World]! shouted the sailors." In "Dr. Williams' Position" (1928), EP singles out this chapter as one in which "the element of form emerges." Nevertheless, the passage does not appear in the *Active Anthology.*

printed in London: Between 1931 and 1940, seventeen new books by EP were printed in
London, ten by Faber and Faber, where T. S. Eliot had become an influential editor and
company director.

the VanDoren fambly: The Van Doren family was a powerful influence in New York
literary circles. Carl Van Doren (1885–1950), a professor of English at Columbia
University, was literary editor of *The Nation* (1919–22) and of *Century Magazine*
(1922–25), and editor of the Literary Guild (1926–54). His brother, the poet Mark Van
Doren (1874–1972), also taught at Columbia and served as literary editor of *The Nation*
(1924–28). Irita (Mrs. Carl) Van Doren (1891–1966) edited the *New York Herald Book
Review* from 1926 to 1963.

MY last two new books: How to Read, published by Desmond Harmsworth in 1931, and
ABC of Economics, published by Faber and Faber in 1933.

the XXX: A Draft of XXX Cantos (New York: Farrar and Rinehart, 1933). See "Biographical Notes" on MacLeish, Archibald.

"Portrait of a Woman in Bed": First published in *Others* for December 1916, this poem
was chosen by EP for inclusion in *Profile* (1932).

59. TLS-1

March 15, 1933

Dear Ezra:

I've selected twenty one typewritten pages of verse for you. They go forward
to Zukofsky today. They may not be exactly what you expect but I refuse to go
back over the old books to rake up "favorites". I have made this selection from
my present, unpublished, volume. If you don't like the group and there is time I'll
make another for you or add to this one. Twenty pages do not after all give much
leeway. But I for myself find the group excellently representative and would wish
that it remain as it is.

What shall you say about me? That I have a volume of verse which I have been
in the process of making for the past ten years, that it is the best collection of
verse in America today and that I can't find a publisher – while, at the same time,
every Sunday Literary Supplement has pages of book titles representing the
poetry of my contemporaries. And when I say I have sought a publisher I mean
just that for I had the best agent in New York, Brandt & Brandt fairly comb the
city for me last year. I'll try again this spring.

This must mean something. No doubt it means that my conception of poetry is
not that of my contemporaries either in the academies or out. This should be a

distinction. It means that I believe poetry to be the mould of language as of feeling in any world and that its importance as a mechanism for correct thinking makes it too difficult for ordinary use. Not that my own work is anywhere near what it shd. be & that it is my constant effort to make it.

I don't care what you say. Any one of the poems, or some one of them, should be capable of saying all that is necessary.

But I've had a letter recently from a young fellow named Brittain who first sent me a short story and then a long poem both ov [*sic*] which are on the verge of being very good indeed. I believe him to be very young as I know him to be somewhat influenced by Eliot. I immediately threw up a red flag warning him to come to life if he wanted me to help him and to get off Eliot as soon as he could. When I know more of him I'll say more. He looks to be worth watching. He gives me something to say at least in reply to your query about – Any new ones coming along? I'll report later on.

Yrs.

Bill

Thanks for the working drawings etc. re. the catamaran.

a volume of verse: Collected Poems 1921–1931; see Letter 51 above. Brandt and Brandt were also the literary agents of e. e. cummings.
Brittain: See "Biographical Notes" on BRITTAIN, ROBERT.
catamaran: WCW had inquired about the unusual design of the *patino,* or pontoon rowboat, used by Rapallo residents and holidaymakers on the Gulf of Tigullio. EP sent a detailed, four-page description of the boat's construction, including diagrams, precise metric measurements, and safety tips (Rutherford). See Reed Whittemore, *William Carlos Williams: Poet from Jersey* (Boston: Houghton Mifflin, 1975), pp. 116–17.

60. TLS-1

March 23, 1933

Dear Ezra,

Fer the luv of God snap out of it. I'm no more sentimental about "murika" than Li Po was about China or Shakespeare about Yingland or any damned Frog about Paris. I know as well as you do that there's nothing sacred about any land. But I also know (as you do also) that there's no taboo effective against any land

and where I live is no more a "province" than I make it. To hell with youse. I ain't tryin to be an international figure. All I care about is to write.

When I write badly, sock me, I like it. But you gotta agree that the sort of thing you pointed out to me in your last, the "dark kisses" sort of thing, is not the first thing that hits you in my work. I acknowledge, however, that it does occur – but less and less frequently – It won't occur again. It's less than half of one percent anyway.

I'll be sending some typescripts soon to augment the ones which I presume Zukofsky forwarded yesterday. Go ahead with your selections from Spring and All

(wait a minute, I can't chew gum and smoke a cigarette at the same time) fer myself I – well, I admire your choice – adding only the ones I added in the script Z. sent you. I must confess I do like the ball-game – Is that sentimentality? So – s – o – o – o – o! Let's say: (*ing my preferences) I

By the way, Floss almost dropped dead at the expression of your love!

– once again: I* III IX* X XI XII XIV XVII XVIII* – and the ball-game at least of those I sent you

Soberly, I'm bound to agree that your criticism about The "soft spots" is valid. No doubt an immediate reaction from proximal pals would be the greatest thing in the wurrld for me. But, writing the way I do, soft spots must occur. I cannot stop for them. I *must* count on the well inclined reader. In the end I've got to get over the bad slips but I can only get over them by writing, chucking up the diamonds with the marl. If I didn't do it this way I'd be hamstrung, nutted, sunk in two minutes. But I do realize the difficulty.

Thanks fer wishing twenty more years life to me. In that time I may school myself to a purer product – also less of it.

Yrs.
Bill

Li Po: Seven poems by the Chinese master Li Po (*c.* 701–762) are among those translated by EP in *Cathay* (1915).

some typescripts: These additional poems were sent to EP with a letter from WCW dated March 24, 1933 (Yale).

the ball-game: "At the Ball Game" is section XXVI of *Spring and All;* it does not appear in the *Active Anthology*.

my preferences: This list does not correspond to the contents of the WCW section of the *Active Anthology*.

61. TLS-3

5 April [1933]
still running

Deer Bull

Noo poems to hand and a damn fine set/ to which – as you adumbrated – my crit. of yr/ earlier efforks do not or do less apply.

MUCH BETTER, more interesting fer you, me, an' everybody if I can run 30 pages of your inedits, or nearly so/ or at least of stuff that has only been printed in mags. and not in books.

Z/ says you agree to omit footnote.

Did he or you say something about the Ball Game.

I think the Portrait of the Lady the least interesting simply in *confronto* [comparison] with yr/ other stuff. The theme HAS been treated before. You have a lot of stuff that is certainly of more INTEREST (not talkin about the way it is done)

I shd. like thirty pages. Can you send on another fifteen.

Of this lot I shd. drop Portrait of Lady

Foot note

AND Ball Game

And replace them 4 pages by 15 others.

I DONT think the footnote and the Ball Game are up to the others.

The portrait of lady aint a patch on the "woman in bed." I am NOT saying anything about how its done. Its just less interesting because lots of young lads has seen lasses arses BEFORE.

Let Mr Leippert have you write it.

This group in me anth// shd. be a lancet or whatever, to cut in and open up interest; NOT to terminate ANY part of the interest aroused.

Did you read the Reznikoff mss/   mostly Lustra 1916, VERY cleanly done, but no advance in methodology.

Just as good what I did then.

I go'r job to cut out a bit and find something NOO. I spose by stickin to Hebe element I may be able.

NAOW what the hell am I to do about Tyler, who writes better than the rest but apparently WONT write about anything but buggary, in the pureent [*sic*] greek spirit/ not smut, not suggestion, but just straight honest gawd how good it is to buggah (in perfectly decorous language).

Seems to me (as editor) that might raise irrelevant discussion. After all the anth/ aint a reeligious revival meetin' either for Zionism or for Japanese noble affections.

I dare say he might make a few converts . . . .

He ought to have a TREEmenjus success in some quarters or nattiche [buttocks] or hind quarters or whatever you call 'em, but cd. be the better inserted apart from a methodological anth. containing non = soderastic poems by non- = soderasts.

Perfectly obvious that yr/ book is the best stuff now lyin unprinted in America. Aint I said as much on earlier occasions...or words that wd. imply so.

y

E

Z/ says: See Pound/Zukofsky, pp. 144–49.

footnote: WCW sent "A Foot Note" to *Poetry,* where it appeared in October 1933.

Portrait of the Lady: WCW's "Portrait of a Lady" was first published in *The Dial* for August 1920. It does not appear in the *Active Anthology.*

"woman in bed": See Letter 58 above.

Mr Leippert: James George Leippert, also known as J. Ronald Lane Latimer, was editor of *The Lion & Crown,* a Columbia University literary magazine that began in the fall of 1932. He later edited *Alcestis: A Poetry Quarterly* and founded the Alcestis Press, which published two of WCW's books: *An Early Martyr and Other Poems* (1935) and *Adam & Eve & the City* (1936).

the Reznikoff mss/: Nothing by the American Objectivist poet Charles Reznikoff (1894–1976) appears in the *Active Anthology.* Barry Ahearn speculates that the manuscript sent to EP may have contained "selections from the poems included in *Jerusalem the Golden*" (1934); see Pound/Zukofsky, p. 145.

Lustra 1916: This collection of EP's poetry gathered the work of his Imagist period.

Tyler: See "Biographical Notes" on TYLER, PARKER.

62. TLS-1

Octo. 3, 1933

Dear Ezra:

No, I haven't heard of the French Revolution (1933) only of the Cantos. Yes, I've read something of Douglas and something also of his American backers. The world's been looking in a convex mirror for some years, old darling, we can't most of use [*sic*] make out clearly more than the tip of the nose. For my own part I have no organized theories. My observation is that the too close organization of theories is likely to make one blind to what's taking place. But maybe I am getting rather too fascinated with the tip of my nose. Hope not but it may be so.

Yeah, I've heard of Roosevelt. He still has a few backers among the rich – but my guess is that he's losing them fast – to his credit. And I'll go this far with you that it's the question of credit that is blocking him. How will he unhorse the boodle-holders without turning radical-proletarian: an imbecility in this country, I agree with you. He's in a tighter hole every day to my way of feeling.

But fer ol' time's sake don't imagine I've turned New Masses. I'm fighting their stupidity every day and they are agin' me lock stock and barrel. All I claims is that I knows my material and I puts it down as I sees it. To witness, the enclosed with letter accompanying it.

We'll probably go ahead with Zuke's publishing scheme or some form of it. They want to bring out my "new" poems first. Quien sabe [who knows]? It may drag it's [sic] carcass along for a year. No great hopes here though I may be mistaken. We are counting on your backing. Thanks for the news of the [Active] anthology which I had begun to despair of.

Affectionate regards all around.

Yours
Bill

Douglas: See "Biographical Notes" on DOUGLAS, CLIFFORD HUGH.
New Masses: American Communist periodical; see Letter 31 above.
the enclosed: Unidentified.
Zuke's publishing scheme: The Objectivist Press; see "Biographical Notes" on ZUKOF-
SKY, LOUIS.

63. TLS-1

Nov. 8, 1933

Liebes Ezrachen:

When you go off the handle about the economic situation, though I acknowl-edge you may be in the right, you are all wet to me. But when you write as you have written in the preface to the Active Anthology you are superb. You do hold the lamp and it is lit. I am enheartened (is that a word?) and bound to proceed. It is especially good for me to have you point out where an American writer may and does fall into a colonial attitude. But, were we to follow you, I think we should be the only people on earth who did not believe that they alone were carrying the light. In that way we shoud [*sic*] lead the world, which would not be a colonialism. Possibly a fact. Never English or French.

Floss, who seldom sees what isn't there, likes your anthology: Businesslike. Focussed. Achromatic. Non-hazing.

We're going ahead with our Objectivist's Press. They, the others, wish to have my book of verse as the lead. It will cost more than I'm eager to put into it but the gesture must be made. Not that I'll be without help.

Tomorrow I speak to "the Poetry Club" N. Y. U. [New York University] on "poetry". My title: Love and Poetry or The Trick of Writing. Thank God you won't be there. Not that I think you have passed the age when you might listen!

I'm spreading the news re. the anthology whereever [*sic*] I can. i.e. the Modern Poetry Class of Texas College of Arts and Industries. Kingsville, Texas.

> Affectionately
> Bill

off the handle: An undated carbon copy of the letter to which this one is a response is housed at Yale. In it, EP argues, *contra* Letter 62 above, that "Douglas C. H. or Gesell are no more systems in the pejorative sense, than the effect of whatever and whatever else in a set of test tubes."

the preface: "Praefatio, aut tumulus cimicum," pp. 9–27. The Latin literally means "Preface, or heap of lice," but a better translation might be "Preface, or can of worms."

cost more: WCW gave the Objectivist Press a subsidy of $200 to underwrite the publication of *Collected Poems 1921–1931*; see Mariani, p. 340.

64. TLS-2

[November 17, 1933?]

Deer BHULL

Wet or dry/ God damn it if the amurkn pooplishing shistum werent solid dung/ my J/M wd. be in print. written in Feb.

and right or wrong it god damn well SAYS what has happened since, and nowt that HAS happened contradicts it.

What F. D. [Roosevelt] has accomplished has gone ON THAT LINE . . . F. D. is full of fuzz, or only says what the boops can digenst [*sic*].

Also this years consegna [declaration] and Muss's speech on econ/ three days ago.

ALL go on the lines of my Volitionist economics.

I am not merely a highschool kid who has read/ [C. H.] Doug[las]/ an I am not stoppin INSIDE Doug/ any more than I stopped inside Yaets [W. B. Yeats] and Fordie Madox [Ford].

as fer cat/piss

Praps/ yew strictly literary dilletantes cd/ expand onto at least the university system. and the teaching (or ??? what you wont) of licherchoor in out [*sic*] yoniworsities   clipping Shane Lesli to U. of Penn.

God damn it/ have you no sense of sanitation/ poisoning of wells/

pumping this infection into yet another new corp of students. . . .

IS there NOBODY with spirit enough to tackle the chronic putrefaction of american education and americ/ univs///??

Be anti social/ stick back in the aesthetic era of ole Gourmont (for whose generation there may have been nothing to do but stop upstairs in the viory [*sic*] tower)??

BUT if you cant understand economics and general life outside literchoor// at least look at what happens to the kids IN THE Colleges: and what kind of pewk and sawdust is given 'em . . .

GET to a printing press// get N. Y. to remark on Phila// stir up something...shit on Josh/ and Felix and whomever. . . .

I shd/ take the line "Obviously no literate students or students with an interest in writing can have entered the Univ. of P[ennsylvania]. for some time, otherwise it wd. be imposs[ible] that . . . etc. . . .

Fer Xt'zake bring up some kid to DO a little WORK. . . . .

Get the Insulls *out* of american education.

yrs E.

Wet or dry: The United States went from "wet" to "dry" when Prohibition officially ended on December 5, 1933.

my J/M: EP's *Jefferson and/or Mussolini: L'Idea Statale: Fascism As I Have Seen It* was finally published in London by Stanley Nott in July 1935. In it, EP argues that Mussolini has come closer than modern American presidents to embodying the ideals of Jefferson and the American Founding Fathers.

Muss's speech: See "Biographical Notes" on MUSSOLINI, BENITO.

my Volitionist economics: EP's *ABC of Economics,* published in London by Faber and Faber in April 1933, sets forth the principles of "volitionist economics."

Shane Lesli: Sir John Randolph Shane Leslie (1885–1971) was a prolific writer in many genres. His review of Joyce's *Ulysses* in the *Quarterly Review* for October 1922 had attracted EP's scorn; see Pound/*The Little Review,* p. 291. Leslie was apppointed Rosenbach Fellow in Bibliography at the University of Pennsylvania in 1933–34.

ole Gourmont: See "Biographical Notes" on GOURMONT, REMY DE.

Josh/ and Felix: Josiah Penniman and Felix Schelling, professors at the University of Pennsylvania; see Letter 52 above.

Insulls: At the height of his career, utilities magnate Samuel Insull (1859–1938) was on the boards of 65 American companies worth $2 billion. His empire collapsed dramatically in 1932, and he was indicted for mail fraud.

65. TLS-1

Feb. 16, 1934

Dear Ezra:

Whatever happens to Social Credit, re. the general lack of intelligence not to say the supine stupidity of those controling [*sic*] education, we agree. This is just to say that I have read the Harkness Hoot and salute you for your part in it.

Laughlin has replied to my first letter and I to his next and he to that and I to his last. I even sent him a few hundred words which he says he will print. He may drop in to see me in March.

Don't overlook, The Magazine, Calif. Bank Bldg, Beverly Hills, Calif. (attention of Mr. Kuhlman) They have taken the eight unpublished chapters of my White Mule to publish and pay for them once a month. The first is to come out in March. These with what appeared in Pagany constitute the first 5th. of the book. I'll be fortunate if I ever succeed in finishing it.

Do you see Miller's Blast. I do a short story for him once every three months.

But this is principally to say that I hereby reaffirm my allegiance to you on the score of a general orientation of knowledge and the bitching it gets at the hands of those who should know better. Something I am working on and which you may see later will perhaps explain why I am sensitive to the Harkness Hoot thing at this time.

Regards all around. More when there is more.

Yours
Bill

the Harkness Hoot: EP's essay "Abject and Utter Farce," an attack upon American higher education, appeared in the *Harkness Hoot: A Yale Undergraduate Review* for November 1933.

Laughlin: See "Biographical Notes" on LAUGHLIN, JAMES.

The Magazine: Edited by Fred Kuhlman, *The Magazine: A Literary Journal* ran from

December 1933 to June 1935. WCW's first contribution to it, in January 1934, was the short story "Life Along the Passaic River." The eleventh chapter of *White Mule* appeared in the March issue, and Chapters 12–19 followed at regular intervals until *The Magazine* ceased publication.

Miller's Blast: Edited by Fred R. Miller, with WCW as advisory editor, *Blast: A Magazine of Proletarian Short Stories* ran from October 1933 to November 1934. Each of the five issues carried a short story by WCW.

Something I am working on: Probably *The Embodiment of Knowledge;* see Letter 40 above.

66. TL-2

[April 1934?]

Deer WilYAMM

EXcellent artcl/ by you in Year Magazine. Section 2.

(But also excellent page by Munson in New Democracy. Jan 1. remplying [*sic*] to Doug Critics.)

The excellent artcl/ by W/C/W appears to me to say WOT I have been saying fer night [*sic*] oner 20 years.

Or as Bert Hessler used to say "Might as well agree with Ez cause in the end you'll have to from sheer exhaustion.

Wot ever become of that guy? didJa know him?? U[niversity of]/ P[ennsylvania].'05

That being so. (vide supra [see above]). Will you kindly take the following on faith/ until providence sees fit to vouchsafe unto thee the LIGHT.

or if not/ will you at any rate ADMIT that live ideas ought to be discussed openly and articulately (not merely kicked en bloc [in a lump])

AND that a very good guage [*sic*] of the liveness of an idea, is the solidity with which shits BLOCK the printing of it.

Wich beinKKK the kase. will you note that the following ideas are suppressed almost everywhere NOW.

and that we shd/ therefore seize every idea of printing them either as FACT or as question. It dont matter much which so long as they are discussed and people forced to think about 'em.

One I never do put save as a question.

ennyhow/ Ill putt em on sep[arate] sheet.

and trust you will see to getting em printed REPEATEDLY.

as woozle or whatshis name sez/ some things is dead and come [*sic*] battlz won etc.

GIT on to the next.

I.

Should the rent on money be paid by the people who have it or by those who haven't?

II.

The deficit of purchasing power is NOT static.

Every industry under the present system creates PRICES faster that [*sic*] it distributes the power to buy.

Footnote. The first really scares the pants off 'em. The second they wont think about.

Trob [trouble]/ with proletaires is that THE MARXIST literature WAS written by Flaubert. The job is done. Of course they cant do it now/ the pore simps are 60 years late. The tee/rain has WENT.

EXcellent artcl/: WCW contributed to a symposium on "The Status of Radical Writing," published in *A Year Magazine: Section Two* in April 1934. In this piece, he speaks of "the sluggardly offenses committed against good writing by the 'old reliable literary magazines'" and says that "Compared with Europe America is completely bare of books and they cost too much for every damn fool reason. So we don't read. . . . Therefore we don't know what Europe has done before us" (pp. 133–34).

page by Munson: Gorham Munson, "Douglas in Reviewerland," *New Democracy* 1:9 (January 1, 1934), p. 8.

Bert Hessler: See "Biographical Notes" on HESSLER, LEWIS BURTRON.

the following ideas: EP included these points in a number of the letters he wrote in the spring of 1934; see, for example, Pound/Cutting, p. 106.

woozle: Unidentified.

67. TLS-5

[October 1934]

Deer Doc/

Want yr/ attenshun fer pressin' case (humanity's) now that Miller has opened up his mag/ with my antiseptic if anon/ remarks frum Noo Eng/ Wkly.

Can you get it OVER to 'em, that labour party etc/ & come/ewe/nists are giving hoarhound drops instead of pittressin [*sic*] / and itza scientifik age.

Receipt for Proletarian story// one tough shituation and a shob///

was being done long before 1917.

They don't learn to write/ they are bloody bores/ all except the rugged ole lady's doc/ from Ruggerforg.

The prolet/ storys never ask WHY is the situation TOUGH. and the monotony iz because the answer IZ allus the same/

NOT enuff money.

(it is so monot/ that it bores me to mention it.)

DeKruif has bust into Ladies Hum Choinul/ that's teachin the million where we get a hundred/

Seton has pushed gobbits of my ABC econ/ into a novel of war and strikes/ hope it will git by.

In the hinterhum// will you ANSWER my V/E/ questionnaire/ and will you seereeyus// consider the following minimum program for action/ or the axioms on which to base it.

I. If the govt. owns crops and live stock sufficiently to order their destruction it owns 'em quite enough to issue orders for their delivery, I.E. currency paper (money) against 'em.

II. Get in touch with DeKruif (quietly) and with the *Gesell paper "The Way Out" 309* Madison St. San Antonio, Texas.

Gesell's Nat/ Econ/ Order has had to go to Texas to get pub[lishe]d/ in English// the rural disciples are bone ignorant of everything save the logical cohesion of their particular Koran, and have to be eddikated.

put up a yell about that BLAST ough [*sic*] to have one page of news.

They don't know that

II. You can NOT have reemployment/ you have got to recognize the diminishing need for labour. From mere econ/ or money or bookkeepibg [*sic*] angle it dont matter who does it. from angle of human justice, it shd/ be divided/

must come to 4 hour day. (gradually, I suppose)

III. Stamp scrip. (DouG or no Doug/

all these economists try to be solo tenors/ Science don't move that way.

Doug/ has established the main basis of value as CULTURAL HERITAGE/
he writes me that the stamp is a burdensome TAX/
moth balls/

I wrote him "a tax, if you insist, but a tax on sabotage" no comback [sic] on
that yet & ther'z been time for answer

cant stop fer an 60 year old Major/ any more than science stops because Koch
and Lister didn't find radium.

Gesell does NOT go the whole of Doug/ but stamp scrip is the NEXT step/
and dividends paid in s/s/ can come after it.

None of the bastuds seem to see that TWO kinds of money/ and the proportion
between fixed and demurrage money can do a great part of what Doug/ aims at
with his adjusted price/

the main thing being that s/S is comprehensible//

immediate danger is that it is so EASY to understand, that a lot of dumb
bunnies go Gesell/ and start crabbing antiseptics and vaccine etc. just because
they have found pitressin//

If you don't see this/ fer garzake ANSWER/ and if you agree, GIT AXSHUN.

In yewth we cd/ set in the daisy fields/ but at 50 we got to take up the white
man's/ I mean we have got to work ON the bastuds who are actually making the
laws, put this into literary lang. I aint got time. and deciding what is to be done
NOW, this week.

IV. No more biolog/ research for remedies cheaper than food (You orter read
de Kruif's stuff. I don't know whether he ought to be taught to write or not/ if he
wrote any better it might go to [sic] fast, bee [sic] too good to get into big time
circ/

Lemme see if I can condense. (p. 2)

I. stands as is/

II. No more blah about reemployment. Shorter hours, same pay.

III. Stamp scrip. leading to dividend.

IV. No more biolog/ research for remedies cheaper than food.

get miller to see it & give short manifesto.

The last one you might boost/ you ought to read DeKruif/ and help get him
under the skin of the communists and highbrows who merely crab his style
(which is bloody..) but which gets into the big circ/ where we dont.

To pull our weight at our age/ we have got to come nearer action than we cd/ at
25. At 25 an attempt to get into action wd/ have been mere waste of our time/
utterly futile & wd have prevented our doing our jobs.

My score since Aug/: interview Gazetta [sic] del Popolo.

half col/ Morning Post/ followed by 2 short letters/

2. cols/ El Sol Madrid/ quoting the 8 Questions.

Answers to question from Warburg/ Cole/ Buchi/ B. U. F. etc.

the bootlegged stuff in S' [Seton's] novel. (don't mention this, there is no indication/ the reader cant know where it comes from. we hope it will get past the Brit/ Dailies.

Noo Masses and the proletaires can't ANYhow ever know anything but the disease and its symptoms/ science has got to find the serums/

and gradually teach the sister in law to use boracis borasic/ etc.

The god damn ignorance of the N/Y. "Writer's Union" is enuff to make a rattle snake pewk.

let Miller be proletarian/ O/ K/ but with a program of ideas and measures that wd/ be some USE to the proletaires. If you can do better than these 4 points/ lemme SEE it. A program MUST be kept up to date/ and cant be lot of complicated ideology (as New Dem[ocracy]/ tends to seem).

> yr
>
> EZ
>
> P

[Encloses printed questionnaire entitled "Volitionist economics"] Gettum printed anywhere you can/ fer see if the god damn profs/ UNDERSTAND anything, or have merely memorized wot they heerd in kawlledge.

If T. C. Wilson write you/ be good/ he is etc/ worthy of yr/ eeesteam.

my antiseptic if anon remarks: In "Murkn Magzeens," *New English Weekly* 5:10 (June 21, 1934), pp. 235–36, EP asserts that "Fred Miller is for the moment about the best of the independent editors of fiction." Miller reproduces part of EP's article, without naming its author or source, in *Blast* for October–November 1934, under the title "Testimonials from England."

pittressin: A drug used to strengthen contractions in childbirth.

DeKruif: See "Biographical Notes" on DE KRUIF, PAUL.

Seton: The English novelist Graham Seton (Graham Seton Hutchison, 1890–1946) incorporated passages of EP's *ABC of Economics* (1933) almost verbatim into his novel *Blood Money* (London: Hutchinson, 1934). In 1936, Seton Hutchison became the head of a small political group called the National Workers' Party, whose slogan was "King-Race-Empire."

V/E/ questionnaire: EP's "Volitionist economics" questionnaire consisted of eight economic principles printed on the left side of a one-page broadside, with space for responses to them on the right. It is reproduced in Noel Stock, *The Life of Ezra Pound: Expanded Edition* (San Francisco: North Point Press, 1982), pp. 321–22. Beginning in August 1934, EP distributed the questionnaire widely to bankers, politicians, and writers all around the world.

the Gesell paper: See "Biographical Notes" on GESELL, SILVIO.

4 hour day: Beginning in 1931, EP advocated a shorter working day as a solution to the problem of mass unemployment. Rather than a dole, he favored cutting shifts from, say, eight hours to four, so that twice as many workers could share the available jobs. Full wages could be paid to each shift, with governmental subsidies for employers who could not otherwise afford to meet doubled payrolls. See *ABC of Economics* (London: Faber and Faber, 1933), pp. 20–21, 42–45, 54–56, 74, and Pound/Cutting, pp. 89–90.

stamp scrip: See "Biographical Notes" on GESELL, SILVIO.

CULTURAL HERITAGE: In a letter to Paul De Kruif of March 10, 1935 (Yale), EP explains that Douglas' concept of the cultural heritage includes "ALL PAST inventions . . . agricultural improvements . . . civilized habits . . . developed services, means of transport and communication, the time-saving implied in said manners."

he writes me: In a letter to EP of September 3, 1934 (Yale), C. H. Douglas writes: "Gesell's proposals seem to me merely a continuous and heavy tax." EP replied in a letter to the London *Morning Post* for September 21, 1934.

Koch and Lister: The German bacteriologist Robert Koch (1843–1910) identified the bacillae which cause, and helped develop vaccines to prevent, tuberculosis, anthrax, and Asiatic cholera. The English physician Joseph Lister (1827–1912) revolutionized surgery by his discovery of the antiseptic treatment of wounds. Radium was discovered by Mme. Marie Curie and her husband Pierre in 1898.

dividends: In the Social Credit program, the National Dividend was a direct governmental payment to consumers, intended to rectify the imbalance between consumer purchasing power and prices brought about because private banks charge excessive interest or usury for the use of money and credit. Douglas also recommended a system of price controls, which he called the "adjusted price." EP wanted to combine Douglas and Gesell by issuing the national dividends in the form of stamp-scrip currency.

Gazetta del Popolo: Gino Saviotti, "Il Poeta Economista: Colloquio con Ezra Pound," *Gazzetta del Popolo* (Turin), August 15, 1934.

Morning Post: The following items by EP appeared in the London *Morning Post* during September 1934: "A Poet's Questions for Economists: Mr. Ezra Pound's Posers" (September 3); "Volitionist Economics" (September 11); and "Demurrage Money: Mr. Ezra Pound Explains" (September 21).

El Sol Madrid: Adolfo Salazar, "Ensayos" [review of *ABC of Reading*], *El Sol* (Madrid), August 26, 1934, p. 2. The eight points of the Volitionist questionnaire are quoted at the end of the article, and EP's postal address is given for replies. Earlier, Salazar had interviewed EP for the issue of *El Sol* dated May 27, 1934, p. 5.

Warburg: James Paul Warburg (1896–1969) was a financier, inventor, composer, and the author of *The Money Muddle* (1934), which EP reviewed in *Time and Tide* for August 11, 1934. EP sent Warburg the Volitionist questionnaire with a letter dated August 27, 1934, and Warburg replied on September 11 (Yale).

Cole: George Douglas Howard Cole (1889–1959) was a socialist, an economic researcher, and a Reader in economics at University College, Oxford. Cole answered EP's questionnaire in a letter of August 23, 1934 (Yale).

Buchi: John Henri Buchi was the author of *Free Money: A Way Out of the Money Maze* (1933) and a leader of the Free Economy Federation of Great Britain, a Gesellite organization. He corresponded with EP from August 12, 1934, to June 22, 1935, and answered the Volitionist questionnaire on August 29, 1934 (Yale).

B. U. F.: The British Union of Fascists. Some of EP's correspondence with the organization between September 1933 and the spring of 1934 is housed at Yale. The B. U. F. was sympathetic to the Social Credit and Free Economy movements, but its answer to the Volitionist questionnaire does not appear to have survived.

the N/Y. "Writer's Union": A group of leftist authors who advocated a Federal relief project for writers. In a letter to Parker Tyler of May 1935, EP dismisses the organization as "merely a union of retrospective communists"; see Pound/Tyler, p. 17.

T. C. Wilson: The American poet, short-story writer, and editor Theodore Carl Wilson (1912–1950) taught at Oglethorpe College in Oglethorpe, Georgia. With EP and John Drummond, Wilson edited "Poems by One Hundred and Twenty-Six Outstanding Modern English and American Poets," *Bozart-Westminster* 9:1 (Spring–Summer 1935).

68. TLS-1

Oct. 23, 1934

Listen here Ezra:

Aw what's the use, you wouldn't understand. But anyhow, I can't answer your questions and I don't know how to forward your political ideas. It don't mean a ting to me. Sure, I'll embody anything I kin get hold of in the teknique of a, poem – ef I wuz writin eny. But as fer action as action. Taint in me. No use gettin mad. That won't get eider uv us anywhere. Ef you want action kum on back here and get it. You won't have any trouble finding it.

But when you sez you haven't got time to straighten out your own sentences and ask me to do it. As I sez? Oh well, what's the use of talking to a guy like that.

More another time but not now.

Yrs.
Bill

69. TLS-3

27 Oct. [1934]

Waaaal ole Wokunkus the Wombatt//

I am so god DAMN fed up with the sabotage of ALL living thought in the Eu S/ AH (and to hell with Frankie's Banks)

That I am ready AGAIN to start where I started in 1917 with the Litl/ Review/

I. E. to work like hell on HALF of a skimpy little 32 page shoddy magerzeen for TWO years. purrvided I controll [*sic*] ONE HALF of the contents.

This sounds like an ole gramphone disk BUT I might pint out that I have NOT been in this staterMIND since 1927/8 when I run Hexile/ fer to print you and Adolphe/ and prod/ on the dying PIGS.

Just had a good letter from Miller (very undigested as to knowledge and ideas;

I think he is doing best poss/ for short stories/ BUT that aint the whole show/

The full mental MEAL deemands more than that/ N[ew]. Dem[ocracy]/ is ok. as chappel for Douglasite methodists/ BUT THAT aint enuff.

Miller wants me to write a sassay on yer/ prose/ NO USE. No use my doing just a stray blurb/ everybody who reads me at all knows what I think of ole Doc WullYUMZ.

Barry still thinks "Forchoon" or Yale PEE/ress is about to be about to be about get [*sic*] to be getting ready to print some Frobenius.

Things are SO god damn stagnant with peepul wantin AUTOBIOGRAAPHY of E. P. and reminiscences of E. P. and what E/P/ thought in 1912 and what about what E P/ thought about JJHeezus Joyce in 1913

FAHRTZ!!!

Why not have a li'l meetin' place fer the blokes that are ALIVE *in 1935*??

(Not merely a group of Bob McA[lmon]'s cluck/chickens or peepul just reading what I recommended in 1919, such as [C. H.] Doug[las]/

Cumming's EIMI a bloody sight better than Jamie's last glooks/ or than Gertie [Stein] ever could be/ The blighter HAD something to say/ and damn well said it.

End of the Rhoosian cycle/ like Jimme Joycey wuz end of Keppitulist shit-opisspottt.

Use yr/ bean AND a postage stamp.

The live annimals [*sic*] ANNO THIS YEAR

are

Billyum Bullyums (I putt you foist to excerpt yr/ anxiety, and open yr/ mind to the rest of the list.

Leo Frobenius (even if his front name IS Leo)

Cocteau the hop

Crevel (probably, at least he was and is too young to be dead yet)

Cummings the Kumrad/

Ole EZ/ still steamin' at every pore.

young Loughlin, I beleev/ any how he is due here in a few days and I'll know.

I'd accept Miller as chacer [*sic*] of short stories/

I think he za Goodator [*sic*]/ wdnt ask anyone better to run the short stories/

not yet educated enough/ not got enough historic knowledge etc/ to be trusted with general ideas/ which anyhow, he has sense enough to omit from his own mag/

If you have any other nominates/ name 'em. IF you see any propulsive energy in any of our late allies/ tell PaPAAAAAAAAA.

I can't stop fer stiff legs/ no place fer personal ties in this war . . .

only way to keep mind alive is fer it cut off the daid branches.

I hope they had th' deCENcy to send you 31/41 on pretense that you wd/ review it/

you don't HAVE to/ only I whope you will see it/ and exkuss yerself at leat [*sic*] in privik. If I don't know more N I did, then fetch in coROner.

In view of Miller's letter/ might be more USE if I wrote to Yale Press IF you are in any way held up for pubctn/

Mule; will have to wait till finished, I shd/ think/ but what bout short stuff, case notes etc/ nuff of that fer a BUKK yet???

Answer re/ lil magg/

say what you SEE as available// both as resources and as Matiere a imprimer [material to print] . . .

Objectivist printing too good/ even if it costs no more than bunf printing, it don't look near enough to the ground for what I am now discussing. Also can magazine on continual segregation and exclusion////

yrz

EZ

Frankie's Banks: The Glass-Steagall Bank Act of 1933, passed and signed into law during the first hundred days of President Roosevelt's administration, created the Federal Deposit Insurance Corporation, which offered financial protection of deposits in all banks that qualified for FDIC membership by meeting certain federal standards. Eventually, nearly all U. S. banking institutions became FDIC (or ''Frankie's'') banks.

Adolphe: See ''Biographical Notes'' on RODKER, JOHN.

Miller: In a letter to EP of October 17 [1934] (Yale), Fred Miller, editor of *Blast,* says: ''I wonder if you could be prevailed on to do a short critical piece about the proletarian stories of Bill Williams; staying clear of the Douglasite economics!''

Barry: See ''Biographical Notes'' on BARRY, IRIS. In a letter to EP of October 11, 1934

(Yale), Barry reports that *Fortune* magazine is considering an article on the work of Leo Frobenius by his American assistant, Douglas Fox, and that Yale University Press is considering Fox's translation of Frobenius' *Schicksalkunde* [customs having to do with fate]. Neither the article nor the translation was accepted.

Frobenius: Leo Frobenius (1873–1938) was a German anthropologist and archaeologist who studied the tribal cultures of Africa. His major work was *Erlebte Erdteile,* 7 vols. (1925–29). EP met him in 1927 and was influenced by his concept of cultural ideas in action, or *Paideuma.*

Cumming's EIMI: See "Biographical Notes" on CUMMINGS, EDWARD ESTLIN.

Jamie's last glooks: Joyce's "Work in Progress," published in 1939 as *Finnegans Wake*; see "Biographical Notes" on JOYCE, JAMES.

Cocteau: See "Biographical Notes" on COCTEAU, JEAN. "Hop" is a slang term for opium.

Crevel: The French surrealist poet René Crevel (1900–1935) was the author of *Les pieds dans le plat* [feet in the mouth] (1933). EP's wording here seems almost to anticipate Crevel's imminent suicide.

Loughlin: See "Biographical Notes" on LAUGHLIN, JAMES.

31/41: Eleven New Cantos XXXI–XLI by Ezra Pound was published in New York by Farrar and Rinehart on October 8, 1934.

Miller's letter: In his letter to EP of October 17, Fred Miller says of WCW's fiction: "Here's a writer with everything, no contemporary fictioneer in the USA comes anywhere near him and ain't it about time SOME appreciable bloc of the 'reading public' was catching up with him?" The Yale University Press had recently published EP's *ABC of Reading* and *Make It New,* but book publication of WCW's *White Mule* (1937) and *Life Along the Passaic River* (1938) had to await Laughlin's founding of New Directions.

70. TLS-3

No, I did not receive the new Cantos. I'd be mor'n pleased to give you my feeble slant on them.

Nov. 14, 1934

Dear Ezra:

's O.K. with me if you want to get up another blast into the blue but don't try to make me into another liter'y effigy in the long list of straw men. I'll send you anything I have any time I have it but I'm too Gad damned busy even to scratch my ass where it itches for any thought but composition. I simply don't give one fuckin' damn what happens. I write when I writes and I gets it printed when I can and that's all I care – just at present. But what I has you kin have – if and when you want it.

Now let's see what there is: but before that I want to agree that Objectivist press was no good, too expensive, too everything it shouldn't have been. Not that I want to place blame on anyone (because I like the guy) but [Charles] Reznikoff had it too much in his own hands   but that's old stuff. Nothing went as it was planned, no one could keep close enough to the job so it just fell to Rezzi. I give him credit for seriousness and conscientious energy. It should have been six books, smaller, on cheap paper, etc. etc. costing half the price. Thus we learn (maybe).

Just (the other day) learned of Orage's death. That's bad in every way for I liked his stuff. It's bad for me too as he, along with a certain Nott, had hinted that an english edition of my In the Am. Grain might shortly be brought out. That's that.

To return to myself: (1) The first book of White Mule is about finished, 24 chapters, 12 to 18 typed pages each, 300 to 450 typed pages, not a big book but a book in any case. It will be called, White Mule – The First Year and More. It takes the damned brat up to the end of her first summer vacation, aged 16 months. It also ends a phase in her old man's affairs. I had intended to canvass the N. Y. publishers again through an agent but – as I sez: I don't give a damn, either way. (2) Aside from that I have another book of poems almost roughed out. This time it's going to be preceeded [sic] or accompanied by prose somewhat in the manner of Spring and All; not quite the same though and with prose of a wholly different quality, much more to the point and entirely about writing and *an* attitude toward it which may be called the classic attitude – as broad as a shot in the pants – (pardon me) as broad as learning might have been and is in the practice (not in the shit-criticism) of poetry. I want to make the chain perfect from the beginning up to today with appropriate quotations from the mouthes [sic] of "the babes" themselves. Vita Nuova and all that – as much as I know of anything. (3) Case notes there are, here and there, but little unpublished. As you may or may not know I have the first chapter in a book to be published Dec. 2 this year – America and Alfred Stieglitz. My assignment was "the cultural background" – about 10,000 woids. We had luck in that The Literary Guild chose the book for its cash – maybe as much as $150 – they say. Anyhow, there's that to republish if anyone wants it. I'm not suggesting, just enumerating. (4) Then there are the short stories all of which have come out in magazines. My only suggestion there would be a book of stories selected from Blast, mine and Fred [Miller]'s along with any others. I don't think there are enough of mine for a book and I haven't time now to write any more – though you never can tell. I never know when the disease may strike me.

(5) Your direct question merits a paragraph for itself. As to "case-notes" – speaking more fully – I can't recall what there are. I do have a mass of miscellaneous stuff dating back to my as yet unpublished notes on your cantos, reams and reams of chance jottings, vague notes on everything imaginable but little that's digested. God, there's a bushel of it. I once wrote a sort of attack on the scientificallity [sic] and philosophicality of the age with the general – to say nothing of religion – with poetry as the inevitable and neglected alternative. When I say poetry, I don't need to tell you I mean, the life of which poems are the record – the partial record. It may be this which now in its later, more condensed form I am to put among the poems in the next book of poems. The first shot at the thing lies in a drawer, it is loose, undigested, unarranged. If you care to waste the time on it I'll send it to you. It is at least legible having been typed out by my amenuensis [sic] – the owman [sic] who's [sic] kids I have cared for for ten years in compensation for her typing. I speak of this mass of stuff only because you started it. It is probably very bad, sophomoric – anything you like – it raves in places at it knows not what – incoherently. Maybe you in your all-seeing goodness could make a selection. I'd never ask it of anyone but myself. Do you want to be my literary executor? I mean it. Yes or no. I have some good books too. I hate to bother my sons. One should keep such things more in the horizontal family of the one generation than in the vertical one of his family by birth.

There may be other chance notes but I can't think of any for the present.

My mother is getting old. She is lame, hears little and sees only with difficulty. I took her to the oculist this morning, she has cataracts on both eyes. She is lively though but groans at night when it is cold. My kids are away, one at college one at Prep School in Pennsylvania. I miss them like hell – and should like to bust them in the jaw sometimes for their dman [sic] foolishness. The older shines at English – God help him. The younger admires his brother and probably end [sic] by shining at English also – though swimming is his forte to date. Floss had a serious operation this summer but came out of it in good shape. Less and less do I feel the cuntish call. The energy, I think, is unaffected thereby. Perhaps the conservation is essential. I am a little in doubt as to whether or not it's an interim or a permanent change of life. In many ways a change for the better.

I can add few of the young to your list except Josephine Herbst, wife of John Herrmann of "What Happens". She has written a novel I like. Just out, The Executioner Waits. I was surprised as I tried to like her for a long time without success. She has come along slowly and isn't young – but she has done something this time. It is writing to be saying something and saying it by writing it not just by saying it's so. Deep stuff. Makes me feel as though the floor had been cut away under my feet. Not heavy stuff, just stuff that opens up the void and makes you feel that there's no parachute but some extraordinary sort of intelligence – not from a skull in a gravel pit.

I haven't anyone else to add. I went to a liter'y tea to meet Edw. O'Brien a week or two ago. What a gang of cut-throat [*sic*]. They were positively trampling each other to get near the innocent (comparatively) looking publishers who were there. I didn't see one human being present – aside from O'Brien. Yes, one young man did escape early but I couldn't catch his name. What's the matter with your old friend in England Wyndham Lewis? Not that I give a damn but he is quoted now and then in oracular fashion. I suppose you're really interested in this neck of the woods.

'Nuff for the present. I got woik to do.

Regards to Dorothy. Please tell her Floss is really better after a serious illness.

Yr ol fren
Bill

my feeble slant: WCW reviewed EP's *Eleven New Cantos* in *New Democracy* for January 15–February 1, 1935.

Orage's death: See "Biographical Notes" on ORAGE, ALFRED RICHARD.

Nott: See "Biographical Notes" on NOTT, STANLEY CHARLES.

White Mule: A fictionalized account of the history of Florence Herman Williams' family, re-named Stecher in the novel. It begins with the birth of the protagonist, and describes the struggles of her immigrant parents, Joe and Gurlie.

another book of poems: WCW published no book that fits this description.

Vita Nuova: The *Vita Nuova* (*c.* 1290) of Dante affords a precedent for the mixing of poetry and prose. The connotations of the title (New Life) also appealed to WCW; see Thirlwall, p. 141.

America and Alfred Stieglitz: See "Biographical Notes" on STIEGLITZ, ALFRED.

a sort of attack: The Embodiment of Knowledge; see Letter 40 above.

my amenuensis: Mrs. Johns; see Mariani, pp. 308, 350.

My kids: William Eric Williams was attending Williams College in Williamstown, Massachusetts, and Paul Williams was enrolled in a private academy in Mercersburg, Pennsylvania.

a serious operation: Floss underwent abdominal surgery on August 16, 1934; see Mariani, p. 361.

Josephine Herbst: The Executioner Waits by the American novelist Josephine Herbst (1892–1969) was published in New York by Harcourt, Brace in 1934. A saga of the Trexler family, the novel provides a panorama of American life between the end of World War I and the Depression.

John Herrmann: The American novelist and labor-union organizer John Herrmann (1900–

1959) was associated with WCW's *Contact* magazine and with Robert McAlmon's Contact Editions. Herrmann's works include *What Happens* (1926), "The Big Short Trip" (1932), and *Summer Is Ended* (1932).

Edw. O'Brien: From 1915 to 1940, Edward J. H. O'Brien (1890–1941) edited a popular annual entitled *The Best Short Stories of* . . . [the year in question].

71. TL-4

[January 1935]

Deer Bull

Why the wayward perversity amid the laurels/ Defeated me YARRSE!

Is a hoos [*sic*] defeated for leaving thistles for clover?

The DEFEATED as I have seen 'em, are the yanks who try for Europe and can't make the grade/ or who set down in buffalo, in lavender melancholy, opinin thet "life has passed em by".

The failure to recognize colonial status, is a lack of objectivity. The acceptance of colonial status is a damn nuther matter/ BUT to inhabit a gang of simps who will neither try to make a nation, nor admit the absence of essentials for a LIFE is just shifless.

To make an "asylum" in the West, fer freedumb/ fer thought/ is one damn fine aim/

but to mug round masturbatin' and pretending that the JOB IS DONE, is just Canby and piffle.

Also it took VAN BUREN in lace ruffles to put Andy Jackson over. It took all the pair of 'em cd/ do, and they warn't bickering over patent rights or which of 'em cd/ self = suffice.

Team worrk, my buckyo.

And all the tin wreaths on Andy. The HERO ov New Orleans AFTER peace had been signed/ but bloody good thing he won it, otherwise the peace wd/ have been unsigned or emended to leave the bloody britons lards of the bayou.

the highly questionable conqueror of the Seminoles//

waal/ wall/ and that wasn't in the name of the noble savage; and the inspiration of alligators and other exotic fauna.

Dig in; by [*sic*] beamish dago. Have roots/ roots is O. K. all jake with yr/ uncle.. but dont git yourself HAD by the local imitation of Bloosmbury [*sic*]. There aint one other collyBORE/ator in the Steiglitz [*sic*] who has ever looked fact in the face. All trying to palm off the second rate, and to avoid the international criterion.

Intelligence is international, stupidity is national and art (meaning paint, and spatical [*sic*] art) LOCAL.''

Frankie has mebbe pushed out the N. Y. bankers/ and ay [*sic*] be throwing the whole people bung down the shit house to INTERNATIONAL bank controll [*sic*]. Which is la merrdre [shit]. Bigod, you get up and fight against any plop into the Leg of Nations, the Limb of Satan, Woodie Wilsons' arsebag / so long as bastids in Geneva are preaching the COMMODITY theory of money.

so long as VonMises is telling honest to gawd young american stewdents that money is a commodity.

(Parenthesis, do you know anything about masons, or do american masons know whether they are likely to be HAD by the Grand Orient?

That is a private question, no use to broad cast [*sic*] it. But fer krizake keep yr/ EYE open/ and dont get it woolled over by pretty theories about the geomprphic [*sic*] survey.

I have told yew moren onct that I am interested in civilization, and that I dont care a fhahrt whether it is in Peoria or Persepolis/ in OUR TIME is a locus, just as well as in any spatial area.

OUR TIME oughtn't be arse blow any other. and no parrochial fog ought to cover it.

A man's physical presence is infinitely less than his imaginative presence. he can shift the former in a day or in six days.

I am much more present in Rutherford at this moment than in Chiavari or in the next valley.

Also/ to changer yr/ ijees/ AT THE AGE OF 12 I saw Venice and decide [*sic*] it was O/K/ that I wd/ get back to it as soon as possible. Fail to see any defeat in his [*sic*].

You might ovbseve [*sic*] (orig/ or via Frobenius) cunt = al tendency to enclose and the cock = al tendency to move OUT.

Yr/ parents moved out, and planted th infunt Willum in alien field.

You might also observe that the infunt Wm/ having no RACIAL unity, grabbed a geographic branche [*sic*] and held on/

the egregius Ez/ having 15/16 racial unity, and the 1/16 merely adjancent [*sic*] oisish [*sic*], had no need of superfluous unity of location/ no fear complex about gittin lost if he traversed a geo/ or polit/ frontier. wot the HellBO!!

Why shd/ I wish to live among polish semite/ gents with teutonic monikers/ sweede [*sic*] etc/ or in defective climates.

Do follow yr/ own prinCiplz and USE words. Deafeat [*sic*]? failure in effort, failure to do something you set out to DO /

not failure to arrive in S. Francisco when you started for New York.

Izza wild hoss DEFEATED when it goes to pasture instead on [*sic*] starvin on a mountageous rock??

Order, kum teh ORDER

laurels: This letter is a response to WCW's essay "The American Background" (see Letter 70 above). In a passage on p. 30, WCW says, "To many writers the great disappointment of the years just after the war was that Amy Lowell, while sensing the enterprise of a reawakened local consciousness, touched it so half-heartedly and did so little to signal plainly the objective. . . . Pound, defeated at home, did far better, in reverse, from abroad."

an "asylum": This is not a quotation from WCW's essay, but an ironic pun.

Canby: See "Biographical Notes" on CANBY, HENRY SEIDEL.

VAN BUREN: See "Biographical Notes" on VAN BUREN, MARTIN. His name does not occur in WCW's essay on "The American Background."

Andy Jackson: See "Biographical Notes" on JACKSON, ANDREW. On p. 15 of "The American Background," WCW writes: "Only Jackson carried the crudeness of his origins successfully up to the top by the luck of battle, and for a short time only. And when he did, as Ezra Pound has recently pointed out, it was Jackson who, because of his basic culture, was able first to smell out the growing fault and attack the evidence of a wrong track having been taken, the beginning raid on public moneys by private groups, which he turned back for a few years."

tin wreaths: EP here echoes the third section of his poem *Hugh Selwyn Mauberley* (1920), in which he asks, "What god, man, or hero/ Shall I place a tin wreath upon!" The phrase is an ironic inversion of one in the Second Olympian Ode of Pindar, who asks, "What god [TINA THEON], what hero [TIN' EROA], what man [TINA D'ANDRA] shall we praise?"

Bloosmbury: The neighborhood of the British Museum in London was the haunt of many free-spirited artists, writers, and intellectuals in the decades just before and just after the Great War. Thus "Bloomsbury" became synonymous with a cultural milieu of monied, artistically inclined, politically liberal, sexually emancipated, and rather precious individuals.

the Steiglitz: See "Biographical Notes" on STIEGLITZ, ALFRED.

Intelligence is international: This dictum by the French Fauvist painter Maurice de Vlaminck (1876–1958) was reported in Fritz Vanderpyl's essay "Maurice Vlaminck," *The Dial* 69 (December 1920), p. 591.

Frankie: The Glass-Steagall Bank Act of 1933 curbed the power of large New York investment houses such as J. P. Morgan and Company. Early in 1934, however, President Roosevelt and his advisers drastically devalued the dollar against foreign currencies. This caused EP to suspect that the U. S. Treasury was colluding with overseas banking interests.

the Leg of Nations: The League of Nations was created at the time of the Versailles Treaty of 1919, as the first step toward a world government that would prevent future international conflicts. Although the plan was largely an initiative of the American President,

Woodrow Wilson, the United States Senate refused to ratify the treaty by which the U.S. was to join the League. In January 1935, a group of senators led by James Pinckney Pope of Idaho revived the idea of U. S. membership in the League. Again, the proposal failed.

VonMises: The conservative Austrian economist Ludwig Edler von Mises (1881–1973) was professor of International Economic Relations in the Graduate Institute of International Studies at Geneva from 1934 to 1940.

masons: Freemasonic lodges in France, Italy, Spain, and South America are known as Grand Orients. They have traditionally been more anticlerical, politically radical, and open to Jews than the lodges of Germany, England, and the United States. In late-nineteenth-century France, many religious, social, economic, and political ills were blamed upon a Jewish-Masonic conspiracy, supposedly centered in the Grand Orient of Paris, to destroy Christianity and rule the world. The existence of such a conspiracy was reaffirmed by the spurious *Protocols of the Learned Elders of Zion* and by much anti-Semitic propaganda of the 1920s and 1930s.

Peoria or Persepolis: Peoria, Illinois, was the home of *Direction,* a little magazine edited by Kerker Quinn to which both EP and WCW contributed in the autumn of 1934. Peoria is also a byword for middle-American attitudes and values; according to a popular adage, if something new will "play in Peoria," it will succeed anywhere. Persepolis was the ancient capital of the Persian Empire of Darius and Xerxes (5th Century B.C.).

Chiavari: A town near Rapallo on the Ligurian coast of Italy.

Frobenius: For Leo Frobenius, see Letter 69 above.

72. TLS-1

Jan. 14, 1935

Dear Old Sock:

The cartoon returned herewith. Not bad. But how in hell I ever got into it is more than I can say. Must be someone who knows my publisher.

Your judgement, too, is superficially correct. No doubt if my cocky ancestors had been driven by penury to Tasmania I'd be sticking up for that spot in the sun also – perhaps. I know it looks attractive to say I stay where I am out of fear – which is more or less true. But there are all kinds of fears. Sometimes we fear to lose what we hold precious more than we fear to lose ourselves. I have never had any illusions about places. They mean nothing to me. I know that I will be the same in any of them. Granted, I'd enjoy seeing those I love and admire more often than is possible here but here I have the materials I am familiar with with which to work. One balances the other. I wish it were different. I have found by trial that I work best here – in spite of the drawbacks.

Thanks for the Vlamink [*sic*] dictum, I'd seen something like it before. Stupidity can also be international.

You never were a lover of the flora and fauna of any place. You couldn't even tell the difference between lilies-of-the-valley and burdock. You do seem to have an affection for olive trees and a few of the well known flowers. That's you. I have a quasi-scientific curiosity about vegetables, I put it broadly – to please you. The damned fish in the river are probably of a curious sort. That's why I stopped to see if I could catch one. I'll come along in time. And, by the way, that mountain wasn't named. Wouldn't it be funny if it should turn out to be some other one which you had better have been climbing?

It'd be fun to drop in on who's this in London for a short talk, on Bob [McAlmon] in Barcelona – if he could spare the time to be civil – to spend a week or two in Paris even to visit Rapallo – not many can do it.

I'm doing a criticism of your Cantos, the new ones, for Munson's sheet. I admire you, old cock, you can believe that but I ain't you and nothing could make me you, not even my desire to be so did I have such a desire. From my study of plants I find that nature is various and genius about evenly divided between them all. But even that does not kill regret nor cure desire.

My best to you.

Bill

the cartoon: Unidentified.
the Vlamink dictum: See Letter 71 above.
a criticism of your Cantos: See Letter 70 above.

73. TLS-1

Feb. 1, 1935

Dear old pal of mine!

Well, I suppose the pore ol' British, being relatives of me father, have to have some instruction – sooooo I'll start off by sacrificing the enclosed masterpieces to 'em. 3 poems   But grudgingly. Why in hell should I sacrifice my hard screwed to life children in order to save their blasted hides?

So take 'em and say thanks.

If I get more time this afternoon I'll see what else I can find – after I get a taste of the deeelicious cream puffs I saw my wife making for her damned ladies that she has to entertain once in a while so her husband can reap a harvest by being popularly supposed to be an intelligent and discriminating physician in this here daintily balanced suburb.

All I asks is that if you don't happen to agree with me that these are poems, that you'll say so clearly and let me dispose of them elsewhere.

I haven't touched the verse technique recently, I've been too busy getting the White Mule harnessed up for delivery. Last week I got heeeem off, to an agent (nice gal!) who says maybe yes, maybe no: 319 typed pages (double space) 22 chapters. Takes the cheeeild up to the tender age of 15 months. I like the book as well as anything I have done with prose.

Thanks for the impetus that sent me digging into my notes for the poems. I'll do everything I can to get you at least a paragraph or two every two weeks.

My best and my appreciation for the opportunity to shove my pen in the service of a blind, stupid and generally unwilling humanity. "They lack *wit,* more than anything else." said an old associate of old artists to me this morning. "Oh they're smart enough, it isn't that, but they're witless, that's what's the matter with them."

> My distinguished salutations
> Bill

the enclosed masterpieces: The three poems are "View of a Lake," "Invocation and Conclusion," and "Genesis." EP may have asked WCW, in a letter that has not survived, to contribute to the *New English Weekly;* but none of these poems appeared there.

an agent: Possibly Mavis McIntosh of McIntosh and Otis.

an old associate: Possibly WCW's wife, Floss.

74. TL-3

16 Feb [1935]

Waal/ me yole CRUMBO!!

That is a very fine bit of sloggin! Fer Ezry 'ome and cuntry!! HooRAY; HHOOOray!

an if I spend all me time ritin epiks and boostin social credit/ WHEN do I eat . . .

gHEEZ/ time I looked fer the gate/ recepits [*sic*]!! waaal///pass thet.

In the mean time, wotter bout licherchoor. I have ope'd the N/E/W/ to kumrad cummings.

AN fer all use of language AS COMMUNICATION, I reckon th pyper is now open. At any rate HOPE to make it as strong as Egoist or Little Review. (dunno how far I can get . . . or how much left-over from O/R/O's [*sic*] lichery epotch will remain, in spite of me.

BUT, as Blast is dead; etc. do send on whatevr live stuff there is.

Zuk[ofsky]/ seems to have dried up/ and I dunno/ them thaaar jews/ can't find any trace in Abolitionist movment [*sic*]/ and they dont seem to cotton to counter-usury.

communists just DUMB/ and jews akin to communists (even if never heard of Moscou [*sic*]).

we WANT more of Wm Yam Wms/ in the N. E. W.   send all "modernistic" mss to me.

I dunno whether Marianne wd/ be useful in London or not/

New Democ/ dont seem able to get the licherachoor going/ prob/ better not to try it. at any rate N/E/W/ has room for about all that is worth bothering about/ I shd/ fink (hey WOT??)

I want to do a 32 page/ Soc/ Credit anth/ late in the year (or poss, it wont git printed till 1936) sprung time.

I also want to get the fact that LIVE writers exist (and the names of all of 'em) into N/E.W/ pubk/ by Xmas.

a fair part of the BRIEF list has been lined up, and chance of having 'em in, or reported on.. aint so worse.

Anyhthing [*sic*] you have to say re/ my Amurkn Notes, please send me/ also any dope on the amurikaaaa. econ/ and polit/ or the pussycologic resistence [*sic*] AZ seen by Wm/ Crumbo McCarlos BillYamps.

Someday; somebuddy, somewhere; might some what indi(some) cate the hist/ of contemp/ poesy in my anfologies/

Imagistes, Catholic, Profile, Active (plus the encloraged marginals). at times when I haven't been pushing one or anuvver periodicl// whether for 20 years there has been a time when I have neglected to get good stuff printed sooner that it otherwise wd/ have.

Did I ever quote you that jem of Mike G's: "How *can* you say you had Aragon published in England?"

why don't you see more ov th Kumrad? e: e: c[ummings]/ 4 Patchin Place// very human, you don't HAVE to be clever ALL the time he around.

Wot th hell"z bekum of Bob [McAlmon]? drunk all the time, and too sulky to write, or WOTTELL?? Tell him to send on something an English printer can print wiffout gettin pinched.

See any way I kin pick up a couple of hundred shrunk kundrum dollars?

NOT that I am going to stop work to earn 'em. But still, you might hear of something.

Ole Rouse is a makin a llovely traduction of the Odyssey (he did it fer kids, condensed, now doing it fer adolescents and pubertized.)

Buntin' sweatin' away at Firdusi, which he aint yet found a way to make readable. Dirty dumb middle eastern fat heads.

---

sloggin': EP is responding to WCW's review of *Eleven New Cantos* in *New Democracy* 3:10–11 (January 15–February 1, 1935), pp. 191–92. In it, WCW praises EP's attack upon usury and says that *The Cantos* "should become an Index of the Damned and Damnable, the anatomized *Inferno* of our lives today."

kumrad cummings: See "Biographical Notes" on CUMMINGS, EDWARD ESTLIN.

O/R/O's lichery epotch: See "Biographical Notes" on ORAGE, ALFRED RICHARD.

Blast: See Letter 65 above.

jews . . . in Abolitionist movement: In a letter to Hugo Fack of December 1934 (Yale), EP says, "re/ jews, have never been antisemite, but things do pile up. Is there any trace of jews in abolitionist movement? I doubt. They were all over the south foreclosing mortgages after 1865. No jews in any ECON refor/ or monetary reform." See also Pound/Zukofsky, pp. 157–60.

Wms/ in the N. E. W.: WCW's last published contribution to the *New English Weekly* was the "Jacataqua" chapter of *In the American Grain,* which appeared in the issue for January 3, 1935. He broke with the journal in March; see Letter 78 below.

Marianne: Marianne Moore's poem "Smooth Gnarled Crepe Myrtle" appeared in the *New English Weekly* for October 17, 1935.

New Democl: On EP's recommendation, James Laughlin became the editor of a literary page in *New Democracy*; it began in the fall of 1935 and was called "New Directions."

Soc/ Credit anth/: See "Biographical Notes" on NOTT, STANLEY CHARLES.

Amurkn Notes: "American Notes" was the title of a column on American affairs that EP contributed to the *New English Weekly* at irregular intervals between January 1935 and April 1936.

my anfologies: Des Imagistes (1914), *Catholic Anthology 1914–1915* (1915), *Profile: An Anthology Collected in MCMXXXI* (1932), and *Active Anthology* (1933).

that jem of Mike G's: The American novelist, playwright, and social critic Mike Gold (1893–1967) became the editor of *The New Masses* in 1928. In a letter to EP of January 30, 1934, Gold asks, "How can you say you had Aragon's poem printed in London when Aragon would like nothing better than to blow everyone [*sic*] of you Fascists off the face of the earth" (Yale). Gold refers to "Red Front," a poem by the French surrealist and Communist writer Louis Aragon (1897–1982). e. e. cummings' translation of "Red Front" appeared in EP's *Active Anthology*.

Ole Rouse: A prose translation of Homer's *Odyssey* by the British classicist William Henry Denham Rouse (1863–1950) was serialized in the *New English Weekly* and published in book form in 1937.

Buntin': See "Biographical Notes" on BUNTING, BASIL.

75. TLS-1

Broadside & letter to hand today. Whatever I can do I'll do. Cummings doesn't much want to be seen.

Feb. 25, 1935

Dear Ezra:

Some more stuff goes forward with this. If you're not interested, say so.

The long poem in the batch I last sent is the weakest. I did it in a hurry – which is no excuse and none intended – but I am sorry I let the thing go as it was. It inclines me to say now that I'm in no shape just at present to be sending you new stuff every two weeks. I can't write fast enough – what with the other things I have to do – to keep up with the literary demands made on me. I haven't a poem anywhere around any more – with at least five demands being made on me for new work (without pay, of course!) It can't be done.

Then, God damn it, when I do send a poem to a pay mag and it's accepted, the bastards keep it in a draw [*sic*] for a year or more. I did one for New Republic for which they paid me $11. last fall. But it ain't seen light of day as yet. So I did them another (not too hot) for which they paid me $6. – so that the first one might appear at once – but no action. I sold a good poem to Esquire over a year ago and it hasn't come out yet. Then I sold an Elegy for D. H. Lawrence which Poetry: a Magazine of Verse grabbed last summer. It is coming out, probably, in March. But it was going to head the issue – only Yeates [*sic*] sent them a play so my poem gets the back pages. I told them that all they needed was to have something by Xerces [*sic*] and Zukowsky [*sic*] and they'd have thr [*sic*] whole tail end of the alphabet cornered.

Recently I've been waiting for an order then sitting down and dashing off the first thing that comes into my head. That's bum dope if continued too long. Last night, half drunk I produced this at 1 A. M., for the Oxford (England) English Journal – or some such name. They asked me to interceded [*sic*] for them with you. I never heard of them before; they seem to think you orter send something.

I forgot to say I sent a prose story effect to N. E. R. at just about the time you asked me to send you things for them. You may see it there – medde [*sic*] not – but if you do you'll understand.

Anything I can shake out of the hat I'll ship as usual to you but don't count on a regular two week budget.

Everything still tastes the same – and in reasonable abundance can be enjoyed as usual.

Wish I could get over there. Love to Dorothy – to hell with you.

Bill

Broadside: Unidentified.

more stuff: This group of writings has not been identified, but it apparently contained "Proletarian Portrait"; see Letter 76 below.

The long poem: "View of a Lake" was published in *Artists' and Writers' Chap Book,* May 3, 1935, p. 28. The published version differs somewhat in punctuation and wording from the typescript version sent to EP with Letter 73 above.

New Republic: WCW's poem "The Yachts" appeared in the *New Republic* for May 8, 1935; "To a Dead Journalist," in the number for July 31, 1935.

Esquire: Nothing by WCW ever appeared in *Esquire.*

an Elegy for D. H. Lawrence: Lawrence had died in 1930. WCW's "An Elegy for D. H. Lawrence" appeared in *Poetry* 44:6 (March 1935), pp. 311–15.

a play: The same issue of *Poetry* opened with W. B. Yeats' play *A Full Moon in March,* pp. 299–310.

Oxford . . . English Journal: The journal to which WCW refers has not been identified.

N. E. R.: No short story by WCW appeared in the *New English Weekly* in 1935.

76. TLS-2

March 5, 1935

Dear Ezra:

Who the hell is Eliot, that shit ass. I don't want to get on in England if it has to be at the cost of getting a "yes" from that pot of addled ewe's snot. He can't begin to know anything that is of the least importance to me. His knowledge isn't even of the kind that could affect me. Take him and stand him by the trough he's used to if he knows which end belongs over it.

But for you, carissimo [dearest], I reserve only the most sweet smelling syllables! Muchas gracias [many thanks] for the proper criticism of the gal holding a shoe in her hand looking for the nail in it (use that as the title and let the good follow) No. Drop it. It isn't of any value.

I'll look into this matter of "garment". In this benighted land they speak of "the garment workers striking" etc. etc. I surely can't call it a one piece suit.

It is quite true, poetry can't be what it was and can't in any case be at all without much more thought than I've given it of late. I know where I want to go with it as I realize that these chance images I've been throwing off now and then are not serious attacks. When shall I be able to attack again seriously? I seem to be in a transition period of a major sort. I've felt a need to look more seriously than ever before into the body of the matter. I've got to know more, read more, think more, work piecemeal for unrelated effects in a more acute manner – before I can do what I wish only to do. The drive of people wanting something to print has debauched me to some extent. I've got to stop and tell them to go to hell. I've got to tell them I'm too busy writing to write anything for them.

The tone of your last letter was unusual for you and quite you for that reason. I felt moved by your solicitousness – but I've got my own ideas.

A letter from Wilson says he is including at least one of the things I sent you in his new anthology I'll have him not use the big woman with a nail in her ass ["Proletarian Portrait"] –

Say, 'd you ever hear of a guy named Henry V. Miller who wrote a book called Tropic of Cancer? Now there's a book would warm the cockles of your heart. I'm not going to say its great but I am going to say it's grown up in a way America little understands and it is well done. (Obelisk Press, Setp. [*sic*] 1934) I wonder if you'll see in it what I enjoy?

Anyhow, thanks for your kindness. But I wish to Christ you would lay off censoring me too carefully in the very generous wish to make me acceptable to England. Crap!

Yrs
Bill

Paul Rudin, do you remember him? was just here. He sends his best to you. He said he saw somthing [*sic*] of yours he didn't know where but thought it was in Esquire. Didn't have time to finish reading it.

Please believe that I greatly value your specific criticisms and have endavored [*sic*] to profit by them.

Wilson also liked the shorter piece herewith

No time.! No time! The Japanese are upon us! And we, Good God, distrust each other.

No comment just yet on your American notes.

Eliot: The letter to which this one is a response has apparently not survived.

the gal holding a shoe: This poem had already appeared under the title "Study for a Figure Representing Modern Culture" in *Galaxy: An Anthology,* ed. Beatrix Reynolds and James Gabelle (1934). Retitled "Proletarian Portrait," it appeared in *Direction* for April–June 1935 and in WCW's *An Early Martyr and Other Poems,* published in September 1935.

"garment": The poem in which this word figures or figured has not been identified. Likely candidates are "An Early Martyr" and "Late for Summer Weather." EP's objections may have prompted WCW to delete or alter the word.

new anthology: For T. C. Wilson's anthology, see Letter 67 above. It includes three poems by WCW: "Late for Summer Weather," "An Early Martyr," and "Invocation and Conclusion." The last of these was sent to EP on February 1, 1935; see Letter 73 above.

Henry V. Miller: The American novelist Henry Valentine Miller (1891–1980) was the author of *Tropic of Cancer* (Paris: Obelisk Press, 1934). In a letter to Louis Zukofsky of March 1, 1935 (Texas), WCW describes it as "a whore with her pants off for purity and candor. A swell book. Floss and I are reviving our drooping spirits nightly with it and – "

Paul Rudin: For Paul Rudin, see Letter 26 above. During the 1930s he was employed as a sculptor by the Works Progress Administration.

Esquire: Between August 1934 and January 1936, EP published eight items in *Esquire* magazine, edited by Arnold Gingrich (1903–1976). Four had appeared before the date of this letter.

the shorter piece herewith: Unidentified, but possibly "Late for Summer Weather."

the Japanese: Japan had seized Manchuria in 1931. Throughout 1935, diplomatic tensions ran high as Japan sought to extend its control to the northern provinces of China. WCW expressed his concern over Japanese expansionism in *New Democracy* for October 15, 1935; see Mariani, p. 382.

your American Notes: See Letter 74 above.

77. TL-3

[March 1935?]

Waaal Doctor Williamz/

Yr/ unoozuly vigorous epistl of the whateverth' is vurry welcome, and whatta pity you know the Rev/ Possum only by public excrement and not in the free and easy of privik correspondence/ in fact not the author of Old King Bolo's big black Queen etc/ which vein isn't yet run out/ beyond which I don't remember what wuz the context.

A one piece suit wd/ have kept the line readable.

"Your mother frequently uses the word garment" sez Olga on reading yr/ letter. which is a poem in itself, in a way

The garment woikurs dont however speak of wearing 'em/

I first thort there wuzza beeweetful noo poem begining [*sic*]

    etc etc

    etc.

and am sorry there ain't as I take it the emend is to run on from wherever/

nevertheless a lot of yr/ poems DO begin that way. and 98% of all printed verse wd/ be improved by not only begining [*sic*] but continuing IDEM [in the same way]

Of course its Possum's fault in a way BUT, if you regard them gymnastics as NOT = writing, but axshun, they have enabled him to publish my woiks in England.

so perhaps there is an anagogic sense/ or a subterranean action, entirely independent from the surface or normal significance of the words AS langwidge of human beings. Bromide to putt hawds [*sic*] to sleep and sops for British dogs in the manger.

Tho the nobl [*sic*] Hargrave sez/ "wot a lot of dead cod about a dead god."

I wunner wot'll think of Alf Venison, fer a change?

My "Impact" is set up/ as per Stan Nott's announcement. and my Jefferson/ Muss, at last conthracted [*sic*] for.

And Nott sez he will start thinkin about a seereez of Pankfleks. Ta Hio/ Fenollosa Writ/ Character/ etc.

Yaas, give my regards to Rudin, wot he Doo/din? He iz responsible fer a unknown work by E/P .. I don't spose he knows I went on cuttin up some of that rock he left lyin' about. Ole Marie the char lady she thought it was sauvage or primitif or something/ waal it aint NO Mrs Whitney jitney. ANYhow/ and the wrist woik is just like playing tennis. Whatta pity I aint time [*sic*] to be versatile.

YAAS, Hen VIII Miller/ I did a review of his book, and *hope* the Criterion will print it.

I thought I told Hen/ to send YOU the vollum, waaal naow mebbe he did. The TROPic ov CANSIR

I dont care a fht/ about making you acceptable to Hengland. I merely decline to PRINT you any more *in* that fog/bound ringaround UNTIL you can knock the lizzards [*sic*] cold. jehGIT me?

Wot a man writes he WRITES, but the question of printing it is altogether a public etc/ etc/ governed by vastly other konSiderations.

azi I have said, my last chapter on a few decades of befuddled hedonism.

Gertie [Stein] wdn't empty a piss pot to save the bleedin world. She knows more than the absoloot simps/ but is contemptible as a character. Nice subject for Harvard and Bloosmbury [*sic*].

N[ew]/ E[nglish]/ W[eekly]/ is being run for a particular job/ and to GET ACTION, every page that don't work toward that, is so much waste, and even sabotage.

I like the saasay [essay]; but I don't WANT to bother social creditors with it. Trouble enough keepin the bastards mind on the JOB/

what do you notice with human beings, cant keep their minds on ANYthing long enough to do it decently.

kids with a lawn momer [*sic*], puppydog chasin a leaf..

Writers congress/ thats more active.. all of 'em boneheads except ole Steff/ who is there emeritus and from fidelity.

OUR job to GET the program (three years WORK) into the heads of people who will ACT.

Time enough to clean Gertie's tea kettke [*sic*], and take out professorial sediment, later.

SHIT . . . every construstive [*sic*] author I have ever mentioned has taken years to putt across. let the old tub wait, she's made her haul in the Provinces.

ONE of the main duties of a critic/ is to PICK the subjects for [rest of letter missing]

Old King Bolo: Old King Bolo and his Big Black Kween are characters in a series of ribald, racist poems that T. S. Eliot enclosed in private letters to friends; see Eliot, pp. 42, 125–26, 206, 455, 568.

Olga: The American violinist Olga Rudge (1895–) met EP in Paris in 1923. She became his mistress and bore his daughter Mary in 1925.

Hargrave: See "Biographical Notes" on Hargrave, John. The source of this quotation remains unidentified.

Alf Venison: The Cockney speaker of a series of Social Credit rhymes written by EP, published in the *New English Weekly* from February to October 1934, and collected in *Alfred Venison's Poems* (London: Stanley Nott, 1935). The name plays upon that of Alfred, Lord Tennyson.

"Impact": See "Biographical Notes" on Nott, Stanley Charles. In a letter to EP of February 27, 1935 (Yale), Nott says he will be sending proofs of *Social Credit: An Impact* "in a day or two." The pamphlet appeared in May.

Jefferson/ Muss: The negotiations that took place between EP and Nott over the contract for EP's *Jefferson and/or Mussolini* are preserved in their correspondence at Yale.

a seereez of Pankfleks: See "Biographical Notes" on Nott, Stanley Charles.

an unknown work: In a letter to his father of October 30, 1922 (Yale), EP writes: "Stimulated by the number of things the adolescent Rudin does not comprehend, I have spent two days chipping a block of marble myself. It will not be a chef d'oeuvre, but I have even less respect for bad sculpture than I had before I tried stone cutting.''

Mrs Whitney: Gertrude Vanderbilt Whitney (1875–1942) created a number of monumental public statues. She was also a major collector and patron of the arts; in 1930–31, she endowed the Whitney Museum of American Art in New York. *Jitney* is a slang term meaning cheap and shoddy.

a review: EP's review of *Tropic of Cancer* was not published but survives in manuscript at Yale (Pound Archive, Series V, Box 103, Folder 3879).

my last chapter: Chapter IV of *Social Credit: An Impact.*

Gertie: See ''Biographical Notes'' on STEIN, GERTRUDE.

Writers congress: The American Writers' Congress met on August 26–27, 1935. Its principal action was to create a League of American Writers to affiliate with the International Union of Revolutionary Writers. In ''An 'American' So-Called 'Writers' Congress,'' *New Democracy* 4:6 (May 15, 1935), p. 100, EP describes the organization as ''a group of mainly third-rate authors, backed up by emeritus Steffens and the dundering muttonheaded Dreiser. . . . A congress from which all economic thought is to be excluded and nothing but the Marxian talmud be used as text and dogma.''

ole Steff: The American journalist Lincoln Steffens (1866–1936) published eyewitness accounts of the Russian Revolution in 1917. EP met Steffens, and heard him talk about his Russian experiences, at William Bird's house in Paris on October 29, 1922. Steffens is quoted in Cantos 19, 84, and 113.

78. TLS-1

March 25, 1935

Fer Chri' Sakes:

Keep your eye on the ball. You wouldn't know a split personality from two balls in a bag with a label tied to 'em. I send you a clipping from a small local paper *because* it mentioned a man from Hamilton College who may have been a contemporary of yours there and because he said the banking interests conspired in Montreal (successfully) to have Lincoln murdered. And you come back and say the editorial in the paper says – etc etc. Nerts to you.

AND since you do not intend to use the two or three pages about qualities of knowledge (bearing directly on the economic situation today and having nothing particular to do with Gertrude Stein) WHY didn't you enclose it with your letter and RETURN IT as I asked you to?

What are you setting yourself up to be, a censor for yours truly? I'm not asking you what to write especially since you don't seem to be able to understand plainly written sentences. If you can't tell the difference between yourself and a trained economist, if you don't know your function as a poet, incidentally dealing with a messy situation re. money, then go sell your papers on some other corner. What in hell's all the fuss about? ''To make the world better for the artist!'' And what in hell is the artist going to do with his world once it has been made better for him? He's going to do [*sic*] shove it up his ass for all the good it is going to do him if he hasn't learned to live in it and report it in ANY age during which he happens to exist. Does it have to be specially prepared for him before he can use it? Is that, at the least, to be his major function – to make the world better for himself as an artist? You give me a pain in the ass.

I'm sending you no more writings. Send back the things you have. If there's anything I want the N[ew]. E[nglish]. W[eekly]. to see I'll forward it to them direct. After all the greatest things Orage might have instructed you in, the things that made him GO, have never entered your consciousness. Why don't you quit writing for a year and look around a bit. It'll do you good.

Yours

Bill

split personality: In a letter to WCW of March 11, 1935 (Yale), EP says, ''PULLL ep yer SOX, Pop Willyums. Or I shall have to treat yew azza deeVided pussunalitty.'' The division to which EP refers is between WCW as doctor and scientist, on the one hand, and WCW as economist and social observer, on the other.

a clipping: Unidentified.

the two or three pages: The typescript of WCW's ''A 1 Pound Stein''; see Letter 77 above and ''Biographical Notes'' on STEIN, GERTRUDE.

79. TL-4

[October 1935?]

My Dear ole Rip van BullwinKle:

There is nothing in yr. opening page to contradict what I have said in the book and ALL those points have been answered AGAING [*sic*] and again by Soc[ial]. Credit writers, Gesell and even old whats his name the Postmaster in Californy.

AND on my Volitionist 8 Questions I give the measure.

I think you are defending your own mental tiredness.

Muss. is having a war. All right. We got Louisians [*sic*]. and a war in Africa is better than one in Europe which ALL the buggaring gun makes [*sic*] wanted.

ANYhow. what's italy to you. If you cd. read wop. you might learn something from Odon Por's article in Civilta Fascista for May.

AND it is loony to judge Italy as if Muss. were alone in Europe with no international finance.

Food consumption IN Italy has about doubled, per capita.

AND the grain is now about enough for home use. Give the guy a break.

I dont TELL YOU about Russia or the N. Y. slums.

[line or lines missing] by cutting up the COW!!!

Until the administration examines currency controll [*sic*]. Leagally [*sic*] congress job and no need to bitch the constitution. The administration is a bleeding arse and its members mere piles.

All god damn evasion, like the pacfist [*sic*] socienties [*sic*]. one red herring after another.

and I thoroughly believe you when you say he didn't mean to get any real results.

IF the buzzard wd. read any decent econ. books. or get in someone who knows at least a little economics NOT in the interests of finance but in the interests of the people.

NONE of his god damn shitten cabinet can or dare answer even my elelemtary [*sic*] questions.

Money against AS MUCH GOODS AS ARE WANTED, and NOT against the air in an air cusion [*sic*] with Barney or Vanderlip or Morgan holding the tube and ready to deflate it.

That is the choice.

Yr. first page sounds like you never heard of an INDEX. or as if the price of gold was stable by ANY bloody measure whatever or ever had been. NUTS. me boy, you are feelink th heat.

About IMPACT. CAN I tell it ALL in 31 pages.

or did I putt over a fair amount of ginger fer the longth of the pamphlekk.

Footnote on page something or other covers the question "no advocacy of return to private money"

English dont even know it has existed. Fact. hundreds of 'em have NEVER HEARD of it. The bastids never had a Jackson van Buren epoch.

My shootin at the murkn ersatz [imitation] mind wuz done in Esquire.

Money ought to be good money WHOEVER MAKES IT.

to be good it must be against WANTED goods and/or services. the STANDARD of measure has got to be MATERIAL in the sense it shd. be

a given WEIGHT of something

= b in PROPORTION to other things.

hell thats not clear. say

  one ton coal

  or

  one bushel wheat

  or

  forty lb. cod fish salted.

  or

  ten bushesls [*sic*] fresh peache [*sic*].

A commodity standard ALTERNATE to and you got to have a controll [*sic*] office to hit an average. WHICH every modern economists [*sic*] thinks.

FOOD PRICES ARE controlled here. Market [word illegible] are controlled or fixed n computed by chambers of commerce.

The present system (as you know and wd. admit if it weren't hot, is strangulation of exchange BY finance.

AND dictatorship by frankies banker delegates is NOT the answer.

Oh well my old book on Jeff. Muss is set up and been proof corrected. mebbe it will git printed sometime.

That related to Feb. 1933.

AND nobody meets my statement

IG [*sic*] the bloddy [*sic*] ass of a govt. omed [*sic*] them hawgs an crops enuff to order destrution [*sic*], it owned em enough to issue orders for their delivery.

YOU HIT is [*sic*] square when you say Roos[evelt]. dont WANT to do anything real. the remedy of an ADEQUATE issue of money, NOT AS INTEREST BEARING DEBT, is so clear only the desire to avoid it exlpains [*sic*] the caniNITT attichood.

and so forth. loovely wather here. too warm fer the EZquimos but O.K. for EZ.

Again re. yr. page 1. A. I dont advocate private money save as pedagogy:

banks and state not ABSOLUTELY necessary prelud [*sic*] to issue of money that will function.

profiteering by trading cos. granted. but the value of the lumber wd. have been regulated (loosely by [?] market price at given time, as the valloo of gold or a foreign currency.

Rip van Bullwinkle: In Washington Irving's tale "Rip Van Winkle" (1820), the protagonist falls asleep for twenty years and wakes to find the world transformed.

yr opening page: In a letter to EP of August 26, 1935 (Yale), WCW praises EP's *Social Credit: An Impact* and says, "I'd like to do a review of your book . . . but where could I get it published? I may do it anyhow and send it to you." Letter 79 appears to be EP's response to that unpublished and now vanished review.

the Postmaster: Louis Herbert Bannister was U. S. Postmaster at Al Tahoe, California, and the author of *When We Become Scientific: This book gives the cause of financial panics, and offers a Scientific Remedy* (Pasadena, California: L. H. Bannister, 1933). EP cites this book approvingly in articles published during 1935 in *Esquire,* the *New English Weekly,* and the Santa Fe *New Mexican*; see Pound/Cutting, pp. 178–80.

Volitionist 8 Questions: See Letter 67 above.

Muss.: Benito Mussolini ordered the armed forces of Italy to invade Abyssinia (Ethiopia) on October 3, 1935.

Louisians: EP compares the invasion of Abyssinia to Andrew Jackson's victories over the British at New Orleans and over the Seminole Indians of Florida, both of them highly popular but of dubious legality; see "Biographical Notes" on JACKSON, ANDREW. In an undated letter of 1935 to WCW from Venice, EP writes, "Abyssinia a nuissance [*sic*] but it ENDS a cycle. seminoles, Louisians, necessary regrettable, in some ways" (Yale).

Odon Por's article: See "Biographical Notes" on POR, ODON.

the grain: A major goal of Mussolini's agricultural policy was the planting of enough grain to end Italy's dependence for its daily bread upon foreign imports.

Barney: Bernard M. Baruch (1870–1965) was a wealthy financier and an economic adviser of several Democratic presidents.

Vanderlip: Frank Arthur Vanderlip (1869–1937) was president of the National City Bank of New York and a prominent member of the Committee for the Nation to Rebuild Prices and Purchasing Power.

Morgan: John Pierpont Morgan, Jr. (1867–1943), was the head of a major New York banking house.

Footnote: On p. 14 of *Social Credit: An Impact,* EP writes: "I am not advocating a 'return' to private money in place of government money."

Jackson van Buren epoch: See "Biographical Notes" on JACKSON, ANDREW, and VAN BUREN, MARTIN.

Esquire: On EP's contributions to *Esquire,* see Letter 76 above.

frankies banker delegates: The Banking Act of 1935 centralized and strengthened the powers of the Open Market Committee of the Federal Reserve Board, which determines purchases and sales of government securities. The legislation weakened the authority of regional Federal Reserve banks in making appointments to the Committee, and strengthened that of the President.

old book: For EP's *Jefferson and/or Mussolini,* see Letter 64 above.

hawgs an crops: To restore prosperity to the agricultural sector of the U. S. economy, the Roosevelt administration sought to raise farm prices by constricting supply through the purposeful destruction of livestock and crops.

lumber: EP's grandfather Thaddeus Coleman Pound (1832?–1915) was a Wisconsin lumber baron and railway magnate. His company printed the paper currency with which it paid its employees, thus anticipating some of EP's ideas about the nature of money and credit.

80. TLS-1

On second thought I'll not send the poems just now as you seem to be moving about. When you are again in Rapallo – or settled elsewhere will you drop me a card?

W.

Oct. 29, 1935

Dear Dorothy:

Rome must be something to witness in its new glory. Should I ever find it possible to travel again Rome will be one of the first places I want to see – though I have always wished they would tear down the big Victor Emanuel [*sic*] monument.

I'm glad you liked Old Doc Rivers and some of the other stories. It was thoughtful of you to write. I have such difficulty getting published that of late I have almost forgotten that I am a writer. It may seem odd in the next breath to say that I have just had a book published, but that is the exception that proves the rule. The book is a small one more or less privately printed. I am sending it to you in this mail. The thing I really want to see in print is White Mule, a story of a child's life – in any number of volumes. The first volume of about 300 pages is now finished. But do you think anyone wants it? Yet all who have read it in the script seem pleased.

Curiously enough I too have had the urge to read Gibbon's Rise & Fall. First time I ever felt in the lest [*sic*] interested. I'll probably never get much further, no further than a taste of it surely.

Met a certain McLean last evening, a friend of Ezra's I think. At any rate he has lived in Italy. It was at a Social Credit meeting at which policy was being discussed. There's plenty of activity along Social Credit lines in America today. The general public is at last beginning to be informed but nothing very hopeful for general action has developed as yet.

Yes, I read Ezra's J. and/or M. and liked it. There is a review of it by me in one of the recent New Democracy issues. I also read recently a novel by one John Hargrave which I enjoyed and reviewed for the same paper - to be published soon.

My boys are at college. Bill, the older one, is a senior at Williams College in Massachusetts while the younger one, Paul, is a Freshman at the University of Pennsylvania. Both seem to have normal appetites. The older one plays soccer, the younger swims on the team. They have not, as yet, particularly distingusihed [*sic*] themselves as students but they do well.

Florence is in better health than has been the case in many years while I suffer and enjoy much as usual – fitfully, as I work. By the way you might tell Ezra that an old friend of mine whom he may remember, Charles Demuth the painter, died recently.

I didn't mean this to turn into a chronicle. Best luck and – drop me a line again when you will.

Sincerely

Bill

Old Doc Rivers: WCW's short story "Old Doc Rivers" appeared in *The Knife of the Times and Other Stories* (Ithaca, New York: Dragon Press, 1932).

a book published: WCW's *An Early Martyr and Other Poems* was published in New York by the Alcestis Press in September 1935 in a limited edition of 165 copies.

Gibbon's Rise & Fall: The English historian Edward Gibbon (1739–1794) published his six-volume study of *The Decline and Fall of the Roman Empire* between 1776 and 1788.

McLean: Alan McLean was the son of American parents who lived in Rapallo. For a time, he ran a travel agency there; but in 1934 or 1935, he returned to the United States, where he became active in the Social Credit movement.

a review: WCW's review of EP's *Jefferson and/or Mussolini* appeared in *New Democracy* for October 15, 1935.

a novel: See "Biographical Notes" on HARGRAVE, JOHN.

Charles Demuth: Charles Demuth (see Letter 8 above) died in Lancaster, Pennsylvania, on October 23, 1935. WCW's elegy on him, "The Crimson Cyclamen," appeared in *Adam & Eve & the City* (1936).

81. TLS-2

8 Feb. 1936

Deer Bull

Awakin frum pleasant dreams that had not gone too far I purrformd a act of mental correlation that you flat footed medicos haven't worked at ENOUGH.

I onct did a purrface at the end of trans of Remy/ and I once mentioned part of a idea to a jew (not Berman) endocrinologist.

and YOU have – lemme admit it) ruminated on the shape of the female pudendum. Why pud/

to the gloire [glory] and decor of that port of felicity.

WAAL/ there wuz also a Spanish bloke wot made a large reputation pokin' the end of the trigemini nerve in the NOSE.

WHAT the hell/ history is written and character is made by whether and HOW the male foreskin produces a effect of glorious sunrise or of annoyance in slippin backward.

Someone diagnosed [George Bernard] Shaw years ago by saying he had a tight foreskin/ the whole of puritan idiocy is produced by badly built foreskins.

Criminology/ penology shd/ be written around the cock.

The dissecting room shd/ lay off that chaotic bucket of sweetbreads from the skull and start research from the prong UPward.

The lay of the nerves/ etc.

This dont blot out endocrinology/ but it is the fount of aesthetics/

means microscopic attention/ dissection and micro/photographic enlargements/

killers etc/ shd have their prongs photoed post mortem [after death]/

I supposed something must have been done/ but not enough/

our littie brown brothers in Japan might take to it scientificly/ some very nasty europeans certainly will

but it shdn't be left to mere brutes INCAPABLE of understanding the licherary and musical consequences, in their upward reaches.

Wot I said to the endocriner wuz that jews having been circumcised fer centuries/ it must have had some effect on the character/

Not havin a foreskin he resented the suggestion/

BUT there is somethin' the jew aint got. admittin his talents.

waaal/ verb/ sap [a word to the wise]/

now develop it.

by the way yr/ las' poem in that book aint very unambiguous.

Why limit it to the so vastly inferior fluid.

"A quarent ans et force ma gourme jecté"

yrz

EZ

a purrface: EP's translation of Remy de Gourmont's *The Natural Philosophy of Love* (New York: Boni and Liveright, 1922) carried a "Translator's Postscript," in which EP speculates about the physiological connection between cerebral and sexual powers: "it is more than likely that the brain itself, is, in origin and development, only a sort of great clot of genital fluid held in suspense or reserve" (p. 169).

endocrinologist: Probably Doctor Edgar Obermer of 14 Gower Street, London, who examined Olga Rudge in July 1929 and prescribed a regimen of exercise, hydrotherapy, and medication (Rudge Papers, Yale). Obermer was the author of *Individual Health* and *Health and a Changing Civilization* (both 1935).

a Spanish bloke: Unidentified.

yr/ las' poem: The last poem in WCW's *An Early Martyr and Other Poems* is entitled
"You Have Pissed Your Life."

"A quarent ans: A rough translation of this line might read as follows: "Forty and fit, my
wild oats sown." The source is unidentified. EP quotes the same line in a cancelled
manuscript passage of Canto 49 (Yale), where it describes Lord Byron; see Massimo
Bacigalupo, "La scrittura dei *Cantos,*" *Lingua e letteratura* 16 (1991), pp. 62–63.

82. TLS-1

Feb. 27, 1936

Dear Ezra:

They say Bobby Burns had three balls or an extra artery to the general sphere of
his dynamo – but it killed him in the end. It seems as simple as that. And if cutting
off the loose hide over a few thousand years has altered the Hebrew character – I
doubt it. By all the laws of heredity it should have affected the women and they
are as bad as the men today, or worse.

It ain't the skin that makes the difference in the man, it's the stick in it that does
it. A reglar guy rips in even if it takes half the works away, ripping him wide
open. Next time it hurts less and finally it feels comfortable even most delightful
– as you intimate. But they're clipping the Irish, the Scotch the Scandinavian and
the colored today almost as much as the Jews. What is needed is the opportunity,
a place, a chance to come out of it not whole in cock which is nothing – but with a
reasonable chance of not being castrated by a wife or the law or whatever. That's
the barrier that makes shit of it for man: divorce, torment of mind – and if not then
dray [*sic*] rot. I'm sure I couod [*sic*] get along with or without a foreskin – but one
grows weary of the calamitous, faked up consequences of a simple, salutary,
hygienic and possibly, genius provoking exercise of the whole psyche – Aw
nerts. Ain't you gettin yours?

I'm glad Nott has gone ahead with your Ta Hio. I have no idea what he's doing
of mine. If there's anything - It's gone. Interruption.

No use talking any more. I distrust my own enthusiasms. I cannot answer your
questions. No magazine publishes anything that I know of and it becomes more
and more so. The young look nice in pictures and get a certain deceptive publicity
– but it's my own fault if I don't go out and meet them and teach them. I fear they
are not growing wiser but less and less informed. They are all Communists
completely filled with the "idea" and have lost all touch with the work as a
possible construction – that is in this so called country.

Anyhow, as you sez It's raining. No nooze. Bob McAlmon sojourning with his brothers in Texas –

Yours

Bill

Bobby Burns: The Scottish poet Robert Burns (1759–1796) is known for his many amours.
your Ta Hio: Ta Hio: The Great Learning: Newly Rendered into the American Language
   by Ezra Pound (London: Stanley Nott, 1936).
McAlmon: See "Biographical Notes" on MCALMON, ROBERT.

83. TLS-2

28 Ap 1936

Dear WhallaHoolah

DAMN and again S/S/S etc. bloody a social disorder that provides in 30 years NO decent publishing house and nothing but LOUSES.

If they wun't print MULE, what the hell! the [*sic*] deserve unadulterated Hollywood. and be blowed to 'em.

I cant find the bakk number of Nude Emoc/ but suppose you refer to a narticle ESQUIRE wouldn't print.

There ARE all the Esquire articles and I shd/ think at least SIX Ging/ wdnt print. mebbe I cd/ find copies.

Faber is lookin for innocuous licherchoor/

and the dramatist has just asked for review of BRIDGES collected po/humps. fer Criterion

wich I am *not going* to do.

Waaal he can't help it. He has got more of me pub[lishe]d/ in England than that sink of Sodom wd. otherwise have printed.

The Kulturausfuhrung [cultural exhibition] of the U. S. A on the occasional screen with all that is unconsciounsciously [*sic*] there registered . . . is not a "come home"

How damn much MULE is there/ and what about the ALKESTIS, aint they steamin full ahead to the gee/lory ov ole Bull the Walrus??

I unnerstan Mr Frost has fallen

Does the co/ed invite mean you iz supposed to be safer that that Carolina bloke who is expecting at 96??

or wot OH?

Waaal, I come up again the champeen ov Italy in tennis doubles las' week. (I mean speaking ov BALLS)

few years ago I though [*sic*] them turneymink days wuz over.

to git back to lettice, I can string together all any damn pubr/ will PRINT. thet IZ the priblum.

The British Italian Bulletin is givin me full steam ahead.

Takes economics hotter than the Stew Eng/ Weekly will stand.

I also thought of a new triptych/ the Return of the Native/ i.e. four articles 1. on Douglas/ 2. a Lenin/ 3. Stalin

BUT wot i need is a Economic Eliot to start a pub/ing firm

What is DeKruif up to? his damn pubrs/ haven't sent me the book.

You nevur wuz one to set round a wheedlin the commercials.

Do you ever see Hickok? or the lunatick Streater [*sic*]?

and when wuz you to Passaic with a highly embossied address?

Wouldn't Hen Miller's OBELISH [*sic*] people do MULE?

Of course Joe Gould, he aint printed. And Hen James he said to EZ said HE, "strange how all taint of art of literature..eh semms . . . eh. to shun That con timent [*sic*]

I dunno if I onnerstan yr/ suggested title fer polecatical or economik essays.

I see there is still a lot of hot mama sentimental piffle by hysterics writ/ against Italy in the American usury press and million circulations.

Y

EZ

MULE: For WCW's *White Mule,* see Letter 70 above. In a letter to EP of April 7, 1936 (Yale), WCW says: "I simply can't get my White Mule published. And this time I have been everywhere with it."

a narticle: ". . . The Movement of Literature," *New Democracy* 5:4 (October 15, 1935), pp. 62–63. In his letter of April 7, WCW tells EP that a "useful book" of his essays could be made if they were all in the style of this piece.

the Esquire articles: See Letter 76 above. On the unpublished contributions to *Esquire,* see Donald Gallup, "Ezra Pound's Experiment for *Esquire,*" *Yale University Library Gazette* 67: 1–2 (October 1992), pp. 37–46.

Faber: EP's *Polite Essays* was published in London by Faber and Faber in February 1937.

the dramatist: T. S. Eliot, the New York opening of whose play *Murder in the Cathedral* (1935) is mentioned in WCW's letter of April 7.

review of BRIDGES: Eliot asked EP to review the *Poetical Works* (1936) of the English Poet Laureate Robert Bridges (1844–1930) for *Criterion,* a monthly journal of literature and culture that Eliot had edited since 1922. For EP's refusal, see two letters to Eliot dated April 25 and 26, 1935, in Paige, pp. 280–81.

the ALKESTIS: The Alcestis Press of J. Ronald Lane Latimer published two books of poetry by WCW, *An Early Martyr and Other Poems* (1935) and *Adam & Eve & the City* (1936).

Mr. Frost: See "Biographical Notes" on FROST, ROBERT.

co/ed invite: In his letter of April 7, WCW reported that he had given "a talk and reading to the girls at Barnard" College in New York.

that Carolina bloke: Unidentified.

the champeen ov Italy: Il Mare (Rapallo) for April 25, 1936, reports that in the Third International Tournament of Rapallo EP and his partner Cortese were defeated in doubles, 6–0, 6–1, by Count Mino Balbi and the Italian champion Giovannino Palmieri. Palmieri went on to win the tournament championship in both doubles and singles.

The British Italian Bulletin: Between December 27, 1935, and October 24, 1936, EP published thirty items in the *British-Italian Bulletin.* Carpenter describes the periodical as "an English language propaganda newspaper . . . produced by the Mussolini government for distribution in Britain" (p. 534).

a new triptych: A series of eight articles by EP appeared in the *New English Weekly* between April 2 and July 23, 1936. The first four, entitled "The Return of the Native," have to do with C. H. Douglas and his concept of "economic democracy" (see "Biographical Notes" on DOUGLAS, CLIFFORD HUGH). The last four are entitled "Atrophy of the Leninists."

DeKruif: See "Biographical Notes" on DE KRUIF, PAUL.

Hickok: The American journalist Guy Hickok (1888–1951) worked for the Paris bureau of the *Brooklyn Daily Eagle* in the 1920s and early 1930s. He contributed to the first number of EP's magazine *Exile.*

Streater: The American artist Henry ("Mike") Strater (1896–1988) designed the ornamental initials for the Three Mountains Press edition of EP's *A Draft of XVI. Cantos* (Paris, 1925).

OBELISH: The Obelisk Press in Paris published Henry Miller's *Tropic of Cancer* (1934); see Letter 76 above.

Joe Gould: For Joe Gould and his unpublished *Oral History of the World,* see Letter 43 above.

Hen James: In his essay "The Renaissance II," *Poetry* 5 (March 1915), p. 283, EP reports this anedote in greater detail: "I have heard the greatest living American saying, with the measured tones of deliberative curiosity, 'Strange how all taint of art or letters seems to shun that continent . . . ah . . . ah, God knows there's little enough here . . . ah . . . '"

yr/ suggested title: In his letter of April 7, WCW had suggested that a presentable collection of essays by EP might be called "The Last Gentleman."

84. TLS-3

Nov. 6, 1936

Dea Rezra:

Always delighted to hear from you, I began to think you had gone up into some more rarified stratum than that to which I have grown accusomed [*sic*]. Truly, truly, my friend, you have greatly alleviated the passage of my years – no suppository of cocoa butter could have done better. Don't stop now. My only regret has been that you have not been closer to these here diggins. Dman [*sic*] it to hell, it's been a serious loss to us all that you haven't set your flowers to clambering on our walls. I planted three small clematis vines in my back yard this morning. Very mild weather here so far.

I approve of your proposed manifesto and think that this is of all times the most propitious in which to release it. The american political upheaval having for the moment practically eliminated the Communist Party from our midst it would seem to be THE moment for redirecting sane minds toward the need for an actual radicalism – which would concern precisely the things your nine or ten categories included.

Fer meself – I've at last finisged [*sic*] and had printed the libretto for my american opera: The First President. Serly can't give the time to the music just now – more's the pity – since he thinks he has to get himself up a bit in the world of music befoe [*sic*] he can spend two years on an opus of the sort and size. Soooo, I have enlisted the services of my leetle brother. He (together with three pals) has just be [*sic*] awarded the contract for the first building (the administrative building) of the New York World's Fair to be held in 1939 – if the world lasts that long. The theme of the fair is to be the celebration of the un hund red and fife teeth ana voice ree of the in aug urination of Big Geo. as prusidut of the U nighted Stayts of A merry cugh. And that THAT my deer old back cuspid is the VERRY theme of my opry. Now aint that sumpin? Wuz I wise or wuz I wise? Tell me that? Huh? Wuz I. Huh?

Now, this being as thay r, I asks my brother (and his description of his meeting with the COMMITTEE to sign the contrat [*sic*] of [*sic*] the 580 floor of the Umpire State building is sumpin. Cables for Klieg lights and movie cameras all OVER the floor so you could hardly stand etc etc. – lights to singe the back hair off the participants * [*sic*] rehearsals of what was and waht [*sic*] was not to be said, especially no one must FART!) Anyway. Me brother met the woman who is to be the press agent and he tells her that there is one thing he hez to see her about and she says, Zat so? So it was arranged, and he is to tell her about my libretto and how it is the scared [*sic*] duty of someone to put up the cash so that a composer can write the score and have ot [*sic*] ready to put on the big operatic stage they're to have with a lagoon or river or pond or bay between the singers and the Audience. And then we'll see. If Serly won't do it – maybe one of the boys from the Academy in Rome a few years back, a reputed "genius" and maybe one too, may take it on. So you see!

Meanwhile, the libretto has appeared in The New Caravan 1936 just out last week. I'll see if I can get you one. Nothing to break your heart over but – at least it printed the libretto – and a few other very good things among the bad.

Then there's a new book of poems which I'll send you for whatever you may think of them. This Alcestis Press fellow Latimer (nee Leipert [*sic*]) wants to do a Collected Poems for me – but I dunno whether or not I'm ready for that yet. I got too much I want to do first. Maybe though, if I get bored and want to play do re mi fa sol – I may arrange them for him. He says he'll do a trade edition. I'm sick and tired of DEE LUX impossibilities.

And James Laughlin (bless his heart) has just offered to do my White Mule. *That* finished me. It sure was a bolt out of the blue of almost despair. His impetus has set me polishing (that is, rewriting) the last chapters to make this a definite Book. It is to be Book I and ends with proper regard for an ending. I'm going to like this book. It's put ten years on my life. Out next spring.

Besides which I've about made up my mind to write my mothers story this winter. I have an idea for it that I can't detail now. I've been collecting her sayings and letters for years. You'll see.

And I've done seven new short poems – two of them as good as anything I've ever done, maybe the best.

And then there's that magnum opus [great work] I've always wanted to do: the poem PATTERSON [*sic*]. Jeez how I'd like to get at that. Ive been sounding myself out in these years working toward a form of some sort –

Weeeel, today I went in to Rockefeller Center to see the Book Fair that some one of the Soft Soap Publishing Firms is putting on. I thoought [*sic*] I might learn something. All I got out of it was a belly ache and a view of T. S. Eliot's mug (a photo) advertising some firm or other. What a puss. All he needs would be gauze betwen [*sic*] his ears and he could fly to heaven – a blessed ghost. I don't like him. Then I learned that there has been only one MAJOR American poet since the turn of the century (it turned all right) and that is Edna StVincent Milldewed Millay. That made me fee [*sic*] swell (like a dead dog floating on the Passaic River) GEEZE. What a jernt that FAIR is.

To start with something clean on this clean sheet of paper – glad the basturd is well. Which one is that?

My two guys continue on their merry ways. Bill is now a Freshman in Cornell Medical School New York City. Nice kid. The other is a Soph at dear ol'

Pennsylvania. He has the shits right now and a charley hoss from too much soccer. He doesn't think he wants to be a doctor.

Oh yeah, there's a good guy named Bernard de Voto, he has taken the place of Henry Seidel Canby as editory [*sic*] of the Saturday Review of Literature and MAY come to something. He's got a face like a spoiled potato but they say his heart is in the right place. I'm going to meet him first, through a woman, a real fine woman, and we'll see what happens.

I'm never hopeless as you seem to suggest – but I have always been hopeless of doing anything with other people. I know I am wrong but then, that's the way I am.

You see, I live a very obscure but very complete life in my own petty world. I know its smells and it's bouquets. They are not to be ignored. I tell you when I went in to Rockefeller City today and saw that beeg building and then entered it and rode on the escalator and walked about the shitty show – I tells you my little suburb just bust right our [*sic*] laughing. SUCH a lot of cheap crap I NEVER encountered. There in the kiddle [*sic*] of everything was our old, very old friend Edwin Markham parading his innocent white beard about, wanting to be spoken to and admired. I tell you I was not envious, nor did I waish [*sic*] I had been paraded about the walls to sell for them.

Bob McAlmon in Mexico City drinkin I suppose.

Me Mother is helping me translate an old book I think it was you left here once: El Perro y la Calentura, by Quevedo.

Well, write me again. Floss is fine. Best to Dorothy. I'd enjoy playing you a game of tennis.

Yrs.

Bill

---

to hear from you: In a letter to WCW of October 29, 1936 (Buffalo), EP says, "think how much duller life wd/ have been fer 25 years past if old EZ hadn't had the nereve [*sic*] to be a damn b nuissance [*sic*] onct. in so often."

your proposed manifesto: In his letter of October 29, EP enclosed a copy of a seven-point "Manifesto against TREASON of the CLERKS." It is reproduced in Pound/Lewis, pp. 185–86.

The First President: Since 1933, WCW and the Hungarian-American composer Tibor Serly (1901–1978) had collaborated on an opera based upon the life of George Washington (1732–1799). The opera was never completed, but WCW's libretto for it, entitled "The First President: Libretto for an Opera (and Ballet) in Three Acts," was published in *The New Caravan* for 1936.

my leetle brother: See "Biographical Notes" on WILLIAMS, EDGAR IRVING.

one of the boys: Possibly the American composer Roger Sessions (1896–1985), who was a Fellow of the American Academy in Rome from 1928 to 1931.

a new book of poems: Adam & Eve & the City (New York: Alcestis Press, 1936). For Latimer/Leippert, see Letter 61 above. Alcestis did not publish WCW's collected poems.

James Laughlin: See "Biographical Notes" on LAUGHLIN, JAMES.

my mother's story: See "Biographical Notes" on WILLIAMS, RAQUEL HÉLÈNE ROSE.

seven new short poems: Unidentified.

PATTERSON: WCW had been struggling with this long poem since 1926.

the Book Fair: Sponsored jointly by the National Association of Book Publishers and the *New York Times,* the National Book Fair was held November 5–19 in the International Building on Fifth Avenue. 74 publishers were represented, and 30 authors' programs were scheduled. None of them included WCW or Edwin Markham.

Millay: The American poet Edna St. Vincent Millay (1892–1950) was awarded the Pulitzer Prize for Poetry in 1923.

the basturd: In his letter of October 29, EP reports: "Bastid growin' nicely."

Bernard de Voto: The American novelist, critic, historian, journalist, and teacher Bernard Augustine De Voto (1897–1955) edited the *Saturday Review of Literature* from 1936 to 1938.

Edwin Markham: The American poet, essayist, editor, and biographer Edwin Markham (1852–1940) is best known for his poem "The Man with the Hoe" (1899).

Quevedo: The Madrid poet, novelist, and satirist Francisco Gomez de Quevedo y Villegas (1580–1645) may not have been the author of *El Perro y la Calentura* (1625), which was published under the name of his friend Pedro de Espinosa (1578–1650).

tennis: In his letter of October 29, EP mentions that he has played "3 singles and 3 doubles on tennis ct/ this a/m/ still able to stagger."

85. TLS-1

Dec. 8, 1936

God damn it you Thief –

who's lazy? Come on over here and try your hand at battling some of these currents of liquid shit and see how far YOu [*sic*] get up stream. Take TIME, FORTUNE, the new (?) LIFE, CORONET and all the rest of them who are running the publishing game today and see how much chance you'd have to get hold of a Linotype. You'd land in the mud along with your old pal [Maxwell] Bodenheim and a couple of bum painters and sculptors. And yet you still have the illusion that you'd be permitted to *say* something.

Sure, they give money to "artists" to decorate the walls of this or that place but do you think for one moment they'd permit the artist to SAY anything? Where do you think Hiler is today? Not New York.

At that it isn't a bad idea, to get hold of a Linotype. My own plan was to try to get the gov't to establish a Dep't of Arts and Letters. They left off the Letters. I asked that they give us a periodical in which to pour our helpful work. No answer. I asked for an annual Bulletin. No answer. I suggested subsidies by the gov't to publishers to assist such publishers in printing books they would LIKE to print but couldn't afford, as they protest, to print – in paper covers. And that a committee make an annual selection from these paper books, 5 or 10, for fine printing in boards. No answer. It would have worked.

Come on over here you Smart Alec and let's see what you're hiding in your pants.

Yes, I have the Second Vol. of the Spanitch. 's O.K. to send No. 3 but whar's No. 1? At the moment I'm doing another translantion [sic], prose, El Perro y la Calentura, novella peregrina por [The Dog and the Fever, picaresque novel by] Don F. de Quevedo – 100 pages. I'm up to p. 28 now. Very interesting. More of that later.

The Manifesto doesn't strike me as so hot. I've sent it along. What in hell's the use of my pretending to know anything of Scottus [sic] etc etc.

In reply to your boasting about tennis I'm mailing one of my latest pictures – in a bathing suit, one tip showing. Look for it – and to hell with you. Your last was a good letter.

Yours
Bill

Hope Dorothy is well now.

a Linotype: In a letter to WCW of November 30, 1936 (Buffalo and Yale), EP writes: "The only thing doable INSIDE the nude eel [New Deal] is to get controll [sic] of LINOTYPE machine// you're to [sic] goddam lazy: but you cd/ prod the young on to it . . . then we cd/ get stuff printed."

Hiler: The American painter, writer, and authority on costume Hilaire Hiler (1898–1966) left New York for California in April 1936. There, Hiler painted murals in the Aquatic Park building in preparation for the San Francisco Golden Gate International Exposition of 1939.

my own plan: See WCW's letter to Edward B. Rowan dated August 28, 1934, in Thirlwall, pp. 148–49.

the Second Vol.: Poesías Selectas Castellanas, Recogidas y Ordenadas por Don Manuel Josef Quintana, Nueva Edicion, 4 vols. (Madrid: Gomez Fuentenebro, 1817). EP was given this edition by "a certain Miss Scarborough whom I met in Paris," probably in the early part of 1910 (undated letter to Isabel Pound, Yale). Later that year, he left Volume 2 at WCW's home in Rutherford. WCW included four translations from it in *The Tempers* (1913) and five in *Adam & Eve & the City* (1936), and he quotes from Quintana's introduction in his essay on "Federico García Lorca," *Kenyon Review* 1:2 (Spring 1939), p. 152. See also Heal, pp. 16–17.

El Perro: See Letter 84 above.

The Manifesto: Unidentified. "Scottus" is probably the Irish philosopher, theologian, and translator Johannes Scotus Erigena (*c.* 810–877).

one of my latest pictures: In a letter to James Laughlin of January 1, 1937, EP describes this as a "coloured photo of the Rev. Bull Wms/ et uxoris [and wife] standink by the wide and polubumtious seacoast looking vurry amurikun"; see Pound/ Laughlin, p. 73.

Dorothy: In his letter of November 30, EP reports: "D/ just been to orspital/ but now rizin."

86. TLS-2

24 Jan. 1937

Deer Bull

Thanks for Amdur's (or Ham dure's) thesis volumet, which ought to be entitled "Ole Ez carried into Jerusalem on the Foal of an ass."

"The custom now is" said Dr Johnson "to use *colt* for a young horse and *foal* for a young mare."

Booklet illustrates

American time lag/

conceit and snobism [*sic*] of Am/ Universities.

fixed ideas instilled into jejune [*sic*] stewddents, snobish [*sic*] omission of all ref[erence]/ to W. C. Williams

AND bloody distortion and misrepresentation of London LIFE 1908 to 1914.

Hell, Yeats for symbolism/ Hueffer for CLARITY/ half dozen drawing rooms wherein no whisper of one cenacle arrived.

The main injustice is to Ford/ 2nd is to you.

But if they must blither about Flint/ Tancred and Stroer [*sic*] it is is unjust to OMIT Ernest Rhys, Newbolt, Hewlett, Robt. Bridges

who at any rate WROTE something now and again, and however much one disagreed with 'em, one was at least disagreeing with something.

Nuissance [*sic*] to know whether one ought to publish rectification.

Using steam roller on monkey nut?

job MIGHT be done by reviewers or by some other PH D of Amdur's own size.
Usual time lag/ ANYTHING new is wrong/ anything the professoriate hasn't
yet learned is considered foolish.

There is ONE bit of real criticism/ wonder if it is author's own or a current bit
of collegiate class room opinion/

also two useful quotes from I forget whom.

Than Q fer sending it.

fillet of filly, ces jeunes filles [those girls]

or as Natalie sez: feminine of ecrivain: ecrivisse [writer: crayfish].

YRZ
EZ

Amdur's . . . thesis: Alice Steiner Amdur, *The Poetry of Ezra Pound* (Cambridge,
Mass.: Harvard University Press, 1936), 106 pp. For the letter EP wrote to Amdur after
reading her essay, see Sebastian D. G. Knowles, "Ezra Pound to Alice Steiner Amdur,
23 January 1937," *Paideuma* 21:1–2 (Spring–Fall 1992), pp. 235–49.

Dr. Johnson: In his *Dictionary of the English Language,* 3rd ed. (1776), the English
lexicographer and man of letters Dr. Samuel Johnson (1709–1784) illustrates his definition of the word *foal* with this quotation from Edmund Spenser.

Hueffer: See "Biographical Notes" on FORD, FORD MADOX. EP amplifies this account of
the respective influences of Yeats and Ford in "Ford Madox (Hueffer) Ford: Obit," *The
Nineteenth Century and After* 126:750 (August 1939), pp. 178–81.

Flint: The English poet, translator, and critic Frank Stewart Flint (1885–1960) played a
prominent role in the London Imagist movement of 1912–17. He is the author of *In the
Net of the Stars* (1909) and *Cadences* (1915).

Tancred: Francis Willoughby Tancred was the author of *Poems* (1907). In a letter to
Homer Pound of August 2, 1909 (Yale), EP describes him as "Tancred (stock exchange) who does epigrams of a Horatian-Herrickesque variety."

Stroer: Edward Storer (b. 1882) was the author of *Inclinations* (1908), *Mirrors of Illusion*
(1909), *The Ballad of the Made Bird and Other Poems* (1909), and *Narcissus* (1909).
Amdur (p. 23) notes that Flint, Tancred, and Storer were active in T. E. Hulme's 1909
cenacle at the Tour Eiffel restaurant in London, a forerunner of the Imagist group.

Ernest Rhys: For Ernest Rhys, see Letter 4 above.

Newbolt: The English poet and historian Sir Henry Newbolt (1862–1938) specialized in
naval subjects. EP admired his poem, "Drake's Dream."

Hewlett: For Maurice Hewlett, see Letter 3 above.

Robt Bridges: For Robert Bridges, see Letter 83 above. In 1914–15, EP was interested in
Bridges' experiments with quantitative meter and free verse.

Natalie: See "Biographical Notes" on BARNEY, NATALIE CLIFFORD..

87. TLS-2

7 Feb 1937

Waal me yole Hiram von Kronk von Backhaus

DONT eat so goldam much MEAT. If you got piles, and dont want 'em DONT eat so goldam much MEAT.

I have diminished the pressure on them there anal capillaries or whatever by eatin meat ONCT only per diem [each day]/

and you might git a few endocrine shots in the arm if your''re agein in your underside.

apart that you have that there sloth and *molesse* [flabbiness] wot Kung saiz aint no proper man's ornemunk.

To hekll with Key West/ I prefer May idem [of the same name]

and I aint a fish-killer NO how.

Glad Louis [Zukofsky] is juicin/

and ELJEN [hooray] *tiBORR*/ ELJEN!! T. U. S.

What you cd/ do wd. be to delouse that Chicago band stand. Dew yew XXgpekk to be carried to the skies on bowery bedz of fleas?

Ole Harriet is dead and if YOU dont controll [*sic*] the damn Jesuit the hole dam thing will become a mere shit pile// dungy as ever it waz.

Marianne [Moore] wont make any real effork. waaal; ladies iznt got ballz NOhow.

and she aint even a frustrated maternal..

A decent COMPACT action you, Laughlin, Zuk, cummings (wiff or wiffout Marianne) COULD force the local Dorcas soc/ to INCLUDE

The real stuff and the ONLY stuff that lasts 20 years

Nacherly the hogeaters and local janes will allus be AGAINST real work, they will allus sabotage any real scale of values

BUT that is no reason why it shd/ be complete [*sic*] excluded from feed box.

AND bigod if the artisk dont EAT he ultimately dies/

equally true if he overeats he sleeps// BUT no sech bed of roses is yet in sight..

You howl and yell when *you* dont got printed *presto* and then you wun't do a likk of work toward that thaaar neCessary COhesion, sans [without] which nowt gets did or accomplished.

which means PRINTED, in our time.

Even the aged ElYort izza printin 3 cantos in the Critterun and a vollum of TEN. wiff a 正为

at the end of it

yrz

EZ

piles: WCW signs his letter to EP of January 27, 1937 (Yale), as "Yer old (same old) pain in the ass you always were glad you didn't have."

Kung saiz: The source of this Confucian saying has not been identified.

Key West: In his letter of January 27, WCW says, "If you come to America, the only place I can think of for you is Key West, Florida." EP's "fish-killer" is an allusion to Ernest Hemingway, who had been living and fishing in Key West since the early 1930s.

May idem: American film star and sex symbol Mae West (1892-1980). In a letter to Viola Baxter Jordan of June 8, 1933 (Yale), EP praises West's *She Done Him Wrong* (1933).

Louis is juicin: See "Biographical Notes" on ZUKOFSKY, LOUIS, and Pound/Zukofsky, p. 173.

ELJEN tiBORR: For Tibor Serly, see Letter 84 above. On January 26, 1937, Serly's Symphony No. 1 was performed at Carnegie Hall in New York by the Philadelphia Orchestra under the direction of Eugene Ormandy. WCW was in the audience and reported the event to EP in his letter of January 27.

Harriet is dead: Harriet Monroe died in September 1936. She was succeeded as editor of *Poetry* by Morton Dauwen Zabel.

Dorcas soc: Dorcas is a woman of "good works and almsdeeds" in the New Testament Book of Acts. In English churches, Dorcas societies were ladies' benevolent associations that provided clothing for the poor. Their meetings sometimes included literary readings.

printin 3 cantos: "Cantos XLII–XLIV" appeared in Eliot's *Criterion* 16:64 (April 1937), pp. 405–23.

a vollum of TEN: The Fifth Decad of Cantos, containing Cantos 42–51, was published by Faber and Faber in June 1937. The ideogram cheng (4) ming (2), meaning "right name" or "true definition," appears at the end of Canto 51. It resembles EP's initials, and reappears in many later cantos.

88. TL-2

1 March [1938]

Waaal

I giv yr/ goldarn MULE to a lady wot knowz B from Buzzard, an she sez/ Thazza FINE book.

She sez Cocteau's last is a FLOP   She sez Mule is so good fer the TIMING. I sez woccher mean TIMING?

She sez it takes about long as it wd/ fer to see those poeple [*sic*] and find it out fer yerself.

Pace? sez I, all right she sez "Pace"

Waaal thaZZat, thazza COMpliment, in a world where not more n ten or thirty people know ANY goldam thing about book writin wotever.

Hell, or words to that effek she sez/   As fer young Jas's poscrip/ he orter be smacked/ IMpertinence she sez, pattin his granpop on the head.

I sez WAAALLL, Jas PRINTED it an nobuddy else wd/ and I spose he wuz trying to SELL it.

However. the pace is SLOW/ thazz orl rite/ BUT god damn you/ I sends back a beamish boye/ wiff his starry eyes full of good intentions and JUST apprehensions/ and wot do you DO/ you let him git all gummed up with JoleArses etc/

WHAT is the use. He had sense enough to WANT to stay here/ I sez NO go bak be a man and TRY it/ try to see if anything can be did in the sloppy country

and damn if you UPhold him/ you just go mumpin and grumpin/ and damn if we aint got the usual Am[erican] plus Jolas SUBeuropean MESS.

Joleas [*sic*] at leasts [*sic*] prints JOYCE's vomit/ but then Jas prints Joleas and NO Joyce/

wotter hell WOTTER kuntry.

and wot you EGGspekk me to do about it?

Where do you expect me to sell yr/ damn bukk?

Aint you got any CARBOLIC soap fer the puppies?

Dont doctorin teach you disinfectin?

and so forth/ you ole rapskullyum.

And as fer slowness you an the Possum is a PAIR/ he moves on jest far enuff fer to burn up the wagon.

and you set or stand till you git soot in you belly hairs.

a lady: Unidentified.

Cocteau's last: Possibly the play *Les Chevaliers de la Table Ronde,* which opened in Paris on October 14, 1937.

young Jas's poscrip: The first edition of *White Mule* (1937) carried a postscript by James Laughlin, entitled "White Mule and New Directions." In it, Laughlin declares: "To the editor of New Directions, *White Mule* is a symbol – a symbol of his whole hope and will. New Directions exists only to publish books like this one. . . ."

MESS: EP is attacking *New Directions in Prose and Poetry 1937,* the second of the annual anthologies of new writing edited and published by Laughlin. It contained contributions by Cocteau, e. e. cummings, Eugene Jolas, Henry Miller, Merrill Moore, Gertrude Stein, WCW, and others. In an undated letter to Laughlin (Yale), EP writes: "you have gone too far in obscuring essential differences. Too god DAMNED Amy/ble."

Joleas: Eugene Jolas was the editor of *transition,* the journal in which much of James Joyce's *Finnegans Wake* first appeared. Both EP and WCW found Jolas' editorial policy wishy-washy (see, for example, Letter 39 above); and both were reminded of it by the second volume of *New Directions.* Laughlin dedicated his annual "To the editors, the contributors & the readers of *transition,* who have begun successfully the revolution of the word."

89. TLS-2

March 17, 1938

Dear Ezra:

Thanks for the various recent letters and enclosures. What the hell have you done that I haven't done? I've stayed here, haven't I, and I've continued to exist. I haven't died and I haven't yet been licked. In spite of a tough schedule I've gone on keeping my mind on the job of doing the work there is to do without a day of missing my turn. Maybe I haven't piled up a bin of superior work by [*sic*] I've hit right into the center of the target first and last, piling up *some* work and keeping it right under their noses.

I've interpreted what I could find out of the best about me, I've talked and hammered at individuals, I've read their stuff and passed judgement on it. I've met a hell of a lot more of all kinds of people than you'll even get your eyes on and I've known them inside and outside in ways you'll never know. I've fought it out on an obscure front but I haven't wasted any time.

And I'm not kidding myself that my purpose is to be a great humanitarian. I've kept it coming into the hopper for writing. But the principal thing is that the things I've taken on, to keep myself reasonably free to act as a writer, have been important things under the circumstances. I've had to do it. *I've* had to do it. To exist here at all I've had to do it. It was the only way open to me. I wasn't going to put myself in a position where I could be told what I had to write. I know damned well that if *I* did not stick it out my own way I'd be submerged here. But I haven't been submerged. Not yet.

What do you want me to do, run for the U. S. Senate? The only thing that I fear is loss of time. It hasn't been easy to work around myself so that I could practice my trade with self respect and at the same time work my work around so that I could live and at the same time *make* time for my writing. I've done it, not without difficulty. I could even today double my practice if time weren't my main object. That and to keep alive.

I'll be damned if I'll run away from it or sour myself or give in. I will do what I set out to do. By merely existing *here* I've been able to make myself a rallying point for others. Not that I'm satisfied or, I hope, finished. But I've done it – so far.

All right for you, all right for Eliot to do the things you're doing. Nobody is more willing to hand you the praise due you. But there's more to it than that.

I acknowledge, Laughlin messed up his last New Directions. But don't blame me. I have no way of influencing him and [*sic*] more than you had six months ago. He won't do it again and I was after him the first of all. Until he had the thing out I knew not one word about his plans nor did he confide them to me.

My whole duty seems to me to be to continue to exist here and now. My only regret is that I am so submerged with the labor of living that I can't write as often and for as long a time as I should like to. But to live at all I have had to live as I have been able to do and that has been the most successful and the most effective effort it has been possible to make. That and the slant I have had on the work of you others – in finer coats – plenty rotten underneath sometimes. You'll get over it. Eliot especially needs wiping.

It's a tough game. You know that. One [*sic*] in a while it is possible to make one or two steps ahead. That's about the limit for one life. But the main thing is to keep so that you want to make the step and to keep fighting off the things that would make that spot impossible. It is still possible for me to make a couple of more steps.

Toor a loo, sweetheart.

                              Yours
                              Bill

I was after him: In a letter to Laughlin of January 23, 1938, WCW says of the annual: "there was too much *Transition* like random shooting . . . it should have been newer . . . It's a well gotten up book but NOT sufficiently exciting"; see Williams/ Laughlin, p. 26.

90. TLS-3

                                        April 6, 1938

Liebes Ezrachen:

Heil Hitler!!

Were I not to tell you now you would probably never know that with the daffodils, the squils and forsythia out – it began to snow at about ten o'clock this morning and has continued to snow heavily all day. It was curious to see the forsythia bushes especially, their yellow standing out against the white of the snow.

I opened the cardboard box, containing the radio we had bought for my mother, this afternoon and set it up for her. Of course, she said, I can't hear it the way I would like to. She is nearly blind but can't keep her fingers out of the pot of life. She still wants to tell me what to think and to do. That I ignore her intimations must annoy her. She says that her heart is like a stone. I ask her what she expects. She says she knows all the answers. I suggest that she think of others, even generous thoughts are of value. I don't think she approves of me or my world.

A woman named Dorothy Norman is about to start a new magazine called, or to be called, Twice a Year. She has money. She is a rather beautiful and intelligent Jewess married to a typical young Wall St. broker. I like them both. He doesn't interfere with her. She wants to issue a magazine which will cover the world geographically, artistically, philosophically and morally. She is in no hurry. Her plan is to contact all those she wishes to use for her purpose and to set them to work – if she can. She will pay 1/2 cent a word. At least that is what she told me. She wants me to do an article – which you will have a chance to see later in which I hope to God I shall finish with Eliot forever – so far as I am concerned. Not that I would disturb his corpse if you think it is as bad as that.

The widow of a southern doctor lives in Rutherford with her daughter. She is old and charming. They are descendants of one of the famous Gunning sisters, the most beautiful women, three of them, who were ever introduced (from Ireland) to the Court of St. James. The daughter showed me a miniature on ivory of the Duke of Athlone (?) which Whistler once saw and praised. It is cracked down the center. The estimated cost of repair is said to be $1200. At that it is rather lovely. Photographs have made the art of diminutive personal portrayal obsolete.

The snow is continuing at 8 P. M.

Floss' mother has rented the farm for the summer. That reduces her back taxes to about $1000.

My second son, Paul, has just been elected captain of the 1939 U[niversity]. of P[ennsylvani]a. Swim team.

A young woman of this town was sent home from her position as Physical Training Instructor in a school at Winsted, Connecticut, two weeks ago because of a fever, a dull persistent headache, stiffness of the back of her neck, vomiting and a sore throat. After a week in a nearby hospital when the diagnosis of meningitis was being considered she gave us a positive blood culture for typhoid fever. They have raw milk in Winsted. Her mother is small and dark and has a suspicious nature. We have two nurses on the job. One is tall and is named

Mahlbacker. The mother does not like her – probably because she is so efficient.

Our furnaces, one for the office and one for the house are still being kept alive. Temp. tonight 30 degrees F.

They have asked me to speak (for an hour) at the girls' school, N. Y. C., the first part of May. Also I have to speak at the Bergen County Junior College.

The possibility of an opera on the theme of George Washington's life has interested me for years. I have done a good deal of research on the sugject [*sic*], written a passable introduction to a libretto and perpetrated what to me, now, seems a very, very fifth rate scheme for the whole. It was the best I could do at the time. It had to be written so that I could have a jumping off place when I should really get down to work. Antheil, Serly have both turned me down. A month ago I visited Virgil Thompson [*sic*] with the opera in mind. We had a talk. Nothing more. But it showed me how much work lies ahead of me if I am ever to succeed. No committments [*sic*].

James Laughlin wants to go to press with my complete, collected poems (to date) in June. I am having them typed out now. A final currycombing will be necessary.

The biography of my mother – enclosing in its amber a translation from Quevedo – is well on the way.

You, of course, saw, though you have not mentioned, the recent book of short stories. No matter.

You belong in this country. If you have left no place for yourself here it is largely your own fault. You can't expect to be carried on plush cushions. Certainly I don't want you to pat me on the head or anywhere else. I detest your bastardly Italy today. You complain of the English and their Chamberlin [*sic*] and with good reason, but if you can tell me who is licking whose ass right now between this one and that, explain. Hemingway, with all his faults is in Loyalist Spain. Wish you were there. I think that if anyone needs a change, a new viewpoint it's you. You can't even smell the stink you're in any more. Get out of it. Come over here, go to Conant at Harvard or Gates at Penn and tell them you want to stay here a year.

There's plenty of work for you to do here and plenty who would welcome your contribution to the value of the moment – but there are plenty who are leaving you today – losing touch. Maybe you don't give a damn. That's up to you. Plenty don't give a damn either. But this is where your work should be done.

I wish you were here but I can't make a place for you. I am too little accepted in places where you, with your reputation, might find it possible to enter. Why not try for a Guggenheim Fellowship to study in this country? Now there's an idea. I think it would work. Write to one of the Benets! ? $%# ! ?

Do you remember a person named Gilder who used to be the arbiter of something or other in the gay 90s? in N. Y. WEEEEL, his grandaughter Helena is a member of my son Bill's, class in Medicine at Cornell Medical School in N. Y. A nice kid too. Bill loves to make her life unlivable passing stomach tubes on her, etc. – she came to a cocktail party he gave last month – one of the lamp shades caught fire from a candle.

Perhaps this letter will convince you that I still admire and love you but – GEZUS CHRRRRIST! – you're missing your strokes Comerado [*sic*]! This ain't the old Ez I used to know. You're in the wrong bin. Your arse is congealed. Your cock fell in the jell*o [*sic*]. Wake up!

> Yours little better off perhaps
> Bill

Dorothy Norman: Dorothy Norman (1905–) was one of the editors of *America and Alfred Stieglitz* (see "Biographical Notes" on STIEGLITZ, ALFRED). Her magazine *Twice a Year: A Semi-Annual Publication Attempting a Clarification of Values* first appeared in Fall 1938. WCW contributed an essay entitled "Against the Weather: A Study of the Artist" to the second number (Spring-Summer 1939). In it, he criticizes "the new Anglo-Catholicism" and alludes to T. S. Eliot's *Murder in the Cathedral* as a "secondary" work of "instructed poetry."

Gunning sisters: Elizabeth Gunning (1734–1790), Duchess of Hamilton and of Argyll (not Athlone), and her sister Maria Gunning (1733–1760), Countess of Coventry, came originally from County Roscommon in Ireland. Known as "The Beauties," they were favorite subjects both of King George III and of contemporary portrait-painters.

Whistler: The American painter and etcher James Abbot McNeill Whistler (1834–1903) lived and worked mainly in London.

Floss' mother: Nannie Herman's farm in Monroe, New York, was called Alverheim.

Virgil Thompson: For WCW's opera *The First President,* see Letter 84 above. The American composer and critic Virgil Thomson (1896–1989) created the scores for Gertrude Stein's operas *Four Saints in Three Acts* (1927–28) and *The Mother of Us All* (1947).

complete, collected poems: New Directions published *The Complete Collected Poems of William Carlos Williams 1906–1938* in November 1938.

The biography of my mother: See Letter 84 above.

book of short stories: New Directions published WCW's *Life Along the Passaic River* in February 1938. EP reviewed it in *The Townsman* for July 1938.

Chamberlin: Arthur Neville Chamberlain (1869–1940) was Prime Minister of Great Britain from 1937 to 1940. In "Against the Weather," WCW criticizes the Chamberlain government's policy of neutrality in the Spanish Civil War.

Hemingway: See "Biographical Notes" on HEMINGWAY, ERNEST.

Conant: James Bryant Conant (1893–1978) served as President of Harvard University from 1933 to 1953.

Gates: Thomas S. Gates (1873–1948) served as President of the University of Pennsylvania from 1930 to 1944.

the Benets: William Rose Benét (1886–1950) was a founder of the *Saturday Review of Literature* and served as its associate editor from 1924 to 1950. His brother Stephen Vincent Benét (1898–1945) was a prominent poet and novelist.

Gilder: The American poet and critic Richard Watson Gilder (1844–1909) edited *Scribner's Monthly Magazine* (later renamed the *Century Illustrated Monthly Magazine*) from the mid-1870s to 1909.

91. TL-3

[April 1938]

Young Jas/ falls fer yr/ human touch/ as you leave the supper table in hast [*sic*] to deal wiff two boils and a clap case/

WHEN sense of proportion wd/ tell you that Tweddell might relieve a million cases of pulmonary con[sumption]//

GOD DALMN [*sic*] IT!!

Hem[ingway]/ and his need of subject matter/ all right, he needs subject matter, butt EUROPE never intended Russia to get Barcelona/ The lil boys NEVER had the chance of a snowball in hell/ it is all WASTE and any literate man ought to know that it serves MERELY to delay real revolution by drawing all the dynamism (young ideals etc.) into a blind alley

and selling guns thereby.

NOT that I regret the revolution/ it has diminished the time lag

the cat[holic]/ church has done ILL to Spain, and the living bishops pay for the centuries of darkness/ and some clear up will have occurred.. but at awful cost. Mebbe I will print something on Catalan BASE. clearer than hurried note so az to convince you that Charlie Duff etc/ is NOT a more seereeyus kerrakter than ole EZ/ DMAN [*sic*] it all I know WHO WRITES the accounts that you swallow/ and so forth.

Waal I dunno wots th use in tryin to eddykate yuh.

As fer your IRONY/ the hell Gates and Conant/ IF I tell you to to [*sic*] Bart's horspital and ask 'em to remove the second as[sistan]t/ surgeon cause you wanna JOB they wd/ DO it??

I saw the dean of Harvud in Salzburg/ he sez/ NO new ideas: rule of seniority/ gotta wait fer senior profs to die/ and the younger will then introduce slowly.

As for sedning [*sic*] half Sapain [*sic*] up a blind alley to provide Hem with the kind of subject matter he likes for his writing/

hell/ and the REDS will not attack capital/ wont even use dope about the anti = reds when it trespasses [*sic*] on bank monopoly.

Intellectual cowardice/ when not just plain lack of mind.

The possum does at least run a mag/ that pays for an occasional bit of serious writing/ and participates in a useful firm of pub[lishe]rs/

EF/ amurika dont take you, except as a doctor??

and IF you wdn't be printed at all save for being levered into a but [*sic*] of light in the dim past, by an extra/local implement??

and yr/ kulchur yours [*sic*] ma's and therefore by god NOT N. Jersey produk.?? what price page 2/3 of echos of the american whoosis?

I wonder will Hemites turn to serious revolution now the local Span/ show is waning??

As I remarked in the only free press left/ Adolf has arrested a ROT/schild.. I spose Trotsky dont like that.. or does he/// anyhow Trotsk never tried to bust the internat banks strangle . . .

or did he??

why dont you LIVE in yr/ non = fukn country and send me the reports of the Goldsborough hearings in committee

HEIL Hitler

WHERE the hell DO you live??

       Blissful unconsciousness mid the Daffodil's

       that'z old Bill's

       habitat

       down by the rabbit hutch

       in old Noo Jersey.

Wot a waste of a fine and shining morning

The pleasures of the EYE my dear billbo!! wot price to leave 'em . . .

of course you know nowt of Rossoni and prefer Barney Baruch waaal chakun Shake un to his gout [to each his own].

HEIL Hitler

Young Jas: James Laughlin was in Europe from late March to mid-June 1937.

Tweddell: See "Biographical Notes" on TWEDDELL, FRANCIS I.

Barcelona: For the views of EP and WCW on the Spanish Civil War, see p. 124 above.
EP here criticizes the influence that Soviet Russia exerted over the socialist parties of Barcelona. At the same time, he is sympathetic to the anticlerical strain in Spanish Republicanism.

Bart's horspital: St. Bartholomews was the principal teaching hospital in London.

the dean of Harvud: Kenneth Ballard Murdock (1895–1975) taught English at Harvard from 1923 to 1964 and served as Dean of the Faculty of Arts and Sciences from 1931 to 1936. He was an authority on Colonial American literature. EP mentions his encounter with "dean Murdock" in an undated letter to Gorham Munson (Yale).

Adolf has arrested a ROT/schild: The Austrian banker and financier Baron Louis von Rothschild (1882–1955) was arrested on March 16, 1938, by agents of the Third Reich, who accused him of contributing to the collapse of the Credit Anstalt Bank in 1931. He was released in May 1939, after payment of a substantial ransom. In "Rothschild Arrested," *Action* (London) 111 (April 2, 1938), p. 13, EP writes: "But for a hundred and thirty years no man has laid hands on a Rothschild. And here is the Baron Luigi, pinched like any other absconding cashier with his cash in a suitcase. . . . Trotsky hasn't yet denounced this as oppression of the proletariat."

Trotsky: Leon Trotsky (1879–1940) was a leader of the Russian Revolution. Forced into exile by Joseph Stalin in 1929, Trotsky attracted the allegiance of many dissident Communists in Spain and elsewhere who were repelled by developments in the Soviet Union during the 1930s.

Goldsborough hearings: Sponsored by Representative T. Alan Goldsborough (1877–1951) of Maryland, a bill for the establishment of Social Credit in the United States had been pending in Congress since August 1935. After extensive hearings in 1936 and 1937, the bill died in the House Banking Committee.

Rossoni: Edmondo Rossoni (1884–1965) was Mussolini's Minister of Agriculture.

Barney Baruch: See Letter 79 above.

92. TLS-1

April 29, 1938

Dear Ezra:

Mother says thanks but she doesn't know what you're talking about. I couldn't remember the precise statements to which you refer. Anyhow, she says, it was nice of you to think of her.

If the chief in question discharged his second assistant surgeon and replaced him with someone you recommended without further investigation or reason I venture my expert opinion that he'd be little better than a jackass.

All that you imply, as to responsibility and the individual, going in by the front door and all that – isn't lost on me. You may be right. I think you're wrong.

I think you're wrong about Spain. I think you're letting yourself be played for a sucker by the party in power in the country in which you happen to be living. As for Hemingway, his face is objectionable, I agree there, but he's far from being the issue in Spain or from representing it in his philosophy. You wish to crush out the resistance of a people against the elements of an economic setup which you yourself oppose – only you want to paste your own label on their goods. It happens to be not your particular shade of pink so you approve the destruction. Spain is up a ''blind alley'' because of the blackguards who have blocked their clear highway and made it so. It is you, not Hemingway, in this case who is playing directly into the hands of the International Bankers.

No, I'm not particularly interested in daffodils. There is more to look at than that. ''I know a bank where the wild time (thyme) grows'' just like any other man. Fucking isn't confined to Rapallo no more than is the spray of waters to the Mediterranian [sic]. The girls here still take it straight, all that is needed – and cry for more. They're not bad girls either.

You can get your information about the Goldsboror [sic] bill much more accurately from better informed circles here than from me. Don't waste your energy.

Eliot, you are right, is to be respected for what he does. He's known how to get himself where he can look up out of the poetry trade and get one arm at least into the world. He has also written a produceable play. All that is important. I still detest him.

Many thanks for your frequent direct and indirect communications.

Bill

I know a bank: WCW echoes Oberon's description of Titania's bower in William Shakespeare's *A Midsummer Night's Dream,* Act II, scene ii: ''I know a bank whereon the
wild thyme blows,/ Where oxlips and the nodding violet grows.''
a produceable play: Murder in the Cathedral; see Letter 83 above.

93. TLS-2

May 18, 1938

Dear Ezra:

You maka me smile, you Wop. Your man is a physician such as I am. What do you want me to do, produce a Sanatorium out of my vest pocket for his use? I was in communication with him and have read what he has to say. What he has to say is that he thinks he has observed something and that he'd like a large number of early cases, childhood cases, of tuberculosis to try his inhalations on. And I am to supply him with the cases. He doesn't want a few cases, he wants a large number of cases. And if his gas kills them, then what? And this is what you are exciting yourself about! You need a shave.

But the silly part of it is that, without the vaguest knowledge of the subject, you inflate yourself into the conceit that you can make decisions and condemn and approve of the opinions of others relative to technical matters completely outside the realm of your competencies. What do you want to do, be a hero? On what basis? On the basis of a chance article in an obscure medical journal? There are a thousand such "new ideas" published in technical journals throughout the country every year. Perhaps one of them will be of some value. If so it will become effective only after it has fulfilled the preliminary requisites of being based on clear, technically accurate reasoning *and/or* a thoroughly convincing trial in a few cases. Also, it should be borne in mind that there are already very effective measures in the field covering the same ground and that the real difficulty is not so much a medical one as one of an economic nature. The situation is vastly better than it was twenty years ago and is improving rapidly every day.

It is even possible that the situation may resemble that created by the hundreds of "cancer cures" we see every year. The net result of them has been disaster. Certainly some day we expect to get to the bottom of the situation there also but only by sound proceedure [*sic*]. A streak of luck may occur, granted; some damn fool may stumble on the secret. A way must be kept open for him to present his observations. True. But after he has spoken the final word will be in the hands of experts. Your man has spoken and it doesn't look as though what he has to say is sound.

All this, I realize, means nothing to you. Your principle [*sic*] value is your lack of reason which might permit you to jump the track in time to prevent you from going over the precipice. It's a great virtue. I admire it but I could never follow you. I can only say that occasionally you have landed (by accident) on something true.

I'm not going to see your latest miracle but I tell you what I'll do. I have an old classmate who is Medical Superintendant [*sic*] of a large, public sanatorium for tuberculosis in Pennsylvania. I'll present the story to him and ask him what he thinks of it. If he can be persuaded to see your man I'll be sponsor for him to the extent of getting an interview for him with my authority. I'll let you know the results. Then, whatever happens, for Christ's sake let's agree to shut up about it, one way or the other. If it's good, let the profession work the thing out in peace, if the verdict [*sic*] is that it's dangerous or has been tried without effect long since or something of the sort let that end it.

Meanwhile, since you believe in your innocense [*sic*] that my profession has something important to do with opening boils, ask me to open one on your ass next time and not in your brain.

You are so completely wrong in what you say of the Spanish situation that you have to build up a myth to support yourself that you only get inside information on what is going on and that nobody else knows anything – never realizing that many thoroughly trained men and women of all nationalities are spending their lives in Spain to discover personally what it is all about and that they can write also while you sit in Rapallo and drink in wisdom of the purest and most refined distillation. Crap. You can't get away with that with me. I glance at the papers to see where the troops are today or to try to discover what, under the news, the prize bastards of the world who rule it are cooking up. But beyond that I know what the moves must be, I know, at least, as well as you what the moves mean. You don't have to label them for me.

I only agree with you when you tell me of the concession seekers who are following Franco around and what that signifies. And what concessions are you seeking from Mussolini and Hitler? God help you.

Anyhow, you're my Ezra and you ain't the worst vice I own to. I have my troubles defending you in America these days but I still do it. Go on farting, I'm tough.

Yours
Bill

Your man: See Letter 91 and p. 125 above, and "Biographical Notes" on Tweddell, Francis I. In a letter to WCW of May 10, 1938 (Yale), EP calls him "an ass and an ape and a slacker NOT to go see Tweddell."

a myth: In his letter of May 10, EP says, "I do NOT get MY views from the nooz wypers. I get 'em first hand or at worst from private letters which show direct contact."

Franco: Generalissimo Francisco Franco (1892–1975) was the supreme commander of the Nationalist forces in the Spanish Civil War. In his letter of May 10, EP speaks of "the concession hunters flocking round Franco."

94. TLS-2

April 6, 1940

Dear Ezra:

All right, all right, all right – but before you start to play around with mathematics learn to write legibly, you leave yourself too many loop-holes for mental escape the way you write now. Voorhis is doing everything he can, I received a note from him this morning – that's what reminded me of you and that I hadn't answered your letter.

Let's see an operating statement of your sales for the last three years before we begin to talk about my bad influence on them. You've got a crust to talk that way. To my own knowledge, you've sold more copies of *Culture* since I wrote my short review than you sold since it first appeared. If you don't like the way I behave come back here and fight it. You haven't the nerve.

We're old friends and likely to continue to be so but I think you're slipping badly both in your mentality and in the force of your attacks. It comes from babying yourself and hiding behind a philosophy you know damned well is contrary to everything you stand for, really. I've defended you till I'm sick of it. Why, for instance, try to tell me that your whole initiative hasn't been anti-semitic of recent years? You know damned well it has been so. Tell somebody else such things but don't try it on me if you value the least vestige of what we used to treasure between us.

I have no use for Jews as Jews, their religion is so much shit, just like T. S. Eliot's religion or the Catholic Church. But just so long as the Catholic Church exists so long must and will Judahism [*sic*] exist, theyre identical – in everything but the stuff they dilute the arsenic with. And both are made for the same purpose, to deceive. Certainly men of intelligence are among their backers, what else is the intelligence for – apparently?

I have no news you'd be interrested [*sic*] in by the tone of what you write to me. Why do we waste our time?

Yours

Bill

Voorhis: Horace Jeremiah ("Jerry") Voorhis (1901–1982) of California served in the U.S. House of Representatives from 1937 to 1947. On January 23, 1940, he introduced a bill entitled the "National Credit for Defense Act" (H. R. 8080), which authorized something like a Social Credit national dividend; see Pound/Zukofsky, pp. 204–05.

Culture: EP's *Culture* (also known as *Guide to Kulchur*) was first published by New Directions in 1938. WCW reviewed it in "Penny Wise, Pound Foolish," *The New Republic* 99 (June 28, 1939), pp. 229–30. In this review, he accuses EP of thirty years' anti-Semitism. Responding in a letter to WCW of March 22, 1940 (Yale), EP suggests that WCW's accusation is a "wheeze to keep down my sales." See also Pound/Zukofsky, p. 201.

95. TLS-3

13 May [1940]

My vurry deer ole Hiram Kronk/

You go right up stairs and ask yr/ muvver did you lose yr/ sense of humour when you lost your virginity?

No you did NOT. and a li'l irritation from me never yet did yr/ mind any harm/ wotever effek it has on yr/ bile duct.   and now damn it, I putt yr/ letter out to answer and cant find it/

BUT anyhow/ use a WORD in the same sense/ I mean *you OUGHT* to use a word in the same sense when it refs/ to YOU as when you ref/ it to me.

You say fer 30 years EZ is antisemite/ O. K. IF you admit that in the same sense YOU have been/

i; e; against the masochism & muck that has bitched Europe and Xtianity fer 1900 or however many years/

that don't mean I start pogrums [*sic*]/ Fer 20 years or nigh on/ I advocated strictly ECONOMIC action re/ high finance/

That don't mean I have got to omit NAMES from list of high = swine and the general conspiracy to bitch the whole life of the occident.

Why the hell, by the way; being so god damnd autocthonous [*sic*], and waving the eagle's arse on 4th July/ didn't you ever dig up Brooks Adams "Law of/ Civilization and Decay/"

read it/ I seldom recommend an American author BUTTTT: we are 44 years late on THIS, probably the best buk/ writ in the U. S. after Whitman's 'Leaves.'

at any rate B/A/ had the most vigorous mind in the U. S. in his time/ and the prof[essor]/ snots never mentioned it when we wuz beink eddykated/

waaal, you weren't in the history dept/ and I dont spose MUCK-masters wanted to read a buk that wd/ have made him think, In Ames case I reckon it wuz just plumb iggurunce.

the stinking lack of ANY intellectual life in our goddam onivurstities.

B. Adams may have got coloured by local opinion later/ but in 1896 he was years ahead of any European historiography that I know. Spengler a fahrt left in his wake/ and Frobenius prob/ never heard of him.. such was the shitten inability of our cuntry to MENTION its real writers.

I don't suppose we *could* then have read the protocols/ they wd/ have been too damned DULL; too badly written, and probably incomprehensible UNTIL 20 years of Doug[las]/ and Gesell/

their origin is not the point/ it is their diagnosis of what has (now) happened that makes 'em educative.

You hit the results in the bed-bug ward of that there orspitool. and left the wikid life of the metroPolis.

Now IF you mean to write/ you have got to the time of life when you gotto [*sic*] KNOW more/ gotter know when yr/ view is greek; latin, european, oriental, near east or Confucian

(as distinct from chinese shit which is just a [*sic*] squshy as any other form of excrement.)

DAMN all, it is too long since you looked over the edge of yr/ hummock.

Canonist economics is ONE thing, and church decorations paid for by shares in the Monte Carlo casino are another.

"anti = ism" (of all sorts) is too vague a term fer impolite correspondence.

yrz

Ez P'o

What do yr/ tale [*sic*] hebes say to this? do they say ANYTHING/ did any bleedin bolo/ ever do anything but want labour to earn the interest on state capital, and to split up the general purchase ticket into specific cards for soap, suet and margerine [*sic*]???

? news wyper reports in interim??

Brooks Adams: Great-grandson of John Adams and brother of Henry Adams, Brooks Adams (1848–1927) published his *Law of Civilization and Decay* in 1895, three years after the so-called "Deathbed" edition of Walt Whitman's *Leaves of Grass*.

MUCK-masters: John Bach McMaster (1852–1932) was professor of American History at the University of Pennsylvania from 1883 to 1920. He was the author of *A History of the People of the United States,* 8 vols. (1883–1912), *The United States in the World War,* 2 vols. (1918–20), and studies of Benjamin Franklin, Daniel Webster, and Stephen Girard.

Ames: See "Biographical Notes" on AMES, HERMAN VANDENBURG.

Spengler: The German historian and philosopher Oswald Spengler (1880–1936) was the author of *The Decline of the West* (1919–1922).

the protocols: The *Protocols of the Learned Elders of Zion* ostensibly revealed a Jewish conspiracy to dominate the world. Adapted from a French political satire of 1864, the document was published in Russia in 1905 and used extensively in anti-Semitic propaganda. Its authenticity was called into question by Philip Graves of the London *Times* in 1921, but the fact that its origins were dubious did not affect EP's belief in the validity of its contents; see Carpenter, p. 613.

that there orspitool: The Nursery and Child's Hospital in New York City, from which WCW resigned under pressure in 1909; see Letter 3 above.

Ez P'o: Spelled in this way, EP's name recalls that of the Chinese poet Li Po (see Letter 60 above), as well as the Chinese character P'o3.5 (M. 5354, "sincere . . . substance of things").

this: EP encloses a two-page copy of Representative Voorhis' bill, H. R. 8080; see Letter 94 above.

96. TL-2

14 Luglio [July 1941]

Dear Bull

Thanks fer them kind words/ and herewith a memorandDUMB/ fer yr/ consideration.

What no one seems to remember is the DAMage done England during the Napoleonic wars by simply being cut off from ALL contemporary thought/ same goes for the U. S. now/ I note it in Hika and other magazines. Not only gross ingorance [*sic*] of thought on the Axis side of the line/ which side manifestly increases almost hourly/ BUT gross ignorance of Irish thought/ and of English thought. They have heard of Douglas because I TOLD 'em 23 years ago or 21 years or 20 or whenever/ BUT the [*sic*] are none [*sic*] ignorant of 20 years English thought on guilds that preceded it. Sale [*sic*] for distributism, so far as any of the mag/ I have seen.

Tale [*sic*] Blacam's Sinn Fein, pub/ 1921/ a whole phase of thought IGnored/ whole masses of geo = political thought ignored/ the Acad/ of Soc/ and Pol/ Sci/ is ham IGnorant./   even Bolchevism [*sic*] was not discussed/ basic fact that NO one was really communist/ not in Europe or the U. S./ but the capitalists did not open their papers to serious anaylsis [*sic*] of communism/ The whole occident wants homesteads/ or an equivalent/ plus defence of purchasing power of labour/ espec/ agricultural.

What is sense of Hika giving only one side? / The opposition that you indicate is TIME LAG/ or at least you better figure out how far there is ANY real opposition and how far it *is* Time lag and NOWT BUT time lag.

Communism/ and various other manifestations mere atavism to nomad mentality. oh hell/ NO real knowledge of Frobenius or enything else in the U. S. A.

shd/ be deelighted for any items you think wd/ guide me in the labyrinth

Now that the Japan Times can't get here, I get very little American news, but shd/ welcome yr/ ideas as to what I ought to think about our native land and its rulers. Naturally you object to thinking about its govt. and prefer to consider the

anthromomorphology [*sic*] and composition of the humus and subsoil/ but U keep
on xsposing that the outcroppins results from etc/ or are symptoms of.

waaal; more power to yr/ bloody elbow/   dear Richard [Aldington] seems to
have SUNK (and how). who else survives the tempest?

14 Luglio: This letter was appended by WCW to his essay "Ezra Pound: Lord Ga-Ga!"
    Decision 2:3 (September 1941), pp. 23–24, as evidence that EP had lost touch with
    political reality.

them kind words: In "Dr. Williams Cocks a Snook," *Hika* 7:7 (May 1941), pp. 7, 27,
    WCW writes, "I want to say that Ezra Pound went to Europe to get personal recogni-
    tion, to get recognition for his supreme genius. He wanted to rule because he was
    convinced he knew more than anyone else and so, by God!, had a right to rule and
    would rule."

Blacam's Sinn Fein: Aodh Sandrach De Blacam, *What Sinn Fein Stands For: The Irish
    Republican Movement: Its History, Aims and Ideals, Examined As to Their Significance
    to the World* (Dublin: Mellifont and London: Chapman and Dodd, 1921). In Chapter
    VI, "Gaelic Social Ideals," De Blacam envisions an Irish rural polity based on distrib-
    uted property and co-operative exchange. There would be private ownership of land but
    no surplus private capital. In cities, workers' guilds would be in charge of production,
    and a Just Price would regulate the sale of goods. De Blacam summarizes his program as
    a "vigorous democratic Distributivism" (p. xvi).

Acad/ of Soc/ and Pol/ Sci/: EP became a life member of the American Academy of
    Political and Social Science (Philadelphia) in 1940. For his later relations with the
    Academy, see Letter 165 below.

Japan Times: Between December 10, 1939, and September 29, 1940, EP contributed
    eleven items to the *Japan Times & Mail,* an English-language newspaper published in
    Tokyo.

97. TLS-2

18 Ott [October 1941]

Dear Bull

You live a few doors from deal [*sic*] Viola. mentally, morally and spirichooly.

Certain points will NOT go out of date till they are settled/   thefts from the
public purse, cheatings of the whole nation.

If you don't take up the points I make in the only means of communication
open to me, that's yr/ affair.

You assume my points are twaddle, and decline to find out whether they are so or not.

That ain't SCIENTIFIC, but you never did like medicine/

I spose you cure bunions by intuition/. . . . WHAT is [*sic*] Xt's name DO you know about doctrines that you have NOT read? ideas that you have NOT looked at?

You did not hear. You assumed. Then even Gorham [Munson] told you it was other.

The ole Jersey farmer and the giraffe, AS USUAL.

And then one day comes T. Tzara and he aint Alexander of Macedon . . .

Waaal; yr/ letter is dated August 25/

so I don't know whether you were then going communist or going episcopalian; but I assume yr/ article is full of meat (date of demise not yet ascertainable) There is a lot of meat lying round on the steppes at this moment.

If you have joined Possum and the Archpiscop of Pork in the episcopalian = communist prayer = circle that wd: be *up to date* for N. Jersey, but I do NOt *assume* that you have done so.

Yr/ article is doubtless enlightened (a pale celto = Jersic twilight.)

I am doing a bilingual edtn of the Ta Hio, having translated and [*sic*] excellent novel by the other E. P. (Enrico Pea)

Yaaas, five vols of Morrison chinese-dic[tionary]. spread round on various stands, and the first chapter of the ideograms been zincografato before I left the Eternal City [Rome] on Wednesday.

Why you think Aristotle, John Adams and Confucius are twaddle I don't know. And yr/ opinions of the Athenian constitution are awaited with patience. Not that I allus use the classics, but I do sometime. Wall bless yr/ baldening pate, and gawd save civilization.

> yrz
> Ezra Pound

I don't quite git yr/ remarks on opportunity. Just WHAT DO you mean?

a few doors from . . . *Viola:* See "Biographical Notes" on JORDAN, VIOLA BAXTER. She lived in Tenafly, New Jersey, not far from Rutherford.

T. Tzara: The Romanian poet, playwright, and critic Tristan Tzara (Samuel Rosenstock, 1896–1963) was a co-founder of the Dada movement in Zurich in 1916–19.

yr/ letter: WCW's letter to EP of August 25, 1941, has apparently not survived.

yr/ article: Probably "Ezra Pound: Lord Ga-Ga!"; see Letter 96 above.

meat lying round on the steppes: A reference to heavy Soviet losses in the early battles of Germany's campaign against the Soviet Union, launched on June 22, 1941. WCW misquotes this passage of EP's letter in his contribution to "The Case for and against Ezra Pound," ed. Charles Norman, *PM* (New York) 138 (November 25, 1945), pp. 12–17.

the Archpiscop of Pork: William Temple (1881–1944) was Archbishop of York from 1929 to 1942 and Archbishop of Canterbury from 1942 to 1944. An advocate of the social application of Christ's gospel, Temple was a member of the Labour Party and the Workers' Education Association. He was also chairman of the committee that produced a controversial report on unemployment, entitled *Men without Work* (1938).

a bilingual edtn of the Ta Hio: Confucio. Ta S'eu. Dai Gaku. Studio Integrale. Versione italiana di Ezra Pound e di Alberto Luchini (Rapallo: Scuola Tipografico Orfanotrofio Emiliani, 1942). According to Gallup, B46, "each page has Chinese text with Italian version below."

and excellent novel: EP's translation of the first volume of the four-volume novel *Il romanzo di Moscardino* (1922) by the Italian-Egyptian novelist and printer Enrico Pea (1881–1952) was first published in *New Directions 15* (1955), pp. 86–131.

Morrison chinese-dic.: Robert Morrison (1782–1834) was the author of *A Dictionary of the Chinese Language,* 7 vols. (1815–23). EP's copy is now at Hamilton College.

zincografato: Zincography is a process of printing by means of etched zinc plates.

98. TLS-2

Nov. 26, 1941

Dear Eazy:

Your brutal and sufficiently stupid reference to meat lying around on the steppes at this moment is quite an unnecessary flight of fancy, you'll find far more of it solidly encased in your own head. I used to think you had a brain, no more. It looks more like round steak every time you try to reveal it.

Do you imagine that your position in "the Eternal City" gives you an intellectual advantage of any sort? And what in God's name you think you're talking about when you speak of Jersey farmers? Did you ever see one? Maybe you think your devoted Viola (who was never one of my appendages!) grows potatoes in her back yard.

You're just an ignorant infant trying to batter out the sides of his crib.

Yes, I have read the Athenian constitution. I have also read of the end of Constantinople and the Cantos of Ezra Pound – for the most part. What does that make me? I presume you too have read books. You even adapted some verses from the Chinese once – to make a native guffaw. I presume you were trying to please Viola or one of her upstate cousins.

You ask me what I know about doctrines that I do *not* read. What in hell do you know about the doctrines you *do* read? The presumptive effects of them never for one moment seem to dent your skull – or you wouldn't write such trivial wash. You have, I presume, read all the outpourings of your imbecillic [*sic*] leaders and have swallowed everything they say, spittle and all. Is this or is this not true? Come on, let's have specific statements of just what and whom you are backing. Is it Hitler or Moussie [Mussolini]? Or both? I want facts.

As for Aristotle, John Adams and Confucius! I only wish they were alive, just to see them laugh! Boy! that would be something. They wouldn't even have to castrate you to make you an eunuch. Honestly, you do have the damndest fund of selfesteem [*sic*] and narrow mindedness it has ever been my delight to encounter.

For God's sake (I'm sorry to have brought that up again) can't you see that every word you utter reveals to any intelligent and wellinformed man that you know nothing at all? Had you one grain of understanding you wouldn't rant as you do. You seem to be fighting something off from yourself, hiding yourself behind some sort of mysterious screen which you call enlightenment. You're a wonder. Barnum missed something when he missed you.

I hope your family is holding up under your weaknesses. You need it – badly.

Affectionately yours
Bill

Nov. 26, 1941: Postal delivery to Italy was suspended when the United States entered World War II early in December. This letter was returned to WCW.

Barnum: The American impresario Phineas Taylor Barnum (1810–1891) earned fame and fortune by stocking his American Museum with oddities of nature.

PART FOUR
1945–1951

Pound continued to broadcast over Rome Radio after the United States entered the war. In some speeches he attacked President Roosevelt and urged American soldiers not to fight against Italy; he also made many anti-Semitic remarks. The broadcasts were monitored in Washington, and the Department of Justice prepared charges of treason against Pound, who was still an American citizen. After Pound mentioned "my old friend Doc Williams of Rutherford, New Jersey" in one talk, the F.B.I. interviewed Williams, much to his chagrin. Pound was indicted by a federal grand jury in October 1943.

In May 1945, he was arrested by Italian partisans in Rapallo and turned over to the United States Army in Genoa. He spent the next six months in an Army prison camp near Pisa. In November, he was flown to Washington, D.C., and brought before a federal court. To avoid a possible death sentence, his lawyer entered a plea of mental incompetence. After a psychiatric examination, the prosecution and the judge accepted this plea, and Pound was remanded to St. Elizabeths Hospital for the criminally insane in Washington, there to remain until such time as he was well enough to be brought to trial. He was held in St. Elizabeths for the next twelve and a half years.

Williams resumed his correspondence with Pound, although his feelings about the man were intensely ambivalent. On the one hand, he believed that Pound was guilty of treason, and that he should stand trial, state his defense, and take his punishment like a man. The mental-incompetence plea seemed to Williams a cop-out: "That you're crazy I don't for one moment believe" (February 4, 1946). On the other hand, Williams still cared for his poet-friend, pitied his plight, and did not really want to see him executed.

During the spring and summer of 1946, Williams tried to ease the burden of Pound's imprisonment by writing him long, chatty letters at frequent intervals. At the beginning of his incarceration, Pound was physically and mentally shattered. As in the *Pisan Cantos,* his mind reverted to the past, and his letters summon nostalgic reminiscences of H. D. and Ford Madox Ford in pre-1914 London.

As Pound adjusted to his new circumstances, he regained strength and confidence. With the help of his wife Dorothy, who had come to live in Washington, Pound began to lead a productive life in St. Elizabeths. He wrote and published, received visitors and books, and carried on an extensive correspondence.

He was also utterly unrepentant. He recanted none of his former views or actions. He believed that he had been right about Mussolini, Roosevelt, and the

Jews. Although he probably did not learn of the Holocaust until after the war, he never publicly denounced it. He regarded his broadcasts as legitimate and patriotic exercises of free speech protected by the First Amendment to the Constitution. He therefore considered his imprisonment to be illegal and unjust.

As his energy returned, Pound began to bully Williams as of old about the inadequacy of his reading. Williams, as usual, resented Pound's presumption yet took his recommendations to heart. Before the end of 1946, Williams was once more so furious with Pound that he broke off the correspondence for several months. He could not bring himself to visit St. Elizabeths until October 1947, more than a year and a half after Pound was housed there.

Subsequently, Williams visited St. Elizabeths about once a year. To judge from the evidence of correspondence and a diary kept by Dorothy Pound (now at Indiana), Williams saw Pound on the following dates: October 18, 1947; November 20, 1948; January 21, 1950; June 1950; February 10, 1951; December 1952; April 27, 1954; and May 1954. After that, Williams' deteriorating health made travel difficult for him.

These were years of intense literary activity for both men. Hampered by paper restrictions during the war, New Directions undertook an ambitious postwar publishing program. The first four books of Williams' long poem *Paterson* appeared to great critical acclaim between 1946 and 1951. A volume of his *Selected Poems* paved the way for *Collected Later Poems* (1950) and *Collected Earlier Poems* (1951). Pound's *Pisan Cantos* and the first collected edition of Cantos 1–84 appeared in 1948, and his *Selected Poems* reached bookshops in 1949. It was an impressive burst of publications by the little company Pound liked to call "Nude Erections."

The new books brought celebrity and honors to both authors. Williams received the Russell Loines Award from the National Institute of Arts and Letters in 1948 and the National Book Award in 1950. The Library of Congress invited him in 1948 to become its Consultant in Poetry. Honorary degrees were bestowed upon him by the University of Buffalo in 1946, by Rutgers University and Bard College in 1950, and by the University of Pennsylvania in 1952. Invitations to read and record his work arrived regularly, and after 1947 he was a featured speaker at writers' conferences and workshops around the country. Younger writers gravitated to him for encouragement and inspiration. At last Williams was receiving some of the wider recognition he had always craved.

Meanwhile, Pound again made headlines when a committee of the Library of Congress awarded him the Bollingen Prize in February 1949. The award honored the *Pisan Cantos* as the best book of American poetry published in 1948. Because Pound was an alleged traitor, the announcement provoked a national furor. His selection triggered a wide-ranging debate over the relationship between politics and poetry, and over the role of the national government in fostering the arts. Williams defended the presentation of the award to Pound and was in turn criticized for his stance.

Amidst the glare of publicity, both poets—now in their sixties—began to experience health problems. Pound's were relatively minor, but Williams' were more serious. The Pounds sought Williams' advice on a variety of medical and dental questions, and Williams sometimes sent prescriptions for Dorothy to take to the pharmacy. At the same time, though, the doctor himself was beginning to pay the price for years of overwork. In February 1948, he suffered a mild heart attack; and in March 1951, a stroke—the first of a series. Williams now began gradually to turn his medical practice over to his elder son.

As he withdrew from practice, Williams began to worry about retirement income. He had saved few of his earnings. He therefore decided in 1950, when his reputation was bullish, to seek a publisher who would assure him wider sales and greater profits than he was accustomed to receiving from New Directions. He accepted an advance of $5,000 from Random House for three books of prose, including his *Autobiography*. During the next ten years, Williams published eight books with Random House and McDowell, Obolensky. Nevertheless, *Paterson* remained in the hands of New Directions, and by 1960 Williams had severed his connections with other houses and rejoined Pound and Laughlin at "ND."

In *Paterson,* as in *Kora in Hell* and *The Great American Novel,* Williams made creative use of his correspondence with Pound. Pound's *Cantos* had taught Williams how to incorporate letters and other historical documents into an epic-length poem. As if in tribute to his mentor, Williams includes edited versions of four different letters from Pound in *Paterson*. All four belong to the postwar correspondence; the earliest dates from 1948 and the latest from 1956. All are included in the present edition. Once again, a phase of the correspondence that began in conflict ended in collaboration.

99. ALS-3

Dec. 10 1945

Dear Bill,

I imagine you are following what happens to my poor EP.?

If he needs some cash, can you lend him a little? I will repay you before too long – At present am all held up as they won't give me a new passport – I have applied through my solicitors in London,

Shakespear & Parkyn

8. John Street

Bedford Row, W.C

for a permit to visit EP. & shall come over if possible. I've had all sorts of trouble about getting enough, or any, money here, for daily expenses –

You must know that E. has never been a traitor: he has never broadcast a syllable against his country's Constitution –

They tell me now he is very ill. I get news through S[hakespear] & P[arkyn]. (A[rthur]. V. Moore:) I saw him twice in the camp Oct.–Nov. in Italy: after *five months* incommunicado when I did not even know where he was: it is all monstrous.

Please write him – any thing – if you can find his address..I have none.

Affecly
Dorothy Pound

Laughlin or MacLeish are the best to communicate with.

here: This letter is written from the Villa Raggio, Cerisola, Rapallo.
the camp: From May to November 1945, EP was held at the U. S. Army's Disciplinary Training Center near Pisa. Dorothy visited him on October 3 and November 3.
Laughlin or MacLeish: See "Biographical Notes" on LAUGHLIN, JAMES, and MACLEISH, ARCHIBALD.

100. ALS-1

[January 31, 1946]

"The pure products of America
                    go crazy."

all right ole bull-pup!
   who said it??

però
   mañana
      sara
         otro
            dìa. [*sic*]

Ez P.

The pure products: EP quotes from WCW's poem "To Elsie," first published in *Spring and All* (1923) and reprinted in EP's *Active Anthology* (1933). EP's legal defense rested upon a claim of mental incompetence, as certified by a panel of psychiatric examiners. *però:* Spanish proverb, "but tomorrow will be another day."

101. TLS-1

February 4, 1946

Dear Ez:

That you're crazy I don't for one moment believe, you're not that good an American. And if you're shot as a traitor what the hell difference should that make to you? All it should mean is that you go down to the future, on which you seem to count so much, intact, your argument undamaged. Not many years left anyway for either of us.

Had a letter from Dorothy enclosing a leaflet entitled Introductory TEXT BOOK, printed apparently in Rapallo and showing quotations from various American statesmen, with a note by you. Everything there is O. K. She asked me to get in touch with you. She is trying to come to America.

If there is anything I can do for you let me know. Best of everything.

Yours
Bill

a leaflet: A three-page "Introductory Text Book E. P." containing quotations from John Adams, Thomas Jefferson, Abraham Lincoln, and the Constitution of the United States, with a "Note" by EP, was privately printed in London in 1939. A second edition was printed in Rapallo in December 1945.

102. TLS-3

March 29, 1946

Dear Ez:

I came to Rutherford merely that I might survive, I refused to be sucked in by the maelstrom. Here I have been able to cut down my work when necessary by just saying no. I accept your amende honorable as offered. I wish to Christ you'd been here all these years, that's all I can say, though I can understand the necessity you were under even at the cost of its tragic outcome. Your work, especially your early work, is a landmark; it is work no one has surpassed in our day.

The sad thing to me is that I'm afraid you yourself never properly recognized your own great talents but allowed them to be subverted by something else which must always have been secondary in you. I'm not going to quarrel with you now over that by trying to be more specific. A man doesn't put his life in the balance against the subtlties [*sic*] of the poetic line and yet your life weighed, to your everlasting glory, no more than your poetic genius – had you known it. You wanted more. You still want more.

Mother, who will be 90 the day before Christmas, always asks after you with the most intense interest. She feels you belong to her clan, the artists. She has forgiven you completely for all faults the others have imputed to you, she does not believe them. The old gal has a broken hip, she can't walk. She was operated on for cataracts in both eyes many years ago [1937] with rather unsatisfactory results; she can see but she can't read – all she knows of the news she hears from the woman who takes care of her, who in turn knows what she wants to hear about and cuts paragraphs from the papers which mother, though she can't read them keeps for me and for Ed[gar Williams]. She has in her posession [*sic*] everything in the papers relating to you. Poor old thing, she's deaf as well as half blind. I'm amazed at her spirit.

As to your first paragraph: no one forgives you for what you did, everyone forgives you for what you are. Horace Gregory for instance is doing everything he can to get your work republished. Jim Laughlin is eager to help you. Abd [*sic*] for God's sake you didn't expect anyone to *listen* to your foul-mouthed broadcasts, did you? Some listened until bored to death and then quit. Viola [Baxter Jordan] listened and was fed up with your ranting. I didn't listen at all, the mere fact of your broadcasting at all at such a time was enough for me; I was interested in other things to me far more important. You might as well realize that there is a point in all controversy beyond which a man's life (his last card) is necessarily forfeit. A man accepts that and goes on with his eyes open. But when the showdown comes he loses his life.

There is so much I should have liked to talk over with you through the years –
but not in the mood you were habitually in and not there, where you were, but
here – on the ground. I don't know what you mean by saying a frenchman or an
italian cannot be expected to love England *more* than France and Italy. I don't see
why he should love England at all. I don't – certainly not as a writer, which is all
that concerns us. Especially I don't see why we should love the substitute english
and ape them in our work. I see that we should very definitely love our own
"France" and "Italy" far more than England or anything english or englishoid.
Where the hell have *you* been all these years while you were discovering such
matters?

I acknowledge my life is hell – for a so called intelligent person – I allow
myself to be tormented by stupid detail until there is nothing left of me any more
than there is to a tramhorse after 40 years of dragging idiocy around. However
there is no other way, no other effective way, to get what I want, therefore I take
the bad with the good. I do not pretend that my way is the only way or even the
best way to get on but it is the way I have found. I am particularly annoyed today
as my distorted sentences show. I do not like it.

Parker Tyler has produced a poem which I like and admire called *The Granite
Butterfly*. I have written an appraisal of it for a little mag called *Accent,* to appear
next month. There are 9 "cantos" upon a rather lurid theme of lust and murder
but the effect is very successfully of a work of art, not just another telling of a
sensational story in second-hand imitation poetry. I have called the poem the best
long poem produced in America since the disaster of Eliot's Waste– [*sic*]   eliot
set us all back a generation. Tyler resumes where our investigations were stopped
by that piece of vaginal stop-gap. Why have you never protested against Eliot and
his gleet? Now we have the malady of the franco-gobi St J. Perse to struggle with,
a direct result of Eliot and the failure of men like yourself to stop him. I can't do it
all. But you prefer translations. So be it.

Louis Zokofsky [*sic*], potentially our best poet or best lyrist, had come through
with a small volume, *Anew*. It has in it some of the most adult lines written
anywhere, after music, today. His wife Celia is a composer who has helped Louis
greatly to get away from his fractured language and make soundable lines of his
verse. Unless somebody *points out* Louis' accomplishments not one person will
see them with the overlay of bad Aiken-Eliot-Perse putridity we labor in. There
have not been intelligences enough here to perceive and make clear what the
battle is *for*. Music, clarity, freshness: *Anew*. Poor blind Louis, a Jew, what
chance has he to realize anything without help? No chance at all. Then you go and
make yourself a political prisoner, you ass.

All sorts of little magazines publish new poems by me – some of them or even
most of them of little worth perhaps. I do articles and write stories – such mags as

Arizona Quarterly (1 poem), Harvard Wake (an article on Cummings and 5 or 6 poems), Contemporary Poetry, (2 poems), Yale Literary Review (4 or 5 poems etc etc. A month ago I sent a complete 2 act play (prose) to an agent. Ten days ago New Republic, whether you like it or not, accepted a 4 page poem of mine entitled *Russia*.

It may interest you to know that the Comprehensive Anthology of American Poetry which has used you for so much inexpensive advertising – the bastards! excludes me from its list. Why in hell don't you write to them and tell them you refuse to have your work included unless they include mine also? And it isn't the bastard of a publisher who is really at fault, he's running true tp [*sic*] type and not much more could be expected of him; it's Conrad Aiken, Eliot's backer and ass-licker who is the real nigger in the woodpile. There's where the fight should be made.

The first part of my 4 part poem *Paterson* should be out in two weeks. Laughlin has made a beautiful job of the thing as far as appearances go. The following 3 parts should be out within the year or by next year if I am given any encouragement. Naturally, if the play is produced and brings me in a little cash much more can be done to forward the entire game. The main thing we lack is the right kind of brains, of sensitivity and knowledge. We need more concentration of the means of writing well so that we can defend ourselves. The whole racket in modern second-hand criticism is to prevent the opposition from being *heard*. The means of getting a hearing is monopolized by the dullards as always. We need help and the help runs off to play and to be scratched by "foreigners".

During the entire war the french surrealist group has been living in New York, running back and forth over the country on the snot that runs from Peggy Guggenheim's nostrils which they lick up and thrive on. They boast of their immunity to *all* american ideas but live immured in their own ideas safe from our contamination. Let's not mention names, I hope they have returned to Paris and will remain there until they rot – which will take place long before their deaths if it is not long since well started by now. A crappy and ignorant crew of something out of a dog's stomach. If there is sterility prevalent in the world today you'll find much of it just there. No good to anyone, all they think of is to protect themselves from all contacts.

Will they allow you to have books and magazines which might be sent you? I don't want to flood you with stuff your nerves are not ready to accept – but if you want anything in the way of reading matter I'd be glad to send you what there is.

And for God's sake write so I can read your letter. This last was better than most but I'm not sure yet what you want to say in several spots.

Your old friend
Bill

your amende honorable: In a letter to WCW of March 23, 1946 (Yale), EP says, "Well I *now* after 35 years understand why you chuck'd N. Y. for Rutherford. I mean I see now that you were right *then.* = If that is amende honorable – take it as such." An *amende honorable* is a public avowal of an error, fault, or crime.

your first paragraph: EP's letter of March 23 opens as follows: "Reflectively & calmly I defy you to find 5 cents worth of magnanimity in all the fkn gang you pull with."

Horace Gregory: The American poet and critic Horace Gregory (1891–1982) was professor of English at Sarah Lawrence College. He was a friend and correspondent of WCW and a sympathetic critic of his work. He liked EP's early poetry but not *The Cantos*; see Pound/Zukofsky, p. 227.

a frenchman or an italian: In his letter of March 23, EP asserts that "a frenchman has a right to love France MORE than England, or an Italian, Italy more than England."

Parker Tyler: See "Biographical Notes" on TYLER, PARKER.

gleet: A slimy or watery discharge from the human body.

St J. Perse: The French poet and diplomat Saint-John Perse (Alexis Saint-Leger Leger, 1887–1975) was the author of *Anabase* (1924) and *Exil* (1945). T. S. Eliot gave his work currency in Britain and the United States by publishing an English translation of *Anabase* in 1930.

Louis Zokofsky: See "Biographical Notes" on ZUKOFSKY, LOUIS, and Pound/Zukofsky, pp. 208–10.

Arizona Quarterly: WCW's poem "The Horse" appeared in the *Arizona Quarterly* for Spring 1946.

Harvard Wake: The *Harvard Wake* for Spring 1946 was a special e. e. cummings issue. It carried WCW's essay "lower case cummings" and nine of WCW's poems (not five or six).

Contemporary Poetry: One poem by WCW (not two) appeared in *Contemporary Poetry* (Baltimore, Maryland) for Spring 1946: "The Mind's Game."

Yale Literary Review: The *Yale Poetry* (not Literary) *Review* carried four poems by WCW in the issue for Summer 1946: "East Coocoo," "Ol' Bunk's Band," "The Savage Beast," and "At Kenneth Burke's Place."

a complete 2 act play: WCW sent the script of his play *A Dream of Love* to Tennessee Williams' agent Audrey Wood; but it was not performed until the summer of 1949.

New Republic: WCW's poem "Russia" appeared in *The New Republic* for April 29, 1946. Its rosy vision of a postwar communist society was not likely to appeal to EP.

Conrad Aiken: See "Biographical Notes" on AIKEN, CONRAD.

Paterson: New Directions published *Paterson* (*Book One*) on June 1, 1946. The striking visual layout of the book was largely the work of the printer George W. Van Vechten, Jr., of Metuchen, New Jersey.

the french surrealist group: A number of French writers and artists sat out World War II in New York. They included André Breton (1896–1966), who founded the surrealist movement in 1924; Marcel Duchamp (1887–1968); and Max Ernst (1891–1976). The American art collector and patron Peggy Guggenheim (1898–1979) married Ernst in 1941. From 1943 to 1947, she directed and financed a New York gallery called "Art of This Century," where the surrealists often exhibited their work.

103. ALS-2

31 Mz [March 1946]

Dr Bull

Comfort to know yr. mother is still alive – as if something were left after the cataclasm [*sic*].

(of course here there has been no cataclasm & there can be no understanding until a whole new means of communication is built up – neath which weight I am crushed = I mean need of creating it.) –

anyhow despite blind-deaf etc. still feel that one of those flashes of indestructable [*sic*] charm will come from her @ an odd moment – as it did when I last saw her. = Broken temple – but still a flame in embers of altar.

rest of yr./ letter wd/ need a months work to answer.

go on writing me when you can

only things that pierce the wall are letters & occ[asional]. visit.

you have no idea of my condition.

y
Ez.

when I last saw her: Probably June 5, 1939, when EP stayed overnight at WCW's home during his last visit to the United States before the war.

104. TLS-2

April 6, 1946

Dear Ezra:

I did not get over to see Mother today but when I do go, tomorrow, I'll tell her of your greetings and I know she will be pleased that you remember abd [*sic*] speak of her. She is living in a nursing home presided over by a very kindly (and strong) english woman who picks her up every night around 2 or 3 o'clock to let her piss. I can't imagine the life that this Mrs. [Harry] Taylor leads but she's happy in it and refuses to raise her very reasonable rates even though I urge her to charge more. She won't do it, it's against her conscience. We had Mother here for 18 years but it was too much for us taking meals up day after day and bringing her limping down every evening for supper. When she broke her leg the third time I insisted that she go to this home where she has remained ever since.

We had Paul's wife and two children here while he was at sea, first in the

Atlantic on a destroyer then in the Pacific. They have now put their money, little enough of it, down on a house here in town and have moved away. The day they left Bill, the doctor, was released from his job also with the Navy and turned up from New Orleans where his ship had been decommissioned. He is loafing now adjusting himself to the civilian world again after 4 years of it in the Pacific. It's hard to realize that the terrible grind is over, I for one can't yet think straight even now but expect the deprivation and terror to begin again any day. Bill went out tonight with old friends wearing his civies [civilian clothes] for the first time in the 4 years of his service. I hardly knew him.

Not that I want to go on speaking to you of these things which interest you perhaps not all – but they interest me and so I speak of them.

I am doing what I can to find Nancy Cunard for you. I know few people in London these days but did find one name, for that's all it is to me, which might serve. It belongs to a young Irish poet, Leslie Daiken whose work I admire. He sent me a small book of his poems, Signatures of All Things, to which I am replying by sending him one of my Collected Poems – as soon as I can get it from Laughlin. He hasn't been answering my letter [sic] of late – he may be busy getting his next New Directions edition out and has perhaps cut himself off from the world until that is ready to launch. I'm surmising only. Daiken should know everyone in London, he'll find Nancy if anyone can, that is, if she's about. God knows where she is, perhaps here. We'll see.

I sent your last letters to Zukofsky.

Bob McAlmon is working for his brothers who own a surgical instrument supply house, The South-Western Surgical Supply. We hear from him now and then.

There's no use my going to see you, it would break me up and do you little good I imagine. I think it's bettr [sic] to stick to letters but if at any time the matter becomes urgent please speak frankly and I'll come. Of course it's urgent now but may become more urgent later. Anyhow there's my word.

I go on writing as I've told you – but I don't know what you want to hear. I'm sure you're not interested in my garden or in my casual day. I'm looking forward, as I think I told you, to the appearance of the long first fart [sic] of my poem *Paterson*. I imagine that it will not be particularly noticed, nothing of mine has been particularly noticed – except the brief flurry over the novel White Mule at which time Laughlin, the publisher, had been at pains to be in New Zeeland [sic] skiing when he might have made the book a good seller.

No news of my play, now at an agency. I think I told you of that too.

I hear that Hilda is giving a course at Bryn Maur [sic] this semester in Poetry. Have no idea what it's about or who grought [sic] her here or is staying with her. Bryher, no doubt. I think she has been paying the bills for years.

I'll write you now and then – so long as you care to have me do so but I'm afraid it won't be exciting. My excitements – as about the 5 year old child who is recovering from meningitis, lively enough for me, is [sic] not international news. I'm reading Evelyn Waugh's, Brideshead Revisited. It's a good english novel now a best seller, well written and just that cleverness and keeness [sic] of wit which flatters our provincial senses and makes us feel a little the aristocrat just to hear. But it's good reading. I distrust, however, the Catholic mind behind it. How we are being beset before and behind these days with fat priests crawling to glory on their protuberant bellies! Clare Luces (part owner of LIFE magazine and TIME!) being converted to Catholicism by the various Monseigneuri! Poor decent Jesus, what his memory has had to suffer upon this earth. I wish I might suggest that the Establishment devote its one day's take from the poor of thw [sic] world to feed the poor of the world. Quel bonheur [what happiness] it might be. But we have movies of base-ball playing priests sweetly saving the old farm – and much more. Waugh's novel a subtly reversed edition of the same. And much, much else. There's your chance, old boy, snap it up and be saved.

Tell me what you want me to write about.

> Your old friend
> Bill

Paul's wife: Paul Williams married Virginia Carnes in June 1941. Their son Paul, Jr., was born in August 1942; and their daughter Suzanne, in August 1944. "Jinny" and the children lived at 9 Ridge Road from September 1944 to March 1946.

Nancy Cunard: See "Biographical Notes" on CUNARD, NANCY. In a letter to WCW of April 2 [1946] (Yale), EP writes: "I know mostly who's alive & who'se [sic] dead = but no news of [Basil] Bunting or of Nancy Cunard." In a letter of May 26 (Indiana), WCW was able to send EP Cunard's Paris address. For the resumption of correspondence between EP and Cunard, see Letter 110 below.

Leslie Daiken: The Irish poet Leslie H. Daiken was born in Dublin in 1912. He attended Trinity College, Dublin. He is the author of *Signatures of All Things* (1945) and the editor of *They Go, the Irish: A Miscellany of War-Time Writing* (1944).

White Mule: When *White Mule* was published in June 1937, 500 copies of the first impression sold out quickly. An additional 600 copies had been printed but not bound. James Laughlin had gone to New Zealand with a ski team, and nothing could be done until his return in September.

my play: See Letter 102 above.

Hilda: See "Biographical Notes" on DOOLITTLE, HILDA.

Bryher: See "Biographical Notes" on ELLERMAN, WINIFRED.

Brideshead Revisited: The English satiric novelist Evelyn Waugh (1903–1960) published *Brideshead Revisited: The Sacred and Profane Memories of Captain Charles Ryde* in 1945; the first American edition was published in Boston by Little, Brown and Company in January 1946. It is the saga of an English Catholic family and its ancestral home.

Clare Luces: The American playwright, magazine editor, businesswoman, congresswoman, and diplomat Clare Boothe Luce (1903–1987) was the wife of Henry Robinson Luce, publisher of *Life, Time,* and *Fortune* magazines. On February 16, 1946, Bishop Fulton J. Sheen announced that Mrs. Luce had been received that day into the Roman Catholic Church at St. Patrick's Cathedral in New York.

base-ball playing priests: Possibly a reference to the popular films *Going My Way* (1944) and *The Bells of St. Mary's* (1945) starring Bing Crosby as Father O'Malley, an athletic young priest.

105. TLS-2

April 24, 1946

Dear Ez:

Were conditions different, peaceful and more easy for you (though how could they be easier?) and the past not the past – I'd josh you a bit about your blinding egoism, make a few mental reservations as to your limitations and write you the sort of letter I thought you could understand and let it go at that.

It would be worth it too. To the men who do the creative work in the world, those fastened so hard upon the "local" that their feet fairly grow into the soil there, it is stimulating to feel the breezes of such "translators" as yourself blowing about the temples. It gives an impetus toward a new dedication to duty in a hard battle with materials to have minds such as yours remind us of the goals toward which we are striving. The universal objectives toward which men in all ages have locally striven: to rise from the local until that difficult resistance has been forced to become illumined.

Did you think that YOU were the illumination? But your place is a magnificent one – once you fully realize its dependence on the masteries of others.

Ezra do you not realize the pathetic falsity of your position when, at your age and with your reputed insight into the world you fail to see that there is no limitation in the materials (the local) to a man's flight if he is able to make it? I do not deny the value of your own work, be at least courteous enough to recognize that a man in my position is not limited by what you so glibly call his provincialism. I have no ill will against you but you talk like a second rater when you fail to realize the true nature of my position – or your own.

When I speak of Eliot as a quitter you reply that as between Eliot and me you prefer yourself. Good idea. I like it. But it is neither a helpful nor an intelligent answer. You show merely that you don't know the conditions about which you snap out your "illuminations". Think a minute, if possible. And for once give a direct answer to a question: you never answer direct questions.

Tell me these things: Can you receive books? Can you receive magazines? Are you permitted to receive manuscripts and comment upon them? And if so do you want to have such things sent to you? Certainly you have mind enough left to say yes or no to such simple queries. You speak of the time lag; what are you doing to combat the situation?

Mind you, I'm not attempting to bind you to anything. I'm merely trying to satisfy myself as to your real condition.

It's wonderful to think that you're coming around again to the virtues of old Ford. Where have you been all these years?

No news from Nancy [Cunard]. Always glad to hear from you. I've got a small book coming out soon called PATERSON? Now specifically, am I permitted to send it to you and if so do you want to read it?

> Yours as always
> Bill

Eliot: In a letter to WCW of April 19 [1946] (Buffalo), EP writes: "You blinded by puppygander. Eliot going as far as buggy milieu permits. both of you adaptin local necessity – fortunately DIFFERET [*sic*] locales."

time lag: In the same letter, EP says, "Time lag here gets WORSE not better."

old Ford: See "Biographical Notes" on FORD, FORD MADOX. In his letter of April 19, EP speaks of "ole Fordie – who knew more than any of us."

106. ALS-3

[April] 26 [1946]

D Bull,

1. Yes I can receive books & mags. & mss.

(the god shitten customs house as usual holds up foreign books & pewbs [publications] for 35 cents. to prevent internat. communication. causing delay or possibly block

   that is an affair to COM-bloody-BATT from inside the Frontiers)

2. My Main spring is busted . . . I can not make ANY effort mental or

physical. i. e cannot comment, or trust my 1/2 formed comment, on anything sent me.

IF the goddam mind flows O. K. but if not, NOT & nowt to do about it. also

_____   _____

_____   _____

lacunae [gaps] all over & thru the dam thing.

Hell! I boosted Ford as much as anyone except Goldring – but NOT enough – NOT ENOUGH.

not a case of come *back* to Fordie –

I never left him & he never suggested that I did; @ least once contrasted me with "all" (really *most*) his frieds [*sic*] of 1909–14 as not having double xx'd him.

I was trying to tell you how to combat the evil that Eliot has (*unintentionally*) done & does

yrs

EZ

Dont pull yr. punches in reply.

Goldring: The English poet, novelist, short-story writer, and essayist Douglas Goldring (1887–1960) was Ford's assistant editor on *The English Review*. He later published a memoir entitled *South Lodge: Reminiscences of Violet Hunt, Ford Madox Ford, and the English Review Circle* (1943).

107. TLS-2

7/8/46

Dear Ez:

Flossie vetoed the enclosed letter – but I send it anyway but in a different mood from that in which it was written – for your possible amusement.

Let me try to remember a sentence I learned by heart a day or two ago, it is from an essay by John Dewey, Democracy and America: Vital and thorough attachments are bred only in an intimacy of intercourse which is of necessity restricted in range.

I like that sentence. It means much to me. I was interested when I first began to memorize it to find how many variants could be devised in the wording of it. First I kept saying: *by [*sic*] an intimacy. Then I said: through an intimacy. Finally I found myself saying: limited in range – and – limited in scope. etc etc.

I read the various reviews of books in the [New York] Times Book Review section – a bad practice, I know, but one that helps me here and there to discover at least what has been published. I can't read long treatises such as the various philosophic works of Kirkegaard [*sic*]. All I can do is to pick up what I can from the reviews I read here and there of his outpourings. I am reading the Age of Jackson by Schlesinger – whom, by the way, I asked to drop in on you sometime when he is in Washington.

I have read various short stories by Anais Nin. I have read whatever comes to me of Parker Tyler's writing. Notably of late I have read a long poem of his called The Granite Butterfly. It is very good. I have translated (for Jim Laughlin) some short bits by Eluard – you no doubt saw them in ND 1946. I have read a Western called Billy the Kid. A hot bit of American history which I greatly enjoyed. I see new poems by all sorts of men American, British, French and South American. Zukofsky has done two or three things that I greatly admire. There are many short essays in such periodicals as View though I get a little fed up on the homos at times.

Occasionally I reread one of Shakespeares plays or one of the few other good ones of his time. I read poems wherever I see them, old and new – mostly english and american: anything that comes my way. Recently I have been interested in the new crop of irish peots [*sic*] who are rebelling again De Valera and the Church – as well as against the Yeatsian tradition. Some are first rate.

I enjoy Henry Miller (in spots) whenever I get anything new by him to chew on. His revent [*sic*] Rimbaud article is first rate.

Kenneth Burkes, A Grammar of Motives is good.

But in general I don't find much (as I get little from you) that seems alert to the main problems of the making of verse today. They're all shot (as you are) through too much attention to their "great intellectual sorrows" like Werthe [*sic*]. I'd like to find a poet who knows what it means to sing again, to sing "Anew" as Louis [Zukofsky] says. Nobody can sing much today – yours truly included. They have lost the drift. Rather they have been nutted (you included) by irrelevant ideas.

So, naturally, you conclude: "Poor Bill he ain't interested in ideas." 'S all right with me. But it does seem a waste of time to argue with you bastards. Yet, I must be patient – and work. Work! produce. Better stuff. If only I could do it faster. Too many things block me – you are one of them. If only your intelligence was what it was when you were younger! You were, at heart, more generous then. More alert to others.

I see by today's papers that there is a big and important work out by F. S. C.

Northrup [*sic*] of the Harvard [*sic*] Philosophy Department, The Meeting of East and West. It sounds good – but the poor bastards, great as their reasoning is and deep as may be the ultimate effects of it their own heads are not on the block. If they were themselves on the block they'd cry out agains [*sic*] the offenses of their times in plain words – not philosophic evasions.

We need a lot of direct name calling – starting with the Church and its patent bastards (in the sense of false intellectualizations) like an Eliot. Did you ever see through Eliot. Like hell you did. Talk about time lag. There you have it, right in your own gullet. You *encouraged* Eliot. You saw not for one moment the ultimate implocations [*sic*] of his thinking, his basic Catholicism with all its 13th century drag on present day realizations. In fact you have never to this day pointed out what Eliot really is. Snd [*sic*] I use him only as an instance of your own evasions. There are many other such things in my world.

I've never heard you say anything about Kafka. I have never heard you say anything pertinent to our present day struggles – except Confucius. O. K. – apply it in devastating some thinker in your own environment. You can't do it. Oh yes, I know your answer: You have grown out of poetry into a world of action, a realer world of political and economic conflicts.

All right keed, I'm still battling in my own realm of poetry. "Esthetics" to Mr. Northrup. Let him search in my works for his answers. We need someone with a keener nose than anything present in our world today to catch up with the leads I am attempting so faultily to follow.

And if I grow angry with you it is just that I do not have your help in my work, you a man with what used to be extraordinary perceptions. Now all you do is ask me, What are you reading? What kind of an intellect does that present to me? But, as I say, I must be patient. Not even you properly grasps [*sic*] the real situation.

Cheerio

Bill

the enclosed letter: See Letter 108 below.

John Dewey: "Democracy and America" is the final chapter of *Freedom and Culture* (1939) by the American philosopher and educator John Dewey (1859–1952). It celebrates the political thought of Thomas Jefferson and describes some of the difficulties facing democratic society in the modern era, including the threat of totalitarianism. Dewey is actually quoting himself at this point in his essay; the original source of the sentence is the sixth chapter of *The Public and Its Problems* (1927).

Kirkegaard: Six books by and about the Danish philosopher and theologian Sören Kierkegaard (1813–1855) were reviewed by Richard McKeon in the *New York Times Book Review* for November 25, 1945, pp. 1, 29–30.

Schlesinger: The American historian Arthur Schlesinger, Jr. (1917–) published *The Age of Jackson* (Boston: Little, Brown) in 1945. The book was reviewed by Allan Nevins in the *New York Times Book Review* for September 16, 1945, pp. 1, 26.

Anais Nin: The American writer of fiction and autobiography Anais Nin (1903–1977). WCW reviewed her *Winter of Artifice* in *New Directions in Prose and Poetry Number Seven 1942*.

Parker Tyler's writing: See "Biographical Notes" on TYLER, PARKER.

Eluard: New Directions 9 (1946) presented translations of thirty poems by the French surrealist poet and Resistance worker Paul Eluard (1895–1952). WCW was responsible for six of them.

Billy the Kid: WCW was reading *The Saga of Billy the Kid* by Walter Noble Burns (Garden City, NY: Doubleday, Page, 1926).

View: New York surrealist magazine edited by Charles Henri Ford and Parker Tyler.

irish peots: WCW's friend and typist Kathleen Hoagland was compiling her anthology *1000 Years of Irish Writing: The Gaelic and Anglo-Irish Poets from Pagan Times to the Present* (New York: Devin-Adair, 1947). She includes a generous sample of work by young, contemporary poets, among them Leslie Daiken (see Letter 104 above), Patrick Fallon, Donagh MacDonagh, Ewart Milne, Patrick MacDonagh, Patrick Kavanaugh, Robert Greacen, and Valentin Iremonger. Eamon de Valera (1882–1975) served at various times between 1919 and 1973 as Prime Minister and President of Ireland.

Henry Miller: For Henry Miller and Arthur Rimbaud, see Letters 76 and 15 above. *New Directions 9* carried Miller's essay "When Do Angels Cease to Resemble Themselves: A Study of Rimbaud," later incorporated into Miller's *The Time of the Assassins: A Study of Rimbaud* (1956).

Kenneth Burkes: See "Biographical Notes" on BURKE, KENNETH.

Werthe: WCW alludes to *The Sorrows of Young Werther* (1774), a romantic novel by the German man of letters Johann Wolfgang von Goethe (1749–1832).

"Anew": See "Biographical Notes" on ZUKOFSKY, LOUIS.

F. S. C. Northrup: F. S. C. Northrop was professor of Philosophy at Yale University (not Harvard). His book *The Meeting of East and West: An Inquiry Concerning World Understanding* (New York: Macmillan, 1946) was reviewed by Howard Mumford Jones in the *New York Times Book Review* for July 7, 1946, pp. 1, 21.

Kafka: The Czech-German novelist and short-story writer Franz Kafka (1883–1924).

108. TLS-1. Enclosed with preceding letter.

July 8, 1946

Dear Ezra:

What have you been reading recently, from your letters and the clipping I presume it's the New York Journal American? But you seem to have missed a lot of back numbers. Come on give me the low down so that I can make a proper diagnosis of your condition. You really are cracked. Who the hell do you think you are, asking me what I'm reading and then going off half cocked – before I've even made an attempt to answer you – giving a general opinion on events in general. I don't know why the hell I bother with you at all.

What you need is your daily newspaper from Tokyo that you so longed for a couple of years ago. Damn you to hell I'm sick of you, you can't learn anything.

I'm glad Farrell called, I presume of course you told him everything that's wrong with him, how to improve his style and his mind, for which he is deeply grateful and, besides, is now on the way to becoming a noteable [*sic*] writer like yourself. If you'll stay in your country long enough to learn to ask an intelligent question, which Dora Marsden used to say is the beginning of knowledge, I might find it profitable to attempt to answer you. You just don't know what you're about. I'm sorry but it's not my affair – or won't be so much longer if you continue your assinine [*sic*] gyrations which you fondly believe is thinking. And writing. You can't even make a sentence, not even a phrase that is intelligible – or

I have nothing to tell you. I have many proposals which I am interested in developing, not as abstractions but as objects. Obviously they are none of your business since they have never in any way been your business. You have what you might object to calling "greater interests" – or have you balled yourself up again? Nothing of course is "great", naturally.

I hope you get out of the insane asylum and that you will live and work at your perceptions for many years to come, I wish I could make my beliefs and preoccupations pertinent to you but after a number of trials and failures I'm through. You will discover in what I write, what I read. I will never tell you in any other way. You obviously don't need me. I shall have to do the best I can also without you.

Yours

Bill

the clipping: Unidentified. The letter to which this one is a response has apparently not survived.

newspaper from Tokyo: See Letter 96 above.

Farrell: See "Biographical Notes" on FARRELL, JAMES T.

Dora Marsden: For Dora Marsden, see Letter 8 above. When WCW contributed to *The Egoist*, the leading article was often a philosophical essay by Marsden.

109. TLS-1

July 16, 1946

Dear Ez:

Apart from sending you back to the sixth grade to learn to write a simple declarative sentence my only advice to you would be that you study the prose style of a barred window.

As for Hilda, where else would she be able to learn anything but in Freud's city? Or perhaps Bryn Mawr – or however the hell they spell their Welsh name – where the cash comes from.

Not that I wouldn't like to see you let out – and in the end they'll let you go no doubt for the very shoddy reason that you can't spik english.

Yeah, Fordie could write – that was the Catholic in him. Then there's Bishop Spellman and the excrement in Washington that converted Clare Booth [*sic*] Luce of LIFE magazine to the faith. Now there's a prose style! and a prose stylist! Begorrah!

We did get a tempting recipe for roast pullet stuffed with whole garlics from Ford – whose foibles were often charming.

Bill

Freud's city: Vienna; see "Biographical Notes" on Doolittle, Hilda. For H. D. and Bryn Mawr, see Letter 104 above.

Fordie: See "Biographical Notes" on Ford, Ford Madox. In a letter to WCW of July 10, 1946 (Buffalo), EP asks, "How 'bout ole Fordie? didja learn anyfink from 'im? & have you notic'd Hilda has learned to write (prose)? Vienna a helluva place to go fer it, but better to seek the light than NOT seek it."

Bishop Spellman: For the conversion of Clare Boothe Luce, see Letter 104 above. The Reverend Francis Spellman (1889–1967) was Archbishop of New York; he was made a Cardinal in February 1946.

110. AL-2

1 Ag [August 1946]

You dear old dung-beetle

you ineffable god-shitten ASS
What t hell do you mean fillin Nancy with shit
IF Jefferson was finally quoted on fascist posters WHY? & who told

'em?? who issued a manifesto to say Muss[olini] wd be followed by a RE-PUBLIC?

There are 35 historic FACTS that yr shitten friends dare not print.

You sound like you are jealous of everything near yr. own size.

Possum @ least printed my essay on YOU in his crematorium.

If you want to dig in yr dung of a 25 year TIME LAG

What can save you?

You haven't even got to Brooks Adams 1903 (or '97) let alone thought that has gone on SINCE.

Yr. abuse by generic lable [*sic*] & your drive to suppress opinion which you haven't bothered to ascertain!!!

be yr self

Gawd ellup yuh

& beleev me –

yrz

dung-beetle: Possibly an allusion to Franz Kafka's story "The Metamorphosis" (1915), in which the protagonist Gregor Samsa becomes a dung-beetle. In Letter 107 above, WCW challenges EP on his knowledge of Kafka.

Nancy: See "Biographical Notes" on CUNARD, NANCY. On June 11, 1946 (Yale), Cunard sent EP a blistering, six-page attack upon the entire direction of his career since 1930. EP's reply to Cunard (Texas) was written on the same day, August 1, 1946, as this letter to WCW.

posters: EP had several broadside posters printed in Rapallo, probably in 1944; see Gallup, E2t.

my essay on YOU: EP's essay on "Dr. Williams' Position" appeared in *The Dial* for November 1928, not in Eliot's *Criterion*; see Letter 41 above.

Brooks Adams 1903: For Brooks Adams' *Law of Civilization and Decay*, see Letter 95 above.

111. TLS-1

August 5 or 6 or something
[1946]

You poor dumb cluck:

Instead of sounding off on your pathetic little Ego-tooter why don't you use what is left of your head and try to think a little while? Or, since thinking is something that is probably not possible for you at the moment, why not just try for a few accurate statements? Start with simple things like saying, Did I brush my teeth this morning? or something of the sort. From that you could build up until you felt strong enough to write a letter. Then you might, just might, arrive at a point at which you began to deal with simple statements – on very elementary things! rather than with false but self satisfying wishes.

How delighted you must feel to imagine I had smeared you in Nancy [Cunard]'s eyes. That really must give you a kick. And it must be sweet balm to believe you had made anyone think anything at all much less what you state about the country squire of Monticello [Thomas Jefferson]. Why what a master mind you are to have predicted that Mussolini's stinking corpse would be followed by a republic in Italy! And did someone really see your manifesto? Tell me, darling, what did you predict about Spain and Ethiopia, I am waiting breathlessly to hear? And do you think we should send an ambassador to the Vatican? Think hard and answer these childish suggestions.

So you have read Brooks Adams too – or so I am led to believe. You don't seem to show any evidence of such reading in your literary style. And come to think of it you don't seem to show any evidence of having read him in anything you do or say. In fact I don't believe you ever did read him. I think you must have used some one of his books as an elbow prop once when you were unable to keep your back straight from the weight of your beard. Remember the fall of Constantinople?

Take my advice, Ez, and treat me with more intelligence or you will not even have *one* left in your audience – perhaps, to amuse you, I'd better say 1/2 a person to your credit. For I do still appreciate you in spite of your childishnesses. But you demand too much of friendship. I am half ashamed when I abuse you, knowing your unquestioned abilities, your genius even – but you assume too much. How will you ever be enlightened unless you give the other fellow at least the chance to prove to you that he is a man also? You might even go so far as to say to yourself that perhaps this man who is my friend (by his insistence on a certain sort of loyalty) has a brain and may (God perish the thought!) have surpassed me by far in certain channels. I might even (now get ready for a devatating [sic] thought) I might even LEARN SOMETHING FROM HIM! That'll knock you, I'm sure.

For, after all, isn't that what you expect your friends to think of you? That you are the Helikon to all bright spirits? I admire you most, I think, in that you have been able to remain idle for a lifetime. More power to you – but please keep away from delusions – if you are able. I'm on a vacation in the mountains of western Massachusetts, I wish I might park you here for a year or so – we might still be able to rescue a few remnants of you from the void. Best luck.

                                        Yours as ever
                                        Bill

Mussolini's stinking corpse: See "Biographical Notes" on MUSSOLINI, BENITO.

an ambassador to the Vatican: In May 1946, President Truman named M. C. Taylor to be the first United States Ambassador to the Vatican. The appointment was vigorously opposed by Protestant groups and defended by Catholic groups. Taylor returned to the U. S. in August, and the controversy went on for months.

the fall of Constantinople: Constantinople was the eastern capital of the Roman empire and the center of Greek Orthodox Christianity until 1453, when it fell to the Ottoman Turks.

Helikon: A mountain in Boeotia, Greece, sacred to the Muses.

western Massachusetts: The envelope enclosing this letter is postmarked Charlemont, Massachusetts, August 7, 1946.

112. ALS-1

9 Ag [August 1946]

OK Dr Pedagogue

2 simple questions
1 What do you think of Gesell?
2 Whom do you *agree* with?

y
Ez

What is best book you have read in last 7 years?
or @ least tell me one good one.

Gesell: See "Biographical Notes" on GESELL, SILVIO.

113. TLS-1

Wednesday [August 14, 1946?]

No Ezekiel –

I haven't read Gesell but I shall do so on your recommendation. What have I read in the past 7 years? Let's see – a good deal of medical detail, some of it superb, especially the articles by Dr. Alvarez of the Mayo Clinic. I have just completed Schlesisnger's [*sic*] The Age of Jackson and all sorts of brief articles in the various lesser magazines. I believe there must be some other books, if I could recall them. And I've enjoyed some excellent verse by people you have never heard of I suppose.

In fact it's just such heavy readers as yourself that we have been needing in this environment for the past twenty years, to criticise the various intellectual move-mnets [*sic*] that have been taking place here. Translators are always needed in an active community to act as measuring sticks for the more original minds. That is they'd be useful in such an environment as this if they could be made to learn the language of the place.

I've never been a very good reader of long texts, it takes too much out of me, my eyes I mean. But ideas have a peculiar permeability if they are necessary to an age and one hears of them from many unsuspected sources. My talents, such as they are, seem to lie elsewhere. I have not, for instance read The Bible, I haven't read enough of Freud, I have not read Das Kapital nor any of the landmarks of present day thought – except in the form of excerpts. Have you? I haven't even read War and Peace. In fact I am not a well read man. I am more an observer of the life about me – informed no doubt by certain habits of perception, perhaps inherited, perhaps acquired, which have to serve in place of such other aptitudes as you, let us say, exhibit.

All this is, of course, of no interest to you. Why should it be? I am always reading. I touch all sorts of facets here and there and, if I could remember some of the books I have put behind me recently I'd be glad to tell you about them. They seem mere confirmations of my best perceptions when I do encounter them. You'll never get anywhere by attacking me on that score. Forget it. I have read what I want to read and what I am able to read. My sources are elsewhere – indirect, if you like – and I am always ready to learn where I can, even to learn to read. I can't read much.

I wish you were in circulation again and I hope you may soon be free. I'd like to talk with you (if we could talk intelligently together which I doubt is possible), I'd like, that is, to have you available for what talk we could manage but I haven't the least doubt that you'd run away from this environment just as you did forty years ago at the first opportunity and as fast as you could make it. And I'd be there just as I was then to wish you luck. I've had some interesting reviews of my *Paterson* recently, some good and some bad, as usual – some even presenting the views of Gesell, no doubt.

Yours
Bill

Dr. Alvarez: Dr. Walter Clement Alvarez (1884–1978) worked at the Mayo Clinic from 1926 to 1951. He was editor-in-chief of *Modern Medicine* and the author of *An Intro-*

duction to Gastro-Enterology, 3rd ed. (1940); *Diseases of the Intestine and Some Poorly Understood Disturbances of Digestion* (1940); and *Nervousness, Indigestion, and Pain* (1943).

Schlesisnger's Age of Jackson: See Letter 107 above. In "Letter to an Australian Editor," *Briarcliff Quarterly* 3:11 (October 1946), pp. 205–08, WCW relates *The Age of Jackson* to EP's writings about the Jackson/Van Buren period. WCW also develops his idea of EP as a "translator."

Das Kapital: Published in 1867, *Das Kapital* is the principal work of the German economist and philosopher Karl Marx (1818–1883).

War and Peace: Published in 1865–69, *War and Peace* is the masterwork of the Russian novelist and mystic Count Leo Tolstoy (1828–1910).

114. TLS-2

Aug. 23, 1946

Dear Ez:

I took *No More Parades* away with me on my vacation and read it with strange feelings – shame at not having read it before (especially after Ford's kindnesses), some boredom at times but mostly with tremendous admiration for the man's sturdy craftsmanship. His language (English) made the prose often beyond my understanding since it referred without explanation to manners which were entirely foreign to my thought and also because I simply did not recognize the words. But that was a small matter compared with the style which is serious and determined: that's the only word that seems to express the doggedness of his sticking to his technique. It makes for an aliveness which would never keep him long in the Best Seller class although this particular book reached that because of the bitchiness of the heroine and her extreme fuckability. God how many 'Muricans would have liked to fuck themselves into society through her!

How much of the book is Ford's own history I can't guess but Tietjens seems to be an idealized Ford in many respects. It explains many of Ford's foibles and the extreme difficulty it was to get to the bottom of his social behavior. For instance it would be impossible to know whether or not he was starving to death before you or eating well. I feel upset to think that when he urged me, indirectly, so persistenly [*sic*] to buy one of his wife's paintings (which I did not admire) he may have been asking for bread and butter. I am afraid I was very obtuse, I didn't buy a picture. He went away and was dead after a few weeks. At least he was buried, I suppose, in France where he wanted to be.

I am asking a friend to look up Gesell for me in order to make my approach as easy as possible – not to have to waste time selecting the one book of his (since there may be several) which I should take on. By the way you may hear from this friend one of these days when I decide to let him approach you. His name is David Lyle, a man of amazing reading especially in philosophic-economic theory. I've never seen anything like it. But he's no book-man in his own right. He works practically with employment and other social groups. You'll see. You remember Virgil Jordan, Viola's first husband? He's another.

After another week of relief from my practice of medicine I'll plunge in again for another long labor through the winter. After that, if I survive, I'm turning, I hope, much of the work over to my son Bill. My book *Paterson Part I* is being enthusiastically reviewed in *Partisan Review* and *The Nation*. It is pleasant.

There's something else I wanted to say – what is it? (five minutes) Can't think of it. Time passes and pisses on us all.

Yours
Bill

No More Parades: The second novel in Ford Madox Ford's tetralogy *Parade's End* (1924–28). It centers upon the difficulties of Christopher Tietjens, including his marriage to an unfaithful wife named Sylvia.

Ford's kindnesses: See "Biographical Notes" on FORD, FORD MADOX.

Ford's own history: In a letter to WCW of August 25 [1946] (Buffalo), EP writes: "novel Not autobiog. Tiet. drawn largely from Marwood who died – F. imagined M. in situations of F's experience." WCW, however, was not convinced; in his 1951 review of *Parade's End,* he says of Ford, "he might have been Tietjens."

his wife's paintings: The Polish-American abstract painter Janice Biala (1903–) worked in New York and Paris, where she met Ford on May 1, 1930. She was Ford's companion (not his wife) for the rest of his life, and she became his literary executor.

David Lyle: Since 1938 WCW had corresponded with David Lyle, a former radio operator with a photographic memory, who periodically mailed out newsletters containing his digests of huge amounts of information gathered from many different media.

Virgil Jordan: See "Biographical Notes" on JORDAN, VIRGIL D.

Partisan Review and The Nation: See Randall Jarrell, "The Poet and His Public," *Partisan Review* (September–October 1946), pp. 488–500, and Isaac Rosenfeld, "The Poetry and Wisdom of *Paterson,*" *The Nation,* August 24, 1946, pp. 216–17.

115. ALS-2

Aug 29. 46

Dear Bill,

A line to say that I have finally got over here – I have found a room near St. Elizabeth's – I am allowed to see Ezra three times a week – for about 15. or 20. minutes. I find him terribly shattered by all the horrors he has been put through. He says he has heard from you. I don't know what you suppose he was doing over the radio? John Rodker wrote me recently that he had heard some of it – "I always said there was nothing treacherous in them & if one couldn't criticize a form of civilization wh. seemed damnable, what was the point of free speech anyway" (? is Rodker still under the impression that there *is* "free speech"?) and another friend wrote me, "his crime seems to be that he advocated a sane economy," & that's just about the truth.

Some cantos & more Confucius are coming out this autumn with or through New Directions.

I am able to get Ezra books, & he is allowed paper & pencil – He says he has enough and pretty good food. St. Eliz's have a large herd of cows & an enormous acreage of vegetables – I myself often eat at their Red X cafeteria.

I hope you are still writing? I have lost track naturally these last chaotic years.

Affectionate salutations
Dorothy Pound

I have just enjoyed W E. Woodward's Tom Paine so much: & am giving his "New American History" to Omar, (who has arrived in the U. S. finally) to help him with his American History.

& let me add – that of all I have read of yours, I still prefer "In the American Grain".

D. P.

a room: See "Biographical Notes" on POUND, DOROTHY SHAKESPEAR. The return address on this letter is c/o Mrs. Boyce, 3227 9th Place S. E., Washington, D. C.

John Rodker: See "Biographical Notes" on RODKER, JOHN.

Some cantos: The *Pisan Cantos,* on which EP had worked during his imprisonment in Italy, were published by New Directions in July 1948. *Confucius: The Unwobbling Pivot & the Great Digest* was published by New Directions as *Pharos,* No. 4, in March 1947.

W E. Woodward's Tom Paine: The American historian, biographer, and journalist William E. Woodward (1874–1950) was the author of *George Washington: The Image and the Man* (1926), *A New American History* (1936), and *Tom Paine: America's Godfather, 1739–1809* (1945).

Omar: During the war, Omar Shakespear Pound (1926–) served in the United States Army in Italy and Germany. After the armistice, he became a student at Hamilton College.

116. TLS-2

8–30–46

Dear Dorothy:

It is good news for Ezra that you are here to see him and to bring him what assistance you can. For I see no other release for him from his misfortune than that – unless it be executive clemency. That Ezra is guilty of treasonable activity toward the United States is inescapable nor does it matter in the least what he said in his broadcasts.

When Italy declared war against the United States Ezra had a clear choice before him, to back his country with his life if necessary or to oppose us in our collective effort. To broadcast as he did from enemy territory under enemy pay at such a time is treason. He chose that course deliberately, at cost of his life if necessary. Legally his life is forfeit. Those are the rules of war.

Now, civil disobedience is sometimes justifiable (though I do not think it was so in this case) but it is only justifiable when we pledge our very beings to the moral cause which motivates us. But to dodge the issue after the event is something I cannot admire. If I were Ezra I'd stand up and invite them to shoot me, after all he's a man. He is bound as a man to do just that – unless he is really mentally unbalanced as he may be.

Morally Ezra's position is at least arguably justifiable though I am more than suspicious of his motives knowing his stand on Spain, but that he did not know what he was doing is childish to believe.

I am sorry to have to say all this but I refuse to be misunderstood by Ezra or yourself and we shall get nowhere by pretending otherwise. I intend when the time comes to write to President Truman asking him to look into Ezra's case and to release Ezra by executive order if that be legally possible. After all [Abraham] Lincoln released several boys who had been condemned to death for sleeping when on sentry duty during the Civil War, it seems to me that this case is little different. My only fear is that there may be something in the law which forbids even the President to intervene in such cases while a war is on. Peace has not yet been declared, as soon as peace becomes official I shall write to President Truman.

If you are ever in the region of New York and have the time to do so please come and see us, we'd be delighted to see you when we may talk of these things at greater length.

Sincerely

W. C. Williams

Like many of Ezra's friends I feel myself torn between anger at his official guilt which is unquestioned and unquestionable – with all its deadly implications, in american lives – and my lifelong affection for the man. When I think of what he deliberately chose to do when his country was expending every effort to crush its enemies and complete devotion to the effort was necessary, I wish never to have anything to do with him again. I know his reasons and I reject them. But when it comes to a question of my human affections my whole attitude changes and I am ready to help Ezra in any way – short of disloyalty to my country – that offers itself.

I want to say more, I don't want you to think me hard or unfeeling but it simply isn't possible for me to exculpate Ezra completely.

Bill

President Truman: Harry S Truman (1884–1972) became President of the United States upon the death of Franklin D. Roosevelt in April 1945. WCW followed through on the promise made in this letter by writing to Truman on December 31, 1946, but the request for executive clemency did not succeed (Carpenter, pp. 769–70).

117. TLS-2

Oct. 30, 1946

Dear Ez:

Your predicament has at least done this, it has made the Rev. Eliot vaguely intelligent in his prose; his approach to actuality is only partial, of course, but he shows at least a few symptoms of what might have been a profitable establishment for him. It is strange at the same time how your present position shows him up; he is all but incapacitated but [*sic*] it –. not at all smart, in nothing the brilliant mind – more the surprised student into whose study window someone has thrown

a brick. The second part of Faust perhaps. Too bad there isn't a third part with a
return to the beginning, the actual ebginning [*sic*] when Faust was in fact young,
not the dream. Nobody thinks of Faust actually young or that he was ever young –
and mistaken. Goethe knew better ot [*sic*] he would never have written his lyrics
but the times made him "philosophic"./ Poor dead bastard regretting the past
"beautifully".

   This last letter of yours is the most coherent so far and the most informative
concerning the best of you – or at least the best of you as you, aside from your
words. I understand perfectly your adult concern for government, discipline and
your courageous definace [*sic*] of the spurious, lost in half measures. But you
make an ass of yourself for all that – by misjudging the difficulties and successes
of others: it was stupid of you to attack the president of the United States as you
did – plain stupid. Stupid because you destroyed more good that [*sic*] what
inevitable evil the man represented and because you sided with the most vicious
and reactionary forces in the country in seeking to destroy him – by foul means,
such as attacks on his wife and family – too contemptible to list.

   Nevertheless, right or wrong, government is a major subject for the ageing poet
and your work strikes along the path with some effect, if weak since you step
outside the means of poetry very often to gain a point. You deal in political
symbols instead of actual values, poetry. You talk about things (which you
yourself have sufficiently damned in the past) instead of showing the things
themselves in action. A magnificent opportunity still exists for you if you can
ever bring yourself back from your excited state to the calm which true poetic
achievement demands. I doubt that you'll be astute enough to do it – or indeed
that you'll ever again have the opportunity due to your present position.

   Yes, I read the Harper's article and understood it. There again you act like an
infant. Did *you* understand it? I doubt it or you would not presume to question the
ability of others who could twist you around a little finger where technical matters
are concerned and show you to be the ignoramus you are in most things of which
you boast. Will you never learn *that*? You make a fool of yourself to gain what?
Perhaps self esteem. You must be pretty low to want to gain that kind of self
esteem.

   I haven't seen or communicated with Virgil Jordan for twenty or thirty years.
He's almost as great an ass as you are in economic matters: be he headed around
the circle the opposite way from you. I imagine you're pretty close together by
now: he the great capitalist propagandist back [*sic*] an *enlightened* Wall Street.
What else do you represent?

   I want to rescue you (for myself) because I need you – I being one of the few
who would be benefitted – but I want you whole, the good in you, not a hunk of
bacon fried too crisp.

(I rushed out and found NOBODY in the front office for the moment, which is a blessing – I can go on writing.)

except for the God damned telephone in my right ear!

Eliot's article (in Poetry) is really very good but it contains warnings for you, the same which I have posted, to which you continue to pay no attention. Reda [*sic*] it yourself – the part about Gesell: it will aid your effectiveness.

On the other hand, perhaps you cannot help yourself. In fact I am sure it is the defects of your qualities that annoys us – as Eliot very ably points out.

The great things [*sic*] you have to say to us, as poets, is: READ! Read and learn, learn to hear.

No time for more now. There will be an issue of the Briarcliffe [*sic*] Quarterly in November devoted to my general history etc photos of me with family, a statement as to my position. Might have some interest for you. I don't know exactly what's in it – I hope it turns out at least sensible and not just blah.

Your Canto in Quarterly Review is best of the recnt [*sic*] ones as far as I can tell.

WCW

the Rev. Eliot: WCW is responding to T. S. Eliot's essay "Ezra Pound," *Poetry* 68:6 (September 1946), pp. 326–38.

Faust: The second part of *Faust* by Johann Wolfgang von Goethe (1749–1832) was published in 1832. For WCW's reading of *Faust,* see Williams/Laughlin, pp. 70–71.

This last letter: EP to WCW, October 26, 1946 (Buffalo).

to attack the president: WCW may be thinking of the excerpts from EP's Rome Radio speeches quoted by Charles Norman in "The Case for and against Ezra Pound," *PM* (November 25, 1945), p. 14, a forum to which WCW contributed. In the broadcast of January 29, 1942, EP speaks of "the criminal acts of a President whose mental condition was not, so far as I could see, all that could or should be desired of a man in so responsible a position or office." FDR is mentioned in two other excerpts (April 16, 1942, and May 26, 1942), but the name of Mrs. Eleanor Roosevelt does not appear.

the Harper's article: Probably George Richmond Walker, "Silvio Gesell and Free Private Enterprise," *Harper's Magazine* 193 (July 1946), pp. 91ff. In the letter to WCW of October 26, EP asks: "Did you get the Harpers article? did you understand it?"

Virgil Jordan: See "Biographical Notes" on Jordan, Virgil D. EP mentions Jordan in his letter to WCW of October 26.

warnings: In "Ezra Pound," pp. 335–36, Eliot recalls: "I once complained to him about an article on the monetary theory of Gesell, which he had written at my suggestion for *The Criterion.* I said, as nearly as I can remember, 'I asked you to write an article which would explain this subject to people who had never heard of it; yet you write as if your readers knew about it already, but had failed to understand it.'"

Briarcliffe Quarterly: The *Briarcliff Quarterly* published a special number on WCW in
October (not November) 1946.

Quarterly Review: EP's "Canto LXXXIV" was published in the *Quarterly Review of
Literature* 3:2 (1946), pp. 126–29.

118. TLS-2

7/29/47

Dear Ez:

Fer an amateur I did all rite or so I am led to believe by the plaudits of the
populace. To tell the truth, apart from my prepared address, I didn't know what I
was going to say; I have never taught anyone anything about writing, particularly
about writing poetry, so that on my way to the conference I felt as arid as the
deserts of Wyoming and Utah through which I was passing – which, by the way,
are particularly beautiful in the colors and conformations of their rocks and sands.

Finally the day arrived when I damn well had to say something or sit down
defeated. Well, I sez to myself, there's the poetry of my ol' compatriot Ezra
Pound, if they can stand that they can stand anything, so I let 'em have it. I told
them that I always believed in beginning at the beginning at the site at which I
happened to be standing, what better then than to begin in the general neighborhood of Idaho with the work of a man who stood at the beginning of the modern
movement, what was the matter with beginning with Ezra Pound. Thereat I
attacked the 83d Canto and read it through, stumbling over the places where I was
meant to stumble and making no bones about it. I elucidated where I could and
asked for what help I could get where I was stuck.

The gang of old ladies, young lady poets and G.Is. [soldiers] took it right in
their stride. There were a few bleats but I didn't let them get away with it. I told
them that whatever your private life might be the thing that we were considering
was poetry, to try to find out all we could about it and that I had purposely brought
up your worrk [*sic*] knowing what your reputation was at the moment in order to
emphasize the importance of the art as an art and to get that quastion [*sic*] settled
at the start. As I was the first speaker of the Conference I thus set the mood for the
two weeks that followed. My theory was to knock 'em out at the start and never
let 'em get the upper hand thereafter. They reacted *mit verstand* [with understand-
ing]. I was proud of them.

As I have told you, however, the local paper wrote an editorial or ran an
editorial attacking not ME but the poor guy, a proff at the University, for condon-

ing your traitrous record. Brewster Ghiselin, the man responsible for the whole idea of the conference (a good poet, by the way) wrote a letter in reply which, I must say the paper published in approximately the same location on the ditorrial [*sic*] page at which the attack had been ppplaced [*sic*]. And so the matter passed.

I'll send you a copy of my address as soon as I get one back from the Conference – they are making mimeograph copies for limited distribution to various conference members who seemed eager to keep what I had to say on permanent record. Maybe someone whill [*sic*] want to print the thing later.

By the way, Allan [*sic*] Tate who was one of the Advisers along with myself told me something which may interest you: at one time two years ago he somehow got access through the Library of Congress to the complete transcript of all your broadcasts from Italy during the war and read them through. They were, of course, merely stenographic records and not voice records. Tate said that the copies were definitely of two varieties, sharply marked. One showed you, in your usual blatant style, making flippant remarks about Roosevelt and the "Chews" along with various other comments of the sort. But then there was another class of broadcast, not at all in your usual style, quite separate from the first style of statement, which was completely unlike you and, in his opinion, thoroughly traitrous. In this manner there was talk of "us" and "we" referring apparently to the enemy dictators and their policies.

I don't want to annoy or excite you. I merely report what Tate told me. He is in no way antagonistic to you. After a lapse of a few months he tried again to gain access to the records of the broadcasts in order to check a few points but they had completely disappeared, he could not get to them by any means at his disposal. Someone had removed them from the files.

We are back home after, for me, a tremendous trip. Floss'' sister Charlotte shared the driving with me in my old Buick (1940) which behaved beautifully throughout. At Taos, New Mexico, I or we met Bob McAlmon by agreement he having come up from El Paso for the purpose. I was delighted to see Bob again after a lapse of seven years and to be able to chew the fat with him once more – his address, by the way, is c/o South Western Surgical Supply, El Paso, Texas. He's the same old Bob, a little thinner, perhaps a bit discouraged but still able to make a sharply discerned statement about the people around him. I wish to God I could correct some of his slovenly ways as a writer but have given up hope long since of making him heed me. He just won't or can't get donn [*sic*] to the labor of writing and so he defeats what seems to me one of the major prose talents of our day. I know no one with his keen insight into personalities and with such a biting way of destroying fake and overblown emptiness.

We all had a grand time together visiting the Pueblos as well as Frieda Lawrence at her small ranch on the outskirts of the town. We did not go up the [*sic*] the mountain abode where Lawrence had died nor did we see the yard square concrete block into which his ashes have been compounded but the old gal herself was in good form – over a bottle of white wine.

We came back through Texas and the cities of Oklahoma blossoming in the desert from the products of subterranian [*sic*] wealth –

I'll see that you get the address, my address, as soon as copies of it arrive – if they arrive.

Best

Bill

the conference: From July 7 to July 18, 1947, WCW participated in a writers' conference and workshop at the University of Utah in Salt Lake City; see Mariani, pp. 545–47. WCW delivered his "prepared address," a talk entitled "Our Formal Heritage from Walt Whitman," on Wednesday, July 9.

Idaho: EP was born in Hailey, Idaho.

the 83d Canto: EP's "Canto LXXXIII" was published in the *Yale Poetry Review* 6 (1947), pp. 3–8. In a letter to EP of May 18, 1947 (Indiana), WCW writes: "I read (this morning) your Canto in the YPR & find it very moving – & very beautiful."

an editorial: "Ezra Pound's Fair Words and Infamous Conduct," *Salt Lake Tribune,* July 13, 1947, p. A14.

Brewster Ghiselin: The American poet and critic Brewster Ghiselin (1903–) taught at the University of Utah from 1934 until 1971. He directed the Utah Writers' Conference from 1947 to 1966.

a letter in reply: "Speaker Clarifies Statement about Life of Ezra Pound," *Salt Lake Tribune,* July 16, 1947, p. 6.

Allan Tate: The American novelist, critic, and biographer Allen Tate (1899–1979) also attended the Utah Writers' Conference. From 1944 to 1950, Tate served as a Fellow in American Letters at the Library of Congress. In his *Autobiography,* p. 318, WCW repeats this report about the transcripts of EP's broadcasts, but does not identify Tate by name.

Charlotte: Charlotte Herman Earle was an elder sister of WCW's wife Floss. Charlotte had once been engaged to WCW's brother Edgar.

Frieda Lawrence: D. H. Lawrence died in France in 1930. Five years later, his widow Frieda (1879–1956) had his body exhumed and cremated. Ashes believed to be Lawrence's were sealed in a concrete block housed in a shrine at their ranch on Lobo Mountain, fourteen miles north of Taos, New Mexico.

119. TLS-1

October 21, 1947

Dear Dorothy:

I was keenly disappointed that I had let my visit to Ezra wait until so late in the afternoon. It was my own fault which didn't make me feel any better about my lapse in judgement, I let myself be detained by Lowell over a luncheon which meant nothing at all. Damned foolishness, I'll make it up another time.

Yes, I'll write at once to Oberholzer [*sic*] abopting [*sic*] your suggestion that Ezra be released in my care; under the circumstances, however, I doubt that he'd have the power to act in such a case. We'll see.

I'd gladly lend Ezra the copy of Twice a Year which he wants did I know which copy of that publication he wants to see. It is, as the name implies, a semiannual anthology of opinion and the arts. What particular issue is he interested in? Or rather what article published in Tiwce [*sic*] a Year would he like to read? Say the word.

My medical work has me down. I wish I could get out of some of it. Best to you both.

Bill

my visit: WCW's first visit to EP at St. Elizabeths took place on October 18, 1947. WCW had come to Washington at the invitation of Robert Lowell to record some poems for the Library of Congress (see "Biographical Notes" on LOWELL, ROBERT). WCW describes the visit in an unpublished typescript entitled "The Male" (Yale) and in Chapter 51 of his *Autobiography*.

Oberholzer: Dr. Winfred Overholser (1892–1964) was the superintendent of St. Elizabeths Hospital. In a letter to WCW of October 19, 1947 (Yale), Dorothy suggests that WCW "write to Dr. Overholser & ask whether, as a qualified physician, Ez. couldn't be released in your charge." In a letter to Dorothy of November 4, 1947 (Indiana), WCW reports that Overholser says he cannot transfer EP to WCW's medical care without a legal release.

Twice a Year: For this periodical, see Letter 90 above.

120. ALS-2

[October 23, 1947]

All right ole Bull.

"King Wan worked from where he was at. 止

The enclosed started from Rapallo – (pop. 15,000) & not only but Venice where there wasn't a scrap of V[ivaldi]'s mss – etc. or edtns.) trying to – in fact havin a Viv celebration & mayor of V[enice]. over @ Siena to get 'em off. in fact Vivaldi war Venice vs. Siena.

Why go to Utah when Rutherford cd/ do it?

with larger audience @ less cost.

y

Ez

止 : The ideogram chih (3) means "coming to rest"; but, as EP explains in his translation of Confucius' *Analects,* "there is no more important technical term in the Confucian philosophy than this *chih* (3) the hitching post, position, place one is in, and works from." See Ezra Pound, *Confucius* (New York: New Directions, 1969), p. 232.

Ole Bull: EP may be playing on the name of the Norwegian violinist and composer Ole Bornemann Bull (1810–1880).

King Wan: Wen (or Wan) Wang (*c.* 1231–1135 B.C.) was the father of the Chou dynasty. A model ruler and reformer, he was greatly admired by Confucius.

The enclosed: EP's enclosure was the program of the Fifth Siena Music Week, sponsored by the Chigi Musical Academy in Siena, September 15–19, 1947. Dedicated to the Venetian composer Antonio Vivaldi (1678–1741), these concerts continued the revival of his work begun in 1938–39 by EP and Olga Rudge. They discovered, transcribed, and organized performances of Vivaldi's concerti from unpublished manuscripts in Turin and Dresden.

121. ALS-2

27 Feb [1948]
but it wont git
mailed till Monday

Dr Bull

Sorry you're attached – ergo [therefore] will not send disturbin news re/ the
O. M.

Dizzy wrote (via a (comic) kerakter) some years ago,

"My mind sometimes wants Tone, & then I read _____".

& so on.

now you rest proper. & no more cardiac nonsense – you are still wanted.

yrz
Ez

I yunnerstan the comrad e. e. c[ummings]. njoyd. your O. M. – swat

the O. M.: T. S. Eliot was awarded the Order of Merit by King George VI in January 1948.

Dizzy: The English statesman Benjamin Disraeli (1804–1881) was also a highly successful novelist. The character to whom EP refers has not been identified.

cardiac nonsense: WCW suffered a heart attack on February 10 or 11, 1948, while shoveling snow.

your O. M. – swat: WCW's "With Forced Fingers Rude," *Four Pages* 2 (February 1948), pp. 1–4, was a response to Eliot's lecture on John Milton at New York's Frick Museum in 1947.

122. TLS-1

April 25 [1948]

Dear Dorothy:

May I add to Flossie's letter that I am getting well fast – tho' I am not as yet allowed to drive my car. I had what they call a coronary occlusion – but of the anterior wall rather than of the posterior wall of the heart – a more or less minimal injury from which I am expected to recover without great loss of potential after another month or so. I feel about as always.

I promise you to be careful.

Please tell Ez that I am not a member of the Institute, merely the recipient of their prize.

He knows, I suppose, that they have elected me Advisor the [*sic*] Custodian of Poetry – or whatever it is – at the Library of Congress for 1949–50. Maybe I'll be looking for an apartment down there one of these days. Tell Ez to shove over. Not that I wish to speak lightly of his predicament, which isn't my intention.

Sincerely
Bill

the Institute: On April 3, 1948, the National Institute of Arts and Letters announced that WCW had been selected to receive the Russell Loines Award for Poetry.

the Library of Congress: WCW had also been selected as Consultant (not Custodian) in Poetry at the Library of Congress in Washington. He accepted the appointment, but poor health prevented him from taking it up.

123. TLS-1

May 22, 1948
(More like winter, damn it)

Dear Ez:

Yesterday I climbed to the platform of the American Institute of Arts and Letters to receive the Loines Memorial Award from the hands of Marianne Moore. I was nervous about it thinking I might get a pain in the ribs at the wrong moment but finding nothing was ahppening [*sic*] I even made a little speech in praise of the American language: what it had accomplished at home and abroad. I was thinking, naturally, of you and other Americans who have carried the cross to the heathen English especially.

John Alden, at the Penn Library, perhaps a replica of the original, I don't know, has written saying you have been let out of the hospital grounds. That sounds wonderful to me. Naturally they haven't yet built you a villa under the trees there where you may live rent free for life but it's a good beginning. I wish you always the best – whether or not you deserve it.

My bones and soft parts seem to be gathering a little confidence to themselves once more – tho' I don't yet trust them comepletely [*sic*]. I want to go faster and can't quite make up my mind to ignore advices from the medicos. I don't want to be a softie but when the question of survival comes up I must say I remain in doubt: shall I push myself and find perhaps that I can do much more than they say without damage or shall I wake up apeep among Dante's whirling spheres. (I've been glancing at the Paradiso recently – the spirits seems [*sic*] not to be bored by their whirlings but it sure sounds phoney to me: a very interesting treatise on mathematics – or moderately interesting from this material milieu) (What the hell's the difference between condemning the world from heaven or hell? The old boys, apparently, do not forget their rancor above any more than they do below) (I prefer Scipio's view of the divine void – as reported in Chaucer's dream – to Dante's fancy)

Meanwhile Paterson III is on its way. But Paterson II won't be "released" until June 7. Fer Gawd's sake. Just 1000 copies, what's the sense of trying to make a splurge on that when there won't even be a second edition if they sell out in a week? Well, beggars can't be choosers.

Simpson, from Galveston, keeps up his average very niftily. I like the guy – tho' I know almost nothing about him personally.

Floss has sent Dorothy a copy of the program of the Ceremony at the Am[erican]. Inst[itute]. for Arts and Letters.

Glad to have heard from you. Best as always.

Bill

a little speech: WCW's remarks were published in *Four Pages* 7 (July 1948), p. 3. They are also preserved at Texas on a typed card entitled "Reply to Miss Moore: Am. Institute of Arts and Letters – May 21, 1948."

John Alden: John Eliot Alden (1914–) was Curator of Rare Books at the University of Pennsylvania Library from 1946 to 1950 and the author of *Bibliographica Hibernica: Additions and Corrections to Wing* (1950). His namesake, the Pilgrim Father John Alden (*c.* 1599–1687), was a founder of the Plymouth Colony and the husband of Priscilla Mullins.

Dante's whirling spheres: Moved by the Primum Mobile, the circles or wheels of Dante's *Paradiso* below the Empyrean rotate constantly, thus generating the music of the spheres.

Chaucer's dream: In two dream-vision poems, "The House of Fame" and "The Parliament of Fowls," the English poet and courtier Geoffrey Chaucer (*c.* 1340–1400) draws upon Cicero's "Somnium Scipionis" (The Dream of Scipio, 51 B.C.). In all three works, the dreaming narrator is granted a vision of the cosmos.

Paterson: Paterson (Book Two) was published by New Directions in April (not June) 1948. *Paterson (Book Three)* appeared in December 1949.

Simpson: See "Biographical Notes" on SIMPSON, DALLAM.

124. TLS-1

[October 3, 1948]

Dear Ez:

Yes, I agree, when you speak as you do in one of your Cantos of the shit covered hairs surrounding the ass hole of the world your intent is to convey aesthetic pleasure to *some* audience. But WHAT audience? Granted, you show no irritation in this – or elsewhere in the same vein. It is pure relationship of values finely graded to please and instruct the reader. You and Tex Guinan, huh? Some team.

From this quasi-Paradise I am excluded because of my impulsive self involvement in the machinery of the art – a very, very, very bad blunder in me, I do show my feelings, my pitifully raw places: one should not show one's chaffed hide, it will revolt the possible lector [reader]. Too, too bad. So solly please.

As on your first revisitation of this country in 1909 or so when you found "no writer..who had any worthy conception of poetry" here you haven't progressed much in your understanding of men or situations. At the moment the scab upon your perceptions is still thick and dry. Again, solly to have been so poor a physician to you. You need soaking in hot water, with good yellow soap, head first, for days – as we have to soak the feet of city bums at the municipal hospitals sometimes to get down to the true skin – before you can afford to think again. You know nothing and increase your knowledge each year by leaps and bounds upon the same subject. When will you awaken? Echo: When will you awaken?

When we are both gone, my sorrow and your pleasure will both be weighed indifferently; in the abundance of your gifts perhaps my occasional exhillerations [*sic*] will be overlooked. It won't matter.

Maybe your "Possum" will surpass us both in public appreciation. Won't THAT be sweet to my soul!

Best
Bill

one of your Cantos: In a letter to WCW of September 30 (Yale), EP admits to having prejudices, but maintains that "mine are a source of pleasure and enjoyment WHEREAS you seem to be disturbed or het up by yours." In this rejoinder, WCW recalls the furious scatological imagery of Cantos 14 and 15, EP's "hell cantos."
Tex Guinan: See "Biographical Notes" on GUINAN, "TEXAS."
your first revisitation: Having taken up permanent residence abroad, EP revisited the United States from June 1910 to February 1911.

125. AL-2

7 Oct [1948]

& thaar my deah Wyam

I am in total agree [*sic*] with you. & when he tires he dont fall bak [*sic*] to Ez. but thru back to Browning.

But Ibsen wrote plays. Shaw wrote fakes (level Isadora & Upton) & the sd/ marsupial has been deviluping his stage – not our job but @ least serious play in Family Onion. M. Jean marvelous slight o' and. & occasional great line. as in Antigone.

Stage *aint* writing – it is people moving AND speaking.

J. J.'s play not stage but was try to git back to Ib[sen]. serious.

total agree: In a letter to EP of October 6, 1948 (Indiana), WCW describes T. S. Eliot's
   Four Quartets (1943) as "sadly in the past. I see no carry over from that into anything
   since 1928, rather a regression *because* of muddy mindedness."
Ibsen . . . Shaw . . . Isadora & Upton: Henrik Ibsen (1828–1906), Norwegian dra-
   matist; George Bernard Shaw (1856–1950), Irish dramatist; Isadora Duncan (1878–
   1927), American dancer; Upton Sinclair (1878–1968), American novelist and social
   reformer.
Family Onion: T. S. Eliot's verse drama *The Family Reunion* (1939).
M. Jean: See "Biographical Notes" on COCTEAU, JEAN.
J. J.'s play: James Joyce's *Exiles* (1918) was strongly influenced by the work of Ibsen.

126. ALS-2

13 Oct [1948]

Fer gorzake dont so egggzaggrate   I never told you to *read* it. let erlone REread it. I din't say it wuz (my XT!!) *henjoyable* readin. I sd/ th guy had done some honest work devilupping his theatre technique

That dont necess/y mean making reading matter @ all.

Enny how there must be one hundred books (*not* that one) that you *need* TO read fer yr/ mind's sake

reread *all* the gk tragedies in Loeb. – plus Frobenius, plus Gesell plus Brooks Adams ef you aint read him all.

then Golding 'Ovid' is in Everyman lib.

& nif you want a readin list ask papa. but dont go rushin to *read* a book just

cause it is mentioned eng passang [in passing]. Then of course there is frawgs.
hv. yu read *all* the frawgs fr Willy to M. Jean? (want "CrucifiXion" on loan?? it
aint a ch[urch]. service prob. unobtainable here.

(N. B. Nancy has fergave me & no longer thinks I orter be shot fer not
assassinatin Franco).

& so on

yrz

Ez

Fer gorzake: WCW incorporated an edited version of this letter into Book Three, Part 3 of
   Paterson (1949).

read it: In a letter to EP dated "Yom Kippur: Columbus Day" [October 12, 1948] (Yale),
   WCW writes: "When I read FAMILY REUNION at its first appearance it left me with
   no desire to reread it. But I'm willing to read it agin."

Loeb: The Loeb Classical Library is a joint publishing venture of William Heinemann in
   London and, in the United States, first the Macmillan Company, then Putnam's, and
   finally the Harvard University Press. The series consists of inexpensive, pocket-sized
   editions of the Greek and Roman classics, with the original texts and English translations on facing pages.

Golding 'Ovid': The *Metamorphoses* of the Roman poet Ovid (43 B.C.–18 A.D.) was
   translated into English by Arthur Golding (1536?–1605?).

Willy: The French novelist, translator, and music critic Henri Gauthier-Villars (1859–
   1931) was known to everyone simply as "Willy." A literary entrepreneur of great
   charm, he was the first husband of the novelist Colette.

"Crucifixion": See "Biographical Notes" on COCTEAU, JEAN.

Nancy: See "Biographical Notes" on CUNARD, NANCY. For General Franco, see Letter 93
   above.

127. TLS-1

February 15, 1949

Dear Ez:

In my vast and complex experience there is no simple cure for anything,
especially when it may be due, as in your case, to long standing neglect –
enforced or otherwise. There are dental fortunes established upon some such ill as
that of which you speak.

The one thing you must do, whatever else may be done, and that is you must
take Vitamin C in large doses. I'll send you all you will need if they'll let me do

it, just say the word. Or Dorothy can get 100 or more small pellets of the stuff (100 mgms each) and give them to you to swallow or chew up with your meals. Take them for a month or two, they may help.

But if the teeth need cleaning way up under the gums where tartar has crept up the roots, only an understanding expert can be finally effective. Isn't there some good man connected with the hospital who will take that on? There should be. Ascorbic acid and Vitamin C are the same thing.

Come back at me if there's more you want to know.

I read the various British papers you send me, at least I read here and there in them. They show a certain resistance to political change, what? It is really astonishing that anyone should have, in the past, confused the two languages and the forms suitable in each case to the expression of the national mores. We, as I perceive with greater and greater clarity as I grow older, are not British. Not that I do not admire their resistances.

Paterson III approaches consummation. Shd go to printer in a month or so – as soon as Laughlin gets back from farting around the ski-runs of Davos. But at that I'm lucky. Now only Pat IV remains to be done and I'll be a free man – free to jump off the dock, I suppose. I may try a little prose for a change, finish up another book of the White Mule sequence.

Any change in your status that can be announced? Oh yes, Bill Bird in Tangier with Sally is setting up a press in a pent house on the roof of his native apartment.

Bill

Ascorbic acid: WCW enclosed a prescription for 100 tablets of ascorbic acid.
Paterson III: Paterson (Book Three) was sent to New Directions in April 1949 and published in December.
another book: The third and final novel in the *White Mule* sequence is *The Build-Up* (1952).
Bill Bird: See "Biographical Notes" on BIRD, WILLIAM.

128. TLS-3

Feb 21, 1949

Dear Ez:

Simpson has written from Galveston asking to borrow my Active Anthology. I took it down to send it to him but got stopped by Floss who says that that is just the way we have lost so many valuable books. So I didn't send it – yet. I presume he can be trusted so I'll probably send it to him pretty soon but not until I have found out whether or not I can get another anywhere in N. Y. We shall see.

As a consequence of this request I sat down to the book again after these years and found it so much better than I thought it to be 15 years ago that I can hardly believe my eyes. Compared with anything that is being done today it is simply in another category. Can the world have slipped so far down the scale as this would seem to imply? I'm afraid it is so. But it is the perception the book reveals that is paramount. We have arrived at a stasis that is shocking.

Well, for me the book has come into its own only now. My salutations and felicitations on a good piece of work. I'm afraid I'm a poor reader, it takes me a long time to react, a very long time.

Yesterday I went to Princeton with Floss, to a cocktail party given by Kenneth Burke. He is at the Institute for Advanced Learning on a fellowship that pays him, I think, 400 dollars a month with a house to live in. But he will be there only for 4 months. He is finishing his book on Rhetoric, I like Ken but can't read his books very well, they are too long winded and technical for me.

There I met John Berryman, one of the good younger poets, a skeleton–like man who talks with jerky gestures but knows a good deal about what is worth looking for – either in Virgil or you. I enjoyed talking with him. Malcolm Cowley was there with his wife and several others. Ken wants me to go down some evening t [sic] meet Jacques Maritain who is staying at Princeton in a Renoir like residence. He is not wanted in France and does not want to be in Princeton. Ken believes that he, Kenneth Burke, will end up in the arms of the church – not because he is not enfuriated [sic] by the doctrines of that obsolensence [sic] but because the [sic] so enjoys hearing the seraphim intoning in Latin! He seems vaguely comscious [sic] of some of the resources of the written verse – of which so few are even conscious much less conscious of possible mastery in it.

But occasionally in loose conversation, as yesterday, men begin to say – something really might be done with the line. Or, as Berryman put it, Virgil was resourceful sometimes delaying a key word for two or three lines until by sheer inevitability it brought itself out for the ear. – But that there MIGHT BE something besides routine english verse is still very far toward the horizon for most. They simply emphasize the "thought" and are content there. Few know more than that.

Please tell Dorothy that this is also an answer to her note. Take two of the pellets daily. And, no, Bill Bird did not intimate what he intended to print other than some local jobs to pay for the set-up. The presumption is that there would be more than that if all goes well.

[Autograph addendum on verso of second page] If Dorothy can dig up a copy of *Vogue* for February – at library or dust bin or anywhere other than for cash at a paper stand – look p 213 – for my full page picture. Someone must have a copy of the Slick around. [end of addendum]

Yesterday (was it yesterday or Saturday?) the N. Y. Times and the Herald-Tribune carried the news of your receipt of the B. Prize – with a half column of comment of [*sic*] p. 3 or so. I was mentioned in the Tribune story. As a consequence (sez Bill [William Eric Williams]) the phone was busy all Sunday afternoon with calls from the aforesaid papers – pestering me to make a statement, I suppose. But as I was providentially at Princeton nothing came of it.

I was prepared to say: 1. He is an old friend. 2. I do not share all of his political views. 3. I believe him to be a great poet – our best. 4. As this is a prize given for literary achievement I completely approve of the decision of the Fellows of the Library of Congress to give him this well merited prize.

I might have added: You sons of bitches, what do you think we are, Russians?

So runs the world along – on Washington's Birthday in the tear [*sic*] of grace 1949. And, by the way, I'm enjoying Freeman's, Life of Washington (the first two, of 4 to 6, volumes). Very exciting here and there, very vivid, a sense of reality – the first time the old bastard was made to breathe and seize a good land bargain for what it was worth. He's my basic american hero and has always been so, a little bit dull in the head but nothing the matter with his guts.

Best

Bill

Simpson: See "Biographical Notes" on SIMPSON, DALLAM. For WCW's initial reaction to the *Active Anthology,* see Letter 63 above.

Kenneth Burke: See "Biographical Notes" on BURKE, KENNETH.

John Berryman: This was WCW's first meeting with the American poet and critic John Berryman (1914–1972), who was teaching at Princeton at the time.

Malcolm Cowley: WCW first met the American poet, translator, literary historian, essayist, teacher, and editor Malcolm Cowley (1898–1989) in New York around 1915. His wife was Muriel Maurer Cowley.

Jacques Maritain: The French philosopher, critic, and diplomat Jacques Maritain (1882–1973) held a professorship at Princeton from 1948 to 1954. Coverted to Catholicism in 1906, Maritain was an expert on the scholastic philosophy of St. Thomas Aquinas.

Vogue: The issue of *Vogue* for February 1, 1949, carries a picture of WCW by Joffe on p. 213.

The B. prize: On February 20, 1949, the Bollingen Prize in poetry was awarded by the Library of Congress to EP for his *Pisan Cantos.* The award was reported in the *New York Times* for February 20, pp. 1, 14, and in the *New York Herald Tribune* for February 20, pp. 1, 30. WCW is mentioned in the second of these reports: "Mr. Eliot and Mr. Williams are known to be long-time admirers, if not proteges of Pound."

Freeman's, Life of Washington: Douglas Southall Freeman, *George Washington: A Biog-*

raphy, 7 vols. (1948–57). Washington is the subject of a chapter in WCW's *In the American Grain.*

129. TLS-1

March 1, 1949

Dear Dorothy:

As far as the U. S. Constitution is concerned, though how it got into this discussion I have no idea, I object to that section where it says (according to Ezra's interpretation) a man may speak or act, during an armed conflict with another nation, in such a way as to bring comfort to the enemy.

But if what Ezra is driving at is my statement that I do not share all his political views (which, by the way has nothing whatever to do with the U. S. Constitution) I can only say that I am willing to change my opinions, like any reasonable man, when I am convinced that another opinion or conviction is more to my liking.

The one good thing to say for Ez is that he has not, like the Marxists, traded in convenient lies in order to emphasize his point. My one objection to Ezra's conduct is that he has evaded trial – if he has evaded it. It may be he is ill, as they say, and so will never be able to stand trial. If so he must be treated as an ill person.

But why, in God's name, should anyone at any time expect another to share all his political opinions? What we must all do, in spite of our divergent political opinions, is to unite to support the government when it is endangered. I think you'll find this in the Constitution.

I sent the book to Dallam. I hope he returns it without undue delay as things that are mislaid are often subsequently lost.

I do not intend to enter into political discussion with Ez at this or any time while he is at St Elizabeth Hosp. I write this to you, if you want to show it to Ez that must rest with your judgement of the situation. I'll drop him a note in reply to his recent card.

Best to you both
Bill

this discussion: The letter from EP to which this one is a response has apparently not survived.

a note: WCW's note to EP, dated March 1, 1949 (Indiana), reads: "Dear Ez, Sez you. On the other hand, sez I. Between us lies the sea. as ever Bill."

130. TL-3

April 15 [1949]

Dear Ez:

Glad to hear from you. For the past week I've been watching Mother getting ready to die – in her 93d year. She's not dead yet, not that one, but she's only conscious by moments. That's all she needs, moments, in which to assert herself in her own particular way – by sitting bolt upright in bed (a thing she hasn't done in ten years) and telling off the really wonderful british couple who, "hearts of oak", are caring for her – by God's word. It's a sight all right, no question about that. I'll tell you more about that couple one of these days – a reincarnation of my father sent by divine intercession to carry the old woman into Paradise or Hell or – nothingness, more probably.

But what a fight!

Well, it's early Good Friday morning and I have been standing gawking in the eastward looking bathroom window looking down at our daffodils, out [*sic*] shad bush in white blossom and the starlings bathing at the bird bath – and thinking of you and the eternal poem. The others are still asleep.

Perhaps I have written a few poems, I don't know. I'm happy that you have found a few items in the "Selected" that appeal to you. I am never certain that they have body enough, a sound enough structural initiative to stand by themselves. It really doesn't matter much as far as I'm concerned, I'm fatalist enough for that. For if I haven't written anything such as I'd be happy to acknowledge if I could be sure I know at least WHAT should be written and I'm equally sure that someone will write it, I'd be happy to be a signpost should I turn out to be nothing more.

Yes, there are omissions in the book and "Elsie" did loose [*sic*] her name. I'm sorry for that. The thing is that that poem never did have a name except as an afterthought. It came out in Spring and All where one of the poemes [*sic*] had a name, The name however was obvious so I added it later – then took it away for scatalogical [*sic*] reasons. Silly. It'll be put back at another time. For the odd thing about this selected edition is that though it is liked everyone (so to speak) reminds me of their favorite poems which have *not* been included. Thus we should have a Further Selection which would be quite as sizeable as the first.

Jim [Laughlin] wants to make a BIG new Complete Poems but I'm not anxious to see that at the koment [*sic*]. As one of my ladies said recently: When you want to lie in bed and read poems you don't want to [*sic*] big heavy book that tires you to hold it. – I think she is quite right. My most popular book as [*sic*] been The

Wedge, which, if you haven't seen it is squat, pocket-size, and weighs only an ounce or so. It is very much sought after and nowhere to be found.

It might amuse you for me to take time out to tell you a little of the history of that little book: It was gathered together during the war under the incentive provided me by various GIs who wanted a book of my poems, so their letters said, that they could carry in their pockets. I was determined to supply them with that. So I gathered up what stray ends of poems I had a [sic] found enough to make a small book.

This book I took first, naturally, to Laughlin who said he didn't have paper enough for it, that he had other committments [sic] and that, in short, he couldn't do it. Well, I have a patient, a young man who is employed by a large publishing house in New York, He is a good friend and said he would take the script to another friend etc etc.

The Cript [sic] was then submitted to Raynal and Hitchcock or some such firm. They gave it to their reader, a Harcard [sic] man. This was emphasized, that he was a Harvard man – meaning to imply that this was the Supremem [sic] Court. The Harvard man rejected it. I'll never forget the amusing and slightly shocking circumstand [sic]. My good hearted printer friend brought the script back to me and I could see he was very much embarrassed. "I'm sorry", he said, "but they don't want to publish it". "Why?" sez I? "Do you really want to know?" sez he, lookijg [sic] at me out of the tops of his eyes. "Sure." sez I. "You won't be hurt?" sez he – being a devoted friend. "No." sez I. "Well, then," sez he, this man they gave it to to read says it isn't good enough." Just like that.

After repeating the usual ritual of contempt and exasperation under my breath I excused myself before my friend for HIS embarrassment and swore then, in silence, to show the sons of bitches front and back, first and last that the book would be published.

As it happened I appealed next to the two boys at Cummington – they may have written asking for a script – in fact think they did – but, be that as it may, the occasion arose. They had some excellent paper put away in a cache somewhere on their premises and set to work on the script without delay. I told them the size I wanted, they agreed and after the usual delays consequent upon hand setting the pages were finishhed [sic] and beautifully set.

But how to bind the thing? I had agreed to take fifty copies in case of failure of sales for which I paid in $100. But the binding stumped us – unti, [sic] I went back to my friend in N. Y. who had the job done by a little skillful lying – deceiving his bosses by sneaking it in with something else – always with the feeling I knew he had that it wasn't much of book anyhow but that he wanted to please Doc Williams for having hurt him by telling the truth about his writing.

So within a month I had to resell my $100 worth back to Cummington to supply

orders etc etc as I have said. It's just the SIZE everyone wants. Worth knowing

I wrote a "criticism" of The Pisan Cantos for a small invisible little mag
published by someone at Muhlenberg University [*sic*] in Pennsylvania or Ohio or
somewhere. It is called IMAGI. About 3 sheets. I read the Cantos first! – to be
sure!! You'll see the result when the think [*sic*] is published in May or so.

Poetry is publishing a third installment of my autobiography in their May or
June issue. This bit concerns you and our years more or less together at Penn as
well as the London episode of 1910

Thus begins my Good Friday 1949

Best to Dorothy and yourself for whatever this new year brings

Yrs as always

Paterson III went to press this week. Many other things to tell but the hours pile
up of themselves – yes I'm careless. So is death.

her 93d year: Under the care of Mr. and Mrs. Harry Taylor, WCW's mother did not die
until the night of October 7–8, 1949. After her death, WCW discovered that she was
actually in her 102nd year; see Mariani, pp. 595–96.

a few items in the "Selected": WCW's *Selected Poems* was published by New Directions
in March 1949. In a letter to WCW of April 10, 1949 (Yale), EP writes: "See – lected –
& q[uite]. a lot ov good ones I didn't kno. . . . also some omissions that ought not
sech az Coroner's & wot ever its title in 1st Imgst. & Elsie got her name changed/ 'Taste
good' thazz OK." The poems to which EP refers are "Hic Jacet," "Postlude," "To
Elsie," and "To a Poor Old Woman."

Complete Poems: New Directions published WCW's complete poems in a two-volume
edition: *Collected Later Poems* (1951) and *Collected Earlier Poems* (1952).

a young man: Unidentified.

Raynal and Hitchcock: The Wedge was rejected by Simon and Schuster and by Duell,
Sloan & Pearce. The Harvard reader is unidentified.

Cummington: Harry Duncan and Paul Wightman Williams ran the Cummington Press in
Cummington, Massachusetts. They published WCW's *The Wedge* in September 1944
in a handset, limited edition of 380 copies.

IMAGI: See "Biographical Notes" on COLE, THOMAS.

Poetry: Three installments of WCW's "Some Notes toward an Autobiography" appeared
in *Poetry* for June 1948, August 1948, and May 1949. In March 1910, WCW spent a
week in London with EP.

131. TLS-2

Wednesday
[April 1949]

Dear Dorothy:

Tell Ez my knowledge of medicine permeates everything I write tho' perhaps the specific details hold an interest for the general reader which I do not suspect. In the main, however, the specific knowledge of details gets over unknown to the reader by preventing the erruption [sic] of the usual irrelevancies which the uninstructed mind falls into quite unsuspectingly.

Julian Huxley once wrote a volume of poems exploiting his medical and general scientific knowledge but it was merely fanciful, not serious. By serious I mean, the form was not influenced, merely the old rehash.

I see, by way of the *New Republic,* that I have been compared (this week) by a certain Fitzgerald to a British poet named Empsom or Empson who has spent his life in Beiping and elswere [sic] in China – in other words far from the heart of the British Empire – exactly like myself. He, however, is a classicist – in a very general way; whereas I, to the British public, remain a Yahoo much to my amusement and profit.

Tell Ez the shad are running in the Hudson River and that I took my grandson there today, his spring vacation being on, to see what was going on. We bought two, one "hickory smoked" and the other boned, with the roe separate, a blood morsel. The brother of the rather deaf man who sold me the fish, a man named Herring, painted the "president series" of murals in our town-hall. The fish guy is proud of him, his kid brother. My hands still smell of the fish as I type this – the smoked meat delicious. My grandson could hardly be restrained, after the man broke apart a sample smoked fish, from eating the whole of it – or attempting to. He has decided that when he grows up he wants to live by the Hudson river and fish every day. He wanted to know how old I will be when he is a man. I told him I'd be dead and burnt up. "Oh no," said he, sometimes people can walked [sic] about after they're 100 and even older."

And this is Easter, and the sun is bright and poems in my head are like – or as multiple as the roe of a female shad itself. Gorgeous poems! The best ever!

And hell take the hindmost.

Best
Bill

knowledge of medicine: In a letter to WCW of April 18 [1949] (Yale), Dorothy says, "What beats him [EP] is that you don't see your *specific* medical knowledge is poetic – and no one else has it."

Julian Huxley: The English zoologist, essayist, and poet Sir Julian Huxley (1887–1975) is the author of *The Captive Shrew and Other Poems of a Biologist* (1933). The title poem begins: "Timid atom, furry shrew,/Is it a sin to prison you?"

New Republic: The New Republic for April 25, 1949, carried a review by the American poet and translator Robert Fitzgerald (1910–1985) of the *Selected Poems* of WCW and the *Collected Poems* of the English poet and critic Sir William Empson (1906–1984). Empson lived and taught for many years in China and Japan. His learned and difficult poems are influenced by his studies in mathematics and the modern sciences, and written in tight, traditional forms. According to Fitzgerald, Empson and WCW "represent the extremes of formal difference in contemporary verse." WCW is "an intelligent anti-intellectual," and "no Englishman has ever got the hang of Williams's kind of writing."

Herring: Unidentified.

132. TLS-1

Sept 15 [1949]

Dea Rez:(erection)

Some years ago at about this time of the year, the 17th to be exact, the Constitution of the U. S. wuz adopted by the States and on the same day, some years later, I wuz born – to do what I could fer humanity: pitiful twain.

As far as your complaints are intelligible to me (not your fault) I'd say you lack light and liberty. What to do about that is another thing:

Cold medicines are largely the bunk (like this typewriter). I presume, being confined as you are, that you take some sort of supplementary vitaments (vitamins) there are dozens of good varieties on the market. Squibb's Special Formula is one – tho' somewhat expensive. One a day at breakfast would be worth putting into your guts just on general principles but such a capsule wd be of no use against a cold. Might close your pores tho'.

One old Doc from around here used to say the best way not to cathch [*sic*] a cold was to follow this routine: Take a turkish towel and wrap it around you just under the armpits in the manner of a present day decolté [*sic,* off-the-shoulder] gown. Grab the ends of the towel in your left hand, pulling it tight around you (to prevent the water from running down over your belly) then with your right hand and a washcloth douse your neck and chest with water as cold as it may happen to run out of the tap. Do this every day on arising taking no more time to it than has been used up in telling you of the same. Then take the more or less dry towel and give yourself a brisk rub or until your skin is red from the friction. I still believe that's the best way to tone yourself up – if you'll do it. Few have the patience to persist.

Most times when the mouth and throat are dry on arising it has come about through a person sleeping with his mouth open. All the mucus membranes dry out and, when hawked at, may bleed slightly.

Get your weight down five or ten pounds by laying off the sugars and bread. We're gettin' old, Ez. My complaint is forgetfulness, inability to get from under the load my life has always piled on me – just never have been able to be drastic in that respect with myself as you have: for which I admire you, come what may (And it damn well will come and perty soon too)

I'm sending you something to read which I greatly admire – and you'll probably shit on. So what? Eliot lives! the world is pregnant. Hoooooray!

> Sugar and spice
> Bill

the Constitution: WCW took pleasure in the coincidence that he was born on Constitution Day, the United States Constitution having been ratified on September 17, 1789.
something to read: Unidentified.

133. ALS-3

Dec. 13 [1949]

Yaas som lively itemz
& crizism deaf-eated by lack of page numberz
2,100 ft. = thaz v. interestin' page.
but dont prove there aint no water no where. =
Troubled by wot Dante calls 'muliebria'' in some patches of soft.
the two parts of this note are separate – not sposed to form a unity.
Part 2
recallin' the details of the event
& my erronius impression @ t time

I wd send my best to yr. mother, if I weren't afraid that it is too late.
My father died 2 years or more ago.

yrz fer the ole red sandstone
Ez

I aint nevr seen Bk 2

lively itemz: EP has been reading *Paterson (Book Three)*, newly published and unpaginated.

interestin' page: On the page of *Paterson (Book Three)* facing EP's letter to WCW of October 13, 1948 (Letter 126 above), WCW reproduces a geological tabulation of the substrata found in the drilling of an artesian well at the Passaic Rolling Mill in Paterson in 1879–80. The well reached a depth of 2,100 feet without finding usable water. Continuing his dialogue with EP, WCW paraphrases a passage from the present letter in *Paterson (Book Four)*, Part II (1951): "just because they ain't no water fit to drink in that spot (or you ain't found none) don't mean there ain't no fresh water to be had NOWHERE."

Dante: In *De Vulgari Eloquentia*, Book II, Dante cautions writers of vernacular Italian against using feminine diction because of its softness ("nec muliebria, propter sui mollitiem").

erronius impression: Confused by WCW's premature report of his mother's death in April (see Letter 130 above), EP did not send her his best wishes before her actual death in October.

My father died: Homer Pound died in 1942.

red sandstone: The principal geological formation through which the Paterson well was drilled.

134. TL-3

January 11, 1950

Dear Ez:

It's interesting how many "little magazines" have been turning up recently when it wasn't more than 8 to 10 years ago everyone was bemoaning the fact that due to increase in the cost of printing "pure literature" was about to be extinguished. And books! My God, I'm drowned in them. They flood in (mostly bad) as if they were being distributed gratis [free] by the Post Office Dep't. Never in my life have I seen so many, from all sorts of publishers – and I imagine that not a tenth of the crop are sent to me.

Everyone is writing "poetry". My suggestion is that they start writing a few poems.

Well, I'm glad the kids are active; the colleges are seething with verse. Certainly the interest is there but it's not very well directed. The "English" departments are still predominent [sic]. No one has officially put the quietus on that misdirection of the forces which might lead to an understanding at least have [sic] the lines are to be put together. The feeling for good work is present but without much sense of what shupld [sic] be done with the materials in hand.

One lucky thing is that "causes" are pretty much out of date now. The [sic] do know that to write is to use words and to make them hinge together in SOME way other than to screech after a political figure. But you saw that they gave Viereck the Pulitzer Prize last year. The man has written one fairly good poem but for the most part he stinks, irretrievably has never been on the track of the poem. Not at least to my taste. To me he represents a regression. But he is not representative.

For some reason I've been in demand for talks and readings. The latest, more or less, will be a lecture at the Modern Museum in N. Y. March 20. This could not have happened ten years ago. Then on Aptil [sic] 20 I'm to read again at the T. M. H. A. [sic], the so called "Poetry Center" at Lexington Ave and 91st St. The topic that night will be Paterson Books I, II, III and IV if I have any of it finoshed [sic] by that time. They pay $150 and $100 respectively for the privilege.

Did you get Pat. II? I asked Jim [Laughlin] to send it to you.

New kids are cropping up every minute and the heartening this [sic] is that tho' they haven't done much their interest is pure. I'm delighted. I've seen some wonderful starts and on the right track, an interest in the words, the words, the words, their own words constructed on some sort of scheme related to WRITING on which they are working with someone, you, Gertrude Stein or some other as a preliminary insentive [sic]. I saw some really beautiful "proses" as the guy calls them this week by some young chap in Union City (Weehawken) of all places. That he sent them to me, earnestly, modestly, trustingly was a charming gesture. I've encouraged him to go on.

I'm engaged on a two act libretto for a fantasy upon the Salem Witchcraft incident. I haven't much time to myself and the reading has been a little onerous but with patience I'll do it. A Saltonstal [sic], a relative of the Massachusetts senator has been setying [sic] me on, a woman in her forties with plenty of drive to her. She'll get it produced if I write it and the composer isn't abashed at the difficulties of writing the score. I'll let you know if anything comes of it.

Nothing much else to say. Had a letter from [Thomas] Cole saying he had seen you recently and that he found you looking well. I took your hint and asked him to drop in some time of [sic] he were in New York. He spoke of getting up an "all

America'' issue of his IMAGI at, I think, your suggestion. I told him I'd do what I could to help.

They want me to spend the summer at a place called Black Mountain College in North Carolina to teach there for the summer session. I can't do that – much as I'd like to, But it's at least interssting [*sic*] that they want me and would, I presume pay me a fair fee.

All this just not to waste the envelope in sending the enclosed brochure – if it's a brochure. A catalogue I suppose. Best to Dorothy from us both.

Yrs.

Viereck: The American poet, historian, and political philosopher Peter Viereck (1916–) won the 1949 Pulitzer Prize in Poetry for his book *Terror and Decorum: Poems, 1940– 1948*. WCW reviewed Viereck's *Strike through the Mask* in the *New York Times Book Review* for March 12, 1950, p. 14, but the review does not identify the poem WCW thought ''fairly good.''

the Modern Museum: WCW read from his own work at the Guggenheim Museum in New York on March 28, 1950; see Mariani, p. 605.

the T. M. H. A.: Starting in 1939, WCW made a number of appearances at the Poetry Center of the Young Men's Hebrew Association in New York. The most recent had been a series of four lectures in October and November 1949.

some young chap: Unidentified.

a two act libretto: WCW's *Tituba's Children* draws a parallel between the witch trials in seventeenth-century Salem, Massachusetts, and loyalty investigations in Cold-War Washington. Although it was not scored or performed, WCW's libretto was published in *Many Loves and Other Plays* (1961).

a Saltonstal: Harriet Saltonstall Gratwick was founder and director of the Linwood Music School in Linwood, New York. WCW and Floss visited her home Gratwick Highlands on a number of occasions between 1940 and 1958. Her relative Leverett Saltonstall (1892–1972) was Governor of Massachusetts and United States Senator.

Cole: See ''Biographical Notes'' on COLE, THOMAS.

Black Mountain College: An experimental arts college in North Carolina, where Charles Olson taught from 1947 to 1956.

135. TL-1

[January 1950?]

IN
  venshun.
O.KAY

IN venshun.
and seeinz az how yu hv/ started. Will yu consider
a remedy of a lot:
>   i.e.
>   LOCAL control of local purchasing power.??
Difference between squalor of spreading slums
and splendour of renaissance italian cities.
>   there is ALso the motto to my Gaudier book/ wunner ef yu evr seen that?

IN venshun: WCW reproduces this letter or fragment of a letter in *Paterson (Book Four),* Part 3. The letter is EP's response to a passage in *Paterson (Book Two),* Part 1, which begins, "Without invention nothing is well spaced." This passage, in turn, echoes EP's Canto 45, "With *Usura.*" EP probably read Book Two of *Paterson* for the first time in the latter part of January 1950; for in a note of January 16, 1950 (Yale), he writes, "Than q fer 'Paterson 2.'"

motto: One of the two epigraphs to EP's *Gaudier-Brzeska: A Memoir* (1916) is G. Pauthier's French translation of a passage from the *Tchoung-Young* of Confucius, Chapter 20, Section 12: "*Dès l'instant qu'il (le prince) aura attiré près de lui tous les savans et les artistes, aussitot ses richesses seront suffisament mises en usage.*" (From the moment he [the prince] has drawn all the philosophers and artists to him, his wealth will be adequately employed.) See *Les Livres Sacrées de l'Orient,* trans. G. Pauthier (Paris: Firmin Didot and August Desraz, 1840), p. 170.

136. TLS-2

March 23 [1950]

Dear Ez:

Do you know the ballroom of the Waldorf-Astoria (makes me think of the Black Forest and the fur trade of our colonial period)? It's like the Scala opera house in Milan with all the seats removed and tables seating 10 to 12 put in to replace them. There were 1100 guests, $12.50 a plate and $2. extra for cocktails. Up front was the stage with tiers of tables across the scene mounting to Clifton Fadiman begore [sic] a nattery [sic] of microphones at the top – all just to give me a gold medal worth about $35. dollars.

Anyhoo, as the Canadians say, I got it – fer having writ the best etc etc during 1949, at least Auden who appears to have been chairman of the committee conceded the thing to me which was nice of him along with the others. We had consome [sic] (which I ate in a hurry after being yanked from the table to be photographed 30 times, out of the near, the wrong side of my plate – Floss said everyone was looking at me: I was half conscious of it and remembered something you said about Yates [W. B. Yeats] eating soup as though he were sucking it out of a trough. A piece of sauced fish, a slab of red beef etc etc

and then they had a show on the stage that was terrific: some cute little Mexican wahoo shook her ass until it almost fell off – she was wonderful! The rest stank. The speeches were good at first but Senator Douglas whom I respect for something about him that is rough and ready came out with a statement as to his reading the highlight being Stephen Crane's Red Badge of Courage – which he read while lying in a fox-hole in B. (I've forgot the place in the South Pacific) No, he was reading Dante's Inferno, the seventh circle of hell – and the water gradually creeping up to his ears where he was lying in the rain.

That's all the anthropology I can give you – or want to give you. Most of the time, as might be expected, they acted as if they wondered how I had got into the place among all the gig [*sic*] guys of the book industry. I had to squeeze ebtween [*sic*] tables to get out when my time had come to get up and make my little speech (1 minutes [*sic*], please!) but a few good guys did seem to accept me. Wynfield Townlet Scott [*sic*] of Providence came up and shook hands – and I met Bennet [*sic*] Cerf who would like to get me for Random House.

It's a long story, Ez. But at least for the moment the lime light is on me in a small way. I have to answer reams of letters from strangers, I am asked to speak here and there – for a few bucks but I will say people are very generous with their compliments.

One of the most interesting and intelligent things that have happened to me was a visit, a week or so ago, from a young chap named Woodward from the U[niversity]. of P[ennsylvania]. who is doing his doctor's thesis on my poems. He stayed overnight and talked well – and modestly of his plans. It gave me an opportunity to let go without the usual preliminary explanations. He knew what it was all about so we talked or I talked and talked all one Saturday [*sic*] afternoon (all that was left of the afternoon after I had held office hours and recorded (in my office) an interview with a delegation from the Newark High Schools. Then we had supper and woodward and I talked some more (after going out to supper with friends – where the poor guy chucked his guts he having had the intestinal flu all day without acknowledging it – he was so eager for his interview with me.

Home we went where I (the doctor) dosed him up. put him to bed. Sunday I worked all morning while he was prepaing [*sic*] the plan of his dissertation (you see he is only starting it) During the afternoon he fired his questions at me, I talked some more then took him to Newark for his train to Phily. A really intelligent guy – about 32. Ex nose-gunner, married an English girl he met during the war and has 2 kids.

Evening before last I attended my first "banquet" at the expense of the Am[erican]. Institute of Arts and letters at the So and So Club in N. Y. C. There being now a member of the Institute! I met all the great – that is 50 out of the 250 – all in other words who were at the banquet – including Ann McCormic [*sic*] and Dorothy Thompson. Also Percy Makay or however he spells it. F. P. A. (soused to the gills) Alfred Kreymborg who is also a member, Allen Tate (whom I like) and Lillian Hellman the playright [*sic*] – a good gal. Paul Manship was also there – as far as I'm concerned. etc etc

Gotta go down to breakfast.

I'm getting up a new Collected Short Stories and a new Complete Collected Poems (2 vols) Pat. III is sold out (no more books, that's Jim all over) But will say he is doing a new (smaller) edition.

The only trouble is I HAVE NO TIME ANY MORE TO WRITE. That'll have to be corrected.

Floss is well. Bill's youg [*sic*] wife is pregnant. My grandchildren are a delight to me when they don't drive me crazy and I have the piles.

> Same to you and many more of them
> Bill

the Black Forest and the fur trade: New York's Waldorf-Astoria hotel, completed in 1917, was a property of the Astor family. The first John Jacob Astor (1763–1848) was born in the village of Waldorf in the duchy of Baden in Germany. He became the wealthiest man in North America through the fur trade and purchases of Manhattan real estate.

Clifton Fadiman: The American teacher, writer, and editor Clifton Fadiman (1904–) was host of the radio quiz show "Information, Please" (1938–48) and an accomplished master of ceremonies.

a gold medal: The first National Book Awards banquet ever held took place at the Waldorf-Astoria on March 16, 1950. Three authors were honored: Nelson Algren, Ralph L. Rusk, and WCW, who received the Gold Medal for Poetry for *Paterson (Book Three)*.

Auden: The English poet, playwright, and critic W. H. Auden (1907–1973) had lived in New York since 1939. Along with Louise Bogan, Babette Deutsch, Horace Gregory, and Louis Untermeyer, he was a member of the committee that selected WCW for the National Book Award.

Senator Douglas: See "Biographical Notes" on DOUGLAS, PAUL HOWARD. He was one of three principal speakers at the National Book Awards banquet, along with Eleanor D. Roosevelt and Frederick Lewis Allen.

Stephen Crane's Red Badge of Courage: Published in 1895, this story traces the process by which Henry Fleming, a young Union soldier in the American Civil War, learns courage under fire.

Dante's Inferno: The seventh circle of Dante's Inferno is reserved for the punishment of those who have done violence.

Wynfield Townlet Scott: WCW had corresponded with the American poet and journalist

Winfield Townley Scott (1910–1968) since the early 1940s, but this was their first meeting.

Bennet Cerf: The New York publisher Bennett Cerf (1898–1971) was president of Random House. In March 1950, his firm was trying to woo WCW away from New Directions; see Letter 137 below.

Woodward: Donald Woodward (1921–) served as a bombardier in the 8th U. S. Air Force, stationed in East Anglia. After the war, he became a graduate student in English at the University of Pennsylvania. His doctoral dissertation on the rhythms of WCW's poetry was rejected on the grounds that its style was insufficiently formal. Woodward went on to a successful career in the field of advertising.

Am. Institute: WCW was inducted into the National (not American) Institute of Arts and Letters on May 25, 1950. EP, who had been inducted in 1938, referred to it, in a letter to WCW of [March 1950] (Yale), as the Institute o Farts and Stutters.

Ann McCormic: The English-born journalist and author Anne O'Hare McCormick (1882?–1954) was a foreign correspondent for the *New York Times* and a member of the newspaper's editorial board. In 1937, she became the first woman ever to win the Pulitzer Prize for journalism.

Dorothy Thompson: The American journalist and political commentator Dorothy Thompson (1894–1961) was the author of *The New Russia* (1928), and *"I Saw Hitler!"* (1932). From 1928 to 1942, she was married to the novelist Sinclair Lewis.

Percy Makay: The prolific American poet, dramatist, editor, and translator Percy Mac-Kaye (1875–1956) pronounced his surname to rhyme with *sky*.

F. P. A.: Under the pen name "F. P. A.," the American poet, translator, humorist, newspaper columnist, and broadcaster Franklin Pierce Adams (1881–1960) wrote on books and literary gossip for the *New York Tribune, New York World, New York Herald Tribune,* and *New York Post.* His own books include *Toboganning on Parnassus* (1911), *Christopher Columbus* (1931), and *The Melancholy Lute* (1936).

Lillian Hellman: The American playwright and prose writer Lillian Hellman (1905–1984) is the author of *The Children's Hour* (1934), *The Little Foxes* (1938), and *Toys in the Attic* (1960).

Paul Manship: The American sculptor Paul Manship (1885–1966) is best known for his bronze castings influenced by archaic Greek sculpture, such as the Prometheus Fountain in Rockefeller Center (1933). WCW visited his studio in Paris in 1924.

Collected Short Stories: WCW's *Make It Light: Collected Stories* was published by Random House in November 1950. For the collected poems, see Letter 130 above.

Bill's youg wife: William Eric Williams married Daphne Spence on November 19, 1949.

137. TLS-2

[March 29, 1950?]

Dear Ez:

For no reason at all, for God knows you never tell me anything of your private business, I'll tell you what's happening with me re. the publishing game: Jim L[aughlin]. neither keeps my books in print, nor has enough to sell when the sale of them is on. In short, I make very little cash through him.

Recently he acquired a hot salesman named Dave McDowell, the young chap who put over the recent best seller The Sheltering Sky which Jim published but almost lost out on – due to his almost failure to back Dave's drive.

On top of this Jim fired Dave without warning, saying he couldn't afford to keep him and that anyway Dave could get more elsewhere, which he did, at Random House.

Now Dave says Jim says he can't sell my books. But Dave has answered that by God HE can and will if given the chance. Besides he's furious at Jim whom he accuses of not wanting to sell anything, adding that he, Jim, really wants to operate at a loss for income tax purposes. I know nothing of this, I am merely erporting [sic]. But since I am caught in the middle of this fight I'm interested.

But this, surely; I can't at the close of my life NOT try to make a living at writing. To get time to write as I want to I've got to ear [sic] something more at it than I have earned heretofore. Abd [sic] this is excatly [sic] what Dave through Random House promises.

Now Random House is not Bennet [sic] Cerf – unsavory as his reputation is among writers. And Random House is the publisher of [W. H.] Auden, [William] Faulkner and many another wroter [sic] whom I respect. Poetry is out, that stays with Laughlin no matter what happens. But for the prose, which Jim confesses he cannot move, I am strongly inclined to go to the other house – though not before I have had a talk with Jim who is (as usual when he is wanted) in Switzerland skiing.

There's your meat pie, sir. I hopes you find something in it but Jack-stones [pebbles].

Yes, I attended the first banquet offered me by the Institute of Am[erican]. Letters and was introduced politely enough to all the faces. I remember your speaking to me of this crew before the last war. I can't for the life of me see that it's anything but a club for the convenience of *les arrives* [the climbers]. Doesn't smell too good so far to me. If any *action* comes out of them it'll amaze me – but perhaps I'm missing something.

I read my stuff at The Modern Museum last evening – and had a spotty success.

Jezes! all the kids in the country are writing to me – ane [*sic*] I try to snwere [*sic*] them! It's driving me nuts.

Best to Dorothy.

Yrs

Bill

Dave McDowell: David Ulrey McDowell (1918–1955) worked on the staffs of *Hika* (Kenyon College), the *Kenyon Review,* and *transition.* WCW had corresponded with him at *Hika* as early as 1941. From 1948 to 1950, McDowell worked as sales and promotion manager for New Directions before moving to Random House.

The Sheltering Sky: Published by New Directions in 1949, *The Sheltering Sky,* by the American novelist, translator, and composer Paul Bowles (1910–), sold 25,000 copies.

Poetry is out: Initially, Random House published three prose works by WCW—*Make Light of It* (1950), the *Autobiography* (1951), and *The Build-Up* (1952)—whereas New Directions handled the collected poems and *Paterson.* Later, however, WCW gave Random House two new books of poetry, *The Desert Music* (1954) and *Journey to Love* (1955).

The Modern Museum: See Letter 134 above.

138. TLS-2

December 29, 1950

Dear Ez:

How about an old year letter, this is one. I wus dreamin about two old gals I know, two nurses in the hospital where I work – only they was back of me down in my cellar where I wuz foolin' around (Freudian? of course). All on a sudden I heard them sniggering back of me. I turned around, they were making such a racket about it, and there they were in their voluminous nurses dresses, as starched and clean! One of them was lying on the dirty floor (the younger good looking one) putting up a real battle as the older, heavier one had her down on her back, inside her dress in some way and her old backside rising and falling over her middle in great style. They were having a rare of [*sic*] time of it. You may imagine the state I was in when I worke [*sic*] up over it. An' last week I had a proctoscopic examination (10 inches of steel up my tail end with a light in it and a peek hole for the old doc) to tell me I was not (immediately) to die of cancer. May uv been the cause of the whole episode. But what could the *gal* have been doin?

Haven't got hold of the Domestic Manners book yet. I tried at the local library but they didn't have it. Must look it up in Passaic.

The only trouble is I've finished Paterson Book IV. Cad-wallader is a name to remember, thanks. Might as well send you a copy of The Collected Later Poems but don't want to if "the James" [Laughlin] has already contributed it. Let me know, please.

I'm doing my autobiography – for some reason. Not that I asked to do it. I didn't. They asked me. No plodding job tho' I'll have to get down on it hard sooner or later to keep sloppy sentences out of it. At present I'm just dropping my pants and lettin' fly. No dirt tho', this is to be pure courtesy. Like hell it is. No vituperation however. Just a scattering of bird-shot here and there. No harm to anyone – unless he fergets to shut his eyes. That's up to him. Just bounce off an ordinary buisness [sic] suit.

They tell me you've got fat, over 200 'tis said. Cut that out, young man. Eat greens and cheese, cut vurry thin. No bread, no sugar, no heavy sauces! Ha ha!

Had a nice talk with Marianne Moore at a meeting of the National Institute of Arts and   Farts and fetters – damn close to that, too. Hell with them. She says you've been or [sic] great assistance to her in her translations of La Fontaine. Sahe [sic] says you've been of more help than anyone to her. A tremendous help. She's doing them over now, God knows *how* many of them, for the 3d time.

They tell me Tee Hee Helliot is to teach at Chicago next year. Was a mad Bomb gettin' too close? But what the hell's happened to CHICAGO? I though [sic] there might be some hope there. Now I see even that is facing. Not that the Eeliot couldn't teach 'em a lot, at his best, but will he? I doubt it.

Love little sweetheart
Bill

---

the Domestic Manners: In a letter of [December 23, 1950] (Yale), EP asks WCW whether he has seen the description of the Morris Canal at Paterson in *Domestic Manners of the Americans* (1832) by the English novelist and travel writer Frances Trollope (1780–1863). EP calls particular attention to the sonorous name of Cadwallader Colden (1769–1834), a former mayor of New York City and an ardent advocate of canal-building.

Paterson Book IV: Paterson (Book Four) was published by New Directions in June 1951. At this point, WCW thought the poem was finished.

her translations of La Fontaine: See "Biographical Notes" on MOORE, MARIANNE.

Tee Hee Helliot: In November 1950, T. S. Eliot gave four lectures on "The Aims of Education" at the University of Chicago, but he did not teach there subsequently.

139. ALS-2

Friday the 13th.
[April 1951]

Dear Ez:

Am coming along fine. I am sitting up in a chair & beginnging [*sic*] to write again. This surely was a surprise to me, never thought of such a thing. I was lucky not to get worse; I was, I suppose, trying to do too many things at once. The old machine simply rebelled.

In bed the last week I have reread (most of it for the first time) your *ABC of Reading* with much enjoyment. It is wonderful to realize how stupid the critic can be at times – as in the case of *Sordello*. But there are those in the critical world today, and you know at least one prominent name, whose attitudes lead to much the same sort of shit.

We here in one part of the "English speaking world" thank you for this book.

Best
Bill

a surprise: WCW suffered a stroke on March 28, 1951.

ABC of Reading: A new edition of EP's *ABC of Reading* (1934) was published by New Directions in March 1951.

Sordello: For Browning's *Sordello,* see Letter 9 above. In the *ABC,* EP quotes a passage of the poem and then remarks, "Victorian half-wits claimed that this poem was obscure, and . . . used to pride themselves on grinning through the horse-collar: 'Only two lines of Sordello were intelligible'" (p. 191).

one prominent name: T. S. Eliot; he is also the "irritant" to which EP refers in the following letter.

the "English speaking world": Popularized by Winston Churchill in a famous speech delivered at Westminster College in Fulton, Missouri, on March 5, 1946, this phrase inspired the founding of the English-Speaking Union. WCW uses the expression ironically, because the notion of an "English-speaking world" contradicts his belief in the distinctiveness of American experience and the American idiom.

140. ALS-2

16 Ap[ril 1951]

Banzai al a laa

glad yu r a settin UP. yu keep settin' & don't go rushin' & bustin' yr biler.
ole Jarge Santy iz 88 & sent me a vol –
wot I aint read yet.
vurry leisurly.
you try 'n' act like ole Jarge. & dun't worrit about transient irritants even if
they wear cowns [*sic*] & sceptres.
best to Flos. & tell her to keep yu a-settin

Ez

Banzai al a laa: Japanese acclamation, used in hailing the Emperor and entering battle. It
means "ten thousand years" (of life to you).
Jarge Santy: The Spanish-American philosopher, poet, and critic George Santayana
(1863–1952) may have sent EP his new book, published by Scribner's in 1951 and
entitled *Dominations and Powers: Reflections on Liberty, Society, and Government.* EP/
met Santayana in Rome and Venice in 1939, corresponded with him while in St.
Elizabeths, and mentions him frequently in the later Cantos.

141. TLS-2

June 20, 1951

Dear Ez:

I'm all right – except that I can't talk straight (I feel it inside though they tell me
I SOUND all right); I can't write longhand (and damn poorly on the machine: I hit
the wrong keys); food doesn't like [*sic*] anything but wood; and I when I'm
fatigued from any intense activity (not so damned intense at that) I am prostrated
– with consequent depression, black thoughts, gloomy intimations of death
(gloomy is tautological).
If I take ONE DROP of alcohol my tongue is tied in knots.
But the worst is: What in hell shall I do next? Shall I quit medicine or return to
it? If I quit, my overhead will be out of proportion to my income. If I stick, I
won't be able to write and keep up my practice. And I don't want to move. I like

my home. I can't change it at my age without to [*sic*] most violent dislocation of my habits.

With time (I'm doing nothing now) all these puzzlements will unpuzze [*sic*] themselves. One thing that will help will the [*sic*] fate of my autobiography: if it goes well (brings me in some dough) I'll buy myself off; if it's a flop I'll go back to medicine. It really doesn't make much difference either way. I'll always write.

I read a poem at the Literary Celebration of Phi Beta Kappa at Harvard on Monday, just got back. Floss said I could be heard. Ecclestical [*sic*] atmosphere and my "15 minute" poem was vile in subject matter. Stained glass windows, knocked out, to reveal a fat whore doing a strip tease in a cheap joint at Juarex [*sic*], Mexico. I didn't realize the contrast would be so violent. At least tey [*sic*] applauded though dammed few came up to congratulate me after. One poor old guy pleaded that sitting behind me on the platform he couldn't hear a word I said. Lucky man!

I made an informal speech at the luncheon afterward in which I told them there were only to [*sic*] things to do for the sake of accuracy of language (when "robin" means either of two things in America & England) one of which was to follow Mr. Eliot and the other was to do what I had done: work with the materials (metrical and material) from this end. The result of mt [*sic*] efforts was the horrible example to which they had just listened. With that I left, "to catch a train", they applauded me all during my progress from my seat at the speakers table to the door.

Well, I suppose the ghosts of Emerson, Oliver Wendell Holmes and Jame Russel Lowell [*sic*] must have shaken what flesh remains on their bones loose at my very presence on the august platform they in the past had dignified.

I survive.

> Yours till the hour of death
> Bill

Phi Beta Kappa: On June 18, 1951, at the commencement exercises of the Harvard chapter of Phi Beta Kappa, the American collegiate scholastic honorary society founded in 1776, WCW read "The Desert Music." The poem is based upon an excursion he made to Ciudad Juárez while visiting Robert McAlmon in El Paso, Texas, November 19–22, 1950.

Emerson: WCW evokes three nineteenth-century Harvard poets who were connected with Phi Beta Kappa. Ralph Waldo Emerson (1803–1882) delivered the most famous Phi Beta Kappa oration of all, "The American Scholar," at Harvard in 1837. Oliver Wendell Holmes (1809–1894), who was, like WCW, both a physician and a poet, was elected to the society as a student. James Russell Lowell (1819–1891) presided over a meeting of the Harvard chapter the day before delivering his "Ode Recited at the Harvard Commemoration, July 21, 1865."

142. TLS-1

July 31 [1951]

Dear Ez:

I'll get hold of a copy of the American Mercury in the morning, it's too damned hot to go down town again this afternoon, and see what it has to say. If there's anything I can do or say to give Bob a better hearing, especially if he's been attacked (although I don't know they [sic] should be attacked at this late date) I'll act on it.

Meanwhile my autobiog (for what it's worth) will be out on Sept 17. In it I've spoken frequently and at length of Bob's part in the Paris phase of American letters of those days, what he did for others as well as of his own writings, As soon as I get hold of a copy of the book I'll send it to you. I don't know what you'll think of my statements concerning you. They're factual, as is the whole book, and not interpretive. It's what I saw, I hope you like it.

I've been away for two weeks at the shore, a little shack in Connecticut on Long Island Sound, a very unpretentious place where we have gone summer after summer for approximately 50 years. It rained one week and was as it frequently is at the shore under such conditions, not very pleasant. But the good days were what I was after. I feel much rested.

I'm under contract to write a novel for Random House by next spring. I'm having a terrible time. Why in hell write a nove [sic]? The old trouble still obsesses me. It's fujn [sic] enough to take a set of characters and watch them fuck and eat but what in hell do I care for the landscape? I find myself putting down conversation and letting it go at that, making it twist and turn as the minds (,) appose theselvew [sic] to each other. Oh well I promise not to disgrace you or myself but it sure makes me sweat. THe old values of even Dostoiefsky or even FLaubert are finished. Turgeniev, Stendahl . out. Perhaps there's a new lead in Cervantes. It's the one that most appeals to me: connected incidents – something like that with a group of characters of all ages and both sexes. Oh well. All I want to do is fill 3 or 4 hundred pages without disgrace and going soft.

Bob's address is enclosed. I'll send your letter onto him.

Best to Dorothy
Bill

American Mercury: Robert McAlmon was not attacked in the *American Mercury* during the first seven months of 1951.

shack in Connecticut: The vacation cottage regularly rented by WCW and his family in the summer was located at West Haven, Connecticut.

a novel: The Build-Up was published by Random House in October 1952.

Dostoiefsky: WCW cites four masters of the nineteenth-century European novel: the Russian writers Fyodor Dostoevsky (1821–1881) and Ivan Turgenev (1818–1863) and the French writers Gustave Flaubert (1821–1880) and Stendhal (Henri Beyle, 1783–1842).

Cervantes: Don Quixote (1605–15), by the Spanish novelist and playwright Miguel de Cervantes (1547–1616), has an episodic, panoramic structure.

enclosed: WCW encloses a letter from McAlmon dated July 14, 1951. The letterhead is that of the Hotel Asturias in Cuernevaca, Mexico.

143. TLS-1

August 9, 1951

Dear Ez:

Between being cussed from one side or the other for my lubricity (Marianne Moore and my brother) comes your scarification over my faults of grammer [*sic*]. Don't talk to me of grammer, point out the fault that it may be corrected or ignored. Then a woman that I once helped wants to eat me or murder me, orders me passionately around and when I don't respond abuses me. Attacks my moral and literary integrity. Demands that I see her. Am I not old enough to escape some of these detractors? As far as I know I have never asked you how to write. As far as I know I have never asked a womnan [*sic*] for her intimacy. My brother and Marianne Moore are special cases, they have to be appeased. Placated. They are disabled for one reason or another.

So it goes on. The Autobiography will be out soon that the attacks may be renewed. Have just been reading Suetonius on the lives of the Cesars [*sic*]. August had a notable godfather, didn't it [*sic*]? He lived a long time and died of diarrhoea, quietly in bed. We have much to look forward to.

Thanks for this and that.

Yours
Bill

your scarification: In an undated letter to WCW (Yale), commenting upon *Paterson* (*Book Four*), EP writes: "wot 'bout a l'il grammurh? do voibz agree? . . . do yu git proofs?"

a woman: See "Biographical Notes" on NARDI, MARCIA.

Suetonius: Book II of *The Lives of the Caesars* by the Roman historian and biographer Suetonius (*c.* 70–160) narrates the life of Augustus, who "contracted an illness beginning with a diarrhoea" during a night cruise, and who was "blessed with an easy death." Suetonius mentions no godfather but reports that Augustus' grandfather was said to have been a baker and a money-changer. See *The Lives of the Caesars,* trans. J. C. Rolfe, 2 vols., Loeb Classical Library (London: William Heinemann and New York: G. P. Putnam's Sons, 1928), I, pp. 125–27, 277–81.

144. TL-1

[September 5, 1951?]

WCW

Isn't the real trouble with Sandbag that he would NOT face the real fight Lincoln was fighting. i/e/ vs/ international gombeen men/

You may have read enough of him to find cause to demur, but if so, WHERE does he do it?

[Robert] Frost not even as knowing as Cal Coolidge, prob/ dont know that Cal/ was not merely a peanut.

And of course the attempt to uphold debt system, by pretense that it IS, or is necessary to, the free enterprise system

OUGHT to turn ole Bill's stomach. ALZo

the dirty pinks pretended to attaK KKapTAL, and merely attacked landed property, down to farms men cd/ work themselves.

Sandbag: WCW's review of the *Complete Poems* of Carl Sandburg (New York: Harcourt Brace, 1950) appeared in *Poetry* for September 1951. The review also mentions Sandburg's six-volume biography (1923–1929) of President Abraham Lincoln (1809–1865).

gombeen men: Usurers.

Cal Coolidge: Calvin Coolidge (1892–1933) served as President of the United States from 1923 to 1929.

145. TLS-2

Sept 7, 1951

Dear Ez:

Thanks for your comment on the Sandburg review, I suppose he'll be sore but being so prominent he deserves at least an honest appraisal, at least not the usual hogwash. He can come back at me on any count he may select except that, that I spit-licked him.

You'll be getting my Autobiog in a few days if you haven't already rec'd it. I suppose you'll have lots to find fault with. There are 35 typographical errors in the text to say nothing of other bobbles, blunders. I had almost finished the first (rapid) writing of the thing when I got hit in the head.

When I came out of the hospital I tried to correct the proofs but although I did my best many details escaped me – and nobody else seems to have been worth a damn at picking up the slips – some of them bad.

If there's a second printing they say all errors will be righted. I'm so sick of the book that I just don't give a damn what happens. Floss tells me, besides, that I have left out the most amusing episodes, twisted others. – etc   Shit.

In spite of differences of opinion I still love you. But what are we to say of the world? In our own suburb you can't, so I'm told, do business of any important sort, you can't get liquor to sell, you can't get meat to sell, you can't run a shoe-repair outfit unless you pay tribute to some higher-up. And that is only the beginning, the graft in most vases [*sic*] is taken out at a higher level. The murderous fight that is being waged against the co-ops in Congress by the flour and milling powers employing one of the most flagrantly lawless lobbies (next to the medicos own lobby) in Washington, is something to make you vomit.

I'm reading Witter Bynner's *Journey With Genius,* an account of his intimacy with the D. H. Lawrences during their Mexican period. Very interestingly written, I'm enjoying it.

I'm still alive but not as alert as 'd like to be. I can't relax enough to write, all tied up inside. All I do is stare out of the window. The contract I have with Random House to do a novel irks me, I don't seem to want to get down to work. I can't work that way, I need to be released to slop around as my mind dictates.

Wish you were free but there's nothing I can do about it.

Yours as ever
Bill

the co-ops: On September 10, 1951, *The New Republic* published an article entitled "The Attack on the Co-ops" (p. 8). At issue was a motion before Congress to end the tax-exempt status of many co-operative organizations. The measure was supported by the National Tax Equality Association, a coalition of private industries that competed with the co-ops in agriculture and refining. According to *The New Republic,* Representative Dan Reed of New York described this organization as "an unscrupulous bunch of professional lobbyists and agitators."

Journey With Genius: See "Biographical Notes" on BYNNER, WITTER.

PART FIVE
1952–1963

I f Williams was the dominant partner in the relationship during the later 1940s, the balance tipped back toward Pound in the 1950s. For one thing, Williams' health continued to degenerate, whereas Pound's remained relatively stable. Williams suffered further strokes in August 1952 and October 1958. He was temporarily hospitalized for depression in the spring of 1953, and partial paralysis made it physically difficult for him to read and write.

Nevertheless, Williams fought his afflictions courageously. Under difficult circumstances he produced a remarkable body of new work, including four volumes of poetry: *The Desert Music* (1954), *Journey to Love* (1955), *Paterson (Book Five)* (1958), and *Pictures from Brueghel* (1962). The last of these received the Pulitzer Prize in 1963, after the author's death.

Williams endured political as well as physical aggravations. In 1952 he was again asked to become the Consultant in Poetry at the Library of Congress. He had been offered the position in 1948, but ill health had forced him to decline it. The one-year appointment carried a salary of $7,000 and the prestige of an unofficial laureateship. By 1952, however, Senator Joseph McCarthy's influence in Washington was strong, so the appointment entailed a loyalty investigation by the F.B.I. and other government agencies. Allegations that Williams had once been a communist sympathizer prolonged the investigation. When Williams objected to the entire procedure, the Library attempted to withdraw its offer. The affair ended inconclusively in 1953, after dragging on so long that the one-year term of office had nearly expired.

In the meantime, St. Elizabeths had become a nexus of cultural activity. Pound brought out two more volumes of Cantos, *Section: Rock-Drill* (1955) and *Thrones* (1959). He translated Confucius and Sophocles, emitted a steady stream of contributions to little magazines, and received scores of visitors. He was in touch with some of the most promising writers of the postwar generation: Robert Lowell, John Berryman, Randall Jarrell, Lawrence Ferlinghetti, and Hugh Kenner. Many of these talented figures knew Williams as well.

In addition, Pound attracted a coterie of young disciples. They came from as far away as Australia, and some settled in Washington so as to be near the venerated poet. Their motives and ambitions varied. Some were aspiring writers, artists, and publishers. Some needed to find an authoritative father-figure or to offer themselves as erotic muses. Some were anti-Semites, Nazi sympathizers, and white supremacists. For Pound's politics had changed not at all; he now

285

preached eugenics as well as Social Credit. His well-publicized association with the segregationist leader John Kasper undermined the efforts of Williams and others who were working to secure his release.

Despite his physical handicaps, Williams continued to agitate on his friend's behalf. In September 1956, he was invited to join an American Writers' Group chaired by William Faulkner and Harvey Breit. The group was charged to devise proposals for promoting American culture in the eyes of the world through personal contacts between American citizens and people in other lands. The mandate was part of a Cold War propaganda initiative promulgated by President Eisenhower and known as the "People-to-People" program. In correspondence with Faulkner and in meetings of the group's steering committee, Williams argued that Pound's continued imprisonment damaged America's international reputation and that his release should therefore have a prominent place among the writers' recommendations. In the end, the group submitted no report to the President.

Nonetheless, in the spring of 1958 Pound was discharged from St. Elizabeths Hospital after intensive lobbying by Robert Frost, Ernest Hemingway, and Archibald MacLeish. The head of the psychiatric staff, Dr. Winfred Overholser, certified Pound to be incurable but no longer dangerous. The Department of Justice dropped the charge of treason on condition that Pound leave the United States. Before sailing for Italy, he spent his last two nights at Williams' home. On this occasion, the photographer Richard Avedon took several portraits of Pound and Williams together. These eloquent pictures capture the symbolic quality of their final reunion.

After Pound's return to Italy, he and Williams corresponded very little. Old age, ill health, and depression crowded hard upon them both. Still, their collaborations continued. Williams inserted a poem entitled "To My Friend Ezra Pound" into his final collection, *Pictures from Brueghel;* and Pound included another late poem by Williams in his last anthology, *Confucius to Cummings* (1964). Shortly after Williams' death in March 1963, his wife received the following telegram from Italy:

> Dear Flos, A magnificent fight he made of it for you. He bore with me sixty years, and I shall never find another poet friend like him. My love and sympathy to you,
>
>   Ezra.

The friendship had lasted as long as it could.

146. TLS-1

May 24, 1952

Dear Ez:

Ef you kin see this guy, Ginsberg, do so. He's whatever you want to call him –
but hidden under as fine a heap of crap as you'll find blossoming on our city dump
heaps is a sensitive mind. I like him in spite of himself. See him ef you can.

Haven't written recently for various reasons of state, mainly I've been ill.
Nerves.

Probably be in Washington (Library of Congress job) for the coming year. See
you then if eith [*sic*] of us is still alive.

Best to Dorothy.

Yrs
Bill

Ginsberg: The American poet Allen Ginsberg (1926–) first wrote to WCW from Paterson
on March 30, 1950; this letter and two others from Ginsberg are incorporated into
WCW's *Paterson*. However, EP did not care for the sample of work that Ginsberg sent
him, and the two did not meet until 1967.

Nerves: WCW was on the verge of another stroke, which came in August 1952; see
Mariani, pp. 646–49.

Library of Congress: See p. 285 above.

147. TLS-1

12/31/53

Dear Ezrachen:

Me unable properly to see and write and get about and you immobilized for
other reasons, what do you think we done wrong with our lives that we may warn
the young not to do likewise? Wasn't your pal, the Possum, as you call him, the
wise man to see the trap in time to withdraw in time and gracefully at that and
with profit to himself while we were wallwing [*sic*] in our sins. He made a
complete right about face, and I mean complete, much to his advancement. And
who will be remembered for what we have done with our lives? Why of course
HE will – no matter how pious were our wished [*sic*]. No use, I should tell the
young, to kick against the pricks but rather to stroke the fur the right way to make

it lie down. As between cats and dogs, he chooses cats and with good reason, to be doglike has got us chained up whereas the cats are still abroad and writing clever plays.

Nice to hear from you direct, once in a while news reaches me, as from Cal Lowell, that you are thriving. I wish you the best of health for the new year and if possible your freedom, I don't know how, except for technical reasons, they can keep you where you are much longer, all logic is against it with the country slanted as it is. Best luck and to Dorothy also from Floss and your ol' dormitory mate,

Bill

he chooses cats: WCW alludes to T. S. Eliot's book of light verse *Old Possum's Book of Practical Cats* (1939). Eliot's latest play at this point was *The Cocktail Party* (1950), a drama much concerned with salvation.

Cal Lowell: See "Biographical Notes" on LOWELL, ROBERT.

148. TL-2

8 Ap[ril 1954]

WM/ th WalRuss

Flos/ says (I am glad to read) that yu can stand it.

By now I hv/ forgot wot it was I was askin if yu can stand.

Yu wil be glad to hear Cal Lowell has writ 2 poeMZ without fallin over his feet/ a bit obsKEWer at 1st/ readin, but really got ole Fordie on the page.

Wonder shd/ we mainfest [*sic*]: vs/ the goddam muckers?

Or shd/ we try to find out whether we agree on ANYthing, or on, say, three points/

apart from McC's twenty which Mr Dotty Parker Stevenson can't reply to.

Symptom of DISease/ good guy on hearing Benton's paragraph re/ young men picking each one of 'em one infamy apiece and sticking AT IT till they git rid of it, as Bent/ did with salt tax.

The good guy, having been covered with educational bugwash, sez: "Oh, an obsession."

THAT is what the filth has done to the risin' generation. And wot we OUGHT damn well to cobaltize 'em before we git too old.

I tried "Absent thee from frivolity a while"

on one of our contemporaries, whom I need not name to you. And he replies, POSSibly re/ that sentence, that he dunno wot I mean.

Suppose yu, me an Cal/ WERE to agree on a few points/ WHICH of 'em ought we to let loose in broadside.

Yes, I note you are clearin some dust off Theoc/ O.Kay bei me/

I think my TRAXINIAI has upset our erstwhile colleagues la Famille A/

alzo two octogenarian ladies (VERY l/) and one sexagenarian male are worryin about the COloquial language (I think they call it "slang". Old Genthe had a yoke abaht "serpents".

Kasp/ sez he has at last got Bunting bound/ Tom Scott worth yr/ attention.

what do YOU recommend fer seereeyus reading at my time uv life?

Dave has got Benton bit at bindery/ which yu shall hv/ as soon as it can be got to you.

As to some of these retiring s. o. b. [sons of bitches] each down hiz mousZole/

it AINT the murkn tradition/ note W. Cullen Bryant

and, I shd/ say all of his contemryz/ showing some CARE fer life of the republik.

God DAMN it we need allies against the hoax of kawledge educ/ been going down d o w n DO(bloody)WN fer 50 years.

Hv/ yu seen Schlesinger's Life of Jackson, in pocket edn/ Fordie exposed the hat trick in his attack on Weiniger [*sic*]

BUT at any rate Sch/ has mentioned VanBuren.

I note VanB/ was reading his Benton/ why the HELL did WE never hear tell of these real guys when we WUZ in the formative state.

from which, tankGORR, we haven't separated, tho a helluva lot of our con-citoyenns [fellow citizens] damn well have, IF they ever were in it.

Dont yu think yu cd/ do a boost of Sq/$ series/ basing boost especially on front flap of the Agassiz?

Have them y[oung]. m[en]. SENT yu a copy, an nif not WHY (bloody) Not.??

if they aint I will git on their nekkz.

Oh yuss, the worm L. Pearson (not Drew) was fairly weepin on "Weekend" that he cdN' unnerstan yr/ vollum/

wd/ sombuddy ellup him?

mos' pathetik.

Vyoler (gittin wilder every hour) sez yu wuz on the air?

wot air? warn't mentioned in local air-cat/g

best to yu both

yrz anon/s

Floss says: In a letter to EP of April 6, 1954 (Yale), Floss says, "Bill is hefty enough to take it – and stand it." The surviving correspondence does not clarify her reference.

2 poeMZ: In letters to EP of March 20, 25, and 26, 1954 (Yale), Lowell included several of his poems, among them "Ford Madox Ford" and "An Englishman Abroad (1950)."

McC's twenty: Speaking in Milwaukee on March 19, 1954, Senator Joseph R. McCarthy (1908–1957) charged the Democratic Party with twenty specific counts of "criminal stupidity" and "treason." He challenged Democratic Party leader Adlai E. Stevenson (1900–1965) to plead guilty or not guilty to the indictments. Stevenson refused to comment in detail. Dorothy Parker (1893–1967) was a journalist, critic, screenwriter, and author of humorous and satirical poems and sketches.

Benton's paragraph: Unidentified. Senator Thomas Hart Benton of Missouri (1782–1858) fought for repeal of the salt tax. He is celebrated in EP's Cantos 88 and 89 for his resistance to centralized banking interests.

Absent thee: A variation on Hamlet's dying speech to Horatio (Act V, scene ii): "Absent thee from felicity awhile."

Theoc: WCW's translation of the First Idyl of the Greek pastoral poet Theocritus (3rd century B.C.) appeared in both *The Desert Music* (1954) and the *Quarterly Review of Literature* 7:4 (1954), pp. 255–60.

my TRAXINIAI: EP's translation of *Women of Trachis* by the Greek tragedian Sophocles (496–406 B.C.) first appeared in the *Hudson Review* for Winter 1954.

la Famille A: Possibly Richard Aldington and H. D.

two octogenarian ladies: Possibly Ida B. and Adah Lee Mapel, whom EP first met in Spain in 1906. During the 1950s, they lived in Georgetown and visited EP at St. Elizabeths regularly.

Genthe: The German-American portrait photographer Arnold Genthe (1868–1942) visited Rapallo in November 1938 and photographed EP and Dorothy on commission from *Town and Country* magazine. One of the photos taken at this time has provided the frontispiece for many printings of EP's *Cantos.*

Kasp: See "Biographical Notes" on KASPER, FREDERICK JOHN. In 1956 Kasper and Horton issued Basil Bunting's *Poems,* newly bound from the same sheets or plates used by Dallam Simpson for his Cleaners' Press edition (Galveston, 1950).

Tom Scott: The Scottish poet Tom Scott (1918–1995) is the translator of *Seeven Poems o Maister Francis Villon* (Tunbridge Wells: Pound Press, 1953). EP thought highly of these translations, which Scott sent to him in St. Elizabeths.

Dave: T. David Horton (1927–) had corresponded with EP since 1947. He was a law student at the Catholic University in Washington and visited St. Elizabeths frequently. With John Kasper, he ran the Square Dollar Series.

Benton bit: In 1854 Thomas Hart Benton published an autobiography entitled *Thirty Years' View; or, A History of the Working of the American Government for Thirty Years from 1820 to 1850,* 2 vols. (New York: D. Appleton). An excerpt from Volume I, pp. 187–205, was published in the Square Dollar Series under the title *Bank of the United States* (1954).

W. Cullen Bryant: The American poet, lawyer, and journalist William Cullen Bryant (1794–1878) edited the *New York Evening Post* for fifty years.

Life of Jackson: For Arthur Schlesinger, Jr.'s *Life of Jackson,* see Letters 107 and 113 above. The book was abridged by Donald Porter Geddes for the New American Library edition of 1954. Schlesinger frequently mentions Van Buren, whose *Autobiography* (1920) contains many references to Benton's *Thirty Years' View*, drafts of which were sent to Van Buren for comment as Benton wrote it.

attack on Weiniger: In 1903 the German medical scientist and philosopher Otto Weininger (1880–1903) published *Geschlecht und Charakter*, in which he proclaimed the inherent inferiority of women to men. The book was translated into English in 1906 as *Sex and Character*. In March 1918, FORD MADOX FORD (see "Biographical Notes") criticized Weininger in the second of a group of essays published in *The Little Review* under the title *Women and Men* (republished in Paris in 1923 by William Bird's Three Mountains Press).

Sq/$ series: The Square Dollar Series consisted of paperbound booklets that sold for 95 cents or a dollar. EP approved the contents and wrote the jacket blurbs.

Agassiz: Louis Agassiz (1807–1873) was a Swiss-American naturalist and a professor at Harvard University. In 1953, the Square Dollar Series published *Gists from Agassiz or, Passages on the Intelligence Working in Nature*, selected by John Kasper.

L. Pearson: Leon Morris Pearson (1899–1963) was the host of "Weekend," a Sunday-afternoon cultural program carried by radio station WRC in Washington.

Drew: Drew Pearson (1897–1969) was a nationally syndicated investigative reporter, whose column "Daily Washington Merry-Go-Round" ran from 1931 to 1969.

Vyoler: See "Biographical Notes" on JORDAN, VIOLA SCOTT BAXTER.

on the air: On October 8, 1953, WCW appeared on the CBS television talk show "Author Meets Critic."

anon/s: EP intentionally omitted his signature from many letters written during the St. Elizabeths period, so that they could not be used against him in any future legal proceeding.

149. TLS-1

April 17, 1954

Dear Ez:

I don't even know who Benton is. Never heard of him. Won't you ask some mutual friend to write me acquainting me with the facts. You never will – so that I can understand them.

As far as Dalam [*sic*] is concerned his manifesto, promulgated several years ago now, did not attract me. I can't always follow such things. If you have one around and can see that I get it or he can send it to me anew I'd gladly reconsider it.

The same for Basil Bunting. When I last heard from him via Louis Zukofsky he included in his letter a summary under a Latin title giving a summary of Buntings scholastic accomplishments. It was impressive so I sent it off as it was to Norman Pearson of Yale asking him if he could find a place for him as a teacher of Persian there. He said in reply that no one there was interested in learning the language.

There is a chance that I will be in Washington on April 27, if so I will attempt to run out and see you for a half hour visit. Will you not secure for me the necessary permit? Best to Dorothy – does she remember the evening in the spring of 1910 when with her mother we went to call on Yeats? When we were leaving he turned to some [sic], I think it was Robinson or the Irish player who was there, we were already half out the door: Was that Ezra Pound who was just here? – and on being assured that it was, added: Tell him to wait a while. I'd like to talk to him.

Best luck to you.

Sincerely yours
Bill

Dalam: See "Biographical Notes" on SIMPSON, DALLAM. In a letter to WCW of April 12, 1954 (Yale), EP asks, "DID yu ever giv any thought to that 3 point manifest in Dallam's '4 Pages'?? whether time has come to endorse it openly?"

a summary under a Latin title: An academic job résumé is often called a *curriculum vitae* (course of a life).

Norman Pearson of Yale: Norman Holmes Pearson (1909–1975) was professor of American literature at Yale University and a member of the editorial board of the Square Dollar Series. He was H. D.'s literary executor and was instrumental in Yale's acquisition of many of WCW's papers.

April 27: WCW visited Washington to review for *Art News* the Garbisch Collection of American Primitives at the National Gallery; see Mariani, pp. 683–84. In "Ezra Pound and *Imagi,*" p. 59, THOMAS COLE (see "Biographical Notes") recalls seeing EP and WCW together at St. Elizabeths on Sunday, April 25, 1954.

her mother: The English novelist Olivia Shakespear (1864–1938) was a friend and former lover of W. B. Yeats.

Robinson: Probably Lennox Robinson (1886–1958), Irish actor, dramatist, and manager of the Abbey Theatre.

150. TL-1

[December 1954]

2 be more eggsPlicit.

criks is the buzzards wot yakyaks about awt an' le'rs without bein' abl to
purrJuice any. (vulgarly spelled with 7 le'rs)
    on brook?line [Brooklyn]: wot is a stoic?
    Answer: a stoic iz deh boid wot brings de baby.
    The point wuz that Vals brot me a beeYewteeful vol/ of Gongora here im
buGHousz, and on reading it in the light of intermejit effeks and eggsperience
    I cd/ find NOTHING whatsodam having anyfink to dew with what the gamb
buzzards that TELL about Gong/ in whatever damn hizzeries and crizsms I had
read (not az I read many), had sd/ bout him.
    simply very clear and limpid writing, descriptive, not fervid,
    an I wunn'erd whether the Medical W/ HAD recently looked at Gong/
    or wd/ enliven and pacify his volant [fleeting] and heteroclite perceptions with
doin' so/
    O. K. I await Quevedo's "Dawg".
    si mies te mato.

Vals: Possibly Pedro del Valle, a retired lieutenant general in the U. S. Marine Corps and
    president of the Defenders of the American Constitution. He first visited EP at St.
    Elizabeths in 1954.
Gongora: The Spanish poet Luis de Góngora Argote (1561–1627) is known for his ornate
    and affected style of writing. WCW had written of Góngora and Góngorismo in "Fede-
    rico García Lorca," *Kenyon Review* 1 (Spring 1939), pp. 153–56, an essay EP may
    have seen reprinted in WCW's *Selected Essays* (1954). In a letter to WCW of December
    1 [1954] (Yale), EP challenges the conventional idea of Gongorism and asks whether
    WCW has recently compared "wot he [Góngora] iz with what the criks say about him."
    In his response of December 4 (Yale), WCW queries the word "criks."
Quevedo's "Dawg": In his letter of December 4, WCW promises that EP will soon be
    sent *The Dog and the Fever,* the translation of *El Perro y la Calentura* made by WCW
    and his mother in the late 1930s (see Letter 84 above). The translation was published by
    the Shoe String Press of Hamden, Connecticut, in November 1954.
si mies te mato: Spanish, "if you are afraid, I will kill you." The source of the statement is
    unidentified.

151. TL-1

[June 1955]

1 Ferlingheii [*sic*]
261 Columbus Av. San Francisco 11
wanting poeket series of poeks/ e. e. c[ummings] Rexroth whatso.
34 pages [*sic*] vols.
nacherly no use to ME. BUT what I wd/ do fer the kid, if the idea not allergic,
and if WCW can lend material cause there AINT no room fer permanent posses-
sions in bghsz [bughouse].

It might make the blighters series if there wuz to be W. C. W the poek, his
voices SEEllected by Ez.

Cause Jarrel [*sic*] and eye dont I to I, and no reason why shd/ & the Kosch
gorful

I dunno how yr/ regular pubrs/ wd/ greet the idea. BUT it wd sell their damn
books, not interfere.

Yu cd/ alzo tell 'em Ferl. to do a selection from Fordie, now difficult to
OBTAIN.

Sombuddy wd/ have to do the fotostat or type out the 32 pages of each of yu
as I got NO phussikul strength, and it aint proper/

if yu write em yu cd/ putt in a plug fer Basil the Bunter, that wd. circumvent the
idol of yr. optic Mr Ellyut.

Old Lampman notices that Bryant and Whittier had somefink to say and SAID
it. HE observes the decay of motivation in murkn printed matter.

Yu kno who iz Rex (not roth, LAMPman)?

1 Ferlingheii: The American poet, publisher, and bookseller Lawrence Ferlinghetti
(1920–) was starting his Pocket Poets series, consisting of paperback editions of
modern poetry. In a letter to EP of June 13, 1955 (Yale), he requests a manuscript for a
book of 34–36 pages and says that e. e. cummings and Kenneth Rexroth have already
promised him manuscripts for the series. In the end, Ferlinghetti published, not a
selection of WCW's work, but a new edition of *Kora in Hell: Improvisations* (1957).

Rexroth: The American poet, translator, and critic Kenneth Rexroth (1905–1982) is the
author of *The Phoenix and the Tortoise* (1944) and *The Dragon and the Unicorn* (1952).
To the Pocket Poets series, he contributed translations of *Thirty Spanish Poems of Love
and Exile* (1955). No book by e. e. cummings appeared in the series.

Jarrel: See "Biographical Notes" on JARRELL, RANDALL.

the Kosch: The American critic Vivienne Koch is the author of *William Carlos Williams*
(1950), the first book-length critical study of WCW's work.

Fordie: The Pocket Poets series did not include the work of Ford Madox Ford or Basil
Bunting.

Lampman: Rex Herbert Lampman (b. 1884) was a poet, a journalist with the Washington, D. C., *Times Herald,* and EP's fellow inmate at St. Elizabeths. After his release, Lampman lived in Hollywood, California, whence he corresponded with EP from 1953 to 1960 (Yale) and agitated for his release.

Bryant and Whittier: For William Cullen Bryant, see Letter 148 above. The American poet John Greenleaf Whittier (1807–1892) was a Quaker, an active abolitionist, and the outspoken editor of many periodicals.

152. TL-1

27 Oc[tober 1955]

O William in our hours of ease
the perfect medico to tease
   how oft when irritation bites the toe
we fall on thee for wot we wanna kno.

Waaal they're givin me a differunt salve. and mebbe it will ex-de-hydrate the cuticle.
   mebbe the ole fambly remedy cuttycura wd/ beat 'em to it.
AND so forth.
Pal down the ward wants to know WHY they squirt Thorazine into him? Have yu any modern ideas about THAT?
   have I spelled it right/ I think thazz wot the cullud lady sez is the spellin.

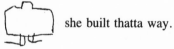 she built thatta way.

   caught sight of Sheri's nude, rep/ of a 17 inch waiste [*sic*] in ceramic, and lawd a mussy.
   "WHAAA yu get that?.!'
S/s art cert[ainly]/ bowls the afros/ plain awe from the male afro when HE saw it.
   yes, garrulous with age/ I am coming to some of yr/ queeries. Must tell Mawgrit A[nderson]/ that the baroness [Elsa von Freytag-Loringhoven] receives homage in Canto, I think it is 95.
   wot else/ ho yuss/ Sandbug [Carl Sandburg] on television/ wotta wreck.
   and as to yr/ pal/ Wally S/ (I mean Stevens) I done TOLE Kenner they ought to

do a obit number and that you were the proper orator/ and I spose he told the slop can/

BUT it wd/ be highly improper for me have opinions of yr/ opinion of a bloke I haven't read

and DOUBT like all hell that yu will be able to PURR-suade me to venture on with such a hellUVAlot I don't know and WANT to find out.

Yr/ error re/ me yole man wuz in a privik letter to I fergit whom which has been printed in the Ez/ Snooze Letter by them californias.

yu were NOT writing for publication and indulged in some airy, and, as it chanced, erronious [*sic*] pfantasy.

O William: EP plays upon a famous passage of Sir Walter Scott's *Marmion* (1808), Canto VI, stanza 30: "O, Woman! in our hours of ease."

Sheri's nude: Since joining EP's St. Elizabeths circle in 1951, the American artist Sheri Martinelli had become his close friend. EP arranged for a book of David Gordon's color photographs of her work, introduced by EP and entitled *La Martinelli,* to be published in Milan by Vanni Scheiwiller in 1956.

the baroness: For the Baroness Elsa von Freytag-Loringhoven, see Letter 25 above. In Canto 95, EP writes, "& Elsa Kassandra, 'the Baroness'/ von Freitag etc. sd/ several true things/ in the old days."

Stevens: The American poet Wallace Stevens (1879–1955), whom WCW had known for forty years, died on August 2. WCW's memorial essay entitled "Comment: Wallace Stevens" appeared in *Poetry* for January 1956. WCW mentioned the article in a letter to EP of October 26, 1955, and sent him an advance copy along with a letter dated October 31 (Yale).

Kenner: The Canadian-born critic Hugh Kenner (1923–) published ground-breaking studies of *The Poetry of Ezra Pound* (1951) and *Wyndham Lewis* (1954). At this time, he was an associate editor of *Poetry* magazine.

Ez/ Snooze Letter: Edited by John Edwards and William Vasse of the English Department at the University of California, Berkeley, the *Pound Newsletter* ran for ten issues from 1954 to 1956. In issue No. 8 (October 1955), pp. 22–23, John C. Thirlwall reproduces a letter of January 18, 1943, from WCW to Babette Deutsch. In this letter, WCW says that EP went to Hamilton College because he "was banished by his father to the sticks for general insubordination of what quality I don't know, probably nothing more than refusing to do anything but what he pleased to do in his classes, perhaps spending more cash than the old man could give him." The letter also appears in Thirlwall, p. 210.

153. TLS-1

Nov. 5, '55

Dear Ez:

Thorazine 200 M. G. M. (Milligrams), S. K. & F., (Smith, Klein & French).
It is a depressant to the nervous system, good in alcoholism etc but the action is
said to be not entirely predictable so that in any specific case it should be used
cautiously. The notable thing about this tablet is the dosage. Around this neck of
the woods a dose of 25 m. g. m. is found to be sufficient! If the guy reacts in the
way you say he does it may be a paraxical reaction which is well known in
medicine due to the excessive dose. If I were his doctor I'd discontinue the drug.

Glad we agree, for once, on the Stevens article. Haven't heard from the editors
of Poetry yet on it, mayde [*sic*] they are of a different opinion.

We're going out to Buffalo next week to visit the Abbotts, he has scheduled a
reading for me at the Library.

I'm deep in the intracise [*sic*] of a short story I'm attempting to compose for no
one in particular. It's a story I promised to write for a patient-pal of mine ten or
more years ago which was interrupted by my illness. She was a young woman
that both Flossie and I were quite crazy about who was murdered by her third
husband. A story, a novel, by a modern Spanish author which is written in a style
I greatly admire, *The Hive,* has whipped my interest to a white hot pitch to get on
with my story again. But it presents a problem as to the composition which I have
not been able as yet to solve – several problems. My difficulty with the sheer
managing of the typewriter is no help to me. Maybe I'll never be able to do the
story. It fascinates.

Best to Dorothy. Floss has had a bad cold.

Yours
Bill

the Abbotts: See "Biographical Notes" on ABBOTT, CHARLES.

a short story: "The Farmer's Daughters" was published in the *Hudson Review* for Autumn 1957. WCW first drafted the story in 1946–47; see Williams/Laughlin, p. 134. It
is based upon the real-life story of Eleanor Musgrove, a friend and former patient of
WCW who was shot to death by her third husband in 1936; see Mariani, pp. 529–30.

The Hive: A novel by the Spanish writer and 1989 Nobel Prize winner Camilo José Cela
(1916–), translated by Arthur Cohen and Arturo Barea and published in New York in
1953 by Farrar, Straus, and Young. Written in a hard-boiled, colloquial style, *The Hive*
presents realistic vignettes of life in a Madrid *barrio* in 1943, juxtaposed in the manner
of a photographic or cinematic montage.

154. TLS-1

May 15/56

Dear Ez:

At least they allow you the priviledge [*sic*] of the open air it being May so that you may walk about on the grass. Men have become so stupid now-a-days that they do not how to enjoy that priviledge without involving their minds with the pursuit of little [*sic*] hard rubber ball to follow. I don't know how you have succeeded in retaining your sanity and humane regard for your fellow man under the circumstances. I sometimes marvel at it. I on the outside almost went out of my wits with the sheer complexity of living. Don't the stupid asses know that civilized men the world over have long since released their war prisoners for the sheer saving of cash for their board and lodging? In this country they are truly more thick headed or indifferent than even the heathen. Let it pass, only under the circumstances you can't let it pass because it involves YOU. At least they in their supidity [*sic*] allow you to walk on the grass.

I seldom send you my poetry any more, don't want to bore you. Here's this. No comment required. C'est de bon coeur, je ne le voes pas [*sic, free of charge, I don't want it*].

Bill

my poetry: WCW enclosed a typed, signed manuscript of his poem ''The High Bridge above the Tagus River at Toledo,'' which recalls a scene from his visit to Spain in 1910. The manuscript is preserved at Texas. The poem was first published in *Edge* for October 1956.

155. TLS-2

June 30/56

Dear Ez:

Thanks for the picher (of the military ducklings), Floss enjoyed it too.

Here's another poem for you. Take it or leave it. After all you're a public figure so that your mental quirks are fair game – even for me.

Me garden's thriving, the gumbos along with the salad and the Swiss chard. But over the glorious Fourth I hope for nothing more than to be left strictly alone.

Mebee I can even work on a poem. But I've had a helluva backache lately. Twill pass or not – as the crow flies.

Been a lot of talk in the literary journals about [James] Joyce.

The weather being fine I presume you've [*sic*] enjoying your usual summer spell in the garden. A garden is a garden wherever you find it – even without gumbos.

Bill

To my friend Ezra Pound

or were he a Jew or a
Welchman
I hope they do give him the Nobel Award
it would serve him right
            – in perpetuity
with such a name.

If I were a dog
I'd sit down on a cold pavement
in the rain
if it so pleased me
to wait for a friend (and so would you)
even if it were January or Zukofsky

Your English
is not specific enough
As a writer of poems
you show yourself to be inept not to say
usurous

W. C. W.
6/30/56

another poem: The poem was sent under separate cover with a note from Mrs. Williams: "Dear Ezra – This inadvertently left out of the envelope in which Bill just mailed the so-called pome to you – Sorry! *Floss.*" The poem was published in *Neon* 2 (1956), p. 8, with "him" in lines 3 and 4 changed to "you" and "Welchman" changed to "Welsh-man." It appears in *Pictures from Brueghel and Other Poems* (1962) with the same changes and with lines 10 and 11 reversed.

156. TL-1

11 Lug [July 1956]

my deaHHH DOKtor Williamz

Have yu ever met your fellow medic and OUR leading sonneteer (unrhymed)?

He was in yester, filled with appreciation, especially of H. D. having written about Freud

(if she had writ about endocrines or eugenics it wd/ be nearer my kettle of fish, BUT MerriLL is deelighted with the results of viennaHHHH).

Well now as he is wanting to DO something, but not to expose me to the hired assassins of his political system.

Why not you tell him to start pinching the baby, and getting me an awning or markee to set under when it rains.

He apparently takes great comfort in the idea that Mr Eliot wanes,

Bryher also feels like a grandma vicariously.

You have lived here longer, I mean on this continent, cumulatively, LONGER than I have. Perhaps yr/ diagnosis is based on wider observation, in fact on closer observation than mine. I allus welKum yr/ views.

devmo/ and best to Flos.

Damn all, I dont believe he left a naddress, but yu cd/ reach him thru [Robert] Lowell.

your fellow medic: See "Biographical Notes" on MOORE, MERRILL.

H. D.: See "Biographical Notes" on DOOLITTLE, HILDA.

Bryher: See "Biographical Notes" on ELLERMAN, WINIFRED. Her vicarious grandchild may have been either H. D.'s *Tribute to Freud* or an actual child born in June 1956 to H. D.'s daughter Perdita Schaffner.

157. TL-1

23 Oc/ [October 1956]

me deer wilBULLyam

Lowell seemed to indicate that mebbe yu got the point of yr ice-pick into Faulkner's mind, after Flos' communication of yr/ kurrySpondents with same.

Now as to KULCH/ so far as I recall, tho I may wrung yu, yu have given NO indication that the Sq/ $ [Square Dollar series]

has reached yr *for interieur* [mental forum]

whereas even the Possum has finally admitted that Plotinus is not Benton or Blackstone.

Rom and Moslem vol/ now out. delay from printer doing cover without sending Dave [Horton] proofs etc/ and it hadder be reDUN.

Blackstone in process, i. e. the brief but essential points, eggstrakted by Gordon who is bein told how to prePare 'em for press.

wot wiff H. D. sheddin post-Freudian graces on the Jale kampuSS etc.

If you are goin to stay serious and DEETatch yrself from the appallingly low level of the rest of yr/ contempteraries etc.

And/or edderkate a younger generation caPAbl of distinguishin wot you have done etc/

BEFORE the centre of light shifts to Melbourne and leaves this effete kuntynunk to Mr. Pressley [*sic*]

(I got nothin gainst the Pelvis, but cummings is enquiring . . .

I shd/ think El. Pr was probably a sign of life (but he hasn't been here.)

BUT not a compleat PAIdeuma [culture]????

if yu got any views on THAT send 'em to kumminkz, who may be takin a plebiscite.

BUTT . . .

I can git Dave to sen([*sic*] yu the latest Del M/ if you wil [*sic*] read it?

Of course there ought to be comPLEAT Benton and Blackstone and more DelMar . . . . I dunno how yu blokes spend yr/ time . . .

> ciao, and saluti alla gent/ma Signora.
> [bye, and regards to the Mrs.]

Faulkner's mind: For the American Writers' Group, chaired by the novelist William Faulkner (1897–1962) and the journalist Harvey Breit (1908–1968), see p. 286 above. On September 15, 1956, Faulkner wrote to WCW among others, asking him to join the organization and to send his suggestions for action. WCW replied on September 24, suggesting that President Eisenhower could best serve the cause of American culture by seeing to it that EP was released from St. Elizabeths. On the same date, Floss sent EP copies of Faulkner's appeal and WCW's reply (Yale). See Mariani, pp. 739–41, and Francis J. Bosha, "Faulkner, Pound and the P. P. P.," *Paideuma* 8:2 (Fall 1979), pp. 249–56.

Plotinus: The Alexandrian Greek philosopher Plotinus (*c.* 203–262) elaborated Plato's idealism into a spiritual mysticism that proved congenial to Christianity.

Benton or Blackstone: For Senator Thomas Hart Benton in the Square Dollar Series, see

Letter 148 above. The English jurist Sir William Blackstone (1723–1780) was the author of *Commentaries on the Laws of England* (1765–69). A selection of his work made by the American poet, scholar, and translator David M. Gordon (1929–) was to have appeared in the Square Dollar series but did not; see Pound/Laughlin, p. 247.

Rom and Moslem vol: Number 6 in the Square Dollar Series was *Roman and Moslem Moneys* (1956), a three-chapter excerpt from the *History of Monetary Systems* (1895) by the American historian Alexander Del Mar (1856–1926).

H. D.: See "Biographical Notes" on DOOLITTLE, HILDA.

Melbourne: Melbourne, Australia, was the home of William Fleming (see Letter 161 below) and NOEL STOCK (see "Biographical Notes"). It was also the site of several periodicals willing to accept work by and about EP: the *New Times, Meanjin,* and *Edge.*

Mr. Pressley: The music and the performance style of the American rock-and-roll star Elvis Presley (1935–1977) attracted national attention in the autumn of 1956. On October 18, e. e. cummings sent EP a postcard (Yale), asking "one (serious) question – who or what is or means a pourainsidire [so to speak] social phenomenon yclept [called] Elvis (the Pelvis)."

158. TL-2

13 Nv/ [November 1956]

Oke Hay my BilBill the Bull Bull, ameer.

Is there anything in Ac Bul 2/ vide enc [see enclosure] that seems cloudy to you, or INComprehensible/

or that having comprehended you disagree with?

The hardest thing to discover is WHY someone else, apparently not an ape or a Roosevelt cannot understand something as simple as 2 plus 2 makes four.

McNair Wilson has just writ me, that Soddy got interested and started to study "economics" and found out what they offered him wasn't econ/ but banditry.

Wars are made to make debt, and the late one started by the ambulating dunghill F[ranklin] D[elano] R[oosevelt] has been amply successful.

and the stink that elevated him, still emits a smell.

Also the ten vols/ treasury reports sent me to Rapallo show that in the years from departure of Wiggin till the mail stopped you suckers had paid ten billion for gold that cd/ have been bought or [*sic*] SIX billion.

Is this clear or do you want DEEtails?

That sovreignty [*sic*] inheres in the POWER to issue money, whether you have the right to do it or not.

dont let me crowd you.

If there is anything here that is OBskewer, say so.

dont worry re Beum,

He didnt say you told him to send me his book, merely that he had metChu. let the young educ the young.

Only naive remark I have found in Voltaire wuz when he found two good books on econ/ and wrote: "Now people will understand it." end quote.

But IF the buzzards on yr (and Del M's) list had been CLEAR I wdn't have spent so much time clarifying their indistinctnesses.

You agree that the offering da shittahd aaabull instead of history is undesirable??????

Bull Bull, ameer: "Abdul, the Bulbul Ameer" was a popular song first performed at Trinity College, Dublin, in the 1850s. In Persian, a bulbul may be either a songbird or poet; an ameer is a prince or commander. WCW incorporated an edited version of this letter from EP into *Paterson (Book Five),* Part 2 (1958).

Ac Bul 2: Academia Bulletin (1956) was produced in Washington by David Gordon as the organ of the Academia Pound or APO, a group of EP's adherents; see Pound/Laughlin, pp. xii, 245–46, 259.

McNair Wilson: Robert McNair Wilson (1882–1963), surgeon and writer of history, biography, and fiction. He was medical correspondent of the London *Times* from 1914 to 1942. He also wrote *Promise to Pay: An Inquiry into the Principles and Practice of the Latter-Day Magic Called Sometimes High Finance* (1934). McNair Wilson corresponded with EP from 1934 to 1958 (Yale).

Soddy: Frederick Soddy (1877–1956) was professor of Chemistry at Oxford University and winner of the Nobel Prize in chemistry in 1921. He subsequently turned his attention to economics, publishing *Wealth, Virtual Wealth and Debt* (1926), *The Role of Money* (1934), and several other influential booklets.

treasury reports: The *Annual Report of the Secretary of the Treasury on the State of the Finances for the Fiscal Year ended June 30* (Washington: Government Printing Office) was sent to EP in Rapallo by Representative George Holden Tinkham of Massachusetts from about 1934 to 1939. The report often contained information on fluctuations in the price of gold during the preceding year.

Wiggin: Albert Henry Wiggin (1868–1951) was President and Chairman of the Board of Chase National Bank, the world's largest, from 1911 to 1930. A 1933 Senate investigation into Wall Street practices revealed that Wiggin had profited from selling short the stock of his own bank and evading income taxes.

Beum: Robert Lawrence Beum (1929–) was an editor of *Golden Goose,* a little magazine published in Columbus, Ohio, and Sausalito, California, to which WCW contributed eight items between 1948 and 1954. Beum sent a book of his own entitled *Twenty Poems* (1956) to EP at St. Elizabeths. In a letter to EP of November 9, 1956 (Yale), WCW writes: "As far as Beum is concerned, I haven't heard from him in more than 2 years. . . . The last poems he sent me were not impressive."

Voltaire: The French poet, playwright, historian, and philosopher François Marie Arouet
(1694–1778) was one of EP's intellectual heroes. The source of the quotation given here
has not been identified.

yr (and Del M's) list: For Alexander Del Mar, see Letter 157 above. In a letter to WCW of
November 5, 1956 (Yale), EP speaks of "Del Mar's remarks on Aristotle, Plato,
Copernicus, Locke, Newton, Smith, Bastiat and Mill." WCW repeats the list in his
letter to EP of November 9, adding the names of Gesell and Mencius and complaining
that "the perverted state of present day economics is due to just that lack of CLARITY
in the names you mention."

159. TLS-2

Nov. 21/56

Dear Assen poop:

Don't speak of apes and Roosevelt to me – you know as much of the IMPLE-
MENTATION of what you THINK (?) you are proposing as one of the Wops I
used to take care of on Guinea hill,

YOU DON'T EVEN BEGIN TO KNOW what the problem IS. Learn to write
an understandable letter before you begin to sound off.

You don't even know the terms you're using and have never known them. At
least you have found a man in ZWECK 2/ who is conscious of the DIFFI-
CULTIES and who unlike you has an intelligent understanding of those difficulties and how to present them. You're too damned thickheaded to know you're
asleep – and have been from the beginning.

You are incapable of recognizing what you mean to prseent [*sic*] and to hide
your stupidity resort to name-calling and general obfuscation. Do you think (?)
you will get anywhere that way – but in jail or the insane asylum where you are
now? Mousolini [*sic*] led you there, he was your adolescent hero, – or was it
Jefferson. You still don't know the difference.

Clear as mud – and for the same reason: too many insoluable [*sic*] particles
suspended throughout the mass.

Never mind, Ez, I hope we can still be friends. You have been of much
assistance to the world as a recorder of facts and I respect and really love you for.
it.

Your letter says more than your enclosures otherwise –

It is comprehensible at least that we may have saved ourselves 2 or 3 billion
dollars debt during the recent war with a valid banking system – but in the rush of

financing our money supply what could we have done other? We weren't governed by crooks as you persist in saying but men who had to employ the instruments that were ready to hand, that they were not revolutionary geniuses may be true but they had a going country on their hands and many enemies such as you to deal with.

I "feel" that much that you say is right. I have tried to follow you as best I can and I am intelligent enough as I tried to follow the teachings of Magor Douglass [sic]. But you don't come CLEAR enough and the only result is further obfuscation: as fast as you open your mouthes [sic] you put your feet in them.

But at best you personally do write poems that are at best supremely beautiful. I'm afraid that for the moment I'll have to let it go at that.

I'll go on reading what I can and when a glimmer of brilliant exposition comes through the fog of your verbiage I hope I will be still alive to recognize it.

Greetings to Dorothy. Have been seeing more of Violer [Viola Baxter Jordan] recently.

Bill

Guinea hill: In American slang, a *Guinea* is an immigrant of Italian or Spanish origin.
a man in ZWECK 2: The second number of *Academia Bulletin* (see Letter 158 above) carried six anonymous definitions under the title "Zweck" (purpose or aim), which derives from a chapter heading in EP's *Guide to Kulchur* (1938). The definitions were EP's, and the text resulted from a collaboration between him and David Gordon, editor of the bulletin. WCW's assumption that someone else wrote "Zweck" amused EP; in a letter to Wyndham Lewis of February 3, 1957, he writes: "Doc Wms complaining of MY obskewrity compliments Mr. Zweck or me on having found someone who can express it clearly"; see Pound/Lewis, p. 304.
the difference: WCW is recalling the title of EP's *Jefferson and/or Mussolini* (1935).

160. TLS-3

Jan. 7, 1957

Dear Ez:

Here's your beginning to the tenzone. when you have noted it send it back, all of it, that Floss may act as custodian. It's fun to play with it.

Did you ever hear of a guy named Kasper? Your name was used along with his in a television broadcast last night. I didn't like it.

I don't know why I should not send you the final report of the committee,

Faulkner's committee on cultural liberty. Here it is though it is not to be releast [*sic*] until it becomes official. Keep it under your hat.

Best
Bill

[Autograph postscript] It's favorable – but not yet time for Bill to release it – Floss

Let him come or go he will not find
any mouse who is not blind

and in a cat's republic votes
for pussies with the sleekest coats

Dear Ez:

Might as well continue on the same sheet of paper. Your letter of congratulation re the prize money rec[eive]d. I'm glad it was given to comeone [*sic*] in the clan, let's exploit it to the full but with both fists up. The sons of bitches would still like to get my hide as, for the moment, they have got yours.

You know better than anyone else that I have been your admirer from the first and have never wavered in my loyalty from the first. Internal fights with you have occurred but between two high spirited companions that is to be expected.

It is acknowledged that much that I have written should better have omitted [*sic*], but that is just part of my individual plan – I regret nothing of it. I couldn't see where I was going. Insted [*sic*] of doing what a more cautious man would have done, retreat to safer ground, within the church or out of it, being impued [*sic*] with a spirit of experimentation, I have ploughed ahead trusting to find my way in the thick of the fight. Striking out left and right I hit at anythind [*sic*] that came up. I have written some worthless things. Tant pis [so much the worse]. It's been hard for me to tell at times what has virtue and what is without it. BUT after floundering around perhaps I find and recognize in my own work what I want to keep. I've never been kidded into believing that I am "the great man" that some of my contemporaries keep talking about. Nut [*sic*] with them.

At the same time I pay attention when a friend such a friend as yourself, and particularly and precisely you, takes me to task – and I will say that thought [*sic*] it infuriates me I have one of my most valient [*sic*] and uncorruptable friens [*sic*] living in the same house with me.

When I have had the chance I'll follow up what you say in the letter about attacking the general misdirections of the entrenched enemy on the boards in control of acabeic [*sic*] opinion. as you point out they are still frozen, intents [*sic*] on not letting ANY information from leaking out [*sic*]. I admire your fight to bust the field wide open and believe me the new generation of students is ready and waiting to do its part. They can't be fooled much longer, that is the most hapeful [*sic*] meaning [*sic*] of thae [*sic*] award that has been given me against the wishes, I have reason to believe, of some of the members of the awardind [*sic*] board. A break has occured [*sic*] in the lines of the enemy. How a man such as Professor Pottle of the Yale faculty, whom I have never met or heard from, (it is he that naminated [*sic*] me for the honor) got away with it I will never know. It was a majority vote that carried it – Auden I am suree [*sic*] voted for me and others, friends of mine, on the board. I'll bet it was close. It is in committee that the battle has to be maintained.

Your Tenzone appeals to me. I have done my gest [*sic*] to follow your lead, I don't know whether of [*sic*] not I have succeesde [*sic*]. If you don't like what I have done, chuck it.

A card from Thirlwall, a Saxon married to a charming Nisi [*sic, Japanese-American*], has sent me a card saying that he has been to see you again. He's a curious guy, not particularly literart [*sic*] but his heart (and intellegence [*sic*]) are in the right place; did he tell you he has written a biography of a distinguishe [*sic*] uncle of his, a bishop in the established church of the last generation, an Englishman selbst verstandlich [of course].

That's enough for now.

Our love to Dorothy.

Bill

tenzone: In medieval Provence, a *tenzon* was a song contest in which rival troubadours strove to outdo one another in composition. For several weeks in January and February 1957, WCW and EP exchanged stanzas of a political satire which has never been published.

Kasper: See "Biographical Notes" on KASPER, FREDERICK JOHN.

final report: For William Faulkner's American Writers' Group, see Letter 157 and p. 286 above. On December 4, WCW reported to EP (Yale) that he and fourteen others had met in New York on November 29, and that WCW's proposal for EP's release was under serious consideration for inclusion in the group's final report to the President. The report was drafted, but it was never submitted.

prize money: Early in 1957, WCW was awarded a $5,000 fellowship by the Academy of American Poets.

Professor Pottle: Frederick Albert Pottle (1897–1987) taught English at Yale University from 1925 to 1966. He is best known as the biographer of James Boswell and the editor of his papers. In 1951, Pottle became Chancellor of the Academy of American Poets.

Thirlwall: John Connop Thirlwall (1904–1971) was professor of English at the City
College of New York. He was the editor of WCW's *Selected Letters* (1957) and the
author of a number of articles and notes on WCW's work. Thirlwall's Anglican ancestor
was Connop Thirlwall (1797–1875), Bishop of St. David's and a prolific preacher and
writer. The biography by his descendant is entitled *Connop Thirlwall: Historian and
Theologian* (1936).

161. TL-1

3 Feb [1957]

didn't the OTHERwise useless Jarrel [Randall Jarrell] do a book on yu, or
zummat.

I think Stock may want to a [*sic*] W. C. W. issue of Edge/ and it wd/ be useful
to have Jarrel

I mean he and [John] Berryman are among the decenter 2nd/ raters/

Stock, will I am sure be doing something re/ *American Grain* busting into
paper back/

HAVE YOU any preference for ten pages of gists from yr/ opus varius prose
vollumz?

sort of quintessence of W. C. W.?

There WAS a selection in Exile, I think, from uncollected ms/

You and Wyndham [Lewis] present prubbulums/ I mean to REACH the uncon-
verted/

out side Mr Kenner's Smithsonian etc.

wot does Bill think is the clearest statement of. . . . no use dodging it/

Bill is PERfectly convinced he had and HAS a message . . . evangelical
term, but find some better word.

It is and was to NOT be swamped by the ideas supposed to be, and quite
possibly really, GOVERNING the aims of Ez/ and/or Possum [T. S. Eliot]
and/or Wyndham and/or evn WBY [Yeats] and the late bro Huffer [Ford Madox
Ford].

It was purty nigh defined in the COlected essays of Bull.

A Edge issue shd/ ?? centre round A. Grain, some stray chapters in that
YuRupp nuvl/ (?), Bulls Essays

& potry you QUOTE wot yu dont yatter about

Bull got any nominations? Yu purty well know wich poemZ I tink is de bes'.

I aint sayin Stock and Flemming [*sic*] WILL tink so.

BUT if yu GOT anything yu think brighter than zummat elsz. now is the time
to come to the aid . . .

wot the old Gynecologist BELIEVES.

Stock: See "Biographical Notes" on STOCK, NOEL. In a letter to EP of February 9 [1957]
(Yale), Stock reports that he cannot produce a WCW issue of *Edge.*

paper back: The first paperback edition of *In the American Grain* was published by New
Directions in August 1956. *Edge* did not review the new edition but did announce its
appearance; see No. 7 (August 1957), p. 29.

Exile: EP refers to WCW's "The Descent of Winter" (see Letter 35 above) but seems to
misremember its content.

outside Mr Kenner's Smithsonian: For Hugh Kenner, see Letter 152 above. He was
employed, not by the Smithsonian Institution, but by the University of California at
Santa Barbara.

COlected essays: WCW's *Selected* (not Collected) *Essays* was published by New Directions in 1954.

that YuRupp nuvl: A Voyage to Pagany (1928).

Flemming: The Australian poet, translator, and technical editor William Fleming was an
associate of Noel Stock in Australia from 1953 to 1957. Fleming translated Sappho and
Catullus and edited the *Mining and Geological Review,* a publication of the Australian
State Mines Department.

162. TLS-1

Feb. 9/57

Dear Ez:

There doesn't appear to be anything in Exile that can be used for your Aussie
friend, not of mine at any rate – I didn't notice anything of Wyndam's [*sic*] either
that looked interesting either [*sic*].

About Jarrell, he wrote a preface to one of my books of poems, I think. Have to
check that:

After asking Floss I find that it was The Selected Poems of which I do not own
a copy!

Jarrell's introduction to those poems, as I remember it, is not altogether favorable. Not that he has anything against me, quite the opposite, but facing my work
he has the disadvantage which all highly schooled men share with him: they know
too much for their boots. I don't know what gets into them, it may be a lack of

modesty – they are so loaded up with information that they can't afford to be simple in their opinions for fear some of their fellows will discover some minute flaw in their information or knowledge.

I like J. and have full respect for his leafning [*sic*] but he's nervous and seems unsure of himself. He's doing a wonderful job at the Library of Congress I hear with the old ladies. He's been out to the coast lecturing and reading his poems and is much liked there. He can take off his shirt and sit on the floor with thw [*sic*] gang so I don't want to throw any rocks in his direction. I'm sure he was among the members of the Academy of American Poets who gave my most recent award, the decision was by majority vote of the committee. He must have voted for me so I dont want to misjudge him.

He has kept a young poet named Corso, a very young poet from the slums of Brooklyn, at his own expense in Washington for the past month, and fed him and bedded him and given him a good overcoat when he couldn't stand it any more. That's something so I don't want to say he isn't all right only he's a high brow . and high brows are not to be trusted.

Don't forget that my English grandmother left the Church of Englang [*sic*] to become a "spiritualis" [*sic*] (later a Christian Scientis [*sic*]) and my fater [*sic*] was a Single Taxer in the 80s. I remember seeing a book by Henry George about the house when I was a boy though I never read it. Read Darwin instead.

There should be a selection from *In the American Grain;* a chapter or two from *A Voyage to Pagany* which I'll be glad to indicate in another week or two; something from Kora in Hell, another edition of which (soft cover) will be out in another month: etc etc . if your interest continues. Salutations to Dorothy.

As always

Bill

Jarrell: See "Biographical Notes" on JARRELL, RANDALL.

my most recent award: See Letter 160 above.

Corso: The American poet Gregory Corso (1930–). For his visit to Washington, see "Biographical Notes" on JARRELL, RANDALL.

my English grandmother: Emily Dickinson Wellcome was WCW's paternal grandmother. When he was young, her spiritualist seances impressed him. As a Christian Scientist, she refused modern medical treatment; see Mariani, pp. 6–8.

Henry George: The American economist and reformer Henry George (1839–1897) was the founder of the Land Reform Union and the author of *Our Land and Land Policy* (1871), *Progress and Plenty* (1879), and *The Irish Land Question* (1881). George believed that all rent charged for the use of land is unjust exploitation. He advocated a single tax of 100% on the unearned increment of land values.

Darwin: The English naturalist Charles Robert Darwin (1809–1882) propounded the theory of the evolution of species. Darwin's major works, *On the Origin of Species* (1859) and *The Descent of Man* (1871), were in the library of WCW's father. See *Autobiography*, p. 15; *The Great American Novel*, section XVI; and Mariani, p. 12.

Kora in Hell: For the new paperback edition of WCW's *Kora in Hell*, see Letter 151 above.

163. TLS-1

Feb. 16/58

Dear Ez:

One of the most effective I know of is Furacin (Eaton Labs., Norwalk, N. Y.) but you are right, Witch hazel oint[ment]., is just about as good for soothing irriated [*sic*] surfaces.

I have heard that Mr. Frost has registerd [*sic*] some favorable sentiments toward you recently. I heard a good story about him as a farmer recently: he bought (when he was younger) a heifer. The farmer, a neighbor, sold him one of his best beasts so that he was more than mildly surprised when Frost wanted to return the cow with the comment that it was no good.

The farmer replied, Let's take a look at it. He looked the beast over and said. How often do you milk this animal. Oh, replied Frost, as often as we need any milk.

We've heard you're writing some beautiful love cantos recently. Congratulations.

Best
Bill

irriated surfaces: In a letter to WCW of February 10, 1958 (Yale), EP asks him to recommend a salve to reduce "a little stiffness . . . in the DUCT, the TERMINAL inch of tubing."

Mr. Frost: See "Biographical Notes" on FROST, ROBERT.

love cantos: Possibly some of those published in *Thrones*.

164. TLS-1

Feb. 24/58

Dear Ez:

When you write in that subdued mood my heart positively bleeds for you – though I know you cannot forever keep up your defiance of fate with that nonchalance which I have always admired. It's a tough racket. Death way [*sic*] be the only end to it. I face every day when I lie down at night a similar conviction, the same that every condemned man faces at the end of his life. For we are all condemned by our fellows because we see through their villanies [*sic*]. We are overpowered.

For a number of months I have been wanting to tell you that I am using in a poem I have been working on, Paterson 5, a letter you sent me a year or two ago a condemnation of Frankin [Franklin D. Roosevelt] and his wife for their actions facing the fiscal neglect of the policies you advocate. Your words are bitter and unguarded. Jim Laughlin will show you the script if you insist on it. I do not promise to delete the letter. If interested write to Jim about it.

Spring will soon be here when you can again enjoy the comparative freedom of the hospital lawns.

Keep your pecker up.
Bill

when you write: On February 21, 1958, EP wrote WCW a reflective, nonhectoring letter (Yale) chiefly about EP's medical interests, past and present.

a letter: WCW refers to Letter 158 above (November 13, 1956). For EP's correspondence with New Directions over this permission, see Pound/Laughlin, pp. 256–57. An edited version of the letter appears in *Paterson (Book Five), Part 2.*

165. TLS-2

26 Marzo [March] 58

Deer BullYum

I am glad you raise the question of the Insteroot (Canby's cronies or crumbs). After the demise of Smeary Butter I was eructed into that BODDY (cf. H[enry]. James 1912: I beeLong to a. . . . . eh . . . . BODDY.

I promptly, within 24 hours nominated you and the reverend kumrad Kumminkx/

and received a rosette/ blue? and gold?

But with the onrush of circumstance, being incarcerated, the conduct of the Canbyites showed marked difference from that of old Patterson. Prex. of the Acad. Soc. Pol. Sci, who write to me in the hell hole stating that I was condiered [sic] an honoured member. etc

the canby crumbs (I believe one s. o. b. [son of a bitch] resigned when they gave a medal to Beard, one of the few historians worth a hoot.)

the Camby [sic] crumbs had neither the courage to expel me not [sic] the civility to communicate with me,

tho my address is no sexret [sic] and even had they addressed Rapallo the notices wd/ have been forwarded.

As sheer pusillanimity, it takes some Hilliering to beat.

Camby as you may have heard did NOT send any letters to Paige when D. D. P, was editing THAT volume.

And I having known perfectly well that I was monkeying with a very large buzzsaw,

in the wake of Walt Raleigh, Tasso and other lights of Parnassus

I have considered that it ill befitted me to put up a howl. re/ the rustic, incult, punkish, pewkish and wormlike behaviour of the secretariat.

If you are drumming up votes for Hilda, you had better ask the shits, how come?

and is Ez still on the elenco [roster] of their sindicate [sic]?

I have occasionally mentioned Ayn Rand/ who had a few words (any resemblence [sic] etc/ to any living bastards is wholly coincidental etc.)

Chatel just told me Fordie did a book on this country, which I had never heard of, re bitchuary like in N. York   name has got away from me, but he promises to bring it in.

The endeavour to teach the banderlog [chattering monkeys] how to HAVE an Institute will need time in its execution.

The work of the Soc. G. Bude in Paris, might consteroot a insPIration. They print serious books, per esempio [for example].

in fact. the last toe hold of culture in France

As a membAH of the Insteroot, (the BODDY), why the hell you aint in the ''ah, er, inner and more secret. . . . eh . . . boDDy gornoze, probably they got a flutist or a ski-jumper, or a Runion [sic] cancer fan)

you WOULD in an effete european country have a right to ask the succerTARry concerning the elimination of yr/ correspondent from their alleged mailing list.

I can hardly vote for H. D. or second her nomination unless provided with the suitable module in triplicate etc.

She is in Svizzeria [Switzerland] where they couldn't annoy her very much.

What is Edith Hamilton's status. Howcum Maranne [sic] a bright star in their diaDAMN, and H. D. still a little prairie flowYer?

GAWD, Monteral [sic], a sense of decorum, for professional decency??

There is an unpolished character named Frampton, who knows purty much what the score is,

whether you cd; stand him or he you,? IF given the editing he wd/ at least cut the cigarette butts and diapers

and leave whatever trace of intelligence either of us may have showin in our strictly informal EPistolary exchanges.

I wd/ willingly throw him a couple of cutletts and the price of a few cocakolas.

BUT yu mightn't like the cut of his jib/ AT least not sunk in beanery wallows.

A titolo di chronica [for your information]/ WHATEVER honours you may have proposed to the isTeROOT, no notice of 'em has ever reached me.

I haven't even a list of the fauna comprising. I remember that nice guy H. [sic] Gilbert Welsh in 1910, quoting: Who are these sonZOV bitches ANYhow? (no connection of the later in Paris Walsh). I suppose they are the kind that put up posters about "Tallulah Bankhead's Play: THE TWO HEADED EAGLE."

but If i err/ KOrect me.

Bill ever ask himself what there is about Xtianity that makes SOME xtns/ use it as an excuse for swallowing every form of pusillanimity? may be it is the habit of asking someone ELSE to deliver 'em.

I spose Buffalo Ab/ knows Mary Bernard [sic] has finally had her Sappho California'd.

Wot ever become of Iris?

best to Flos

y
Ez

the Insteroot: In a postcard to EP of March 25, 1958 (Yale), WCW writes, "By the way. H. D. has been proposed as a member of the Institute of Arts and letters to come up in a few weeks. Aren't you a member also?" EP was accepted into the National Institute of Arts and Letters in January 1938.

Canby's cronies: See "Biographical Notes" on CANBY, HENRY SEIDEL. On January 14, 1938, EP sent Canby a letter in which he proposed WCW, T. S. Eliot, e. e. cummings, and George Santayana for membership in the Institute (Yale).

Smeary Butter: Dr. Nicholas Murray Butler (1862–1947) was President of Columbia University from 1901 to 1945, head of the Carnegie Foundation for International Peace from 1925 to 1945, and winner of the Nobel Peace Prize for 1931. He served as President of the American Academy of Arts and Letters from 1928 to 1941.

old Patterson: See "Biographical Notes" on PATTERSON, ERNEST MINOR.

Beard: The American historian Charles Beard (1874–1948) was the author of *Economic Origins of Jeffersonian Democracy* (1915).

Hilliering: The Pulitzer-Prize-winning poet, novelist, and critic Robert S. Hillyer (1895–1961) attacked the award of the Bollingen Prize to EP in two articles in the *Saturday Review of Literature,* June 11 and 18, 1949. Hillyer was also associated in 1949–50 with attacks upon WCW's political loyalties by Virginia Kent Cummins' magazine, *The Lyric.*

Paige: The American scholar Douglas Duncan Paige was the editor of *The Letters of Ezra Pound 1907–1941* (New York: Harcourt Brace, 1950).

Walt Raleigh: The English poet, historian, and courtier Sir Walter Raleigh (1552?–1618) was imprisoned for many years in the Tower of London on charges of conspiracy against the throne, and was at last executed there.

Tasso: The Italian poet Torquato Tasso (1544–1595), author of *Gerusalemme Liberata* (1581), was locked up as a madman from 1579 to 1586.

votes for Hilda: See "Biographical Notes" on DOOLITTLE, HILDA. She never became a member of the National Institute of Arts and Letters.

Ayn Rand: The Russian-American novelist and philosopher Ayn Rand (1905–1982) was the author of *The Fountainhead* (1943). In this *roman à clef,* many of the characters are modeled upon identifiable public figures, such as Frank Lloyd Wright, William Randolph Hearst, and Harold Lasky.

Chatel: An aspiring young French writer named Jean-Marie Chatel (*c.* 1938–) was a member of EP's St. Elizabeths circle. Chatel was the author of an unpublished novel entitled *The Mind of Pierre Duval.* He later became a psychiatrist.

Fordie: Ford Madox Ford's *When the Wicked Man* (1931) contains an attack on New York publishers.

Soc. G. Bude: The French humanist Guillaume Budé (1467–1540) encouraged the study of Greek in France. In a letter to Wyndham Lewis of February 3, 1957, EP praises "the Soc[iété]. Guillaume Budé, 95 B[oulevar]d. Raspail, started in 1917 to keep greek texts printed with froglation [French translation]. The LAST citadel of frog decency"; see Pound/Lewis, p. 303.

Runion: The American journalist and sportswriter Damon Runyon (1884–1946) was the author of *Guys and Dolls* (1932) and other slangy sketches of New York life. Runyon died slowly and painfully of mouth cancer. His friend Walter Winchell founded the Damon Runyon Memorial Fund for cancer research.

Edith Hamilton's status: The American classicist and writer on Greek mythology Edith Hamilton (1867–1963) was a member of the National Institute of Arts and Letters. She lived in Washington, visited EP at St. Elizabeths, and corresponded with him from 1954 to 1958 (Yale).

Maranne: MARIANNE MOORE (see "Biographical Notes") became a member of the National Institute of Arts and Letters in 1947.

GAWD, Monteral: EP echoes the refrain of "A Psalm of Montreal" (1878), a poem by
Samuel Butler (1835–1902) satirizing North American provinciality. On a visit to
Montreal, Quebec, the speaker finds a cast of the Discobolus hidden away in an attic
because of its nudity. Each stanza of the poem ends with the refrain "O God! O
Montreal!"

Frampton: The American photographer, filmmaker, and critic Hollis Frampton (1936–
1984) became an important figure in experimental cinema with such films as *Manual
of Arms* (1966), *Zorn's Lamma* (1970), and *Magellan* (1972). In a letter to WCW of
March 18, 1958 (Yale), EP proposes Frampton instead of John Thirlwall as the editor of
the EP-WCW correspondence.

H. Gilbert Welsh: For Robert Gilbert Welsh, see Letter 5 above.

Walsh: For Ernest Walsh, see Letter 28 above.

Tallulah Bankhead's Play: See "Biographical Notes" on COCTEAU, JEAN.

Buffalo Ab: See "Biographical Notes" on ABBOTT, CHARLES.

Mary Bernard: The poet and translator Mary Barnard (1909–) was the first Curator of the
Poetry Collection at the University of Buffalo. Barnard's *Sappho: A New Translation*
was published by the University of California Press in 1958.

Iris: Either Iris Barry or Iris Tree, a mutual friend of EP and WCW from Paris days. In his
response to this letter, dated April 13, 1958 (Yale), WCW assumes that EP means the
latter: "Iris Tree as far as I know is still in N. Y. I never see her . . . ."

166. TLS-1

20 Maggio [May 1958]

Deer Bull

thanks fer card announcing future arruvul of dope re/ the Can/Cow.

I had hoped to spend my larst night on these rockbound shores in yr/ paternal
establishment//

and still do, BUTT

complication is that the three of us will be being transported by the eminent
[David] Horton et coniunX [and wife].

which makes 5.

I can sleep on any damn divan, but the rest require bedz.

Have invite fer 5, nine miles from Princeton/

cd/ purrzoombly arrange fer 'em to bed there.

deepending on time of Sailing/

or cd/ hire bunks in Rutherford.

how long by motor from Rootyford to the Wop Line docks?

The Anthologist: Kung to Kumminkz.

means in proportion to Bion and Theocritus, etc. Omitting several victorian worthies,

means one poEM/ a piece fer the survivers, or at most 2.

You have probably fergott yr/ valuable note (undated) listing ten of yourN/ which note I shd/ propose the anth/gist shd/ use as FOOTnote, leading the young suckers to ulterior perusal, from two PTHER [*sic*] poEmz. by W. C. W.

texts of which are not on premises, cause Jas/ [James Laughlin] has MY copies of my former anthologies/

but I reckon I can git the texts from N[orman]. H[olmes]. Pearson/ I *can't* git 'em from Brunnenburg CAUSE the said copies of anthols/ were sent HERE with aim of gittin the whole FOUR E. P.-anth/ reprinted fer the uplift of amurkn yewth kulch etcerAAAA.

Here present yr/ later woikz/ and Jarrel's [*sic*] selects which wd/ be undesirable to repeat from. One aim of anth/ being to jab spots not rendered insensitiv by earlier hyperdermics. or hypo. as may be.

best to Flos

yrz

Ez

card: In a postcard to EP of May 17, 1958 (Yale), WCW promises to send the annual report of the National Institute of Arts and Letters. In a letter to WCW of May 27, 1958 (Yale), EP reports that he has resigned from the Institute.

my larst night: EP was released from St. Elizabeths on May 7, 1958. His last two nights before leaving the United States for Italy, June 28 and 29, 1958, were spent at WCW's home in Rutherford.

three of us: EP, Dorothy, and Marcella Spann, a teacher at a junior college in Washington and an intimate member of EP's St. Elizabeths circle. She was coeditor with EP of *Confucius to Cummings: An Anthology of Poetry* (New York: New Directions, 1964).

Bion and Theocritus: A note on p. 85 of *Confucius to Cummings* explains that the work of the Greek pastoral poet Bion (*c.* 100 B.C.) is not included because there is no adequate English translation of it. Thomas Creech's 1684 translation of one of the Idylls of Theocritus ("The Enchantment") appears on pp. 25–32. WCW is represented on pp. 307–08 by "The High Bridge above the Tagus River at Toledo."

yr/ valuable note: WCW's poem is followed (p. 308) by this note: "Dr. Williams' criticism of himself may be examined in a list of ten poems ('Pastoral' ['When I was younger'], 'Virtue,' 'Nantucket,' 'Between Walls,' 'It is a living coral,' 'Spring and All,' 'Primrose,' 'To a Poor Old Woman,' 'The Sea Elephant,' 'The Red-wing Black-bird') on which he comments: 'This brief selection is as much as the casual reader will find illustrative of what I have been doing with myself for the past 30 years.'"

Brunnenburg: EP's daughter and son-in-law, Mary and Boris de Rachewiltz, purchased

Schloss Brunnenburg in Tirolo di Merano, Italy, in 1948. EP lived there for a time after his return to Italy.

FOUR E. P.-anth: The first four anthologies edited by EP—*Des Imagistes* (1914), *Catholic Anthology* (1915), *Profile* (1932), and *Active Anthology* (1933)—have not been reprinted.

167. TLS-1

May 21, 1958

Dear Ez:

Another milestone past. Whatever is in store for either of us this marks the end of an ugly phase. Take care of yourself in Italy where I understand you are going, don't ever expect to see you again – unless you come to Rutherford before your present departure.

Come if you can. Tell me when your ship sails, the line and name the ship itself. If you have the time plan to spend at least a night with us. We have adequate accomodations [*sic*], in fact you and Dorothy can have a room to yourselves. Anyone you want to bring with you can also be bedded. Your room has also a sumptuous bath not as magnificent as that you used to tell me about in Toledo but what can you expect?

Be glad to see you. Love to Dorothy from us both.

Best
Bill

168. TLS-1

Nov. 26/60

Liebes Ezchen:

You're not worth it but I forgive you nevertheless for all your shortcomings as a friend. My opinion of your recent writing, with few exceptions, up to your translations from Propertius into the AmeriCAN idiom.

I'm giving a friend a letter of intro to you, Mack Rosenthal a really likable fellow, really grown up, which he'll deliver to you by hand during the coming month at Castle Brunnenburg. Be nice to him.

I saw H. D. when she was in N. Y. to receive the citation of the American Academy of Arts and Letters last summer. She's broken a leg during the years and walks with difficulty. I was very happy to see her again.

Floss sends her love to both you and Dorothy. I'm publishing a volume of plays, mostly old stuff, which you'll receive early next year, prose. I haven't heard from you recently, I hope you keep well.

Affectionately,

Bill

your translations from Propertius: EP had done no recent translations of Propertius. WCW is referring to EP's *Homage to Sextus Propertius* (1919), but his thought is incomplete.

Mack Rosenthal: The American poet, critic, and editor M. L. Rosenthal had already written about EP's work in *A Primer of Ezra Pound* (1960) and *The Modern Poets* (1960). On leave from his teaching position at New York University, Rosenthal was in Europe on a Guggenheim Fellowship; but his projected visit to Brunnenburg never took place.

H. D.: See "Biographical Notes" on DOOLITTLE, HILDA. She had fallen and broken her hip in the autumn of 1956.

a volume of plays: WCW's *Many Loves and Other Plays* was published by New Directions in September 1961.

169. Telegram

[March 1963]

Dear Flos [*sic*]

A magnificent fight he made of it for you. He bore with me sixty years, and I shall never find another poet friend like him. My love and sympathy to you –

Ezra

sympathy: WCW died on March 4, 1963.

Biographical Notes

The following notes are not rounded biographical sketches. Rather, they present information selected for its particular relevance to the preceding letters. Names set in capital letters have entries of their own elsewhere in the "Biographical Notes."

ABBOTT, CHARLES (1900–1961). American librarian. He was the director of libraries at the University of Buffalo and founder of the Lockwood Library's Poetry Collection. Beginning in 1940, WCW sold manuscripts and other material to this collection. Abbott helped to arrange numerous readings by WCW at the University of Buffalo, and was instrumental in the university's award of an honorary degree to WCW in 1950. Abbott's wife was Theresa Gratwick Abbott, whose brother and sister-in-law, Bill and Harriet Gratwick, were the proprietors of Gratwick Highlands.

AIKEN, CONRAD (1889–1973). American poet, novelist, critic, and editor. He attended Harvard with T. S. ELIOT and introduced Eliot to EP in London in 1914. He also knew WCW; indeed, on February 27, 1930, Aiken was married to Clarissa Lorenz in WCW's living room in Rutherford (Mariani, pp. 304–05). Aiken's *American Poetry 1671–1928: A Comprehensive Anthology* (New York: Modern Library, 1929) contained seven poems by EP but none by WCW. In 1945, Random House announced that, because of EP's anti-Semitism and treason, his poems would be dropped from a new edition of the anthology, retitled *An Anthology of Famous English and American Poetry* and edited by Aiken and William Rose Benét. Despite an outcry from poets across the country and threats of a libel suit from EP's lawyer, Random House omitted the poems, publishing in their stead Aiken's statement of protest against their suppression. WCW's work was excluded from the new edition as well as the old.

ALDINGTON, RICHARD (1892–1962). English poet, novelist, critic, and translator. He was one of the original Imagists of 1912. In the following year he married HILDA DOOLITTLE and became assistant editor of *The Egoist*. During the Great War, Aldington served in the 9th Royal Sussex Regiment until his demobilization in February 1920. For the next ten years, he was the principal reviewer of books on French literature for *The Times Literary Supplement*. He caricatured EP as "Mr. Upjohn" and T. S. ELIOT as "Mr. Bobbe" in his popular novel, *Death of a Hero* (1929). Aldington was also the editor of *Imagist Anthology 1930: New Poetry by the Imagists* (1930). Separated from H. D., Aldington had a ten-year relationship with the Irish novelist Brigit Patmore (1882–1965), whom EP first met in London in 1909. In 1928, EP found rooms in Rapallo for the financially hard-pressed couple; see Carpenter, p. 465.

AMES, HERMAN VANDENBURG (1865–1935). American historian. He was professor of American Constitutional History at the University of Pennsylvania from 1897 to 1935. He was the author of *The Proposed Amendments to the Constitution of the United States* (1897) and *Outline of Lectures on American Political and Institutional History during the Colonial and Revolutionary Periods,* 3rd. ed. (1908). EP contributed a reminiscence of Ames to *Memorial: Herman Vandenburg Ames,* ed. Edward P. Cheney and Roy F. Nichols (Philadelphia: University of Pennsylvania Press, 1936), pp. 20–22: "After thirty years I still have pleasant recollections of 'Reconstruction' and 'Foreign Relations' courses, part and parcel of the abundant and mellow good humour that pervaded his every act. . . . No man in the university maintained a superior serenity or was freer from heaviness."

BARNEY, NATALIE CLIFFORD (1876–1972). American writer and patron of the arts. Born in Dayton, Ohio, Natalie Barney lived much of her life in Paris, where her salon at 20 rue Jacob was a center of intellectual life and of a sophisticated lesbian subculture. She named EP's "Bel Esprit" (Fine Minds) project, and supported it strongly by enlisting a number of her friends in the cause.

BARRY, IRIS (1895–1969). English poet, novelist, and film historian. Born in Birmingham, Barry became EP's protégée and WYNDHAM LEWIS' mistress. EP helped to place her work in *Poetry, The Little Review,* and other magazines, and he conducted an important correspondence with her in 1916–17 (see Paige, pp. 76–106). Barry later moved to New York and became the curator of the film library at the Museum of Modern Art. There, she developed an interest in the work of the German anthropologist Leo Frobenius.

BIRD, WILLIAM (1889–1963). American printer and publisher. He founded the Three Mountains Press in Paris in 1921. He met EP in 1922 and WCW in 1924. Bird published WCW's *Spring and All* (1923) and *The Great American Novel* (1923), EP's *Antheil and the Treatise on Harmony* (1924) and *A Draft of XVI. Cantos* (1925), and ERNEST HEMINGWAY's *in our time* (1924). Bird and his wife, Sally, later lived in Tangiers.

BRITTAIN, ROBERT (b. 1908). American poet and scholar. As a graduate student at Princeton, he first wrote to WCW on March 19, 1933 (Yale), inviting him to attend a Princeton gathering in honor of T. S. ELIOT. Brittain later taught English at Queen's College, Brooklyn, and edited the work of Christopher Smart. Brittain's poetry appeared in *Atlantic Monthly, Harper's,* and *Poetry,* and was gathered in *Poems* (1950).

BUNTING, BASIL (1900–1985). English poet and translator. He lived in Rapallo from 1930 to 1933 and helped EP compile the *Active Anthology*. Bunting met WCW in New York on January 5, 1931 (Mariani, p. 310). Bunting attempted to translate the *Shah-nameh* (Book of Kings), the Persian national epic by Ferdowsi or Firdusi (Abul Kasim Mansur, *c.* 930–1020). A passage of the translation appeared under the title "From 'Faridun's Sons,' by Firdusi" in *Criterion,* 15:60 (April 1936), pp. 421–23; but the translation has never been published as a book. EP mentions it in Canto 77. Bunting's *Poems* were issued by DALLAM SIMPSON's Cleaners' Press of Galveston, Texas, in 1950 and reissued in 1956 in the Square Dollar Series of JOHN KASPER and T. David Horton.

BURKE, KENNETH (1897–1973). American critic, philosopher, and poet. He met WCW in

New York in January 1921. They became good friends and correspondents, and WCW paid several visits to Burke's farm in Andover, New Jersey. HART CRANE, whom Burke met in 1923, also visited there. In 1945, Burke published a volume of philosophical criticism entitled *A Grammar of Motives*. In 1949, he held a fellowship at Princeton's Institute for Advanced Study to work on a sequel, published in 1950 as *A Rhetoric of Motives*.

BYNNER, WITTER (1881–1968). American poet, translator, editor, and critic. He met EP in New York in 1910 and helped him find a publisher for *Provença*. Bynner came to know D. H. Lawrence and Frieda in New Mexico in 1922 and visited Mexico with them in 1923. Bynner later published a memoir of this acquaintance, entitled *Journey with Genius: Recollections and Reflections Concerning the D. H. Lawrences* (New York: John Day, 1951). In Chapters 25 and 33, Bynner and Lawrence exchange amused memories of the young EP and his affectations.

CANBY, HENRY SEIDEL (1878–1961). American critic, editor, and teacher. He was professor of English at Yale University and the author of books on Whitman, Thoreau, Twain, and Henry James. He was also editor of the *Saturday Review of Literature* from 1924 to 1936 and chairman of the board of judges of the Book-of-the-Month Club from 1926 to 1958. He was secretary of the National Institute of Arts and Letters when EP became a member in 1938. His correspondence with EP is preserved in the Canby Archive at Yale.

CARNEVALI, EMANUEL (1897–1942?). Italian poet, translator, and editor. He lived for a time in New York, where WCW met him in 1919, and Chicago, where he worked for *Poetry* magazine. A victim of encephalitis, he returned to Italy in 1922, where he was hospitalized in Bazzano near Bologna. WCW, EP, ROBERT McALMON, and Harriet Monroe contributed to his support.

COCTEAU, JEAN (1881–1963). French writer, artist, and filmmaker. He met EP in Paris in 1922 and WCW in 1924. Cocteau's French translation of Sophocles' tragedy *Antigone* opened at Charles Pullin's Théâtre de l'Atelier in Montmartre on December 20, 1922, and ran for about a hundred nights. The production featured scenery designed and painted by Pablo Picasso, music by Arthur Honegger, and costumes by Coco Chanel. EP praised the play in his "Paris Letter" to *The Dial* for February 1923. Cocteau was introduced to the serious use of opium by Louis Laloy in 1924, and continued to use it for the rest of his life. He underwent several impermanent cures for his addiction; one of them is described in *Opium: Journal d'une désintoxication* (1930). Cocteau's "Crucifixion" is a long poem of twenty-five strophes, written in 1945–46 and published in Paris by Paul Morihien in 1946. His play *L'Aigle à deux têtes* was written in 1944 and first performed in Paris in November 1946. An English adaptation by Ronald Duncan entitled *The Eagle Has Two Heads* opened in London in the autumn of 1946. A New York production of Duncan's version, starring Tallulah Bankhead as a melancholy queen and Helmut Dantine as a revolutionary poet, had its premiere at the Plymouth Theater on March 19, 1947. It was not a success.

COLE, THOMAS. American poet, critic, editor, and publisher. From 1946 to 1956, he edited a little magazine called *Imagi* in Baltimore, Maryland, and Allentown, Pennsylvania. Both EP and WCW contributed to *Imagi* between 1948 and 1953. WCW's review of EP's *Pisan Cantos* appeared in the number for May 1949. The "All-American" issue (vol. 5, no. 2, 1950) contained work by EP, WCW, E. E. CUMMINGS, MARIANNE MOORE, LOUIS ZUKOFSKY, Wallace Stevens, and Charles Olson. Cole's reminiscences of this period appear in "Remembering Williams and Pound," *William Carlos Williams Review* 7:2 (Fall 1981), pp. 4–20, and "Ezra Pound and *Imagi*," *Paideuma* 16:3 (Winter 1987), pp. 53–66.

COVICI, PASCAL (1888–1964). American publisher and editor. He published EP's magazine *Exile* (1927–28) and the American edition of EP's *Antheil and the Treatise on Harmony* (1927). His firm moved from Chicago to New York in 1928, and on July 1, Covici formed a partnership with Donald S. Friede. Thereafter, relations with EP degenerated. In a letter to EP of September 5, 1928 (Yale), Covici announced that the firm would cease to publish *Exile* after the fourth number. On October 9 (Yale), Friede informed EP that the firm would not publish *Machine Art,* a book which Covici had accepted in March 1927 and for which EP had been gathering photographs of machinery since 1925 (see Gallup, E6e). In a letter to Friede of October 25, 1928 (Yale), EP threatened legal action for breach of contract. Meanwhile, Covici, Friede published RICHARD ALDINGTON's *Death of a Hero* (1929) and *Imagist Anthology 1930* (1930).

CRANE, HART (1899–1932). American poet and essayist. His work appeared in *The Dial, The Little Review, Criterion,* and *transition.* He was the author of *White Buildings* (1926) and *The Bridge* (1930), a work indebted to WCW's *In the American Grain.* WCW met Crane in Brooklyn on December 7, 1929, but did not comment upon his work publicly until after Crane's suicide by drowning on April 27, 1932. Crane's homosexuality may have influenced his decision to end his life.

CUMMINGS, EDWARD ESTLIN (1894–1962). American poet, prose writer, translator, and artist. He met EP in Paris in 1921 and WCW in Rutherford on May 6, 1928. Cummings' play, *Him,* was published in *The Dial* for August 1927, and performed at the Provincetown Playhouse in New York for six weeks from April 18, 1928. The production was subsidized by Gertrude Vanderbilt Whitney, among others. Cummings' *Eimi* (I am) is a travel narrative describing the author's 32-day visit to the Soviet Union in the spring of 1931. It is highly critical of the regimentation and squalor of Soviet society. EP received a copy of *Eimi* in April 1933 and immediately requested Cummings' permission to include excerpts from it in *Active Anthology* (October 1933). EP also praised the book in "E. E. Cummings Alive," *New English Weekly* (December 20, 1934). EP saw *Eimi* as the definitive literary expression of the failure of the Soviet Communist social experiment. Henceforth he jokingly referred to Cummings as "Kumrad" (Comrade). *Active Anthology* also contains Cummings' translation of Louis Aragon's French poem "Red Front," and EP persuaded Cummings to contribute three poems to the *New English Weekly* for February 7, 1935. They are "conceive a man, should he have anything," "Jehovah buried, Satan dead," and "what does little Ernest croon."

CUNARD, NANCY (1896–1965). English poet, publisher, and heiress. She met EP in London around 1914 and WCW in Paris in 1924. In 1928, she founded the Hours Press in Paris, which published EP's *A Draft of XXX Cantos* in 1930. An ardent Loyalist during the Spanish Civil War, Cunard compiled a questionnaire entitled *Authors Take Sides on the Spanish War* (1937). EP's position on the issue was "Neutral." When their correspondence resumed in June 1946, Cunard blasted his politics and the entire direction of his career. Nevertheless, she continued to exchange letters with him until March 1950.

DE KRUIF, PAUL (1890–1971). American bacteriologist, pathologist, and writer of popular books and articles on medical science. EP corresponded with him from August 1933 to July 1940 (Yale), and reviewed his *Hunger Fighters* (1928) in the *New English Weekly* for February 22, 1934. EP converted De Kruif to Social Credit in 1934, and De Kruif acknowledged his indebtedness in the introduction to *Why Keep Them Alive?* (New York: Harcourt Brace, 1936). This book gathered a series of six articles that De Kruif had published in the *Ladies' Home Journal* from February to December 1934. The articles focused upon preventable illnesses among children caused by poverty and the distorted economic priorities of modern society.

DOOLITTLE, HILDA (1886–1961). American poet and novelist, who adopted the pen name of "H. D." She met EP and WCW in 1905 at the University of Pennsylvania. She was associated with EP in the London Imagist movement of 1912–14. She married RICHARD ALDINGTON in 1913 but later separated from him and lived for many years with her patron, WINIFRED ELLERMAN. In 1933–34, H. D. was psychoanalyzed by Sigmund Freud in Vienna. She gave an account of the experience in "Writing on the Wall," first serialized in *Life and Letters Today* (1945–46) and later incorporated into *Tribute to Freud* (1956). Vivid memories of EP, to whom she was once engaged, figure in this account and in H. D.'s *End to Torment* (1979). In the spring of 1946, H. D. was scheduled to teach at Bryn Mawr College in Philadelphia, where she had once been a student; but the visit was canceled when she suffered a nervous breakdown in Switzerland. In 1956, she visited Yale University in connection with a celebration of her seventieth birthday organized by Norman Holmes Pearson. On May 25, 1960, she became the first woman ever to receive the Gold Medal for Poetry from the American Academy of Arts and Letters in New York.

DOUGLAS, CLIFFORD HUGH (1879–1952). English engineer and economist. He began his career as a manager of the British Westinghouse Company in India. After the Great War, during which he attained the rank of major in the Royal Flying Corps, he turned his attention to economics, and formulated his theory of Social Credit in books entitled *Economic Democracy* and *Credit Power and Democracy* (both 1920). For a summary of the theory, see p. 123 above.

DOUGLAS, PAUL HOWARD (1892–1976). American political leader. He served in the Marine Corps from 1942 to 1945, rising from the rank of private to that of lieutenant colonel. He represented Illinois in the United States Senate from 1949 to 1967. In his autobiography, *In the Fullness of Time* (1972), Douglas recalls reading Stephen Crane's *The Red Badge of Courage* while being shipped out to Oro Bay in the Pacific, and reading Dante's *Inferno* in a foxhole filled with icy water during the battle of Okinawa.

ELIOT, THOMAS STEARNS (1888–1965). American poet, playwright, critic, and editor. EP met him in London in September 1914, and was instrumental in the publication of his early poems in *Poetry* for June 1915 and September 1916, and in *Prufrock and Other Observations* (London: Egoist Press, 1917). On June 26, 1915, Eliot married Vivien Haigh-Wood (1888–1947) in London. In the autumn of 1921, he suffered a nervous breakdown under the stress of marital problems and overwork. During his convalescence at Margate, Kent, and Lausanne, Switzerland, he began *The Waste Land*. EP helped to edit the manuscript in January 1922. Fearing a relapse, EP conceived a plan called "Bel Esprit" (Fine Minds) to provide Eliot with sufficient income to give up his job at Lloyd's Bank. Eliot was reluctant to accept such assistance, and the plan was ultimately abandoned. From 1922 to 1939, Eliot edited the *Criterion;* he also became an influential editor and company director in the publishing house of Faber and Faber. In both positions, he was instrumental in the publication of EP's work. In 1928, Eliot announced his conversion to the Church of England, declaring himself a classicist in literature, a Royalist in politics, and an Anglo-Catholic in religion. In 1932–33, Eliot served as Charles Eliot Norton Professor of Poetry at Harvard University. He received both the Order of Merit and the Nobel Prize in 1948. Eliot was a *bête noire* of WCW, who resented the success and influence of his poetry, criticism, and religious views.

ELLERMAN, WINIFRED (1894–1984). British writer and patron of the arts, who adopted the pen name of "Bryher." She was the wealthy daughter of the shipping magnate and financier Sir John Ellerman. She married ROBERT MCALMON in 1921 and divorced him in 1926. Bryher became HILDA DOOLITTLE'S companion and patron.

FARRELL, JAMES T. (1904–1973). American novelist and short-story writer. He was the author of *Young Lonigan* (1932), *The Young Manhood of Studs Lonigan* (1934), and *Judgment Day* (1935). EP met him in Paris through SAMUEL PUTNAM in May 1931. EP admired Farrell's short stories in Putnam's *The New Review* and other magazines, and encouraged him in his work. Farrell later visited EP at St. Elizabeths. Their correspondence (1931–35) is housed at Yale and the University of Pennsylvania.

FORD, FORD MADOX (1873–1939). English novelist, poet, critic, and editor. As the editor of the *English Review,* Ford Madox Hueffer met EP in 1909 and facilitated his entry into London literary circles. Hueffer's critical writings on French prose influenced the aesthetic of Imagism. Parts of his novel *The Good Soldier* (1915) appeared in the Vorticist magazine *BLAST* under the title "The Saddest Story." During the Great War, he served with the 9th Welsh Battalion, attaining the rank of acting brevet major. Suffering from shell shock and lung problems, he resigned his commission in January 1919. Later that year, he changed his Westphalian surname from Hueffer to Ford. He first met WCW in Paris in 1924. Between 1935 and 1939, Ford lived in the United States, and actively promoted the work of WCW. In *Forum* for September 1937, Ford praised WCW's *In the American Grain* and *White Mule*. At Ford's instigation, a group called Les Amis de William Carlos Williams was formed in New York in February 1939. Its members included Sherwood Anderson, W. H. Auden, Edward Dahlberg, Waldo Frank, Marsden Hartley, Christopher Isherwood, JAMES LAUGHLIN, ARCHIBALD MAC-LEISH, MARIANNE MOORE, GORHAM MUNSON, Charles Olson, Katherine Anne Porter, EP, Charles Sheeler, ALFRED STIEGLITZ, Allen Tate, and LOUIS ZUKOFSKY. The group met five times before disbanding in June 1939. Ford left New York for France on

May 30, 1939, and died there on June 26. His memory is evoked in several of WCW's later poems, including "To Ford Madox Ford in Heaven" (1940), "The Birth of Venus" (1948), and "Incognito" (1950). WCW admired Ford's tetralogy, *Parade's End* (1924–28), and reviewed it in the *Sewanee Review* for Winter 1951.

FROST, ROBERT (1874–1963). American poet. His first books of poetry, *A Boy's Will* (1913) and *North of Boston* (1914), were published in London. EP reviewed both books favorably in *Poetry* and helped to place Frost's work in that journal. As Charles Eliot Norton Professor of Poetry at Harvard in 1935–36, Frost said in one of his lectures that the Imagists, and EP in particular, made the mistake of insisting upon visual images only. This drew an angry response from EP; see Douglas Bruster, "'Pound, Frost, and 'Literary Integrity' at Harvard," *Paideuma* 23: 2–3 (Fall–Winter 1994), pp. 237–41. In 1957–58, Frost actively lobbied the U. S. Departments of State and Justice on behalf of EP's release from St. Elizabeths; see Lawrance Thompson and R. H. Winnick, *Robert Frost: The Later Years 1938–1963* (New York: Holt, Rinehart, and Winston, 1976), Chapter 16, and Carpenter, pp. 830–40.

GAUDIER-BRZESKA, HENRI (1891–1915). French sculptor. EP met him in London in 1913. EP bought two of Gaudier's works: a marble group, known both as *Embracers* and as *Samson and Delilah,* and a torso. EP later sat for Gaudier's *Hieratic Head of Ezra Pound.* Gaudier was a central figure in the Vorticist movement of 1914–15, but was killed in the trenches of France during the Great War. EP's memorial tribute to him, *Gaudier-Brzeska: A Memoir,* was published in 1916.

GESELL, SILVIO (1862–1930). German businessman and economist. He made his living by importing surgical supplies into Argentina. Gesell formulated his theories of economic reform, including the use of stamped paper money or stamp scrip, in *Die natürliche Wirtschaftsordnung durch Freiland und Freigeld* (1916). This was translated into English as *The Natural Economic Order* by Philip Pye (Berlin: Neo-Verlag, 1929). Pye's translation was reprinted in two volumes (1934–36) by Dr. Hugo R. Fack, a German-born disciple of Gesell who operated a naturopathic health institute and rest home in San Antonio, Texas. Fack's Free-Economy Publishing Company also produced a periodical called *The Way Out.* Stamp scrip was paper money valid only for domestic use and not linked to the international value of gold. The currency itself was to be taxed periodically by means of a stamp purchased and affixed to each bill by whomever was holding it at the time. The stamp requirement, Gesell argued, would encourage spending and consumption and discourage hoarding.

GOURMONT, REMY DE (1858–1915). French poet, novelist, essayist, critic, and editor. He helped to found the important journal *Mercure de France* in 1889. His works include *Le Latin mystique* (1890), *Le Livre des masques* (1896), *Le Problème du style* (1902), *Physique de l'amour* (1896; translated by EP as *The Natural Philosophy of Love,* 1922), and *Epilogues: Réflexions sur le vie* (Paris: Société du Mercure de France, 1903). EP discovered the work of Gourmont in 1912, and in the following year he wrote about Gourmont's poetry in a series of essays for *The New Age* entitled "The Approach to Paris." He also published essays entitled "Remy de Gourmont," *Fortnightly Review* 98 (n.s.):588 (December 1, 1915), pp. 1159–66, and "De Gourmont: A Distinction

(Followed by Notes)," *The Little Review* 5:10–11 (February–March 1919), pp. 1–19. In the latter (p. 10), EP describes Gourmont's *Epilogues* as "a book of accumulations. Full of meat as a good walnut." But in his activist phase from 1930 on, EP tended to associate the name of Gourmont with pre-1914 aestheticism—"Old rose and mauve," as he put it in a letter of March 12, 1935, to JAMES LAUGHLIN (Pound/Laughlin, p. 41).

GUINAN, "TEXAS" (1884–1933). American actress, singer, and night club hostess. Mary Louise Cecilia ("Texas") Guinan began her career as a star of Western movies between 1917 and 1921. She moved to New York in 1923 and became known as the Queen of the Night Clubs, greeting customers with a line that became a trademark of the Jazz Age: "Hello, suckers!" She starred in a 1929 film based upon her own life, and another such film, featuring Betty Hutton and entitled *Incendiary Blonde*, was released in 1945. Miss Guinan was arrested on several occasions but never convicted.

HARGRAVE, JOHN (1894–1982). English writer, illustrator, cartoonist, inventor, soldier, and political activist. He began his career as an organizer in the English scouting movement, when he founded the Kindred of the Kibbo Kift in 1920. In the 1930s, he became the leader of the Green Shirts, a militant wing of the Social Credit movement. He corresponded extensively with EP (Yale). WCW reviewed Hargrave's novel, *Summer Time Ends* (1935), in *New Democracy* for November 1, 1935.

HECHT, BEN (1894–1964). American journalist, novelist, short-story writer, poet, playwright, and screenwriter. A Chicagoan of Jewish descent, Hecht began his career as a police reporter and later turned to writing prose fiction. EP published a note on his work in *The Little Review*, met him in London in 1919, and described him vividly in letters to Homer and Isabel Pound of January 10 and 23, 1919 (Yale). With Charles MacArthur, Hecht was co-author of *The Front Page* (1928).

HEMINGWAY, ERNEST (1898–1961). American novelist, short-story writer, and journalist. He met EP in Paris in 1921 and WCW in 1924. Hemingway's collection of short stories, *in our time*, was published in Paris by WILLIAM BIRD in 1924; an expanded edition was issued in 1925 by Boni and Liveright in New York. From February 10 to February 20, 1926, Hemingway was in New York to arrange for the publication by Scribner's of *Torrents of Spring* and *The Sun Also Rises*. In 1937, Hemingway went to Spain to cover the Civil War as a newspaper correspondent. He soon committed himself to the Loyalist cause as a fundraiser and propagandist. In 1957–58, he was instrumental in securing EP's release from St. Elizabeths.

HESSLER, LEWIS BURTRON (1884–1958). American teacher and scholar. Born in Nebraska, he took a B.A. at the University of Pennsylvania in 1905 and a Ph.D. in 1916. His doctoral dissertation was published in 1916 as *The Latin Epigram of the Middle English Period*. He taught English at the Universities of Michigan, New Mexico, and Minnesota. Some of his correspondence with EP (1915–16) is preserved at Texas.

JACKSON, ANDREW (1767–1845). American military and political leader. His military victories over the British at New Orleans in 1815, and over the Seminole Indians of Florida in 1818, made him a popular hero and propelled him into the White House for two terms as President of the United States (1829–37). When affirming the importance of MARTIN VAN BUREN, EP liked to point out that Jackson was elected only by virtue of a political alliance with Van Buren. Moreover, Jackson's credentials as a popular hero were somewhat tarnished. His victory at New Orleans came several days after the official treaty ending the War of 1812 was signed, and he conquered the Seminoles by pursuing them across an international border and seizing the town of Pensacola, Florida, from the Spanish, thus causing a major diplomatic furor.

JARRELL, RANDALL (1914–1965). American poet, novelist, and critic. He wrote the introduction to WCW's *Selected Poems* (1949). Jarrell was made the Consultant in Poetry at the Library of Congress from 1956 to 1958, the first such appointment since that of WCW fell through in 1952–53. In this capacity, Jarrell visited the West Coast in October 1956. He gave a number of readings, and he met some of the Beat writers, including Allen Ginsberg, William Burroughs, Lawrence Ferlinghetti, and Gregory Corso. Impressed by Corso's first book of poems, *The Vestal Lady on Brattle* (1955), Jarrell invited the author to visit him in Washington. Corso arrived late in 1956 and stayed for six weeks. Jarrell provided him with food, clothing, and money.

JORDAN, VIOLA SCOTT BAXTER (1887–1973). She was a longtime friend of both EP, whom she met in Clinton, New York, in 1905, and WCW, whom she met in New York City in 1907. In 1914, she married the business economist VIRGIL D. JORDAN; they had three children and were later divorced. From her home in Tenafly, New Jersey, Mrs. Jordan maintained contact with WCW in nearby Rutherford. She also conducted a voluminous correspondence with EP (now housed at Yale and Indiana). See Ezra Pound, "Letters to Viola Baxter Jordan," ed. Donald Gallup, *Paideuma* 1:1 (Spring–Summer 1972), pp. 107–11, and Patrick Moore, "Ten Unpublished Letters from William Carlos Williams to Viola Baxter Jordan," *William Carlos Williams Review* 14:2 (Fall 1988), pp. 30–60.

JORDAN, VIRGIL D. (1892–1965). American business economist, writer, editor, and public speaker. He married VIOLA SCOTT BAXTER JORDAN in 1914; they were divorced in the later 1920s. He was employed by the National Industrial Conference Board from 1920 to 1929 as chief economist and editor of publications, and from 1932 to 1948 as president.

JOSEPHSON, MATTHEW (1899–1978). American poet, biographer, critic, and editor. He attended Columbia University with KENNETH BURKE and GORHAM MUNSON, and met WCW in 1920. As co-editor of *Secession* (1922–23) and associate editor of *Broom* (1922–24), he accepted several contributions by WCW; and as literary editor at Macaulay & Co., he was instrumental in the publication of WCW's translation of *Last Nights of Paris* by Philippe Soupault. Macaulay also published Josephson's *Zola and His Time: The History of His Marital Career, with an Account of His Circle of Friends, His Remarkable Enemies, Cyclopean Labours, Public Campaigns, Trials, and Ultimate Glorification* (1928). Josephson challenged EP in an "Open Letter to Mr. Ezra Pound, and the Other 'Exiles'," *transition* 13 (Summer 1928), pp. 98–102.

JOYCE, JAMES (1882–1941). Irish novelist, short-story writer, poet, and playwright. EP included one of Joyce's poems in the anthology, *Des Imagistes* (1914). EP arranged for Joyce's novel *A Portrait of the Artist as a Young Man* to be serialized in *The Egoist* and published by The Egoist Press (1916). EP also serialized installments of Joyce's *Ulysses* in *The Little Review* until its suppression by the United States Post Office in 1918. The novel was published in book form in 1922 by Sylvia Beach in Paris and by JOHN RODKER in London. EP praised it as the definitive literary representation of the failure of capitalist society. Joyce first met EP in Sirmione in 1920 and WCW in Paris in 1924. Joyce's last novel, *Finnegans Wake,* was serialized in *transition* and published as a book in 1939. EP did not admire it, but WCW imitated it in parts of *Paterson.*

KASPER, FREDERICK JOHN (*c.* 1929–). American publisher and segregationist. He first wrote to EP from Columbia University in 1950. At EP's instigation, he and T. David Horton became publishers in 1951 and booksellers in 1953. They put out the Square Dollar Series of inexpensive paperbacks, for which Kasper selected the contents of a volume of the writings of Louis Agassiz (1953). Kasper went on to become a Nazi sympathizer and a proponent of eugenics. He was an organizer of the White Citizens Councils in 1956–57 and led demonstrations against court-ordered racial integration of the high school in Clinton, Tennessee.

KREYMBORG, ALFRED (1883–1966). American poet, prose writer, and editor. Kreymborg was the principal editor of *The Globe* (1913–14) and *Others* (1915–19), and a co-editor of *American Caravan* and *New Caravan* (1927–36). He was also the author of *Mushrooms: A Book of Free Forms* (1916). WCW dedicated *Sour Grapes* (1921) to Kreymborg.

LAUGHLIN, JAMES (1914–). American poet and publisher. He first met EP in Rapallo in August 1933 and spent six or seven weeks there in November–December 1934. He first wrote to WCW in December 1933 and met him in Rutherford in September 1935. As a student at Harvard, Laughlin was an associate editor and the "Harvard Representative" of the *Harkness Hoot* (Yale), and a member of the editorial board of the *Harvard Advocate,* which published WCW's essay "The Element of Time: Advice to a Young Writer" in February 1934. At EP's instigation, Laughlin founded New Directions in 1936, and eventually became the principal publisher of both EP and WCW. In 1945–46, Laughlin co-ordinated EP's legal defense against charges of treason.

LEWIS, PERCY WYNDHAM (1884–1957). English artist and writer. He met EP in London in 1914, and became his ally in the Vorticist movement. In 1917, an issue of *The Little Review* containing Lewis' short story "Cantleman's Spring Mate" was suppressed by the United States Post Office. In 1917–18, Lewis was assigned to the Canadian War Records project, under whose auspices he made a number of battlefield paintings and drawings. These pictures were exhibited in a one-man London show entitled "Guns" at the Goupil Gallery in February 1919. In *Time and Western Man* (1927) and in a periodical called *The Enemy* (1927–29), Lewis criticized EP and others as misguided romantic revolutionaries. He and EP nevertheless remained friendly and continued their correspondence until Lewis' death in 1957; see Pound/Lewis.

LOWELL, ROBERT (1917–1977). American poet, translator, and critic. He won the Pulitzer Prize in 1946 for his book of poems *Lord Weary's Castle.* He met WCW in 1947 and EP in 1948. As Consultant in Poetry at the Library of Congress in 1947–48, Lowell arranged for WCW to record some of his poems there. Lowell often visited and wrote to EP at St. Elizabeths. "Cal" was Lowell's nickname.

McALMON, ROBERT (1896–1956). American poet, short-story writer, journalist, and publisher. He met WCW in New York in the summer of 1920, and collaborated with him on the production of *Contact* from December 1920 to June 1923. From 1921 to 1926, McAlmon was married to WINIFRED ELLERMAN. With her money, he funded Contact Editions, a series that began in Paris in 1923 and included WCW's *Spring and All* (1923) and McAlmon's own *Distinguished Air: Grim Fairy Tales* (1925). On September 28, 1929, McAlmon came to New York, hoping to interest a publisher in the manuscript of a novel entitled *Family Panorama*. But none accepted the book; see Mariani, pp. 292–94. In later years, McAlmon often stayed in El Paso, Texas, where his brothers ran a surgical-supply company. WCW visited him there in November 1950.

MacLEISH, ARCHIBALD (1892–1982). American poet, dramatist, and diplomat. He first met EP in Paris in the early 1920s. He was instrumental in the New York publication of EP's *A Draft of XXX Cantos* by Farrar and Rinehart (1933). In 1932, MacLeish won the Pulitzer Prize for his poem *Conquistador*. During World War II, he became Assistant Secretary of State for Public and Cultural Relations, but he resigned from that position in 1945. In 1957–58 he helped to arrange EP's release from St. Elizabeths.

MATHEWS, ELKIN (1851–1921). English publisher and bookseller. He published EP's *Personae* (1909), *Exultations* (1909), *Canzoni* (1911), *Cathay* (1915), *Catholic Anthology* (1915), *Lustra* (1916), and *Umbra* (1920), and WCW's *The Tempers* (1913). Mathews' London bookshop was located at 6b Vigo Street, at the corner of Savile Row. He borrowed these place-names for two of the five series in which he marketed volumes of poetry at low prices. The Vigo Cabinet series ran from 1900 to 1918 and included 145 titles. *The Tempers* was Number 7 in the Savile series. In 1916, Mathews raised moral and religious objections to some of the poems in EP's *Lustra*. As a result, the book was published in both expurgated and unexpurgated editions. See Carpenter, pp. 302–05; Gallup, A11; Paige, pp. 80–81; and James G. Nelson, *Elkin Mathews: Publisher to Yeats, Joyce, Pound* (Madison: University of Wisconsin Press, 1989), pp. 158–66.

MOORE, MARIANNE (1887–1972). American poet, essayist, translator, and editor. She first met WCW in 1916, and first corresponded with EP in 1918. WCW solicited her work for *Others,* and EP helped to arrange the publication of her *Poems* (1921) by the Egoist Press in London. From 1921 to 1925, Moore was employed as an assistant at the Hudson Park branch of the New York Public Library. She then joined the staff of *The Dial,* of which she was the principal editor from 1926 to 1929. In 1947, she became a member of the National Institute of Arts and Letters, and in 1948, she presented the Institute's Russell Loines Award for Poetry to WCW. Her English translations of the *Fables* (1668–94) of the French poet, Jean de la Fontaine (1621–1695), appeared in 1954.

MOORE, MERRILL (1903–1957). American poet and psychiatrist. He is the author of *M: One Thousand Autobiographical Sonnets* (1938), *The Dance of Death* (1957) and the introduction to H. D.'s *Tribute to Freud* (1956). WCW admired Moore's sonnets and contributed a foreword that was reprinted in each of his collections of poetry. WCW met Moore in 1952, if not sooner, and Moore became one of WCW's medical advisers on the effects of his strokes. Moore also took a great interest in EP's case. He was a friend of Dr. Winfred Overholser, the head of St. Elizabeths, and visited EP there on several occasions.

MUNSON, GORHAM BERT (1896–1969). American critic and editor. He was an editor of *Secession* and the author of books on ROBERT FROST and Waldo Frank. Munson met HART CRANE in 1919 and became his friend and patron when Crane came to New York in 1923. Munson's *Destinations: A Canvass of American Literature* (1928) contains a laudatory essay on the work of Crane ("probably the most richly endowed of our younger poets") and a mixed assessment of the work of WCW. From 1933 to 1939, Munson edited the leading American Social Credit periodical, *New Democracy,* to which both EP and WCW contributed. Munson also taught at the New School for Social Research in New York.

MUSSOLINI, BENITO (1883–1945). Italian political leader. He was the head of the Italian Facist government from 1922 to 1943. EP met him in January 1933 and wrote *Jefferson and/or Mussolini* later that year. On November 14, 1933, Mussolini made a major speech in Rome, in which he declared the end of the capitalist era and predicted that the parliamentary Chamber of Deputies would be replaced by the syndical Council of Corporations. See *Opera Omnia di Benito Mussolini,* ed. Edoardo and Duilio Susmel (Florence: La Fenice, 1958), XXVI, pp. 86–96, and the *New York Times,* November 15, 1933, pp. 1, 6. On October 3, 1935, Mussolini ordered the armed forces of Italy to invade Abyssinia. He became an ally of the Nationalist forces in the Spanish Civil War and of Nazi Germany in World War II. On April 25, 1945, he and his mistress, Clara Petacci, were executed by Italian partisans and hanged by the heels in the Piazale Loreto of Milan.

NARDI, MARCIA (1901–1990). American poet. She is the author of *Poems* (1956). She corresponded with WCW at intervals from 1942 to 1956, and her letters play an important role in the first two books of *Paterson.* WCW helped her to publish her work in *New Directions in Prose and Poetry* and in *Botteghe Oscure.* In the early part of August 1951, she made a determined but unsuccessful effort to see WCW; see *The Last Word: Letters between Marcia Nardi and William Carlos Williams,* ed. Elizabeth Murrie O'Neil (Iowa City: University of Iowa Press, 1994), pp. 200–02.

NOTT, STANLEY CHARLES (b. 1902). English publisher and expert on Chinese jade art. He was a founder and manager of the *New English Weekly.* After the death of A. R. ORAGE late in 1934, Nott set up a Social Credit publishing firm. In 1935, he brought out three books by EP: *Alfred Venison's Poems, Social Credit: An Impact,* and *Jefferson and/or Mussolini.* EP also planned to edit a Social Credit anthology for Nott's series of "Pamphlets in the New Economics," but the project was never completed. However, ten of the first seventeen pamphlets in the series, including EP's *Social Credit,* were reprinted in *The Social Credit Pamphleteer* (1935). EP also persuaded Nott to undertake a series of cultural pamphlets. The "Ideogrammic Series" began in 1936 with reprints of Ernest Fenollosa's essay on *The Chinese Written Character as a Medium for Poetry* and EP's translation of Confucius, *Ta Hio: The Great Learning.* WCW's *In the American Grain* was to have been the third title, with works by E. E. CUMMINGS, JEAN COCTEAU, and Douglas Fox to follow. But Nott went out of business before these works appeared.

ORAGE, ALFRED RICHARD (1873–1934). English editor, publisher, and reformer. He edited *The New Age* from 1907 to 1922, with EP as a regular contributor from 1911 on. From 1932 until his abrupt death in London, November 6, 1934, Orage edited the *New English Weekly*, the leading British Social Credit journal, to which both EP and WCW contributed. Both paid tribute to Orage in *New Democracy* for December 15, 1934, and EP published a memorial essay in *Criterion* for April 1935. The *New English Weekly* continued until 1949 under the editorship of Philip Mairet and others.

PATTERSON, ERNEST MINOR (1870–1969). American economist. He taught economics at the University of Pennsylvania from 1915 to 1950 and is the author of *The Economic Basis of Peace* (1939). From 1930 to 1953, he served as President of the American Academy of Political and Social Science in Philadelphia, of which EP became a member in 1940. A letter of November 2, 1949, from Patterson to EP at St. Elizabeths begins as follows: "Dear Dr. Pound: You are one of our valued life members. . . ." (Yale).

POR, ODON (b. 1883). Hungarian-Italian journalist and economist. As a Guild Socialist, Por wrote for A. R. ORAGE'S *The New Age* in London. He later served as the London correspondent of *Avanti* when MUSSOLINI edited that periodical in Milan. Like EP, Por turned to Social Credit and fascist syndicalism. He wrote *Fascism* (1923) and other books on the guild and corporate structure of Mussolini's Italy. In 1935, he published a series of seven articles entitled "Cronaca della 'Nuova Economia'" (Chronicle of the "New Economics") in *Civiltà Fascista*, a monthly review published by the Fascist National Institute of Culture in Rome. The fourth in the series (May 1935) devotes several pages to EP's economic thought. Por was still corresponding with EP from Rome in 1961 (Yale).

POUND, DOROTHY SHAKESPEAR (1886–1973). English artist. The daughter of Olivia and Henry Hope Shakespear, she married EP in London on April 20, 1914. Her son, Omar Shakespear Pound, was born September 10, 1926. After EP's imprisonment in St. Elizabeths, Dorothy moved to Washington in July 1946, remaining there until his release in 1958.

PUTNAM, SAMUEL (1892–1950). American essayist, translator, editor, and publisher. He founded *The New Review* in Paris in 1931, with EP as his associate editor. Putnam also planned a series of books to be called New Review Editions. *An "Objectivists" Anthology,* edited by LOUIS ZUKOFSKY, was to appear under this imprint, and Putnam discussed the project with Zukofsky during a visit to New York in August 1931. Upon his return to Paris in November, however, a serious illness obliged Putnam to alter his publishing plans.

QUINN, JOHN (1870–1924). American lawyer and patron of the arts. He was a friend of the Yeats family, by whom he was introduced to EP in New York in 1910. A wealthy collector and benefactor of the modern arts, Quinn subsidized *The Egoist, The Little Review,* and a number of artists and writers whom EP recommended to him. In 1916, Quinn tried without success to persuade the New York branch of Macmillan & Co. to become EP's American publisher.

RODKER, JOHN (1894–1955). English poet, novelist, translator, critic, editor, and publisher. He founded the Ovid Press in London in 1919. Its publications included EP's

Hugh Selwyn Mauberley (1920), T. S. ELIOT's *Ara Vos Prec* (1920), WYNDHAM
LEWIS's *Fifteen Drawings* (1920), and JAMES JOYCE's *Ulysses* (English edition, 1922).
Rodker also published *A Draft of the Cantos 17–27 of Ezra Pound* (1928). His novel,
Adolphe 1920, was serialized in EP's *Exile* (1927–28) and published as a book by
NANCY CUNARD's Hours Press (1929). He also wrote *Memoirs of Other Fronts* (London: Putnam, 1932).

SIMPSON, DALLAM (1925 or 1926–). American editor and publisher. He was the founder
and first editor of *Four Pages,* a little magazine which began in Galveston, Texas, and
later moved to England. *Four Pages* ran for fifteen numbers from January 1948 to
January 1951. WCW contributed three items to it, and his correspondence with Simpson
is preserved at Texas. Simpson also founded the Cleaners' Press in Galveston, which
published BASIL BUNTING's *Poems* in 1950. Simpson later moved to Washington,
D.C., and visited EP frequently at St. Elizabeths. *Four Pages* for March 1948 carried
the following manifesto: "1. We must understand what's really happening. 2. If the
verse-makers of our time are to improve on their immediate predecessors, we must be
vitally aware of the duration of syllables, of melodic coherence and of the tone leading
of vowels. 3. The function of poetry is to disturb by lucidity." The manifesto is signed
by "We, the CLEANERS/ D. Simpson/ L. C. Flynn/ Igon Tan."

STEIN, GERTRUDE (1874–1946). American poet, prose writer, and patron of the arts. She
is the author of *Three Lives* (1908), *Tender Buttons* (1914), *The Making of Americans*
(1925), and *The Autobiography of Alice B. Toklas* (1933). EP met her in Paris in 1921;
WCW, in 1927. WCW's essay, "A 1 Pound Stein," was rejected by EP for the *New
English Weekly* and published in *The Rocking Horse* (Madison, Wisconsin) for Spring
1935. In 1934, Stein made a successful lecture tour of the United States.

STIEGLITZ, ALFRED (1864–1946). German-American photographer, publisher, and gallery
owner. His New York gallery, An American Place, owed its name to WCW's *In the
American Grain.* WCW contributed an essay entitled "The American Background" to
America and Alfred Stieglitz: A Collective Portrait, ed. Waldo Frank, Lewis Mumford,
Dorothy Norman, and Harold Rugg (New York: The Literary Guild and Doubleday,
Doran, 1934). In addition to the editors and WCW, the contributors included John
Marin, Marsden Hartley, Charles Demuth, GERTRUDE STEIN, and Sherwood Anderson.

STOCK, NOEL (1929–). Australian poet, broadcast journalist, and scholar. He was a
Parliamentary reporter for the Australian Broadcasting Company's news service, a news
editor, an advertising copywriter, and a bookseller. A devotee of EP and his work,
Stock began to correspond with him in September 1953 (Yale). A few years later, Stock
founded and edited a Poundian little magazine in Melbourne called *Edge* (1956–58). He
is the author of a major biography, *The Life of Ezra Pound* (1970).

TWEDDELL, FRANCIS I. (1863–1939). American physician. For Dr. Tweddell's ideas about
the treatment of tuberculosis, see p. 125 above. His article, entitled "The Rational
Treatment of Pulmonary Tuberculosis," *Medical World* (January and August 1931),
caught the attention of EP, who corresponded with him from October 20, 1937, to
October 25, 1938 (Yale). See also Omar Pound, "Canto 113: Tweddell, Men against
Death, and Paul De Kruif," *Paideuma* 22:1–2 (Spring–Fall 1993), pp. 173–79.

TYLER, PARKER (1904–1974). American poet, novelist, film critic, and art critic. He was co-editor, with Charles Henri Ford, of *Blues* and *View*. EP contributed to the former in 1929 and corresponded with Tyler from December 1930 until later in the decade; see Pound/Tyler. Tyler's work appears in EP's *Profile* (1932), but EP rejected his contributions to the *Active Anthology* because of their homoerotic content. In 1945, Tyler published *The Granite Butterfly: A Poem in Nine Cantos* (New York: Bern Porter). WCW published an admiring review of it in *Accent* (Urbana, Illinois) for Spring 1946.

VAN BUREN, MARTIN (1782–1862). American political leader. He served as President of the United States from 1837 to 1841. In EP's view, set forth in Canto 37, Van Buren carried on the Populist battle of his predecessor, ANDREW JACKSON, against private banking interests. EP saw Van Buren as an unsung "national hero," and his presidency as one of the "few clean and decent pages in the nashunul history" (Paige, p. 247).

VEGA CARPIO, LOPE FÉLIX DE (1562–1635). Spanish dramatist. As a graduate student at the University of Pennsylvania, EP planned to write his doctoral dissertation on the figure of the *gracioso* (the comical-satirical servant, peasant, or clown) in the plays of Lope de Vega and other Spanish dramatists of the Golden Age. EP also tried to translate Lope's comedy, *El Desprecio Agradecido* (The Grateful Reject, *c.* 1633). The translation was never finished, but EP quotes passages from it in Chapter 9 of *The Spirit of Romance* and mentions it in "Mr. James Joyce and the Modern Stage," *The Drama* 6:21 (February 1916), pp. 122–32. Meanwhile, WCW was trying to translate Lope's *El Nuevo Mundo descubierto por Colón* (Columbus' Discovery of the New World, *c.* 1600). The play counterpoints Columbus' landing in 1492 with the Christian reconquest of Granada in the same year. In *The Spirit of Romance,* EP calls it "the finest literary presentation of Columbus known to exist."

WILLIAMS, EDGAR IRVING (1884–1974). WCW's younger brother. As a student at the Massachusetts Institute of Technology in 1909, he was awarded the Prix de Rome, a three-year fellowship to study architecture at the American Academy in Rome. He joined EP in Sirmione and Verona in the summer of 1911. As a successful New York architect, Williams specialized in libraries and other public buildings, and was one of a team of seven architects awarded the contract for the administration building of the 1939 New York World's Fair (*New York Times,* October 22, 1936, p. 1).

WILLIAMS, RAQUEL HÉLÈNE ROSE (1847–1949). WCW's mother. She was a Puerto Rican of French, Basque, and Sephardic Jewish descent. In her youth, she was a prizewinning art student in Paris. WCW began a biography of her in the winter of 1936–37. He published the introductory section, as "Raquel Hélène Rose," in *Twice a Year* 5–6 (1940–41), pp. 402–12. Initially entitled *Your Grandmother, My Son,* the full version later appeared as *Yes, Mrs. Williams* (New York: McDowell, Obolensky, 1959). WCW and his mother also collaborated on a translation of *El Perro y la Calentura* (1625); this was eventually published as *The Dog and the Fever* (Hamden, Connecticut: Shoe String Press, 1954).

WILLIAMS, WILLIAM GEORGE (1851–1918). WCW's father. Born in Birmingham, England, he grew up in Saint Thomas and Santo Domingo in the West Indies. Upon moving to the United States in 1882, he lived and worked in New York City and

Rutherford and traveled a good deal in Central and South America. His manner was more English than American, and he retained British citizenship to the end of his life; see Mariani, pp. 4–5, 9–13.

WINTERS, YVOR (1900–1968). American poet and critic. He began as a free-verse poet and an admirer of both WCW and HART CRANE. Winters corresponded with Crane, and reviewed Crane's *White Buildings* very favorably in *Poetry* for April 1927. Around 1928, however, Winters renounced experimental modernism and began to advocate neoclassical forms and values. His review of Crane's *The Bridge* in *Poetry* for June 1930 was negative.

YEATS, WILLIAM BUTLER (1865–1939). Irish poet, playwright, and prose writer. EP considered Yeats the greatest living poet of the English language. The two men met in London in the spring of 1909. When WCW visited London in March 1910, EP introduced him to Yeats. Between 1913 and 1916, EP spent part of each winter with Yeats at Stone Cottage in Coleman's Hatch, Sussex. In 1928, Yeats lived for part of the year near EP in Rapallo.

ZUKOFSKY, LOUIS (1904–1978). American poet and prose writer. He contributed "Poem Beginning 'The'" to EP's *Exile* 3 (Spring 1928). At EP's instigation, he met WCW in Rutherford on April 1, 1928. Zukofsky edited WCW's "The Descent of Winter" for *Exile* 4 (Autumn 1928), pp. 30–69. In July 1928, WCW read a draft of Zukofsky's essay "Henry Adams: A Criticism in Autobiography," which appeared in *Hound and Horn* for Spring 1930. In 1928, Zukofsky also began his long poem, *A*, parts of which he showed to WCW and EP as they were completed. Zukofsky spent the academic year of 1930–31 as an instructor in English at the University of Wisconsin, Madison. In 1931, he started the Objectivist Movement with George Oppen, Charles Reznikoff, and Carl Rakosi. The Objectivists founded TO, Publishers, which issued WCW's *A Novelette and Other Prose 1921–1931* (1932), EP's *Prolegomena I* (1932), and *An "Objectivists" Anthology* (1932). The same group founded the Objectivist Press, which published WCW's *Collected Poems 1921–1932* (1934). In 1933, Zukofsky helped WCW make a selection of his work for EP's *Active Anthology*. In January 1937, Zukofsky sent "A–8" to both EP and WCW. Zukofsky's *Anew* was published in Prairie City, Illinois, by James A. Decker in 1946. Zukofsky's wife, the composer Celia Thaew (1913–1980), set many of his poems to music. In 1946, she also wrote a musical setting for WCW's poem "Choral: The Pink Church" (Mariani, pp. 525–26).

Abbreviations of Works Cited

Autobiography	*The Autobiography of William Carlos Williams*. New York: Random House, 1951; rpt. New York: New Directions, 1967
Carpenter	Carpenter, Humphrey. *A Serious Character: The Life of Ezra Pound*. Boston: Houghton Mifflin, 1988
Eliot	Eliot, Valerie, ed. *The Letters of T. S. Eliot: Volume I, 1898–1922*. London: Faber and Faber, 1988
Gallup	Gallup, Donald. *Ezra Pound: A Bibliography*. Charlottesville: The University Press of Virginia, 1983
Heal	Williams, William Carlos. *I Wanted to Write a Poem: The Autobiography of the Works of a Poet*. Ed. Edith Heal. Boston: Beacon Press, 1958; rpt. New York: New Directions, 1978
Mariani	Mariani, Paul. *William Carlos Williams: A New World Naked*. New York: McGraw-Hill, 1981
Paige	Paige, D. D., ed. *The Letters of Ezra Pound 1907–1941*. New York: Harcourt Brace Jovanovitch, 1950; rpt. New York: New Directions, 1971
Pound/Cutting	Walkiewicz, E. P., and Hugh Witemeyer, eds. *Ezra Pound and Senator Bronson Cutting: A Political Correspondence, 1930–1935*. Albuquerque: University of New Mexico Press, 1995
Pound/Henderson	Nadel, Ira B., ed. *The Letters of Ezra Pound to Alice Corbin Henderson*. Austin: University of Texas Press, 1993
Pound/Laughlin	Gordon, David M., ed. *Ezra Pound and James Laughlin: Selected Letters*. New York: W. W. Norton, 1994
Pound/Lewis	Materer, Timothy, ed. *Pound/Lewis: The Letters of Ezra Pound and Wyndham Lewis*. New York: New Directions, 1985

Pound/*The Little Review*   Scott, Thomas L., Melvin J. Friedman, and Jackson R. Bryer, eds. *Pound/*The Little Review: *The Letters of Ezra Pound to Margaret Anderson:* The Little Review *Correspondence*. New York: New Directions, 1988

Pound/Quinn   Materer, Timothy, ed. *The Selected Letters of Ezra Pound to John Quinn 1915–1924*. Durham, N. C.: Duke University Press, 1991

Pound/Tyler   Bornstein, George, ed. "Eight Letters from Ezra Pound to Parker Tyler in the 1930s," *Michigan Quarterly Review* 24 (1985), pp. 1–17

Pound/Zukofsky   Ahearn, Barry, ed. *Pound/Zukofsky: Selected Letters of Ezra Pound and Louis Zukofsky*. New York: New Directions, 1987

Thirlwall   Thirlwall, John C., ed. *The Selected Letters of William Carlos Williams*. New York: McDowell, Obolensky, 1957; rpt. New York: New Directions, 1984

Williams/Laughlin   Witemeyer, Hugh, ed. *William Carlos Williams and James Laughlin: Selected Letters*. New York: W. W. Norton, 1989

Index